About Island Press

Island Press is the only nonprofit organization in the United States whose principal purpose is the publication of books on environmental issues and natural resource management. We provide solutions-oriented information to professionals, public officials, business and community leaders, and concerned citizens who are shaping responses to environmental problems.

In 2003, Island Press celebrates its nineteenth anniversary as the leading provider of timely and practical books that take a multidisciplinary approach to critical environmental concerns. Our growing list of titles reflects our commitment to bringing the best of an expanding body of literature to the environmental community throughout North America and the world.

Support for Island Press is provided by The Nathan Cummings Foundation, Geraldine R. Dodge Foundation, Doris Duke Charitable Foundation, Educational Foundation of America, The Charles Engelhard Foundation, The Ford Foundation, The George Gund Foundation, The Vira I. Heinz Endowment, The William and Flora Hewlett Foundation, Henry Luce Foundation, The John D. and Catherine T. MacArthur Foundation, The Andrew W. Mellon Foundation, The Moriah Fund, The Curtis and Edith Munson Foundation, National Fish and Wildlife Foundation, The New-Land Foundation, Oak Foundation, The Overbrook Foundation, The David and Lucile Packard Foundation, The Pew Charitable Trusts, The Rockefeller Foundation, The Winslow Foundation, and other generous donors.

Making Sense of Intractable

ENVIRONMENTAL CONFLICTS

Making Sense of Intractable ENVIRONMENTAL CONFLICTS

FRAMES AND CASES

Edited by

Roy J. Lewicki | Barbara Gray | Michael Elliott

ISLAND PRESS

Washington • Covelo • London

Library of Congress Cataloging-in-Publication Data

Making sense of intractable environmental conflicts : concepts and cases / edited by Roy J. Lewicki, Barbara Gray, Michael Elliott..

p. cm.

Includes bibliographical references and index.

ISBN 1-55963-930-X (cloth : alk. paper) — ISBN 1-55963-931-8 (pbk. : alk. paper)

1. Environmental policy—United States—Case studies. 2. Conflict management—United States—Case studies. I. Lewicki, Roy J. II. Gray, Barbara. III. Elliott, Michael.

GE180 .M33 2002

333.7'2—dc21

2002011600

British Cataloguing-in-Publication Data available

Book design by Brighid Willson.

Printed on recycled, acid-free paper 

Manufactured in the United States of America

10 9 8 7 6 5 4 3 2 1

Contents

II. Water Cases

III. Toxics Cases

IV. Growth Management Cases

V. Conclusion

Introduction

Roy J. Lewicki and Barbara Gray

Although considerable dispute resolution expertise has been devoted to environmental conflicts in the last twenty years (Bingham 1986, Carpenter and Kennedy 1988, Crowfoot and Wondolleck 1990, Gray 1989, Susskind and Cruikshank 1987, Wondolleck and Yaffee 2000) many of these conflicts remain mired in controversy, tied up in litigation, and riddled with long-standing tensions that defy resolution. As they evolve, these conflicts pit neighbor against neighbor, citizens against business and government, and communities against business, government, and each other; in the meantime, environmental damage accumulates.

Conflicts of this type are characterized by considerable intensity, persist indefinitely over long periods of time, and cannot be resolved through consensus-building efforts or by administrative, legal, or political solutions. We refer to these as intractable conflicts (Burgess and Burgess 1996, Kriesberg 1993). These kinds of conflicts are the focus of this book.

Why do intractable conflicts over environmental issues persist? Why do some conflicts find resolution while others carry on for decades? Why can the same environmental issues be resolved in one locale but remain contentious in others? What is it about certain environmental issues or the people involved with them that makes them more intractable than others? These are the questions addressed in this book.

We selected eight intractable environmental conflicts for extensive study. We selected either conflicts that were long-standing ones with many dispute episodes erupting over many years, or ones that are endemic to communities throughout the United States and show few signs of being resolved. We also included conflicts that were successfully resolved through local consensus-building efforts but which unraveled when these same issues were raised to a national level of debate.

Through many hours of discussion, our research consortium developed a common framework to analyze these conflicts.* Representing seven different universities, we each identified an important intractable environmental dispute, collected data at our respective sites, and brought it back to the consortium for discussion, interpretation, and comparison. We developed a common understanding of what we meant by a frame and by intractability, and we identified several types of frames that were used frequently by our interviewees. By the end of our first year we had developed a scheme for "coding" the frames used by our interviewees in order to make sense of their situations. We elaborated on and refined this coding scheme over the next year. This common framework has enabled us to view each case through a common set of lenses while also capturing each conflict's unique features.

To study the reasons for intractability in these conflicts, we seek to learn how the parties involved make sense of them. Although there are many reasons why conflicts can become intractable (see our discussion in Chapter 2), we believe that one major cause is the way parties use frames in conflicts. We asked people why they believed the conflicts were occurring and what kept them from being resolved. We inquired about their own role in the conflict, and their views of their opponents. We wanted to understand how the players themselves "made sense" of their situations—how they accounted for the persistence of their differences. We refer to their interpretations as *frames*. Recent research on environmental conflicts has shown that parties in a conflict, or those confronting environmental threats and deterioration, often develop considerably different frames about what the conflict is about, what should be done about it, and by whom (Gray 1997, Vaughan and Siefert 1992). We sought to investigate the frames that were salient for our environmental disputants and to learn whether and how these frames contributed to the conflict's intractability.

Our cases cover a wide range of environmental conflicts. We have grouped them into four types: natural resource conflicts, water quality conflicts, conflicts over toxic pollutants, and growth-related conflicts. We studied at least two conflicts in each category. This enabled us to make comparisons by type across the conflicts. Table I.1 provides a brief description of and some preliminary orienting information about each conflict.

The first three cases deal with competing uses for precious natural resources.

---

* Our project is called the Interuniversity Consortium on the Framing of Intractable Environmental Disputes. It was funded (starting in 1998) by The William and Flora Hewlett Foundation.

Table I-1. Overview of Cases Presented in the Book

Quincy Library Group	The Quincy Library Group was formed in 1992 in Quincy, California. Its purpose was to address the conflict between logging and environmental groups over timber cutting in several Northern California counties. The group was successful in achieving a resolution to the local dispute, but came into conflict with state and national groups who also were intent on making policy about these issues.
Voyageurs National Park	Voyageurs National Park was created in northern Minnesota in 1975. However, debate has continued for almost 110 years between motorized users of the park (boaters, snowmobilers, etc.), various natural and cultural resource preservation groups, and local governmental and economic development interests.
Edwards Aquifer	The Edwards Aquifer is a unique underground limestone formation that stretches across a large part of the state of Texas. It is a common pool source of water for multiple counties and cities in the state. Residents, ranchers, farmers, and other stakeholder groups compete for this important water source.
Doan Brook	Doan Brook winds through 9 miles of park, recreational, residential, and urban settings in suburban and downtown Cleveland, Ohio. The case describes a history of efforts to develop a long-term management plan for the brook across multiple jurisdictions and with the involvement of many stakeholder groups.
Antidegradation External Advisory Group	In 1998, the Ohio EPA appointed an external advisory group (EAG), composed of members of the regulated and environmental communities, to advise it on the revision of statewide water quality rules and standards. The group met for eighteen months to discuss and debate these standards and develop recommendations on the new rules.
Drake Chemical Company	Drake Chemical is an EPA Superfund site located in Lock Haven, Pennsylvania. Drake began producing chemical intermediaries in the 1940s, and by the early 1980s, filed for bankruptcy and was unable to comply with then contemporary environmental legislation. Since then, debate has raged between the EPA, local officials, and environmental groups on the appropriate procedures for cleaning up excess chemicals dumped near the site.

(*continued*)

Table I-1. *Continued*

Alton Park/Piney Woods	Alton Park and Piney Woods are two neighborhoods in Chattanooga, Tennessee, that have had a mix of heavy industry and residential uses. In these neighborhoods there are approximately forty small hazardous waste sites that have been declared EPA Superfund cleanup priorities. Neighborhood residents (virtually 100% African American) have come into conflict with citywide environmental activists, industrialists, and city officials over the nature and scope of the required cleanup.
Colorado Growth Project	A wave of economic growth along the Front Range of the Rocky Mountains in Colorado has created a number of conflicts over affordable housing, open space and habitat protection, land use, and general infrastructure overload. The project focused on three different counties—Larimer (Fort Collins), Boulder (Boulder), and El Paso (Colorado Springs)—and the ways that each of these counties has addressed growth management issues.

The first case (the Quincy Library Group) focuses on timber harvesting in the Pacific Northwest, the second (the Voyageurs National Park case) deals with conflicts over use within a national park, and the third case addresses the allocation of water from a common pool resource in Texas (the Edwards Aquifer case). All three of these conflicts have long histories characterized by numerous bitter battles that have left scars on both the parties and their communities. And all three have witnessed dispute resolution attempts that either were unsuccessful or provoked additional conflict at other levels (i.e., the conflict shifted from local to state or federal level). For example, some of the parties in the Quincy Library Group accomplished a successful consensus-building effort at the local level, but the agreement met resistance when the debate was elevated to a national level.

The next two cases address water quality issues. The first (Doan Brook) deals with a long-standing dispute over watershed usage in a major metropolitan area (Cleveland, Ohio). The second (the Ohio Antidegradation External Advisory Group) describes the efforts of key stakeholders and regulatory personnel to establish state-level standards for preventing water quality deterioration. In both of these cases, the parties engaged in consensus-building efforts, but neither of these efforts was successful in resolving the underlying issues in the conflicts.

The third group—two cases—deals with cleanup of toxic pollutants. Both Drake Chemical and the Alton Park/Piney Woods conflicts involve the cleanup of Superfund sites, one in Pennsylvania and the other in Tennessee, but the reasons for their intractability vary considerably.

Finally, the last cases address growth issues along the Front Range of Colorado's Rocky Mountains. They compare and contrast how the debate over growth and development has unfolded in three different metropolitan areas in this region.

In this book, we begin to tell the stories of these conflicts as seen through the eyes of the parties involved. We have tried diligently to capture the diverse interpretations that create the "stuff" of the conflicts themselves. This kind of approach is risky, to say the least, because we have attempted to mold a wide array of individual interpretations into a composite picture of these conflicts. Each individual's perspective is like one view through a kaleidoscope, and no two views are exactly the same. Therefore, the composite picture we have drawn is not only comprehensive, it is also likely to be controversial. In trying to capture the views of all, we may please none of the parties because each has a particular slant on the conflict that the others don't share. This is the risk we have elected to bear, however, in order to reflect these differences in framing and to learn how these different frames intersect to keep the conflicts alive.

Our discussion and analysis will build to the following conclusions:

1. Conflicts are dynamic processes. For intractable conflicts in particular, even though actors change, contexts transform, and the arenas in which dispute episodes are staged shift, the conflict persists. Our data also suggest that framing has much to do with this intransigence and that shifts in frames can make a conflict more or less tractable.
2. Frames act as lenses through which disputants interpret conflict dynamics and these interpretations construct the conflict as more or less tractable.
3. Frames can remain remarkably stable, through many dispute episodes, thereby reinforcing conflict dynamics over time.
4. Frame interactions can either mutually reinforce or dampen the stability of each other and the intensity of the conflict.
5. Frame differences foster intractability in the following ways: often the parties do not frame the underlying problem in the same way leading to repeated skirmishes that never address the underlying issues; limited repertoires of conflict management frames lead disputants to adopt adversarial

conflict management strategies that impede resolution and ramp up conflict; extensive and repeated use of characterization frames polarizes already antagonistic relationships; and finally, the use of positional conflict management frames reinforces characterizations.

6. In natural resource conflicts, ambiguity in the social system coupled with disagreements among the parties about who should be making decisions about resource use and preservation (i.e., when the parties have different social control frames) increases the chances that the conflict will elude resolution.
7. Until some common basis for describing and measuring risk can be agreed upon among disputants, conflicts over toxic pollutants will likely remain intractable.
8. In at least some conflicts, frames can be altered over time, through intentional actions and interventions. These changes in frames can render disputes more tractable.

Research Methodology

In this section, we offer a brief but technical description of our methods. Readers who are interested only in the cases or the broad data analysis process may wish to skip this section and move to the book overview at the end of this chapter.

The cases and findings that we present in this book are based on a variety of data collected from a variety of sources at each conflict site. We examined a broad range of research reports, Senate bills, administrative records, management plans, video clips, Internet Web pages, memoranda, working documents, and formal meeting minutes. We also attended and transcribed interactions from formal and informal meetings, and distributed a questionnaire at one study site. Additionally, we examined over 1800 newspaper articles ranging from stories in local newspapers such as the Lock Haven *Express* and the Hondo *Anvil Herald* to larger ones such as the Houston *Chronicle* and the Minneapolis *Star-Tribune*. We identified relevant articles using electronic data searches, manual reviews of local archives, and contributions from dispute stakeholders. (In one case, over four years of articles were provided by an agency official who had daily clipped local articles because of a personal interest in the conflict.)

Perhaps the richest component of our data consists of transcripts of over 300 one-on-one interviews with individuals actively involved in the conflicts. Interviews ranged in length from forty-five minutes to five hours, with most lasting ninety minutes. The interviews were semi-structured, with probing follow-up questions designed to allow interviewees to express their own perspectives on their particular dispute. Most interviews were audio-recorded and then transcribed verbatim; when this was not possible, interviewers manually transcribed the interviews as they occurred. Each transcript was reviewed for accuracy by the interviewer and, when they were willing to do so, the interviewee.

We chose to analyze the data using content analysis, or the systematic, objective, qualitative and quantitative analysis of message characteristics (Berelson 1952). This practice has a rich historical tradition of use: Krippendorff (1980) found that empirical inquiry into communication content dates at least to the late 1600s, when newspapers were examined by the Church because of its concern over the spread of nonreligious matters. This technique was initiated in the fields of communication, sociology, and journalism in the 1950s and has gained validation as a research tool in thousands of studies examining a broad range of messages (Fan 1988, Krippendorff 1980, Strauss and Corbin 1990). Our approach to content analysis was primarily inductive, although we did develop some preliminary coding schemes from extant literature. Our first step was to formulate research questions based on existing literature and theory. Then we developed a rough typology of frames drawn from the existing literature on framing and conflict analysis. We searched our data for these kinds of frames but also used open coding to identify other frames that appeared frequently in the data (Strauss and Corbin 1990). Our chosen unit of analysis was the "thought unit"—that is, the words, sentences, or paragraphs used to express an identifiable thought.

Over time our preliminary typology was elaborated and refined to reflect the distinctions in frame types in all of our cases. We developed a Coding Guidebook that outlined coding protocols and provided exemplars for each of the codes and its subcategories. Project team members worked together to create and revise the Guidebook until all shared a similar perspective and understanding of the frames. Once agreement was reached, we developed a general description for each frame type. For example, one of our frames was defined as "Characterization" (for a complete list of the frames used in this project, see Chapter 1). After identifying the frame, we constructed key questions to ask and linguistic markers to guide coders in selecting appropriate frame categories. To illustrate: Characterization frames are used to describe thoughts about others. Guiding questions included: "How does the interviewee characterize other people in the dispute?" and "What labels or stereotypes does the interviewee project onto other people and stakeholders?" We also identified the major subcategories for each frame type. Characterization frames were subcategorized as positive, neutral, or negative depictions of others. Identity frames referred to how disputants defined themselves. Subcategories of identity frames included "place-based" identity (the person associated him- or herself with a particular locale) and "institutional" (reflecting an affiliation with a particular institution) among others.

Once the typology was refined, we used it to recode the data. Each site team coded their own data. Trained coders place the data into the categories, and discrepancies were reconciled through discussion. In every case, coding done by one team member was reviewed by a second member to assess intercoder reliability.[†] Finally, the data collected were analyzed and interpreted (Riffe and Freitag, 1997).

Content analysis has four advantages for researchers interested in exploring the ways that people communicate. First, it is unobtrusive. Since messages are analyzed after they have been uttered, the content analysis strategy does not generally run the risk of polluting data sources. Second, content analysis accepts unstructured materials, so that subjects are free to express themselves in their own terms rather than having their responses restricted by, for example, prescribed answers on a survey form. Third, the procedure is context sensitive and thus is able to process symbolic forms and account for constraints and opportunities inherent in a communication situation. Finally, content analysis techniques can cope with large volumes of data, a distinct advantage when dealing with multiple forms of communication (Krippendorff 1980).[‡]

Organization of This Book

Like all other aspects of the work reported on this project, the organization emerged from much debate and discussion. The book is organized into six general areas: a theory section, four groups of cases, each group followed by an integrating chapter that compares and contrasts them, and a final chapter on the conclusions and implications of our research. Within each case chapter, the

---

† Reliabilities among the coders ranged from .72 to .91 with Cohen's coefficient Alpha.

‡ To analyze the frames, investigators at each site independently entered their data into NUD*IST NVivo (Fraser 1999), a software program that facilitates the qualitative analysis of data. NVivo provides a variety of numerical descriptions of the coded data, including the number of frames coded within each category. This allowed us to make sense of the information more holistically by determining what types of comments were most prevalent in the various conflicts.

authors describe the historical development and fundamental nature of the conflicts between the parties. Every case is then analyzed from the perspective of three key frames, as well as other frames that may be integral to understanding the conflict dynamics. Let us say a bit more about each area:

Theory Chapters 1 and 2 describe the core "theory" behind our work. Chapter 1 introduces the notions of frames, framing, and reframing and orients the reader to the roles that framing plays in conflicts. It also presents the typology of frames that guides our analysis and describes our research methodology in more depth. In Chapter 2 we explore what constitutes an intractable conflict. The chapter outlines two essential characteristics of intractability, presents four dimensions on which intractable conflicts can vary, and reviews four major sources of intractability.

Natural Resource Cases Chapters 3, 4, and 5 are the three natural resource cases: Quincy Library, Voyageurs National Park, and Edwards Aquifer. Chapter 6 offers a cross-case comparison of these three cases.

Water Cases Chapters 7 and 8 are two cases on water quality (Doan Brook and the Ohio Antidegredation External Advisory Group). Chapter 9 presents the comparison of these two cases.

Toxic Cases Chapters 10 and 11 present the two Superfund cleanup cases (Drake Chemical and Chattanooga, Tennessee). These are followed by a cross-case analysis (Chapter 12).

Colorado Growth Management Cases Chapters 13 and 14 examine the three cases of growth management in Colorado. Chapter 13 presents the three cases, and Chapter 14 compares the cases and the frames used in each case.

In the final chapter, we present our conclusions about how framing affects intractability of environmental conflicts, along with some recommendations for addressing intractability in practice.

Chapter 1

Framing of Environmental Disputes

Barbara Gray

Imagine two young brothers tumbling in the family playroom. They tussle back and forth giggling as they wrestle each other to the ground. Although they are rambunctious, they do not hurt each other. They are roughhousing—playing. Next, imagine that one of the boys cuffs his brother rather sharply on the ear and the second boy stops cold. Suddenly, they are no longer playing. The fists fly fast and furiously as both boys start to hurt each other and try to win the fight that has emerged.

Why did their interaction shift from playing to fighting? To answer that question, think about their perceptions. At first, they saw their tussle as play; then they saw it as fighting. The shift occurred because they viewed their interaction in a new light. What was considered play initially was reframed as fight when the play became too rough. Their perspective about their interaction changed, or, to use our terminology, they framed their interaction as playing and then they framed it as fighting.*

So what does it mean to say they are "framing" their interaction? Framing involves shaping, focusing, and organizing the world around us. The brothers were having fun until one experienced pain in his ear. Suddenly the frame "play" didn't make sense anymore. Fun does not include pain; in reaction to the pain the first brother reframed the interaction as a "fight" and expressed the result of this reframing by slugging his sibling. Sure enough, his brother responded by framing the interaction as "fight" as well, and the fists flew.

When we use the words "shaping," "focusing," and "organizing" we are talking about framing, and when we use the words "fight" and "play" we are talking about the frames the boys created by framing. Framing is the activity and process of creating and representing frames. It is important to keep in

* This idea was originally presented in Bateson (1975, 177–93).

mind, however, that frames may not be permanent. They can change through future reframing activity. For example, we can frame our favorite hockey player as a "hero" when she scores the winning goal, and as a "bum" when she misses the open net; our parents as "loving" when they pay our tuition, and as "demanding" when they tell us to get a summer job; and ourselves as "studious" when we prepare diligently for an exam, and as "clever" when we pass the exam without reading the textbook.

Environmental disputes are shaped, focused, and organized by the disputants as well as the observers. In this book we argue that the process of framing offers a powerful, if partial, explanation for why some environmental disputes resist resolution. Framing refers to the process of constructing and representing our interpretations of the world around us. We construct frames by sorting and categorizing our experience—weighing new information against our previous interpretations. Through this process we focus attention on an event or issue by "imparting meaning and significance to elements within the frame and setting them apart from what is outside the frame" (Buechler 2000, 41). Framing also involves a representational process in which we present or express how we make sense of things. Constructing and representing, however, are not necessarily separate activities. It is often necessary to represent our thoughts in words to know what we really think of a situation or experience (Weick 1979, 1995).

In addition to being an interpretive process that helps us to understand and clarify what we are experiencing, framing also enables us to locate ourselves with respect to that experience. Through framing, we place ourselves in relation to the issues or events—that is, we take a stance with respect to them (Taylor 2000). Taking a stance involves making attributions about how and why events have occurred (i.e., causality) and who is responsible (i.e., acknowledging or blaming). A frame reflects our interpretation of what is going on and how we see ourselves and others implicated in what is happening.

When we frame a conflict, we develop interpretations about what the conflict is about, why it is occurring, the motivations of the parties involved, and how the conflict should be settled. And we are likely to frame the conflict differently depending on whether we are an observer of others involved in the conflict, a supporter or an opponent of the disputants, or one of the disputants. For example, in the year following the accident at the Three Mile Island nuclear power plant, technical experts from the utility and some citizens held different frames about the risks associated with cleaning up the reactor. The utility was eager to release the radioactive krypton gas remaining in the crippled reactor to reduce any threat of a further catastrophe from keeping the gas bottled up. Local citizens, on the other hand, were worried about suspected health effects from releasing the krypton into the atmosphere. Each framed the potential risk differently.

We all use frames to make sense of the world around us. A frame provides a heuristic for how to categorize and organize data into meaningful chunks of information. When we frame something, we put it in perspective by relating it to other information that we already "know."

Numerous definitions of frames have been provided by researchers in cognitive psychology, microsociology, and sociolinguistics. Cognitive psychologists view frames as cognitive structures in our memory (Bartlett 1932) that help us organize and interpret new experiences (Minsky 1975). In this view, frames are retrieved from memory to guide interpretation of new experiences. The choice of which frame to adopt in a given situation depends on the cues that others in an interaction send as well as on one's own repertoire of memories (Bateson 1972, Van Dijk 1977, 1987). For example, if your friend Tom says to you, "I've been surfing the last two hours" you could frame the meaning of his message in at least two ways. You could assume he meant that he had been "surfing the net" on his computer or that he had been to the beach. Which of these you "heard" might depend on your own frame of reference. If you and Tom have spent time together surfing at the beach, you would likely interpret his message as being about swimming, whereas if you were both computer jocks you would likely assume he had been on the Internet for two hours.

Another perspective suggests that frames are social constructions—that is, they represent agreed-upon "ways to make sense of a situation" (Tannen 1979). When two or more people define a situation the same way, we say they are socially constructing it. Most definitions of frames generally share the fundamental assumption that frames are like road maps that help us to organize our knowledge and to sort and predict the meaning of new information, events, and experiences (Tannen 1979). When people frame conflicts, they create interpretations of what a dispute is about, why it occurred, the other disputants, and whether and how they envision its potential resolution. The frames we construct during a conflict often attribute blame and offer predictions about how the conflict will unfold. And, as we shall see in the following text, framing can also be used to try to influence others to adopt our interpretations of the conflict.

Sociolinguists claim that frames are created when people engage in conversation (Donnellon and Gray 1990, Dore and McDermott 1982) and that disputants use conversations to find out whether or not they share frames. A primary aspect of negotiating, for example, involves testing to see if one's interpretations are compatible with those of one's opponent. Frames, then, are re-created through conversation (Donnellon and Gray 1990, Putnam and Holmer 1992) and reveal how speakers organize what is going on in the midst of an interaction. Frames help us decipher what someone means at any point in a conversation as well as which points are important and which are not (Gumperz 1982). Consider the following conversation:

> Driver: Excuse me, can you tell me the way to get to Bloom Lake?
>
> Old man by roadside: Sure, you go down this road another 3 miles past the Grantley place. You know some say Grantley was crazy. He certainly was a mean ole cuss—killed three of the neighbor's dogs for no reason last year. After you pass Grantley's place, turn left at the next stoplight and go another 2 miles to the lake.
>
> Driver: Thanks.

The directional cues and the initial question suggest that, for the driver, this episode deals with "asking for and receiving directions." Framed in that way, the information the old man provides about Mr. Grantley is subsidiary and even irrelevant. For the old man, however, the conversation was framed as "storytelling" or "characterizing" in which the details about Mr. Grantley were central, and the directions were ancillary. Not only do disputants present their frames in conversations, it is also possible that, by interacting with each other with or without the help of a third party, disputants may also reframe their understanding of the conflict or of the other party. We explore this possibility in the section entitled "Reframing" below.

Research on framing has been conducted at several different levels of analysis—on individual decision frames (e.g., Tversky and Kahneman 1981), on negotiations between individuals (e.g., Donnellon and Gray 1990, Pinkley and Northcraft 1994), and on the intergroup and the societal level (e.g., Schön and Rein 1994, Snow et al. 1986, Taylor 2000). Since all of these approaches are relevant for understanding environmental conflicts, we draw on all three levels to build a comprehensive typology of frames that individuals in environmental conflicts may adopt. (We describe these in detail in the section Frames Analyzed.) However, the second and third levels of analysis—those that occur between negotiators and among different interest groups—are the most useful for linking framing with intractability.[†] We now turn our attention to the effects of framing on environmental disputes.

[†] See Gray, Putnam, and Hanke (2002) for a more extensive review of multiple approaches to the framing of disputes.

Framing in Environmental Disputes

Framing plays an important role in the creation, evolution, and perpetuation of environmental conflicts. Frames are used to (1) define issues, (2) shape what action should be taken and by whom, (3) protect oneself, (4) justify a stance we are taking on an issue, and (5) mobilize people to take or refrain from action on issues.

Frames Define Issues

People use different frames to define whether a problem exists and, if so, what the problem is (Vaughan and Seifert 1992). One area in which these differences in framing abound is in how people view environmental hazards and whether they pose health risks for the community. Parties in a dispute or those confronting environmental hazards develop considerably different frames about what the dispute is about and what should be done about it and by whom (cf. Vaughan and Seifert 1992). For example, people who favor nuclear power tend to frame the issues in terms of economic and technical benefits, whereas opponents focus primarily on psychological risks (Otway, Maurer, and Thomas 1978). Differences also occur frequently in how technical and lay populations frame risks: the former stress prediction and prevention of risks, whereas the latter are concerned about risk detection and repairing damage from risks that have occurred (Elliott 1988). In another example from the occupational health arena, corporate stakeholders framed the health issues in terms of cost and gains, while employees were unwilling even to place monetary valuations on issues they considered fundamental to their well-being (Hilgartner 1985). In still another example, differences were found in whether employees and nonemployees perceived that there was danger from living near an arsenic smelter. Some framed the smelter as hazardous; others did not (Van Liere and Dunlap 1980).

Stakeholders in environmental disputes often base their views on vastly discrepant frameworks of environmental values (Gray 1997, Hunter 1989, Rolston 1990, Vaughan and Seifert 1992, Wildavsky and Dake 1990). For example, distinctions have been made between the "deep ecological" or the "new environmental" paradigm (cf. Dunlap and Van Liere 1978, Hunter 1989, Milbrath 1984) and the "dominant societal" paradigm (also referred to as the "exploitative capitalist" paradigm). Followers of the deep ecological paradigm believe that "humans are an integral part of nature and all natural entities have intrinsic value" (Hunter 1989, 29). They stress the oneness of nature, whereas those espousing the dominant societal paradigm view humans as separate from nature and believe nonhuman life-forms have only instrumental value (i.e., nonhuman life-forms exist only to support human life-forms). Others have suggested that fundamental values or worldviews about society shape where people stand on environmental issues. Four worldviews in particular (hierarchist, individualist, egalitarian, and fatalist) were strong predictors of both risk perceptions and risk preferences (Wildavsky and Dake 1990). These are discussed in more detail under social control frames in our framing typology below.

Other types of frames that factor prominently in environmental disputes are frames about fairness. Such frames involve notions of justice that carry entitlement claims. That is, when disputants believe they are deprived of something they deserve or are entitled to, they may evoke a fairness frame to represent their grievance. For example, if I believe I am entitled to drill for water as part of my private property rights, I am likely to conclude that a tax on how much water I use will be unfair. Another example of entitlement claims rooted in fairness frames can be found in the environmental justice movement. This movement asserts that African American communities in the United States bear a disproportionate share of risk for exposure to toxic materials because the plants that produced the toxic materials were located in these communities (Bullard 1990, Bullard and Wright 1989, Taylor 2000). Proponents of this view use "entitlement" rhetoric to frame their concerns and to seek redress for the health effects that such exposure may have caused.

Frames Shape Actions

Frames not only shape what parties think about the issues, they also influence their preferences for whether and how a dispute should be resolved (Merry and Silbey 1984; Sheppard, Blumenfeld-Jones, and Roth 1989; Vaughan and Seifert 1992). For example, as noted earlier, in conflicts over the risks associated with toxic pollution, if parties frame a problem from a technical perspective, they may prefer to develop an accurate cost–benefit analysis of technical alternatives before taking any action and then base their action on this analysis. In contrast, parties who frame the issue as a health risk may insist on immediate protection from the risk no matter what the cost. These differences in framing are reflected in both the Drake and the Chattanooga cases described later in this book.

Frames Are Used to Protect Ourselves

Different assertions about rights often move disputes into the legal arena, where dispositions about whose rights will prevail are decided. Disputants who feel aggrieved by the actions of others and resort to "rights" framing are likely to seek legal recourse for their grievances. Rights frames are evoked to redress perceptions of injustice or to prevent injustice from occurring.

However, disputants frequently frame their rights differently (Gray 1997). Differences in rights framing can be seen in disputes between ranchers and Native Americans over access to water. Ranchers framed the issue in terms of property rights (as prescribed by state law), whereas the Native Americans based their rights to water on aboriginal possession (as defined by the federal courts). The Native Americans considered these water disputes to be sovereignty issues (i.e., ones that affected the integrity of the tribe as a people) because access to water ensured their survival (Folk-Williams 1988). Their framing enabled them to protect their identity as a separate people.

And, as Ury, Brett, and Goldberg (1993) have argued, "rights" framing is more positional than framing in terms of "interests" and is more likely to escalate the conflict. Therefore, when one or both parties invoke rights framing, it increases the chances that the dispute will end up in the courts.

Frames Enable Us to Justify Our Actions

Once we have adopted a frame, particularly one that helps to define our identity, the frame colors the way we define what is real and what is not. Frames can also shape what we believe "ought" to be or "should" be. If we conform to the expectations set up in our frames, we can justify our own behavior as "correct" or "good." Moreover, we are likely to blame or fault others who fail to live up to our expectations. For example, employees who frame their employers as unfair or exploitive may justify taking extra-long lunch hours or extra "sick days" because they believe they are entitled to make up for their employer's misdeeds (Sheppard, Lewicki, and Minton, 1992).

Frames Are Used to Mobilize Others to Take Action

The role of framing in social movement formation has been considered extensively (e.g., in the environmental and social justice movements). Here framing occurs in two ways. First, participants in social movements use framing in "interpretive" ways to collectively formulate their grievance (Buechler 2000, 41). In other words, framing plays a significant role in creating a common cause, mission, or vision among participants, and a common perception of the enemy. Second, participants in social movements use framing in "intentional" ways to "ripen" movement issues so as to influence others' actions with regard to the issues (Heifetz 1994). Martin Luther King's famous "I have a dream" speech, for example, framed a vision that gave meaning and action to members of the civil rights movement. It was also designed to ripen the issue of civil rights as a social justice issue in larger society. The speech was designed to increase the prospects for social change by mobilizing actors, both inside and outside of the movement. The original Earth Day celebration was intentionally designed to cement a vision for the environmental movement itself and as a way to heighten awareness of injustices against the environment.

When frames are used to mobilize participants for social movements, what gets framed are primarily "grievance claims." That is, the frames convey grievances that individuals have about existing social institutions or practices (such as the disproportionate exposure to toxic pollution borne by African American communities) (Snow et al. 1986). Framing is used in three ways to present grievance claims (Snow and Benford 1988). First through "diagnostic" framing, vague dissatisfactions are transformed into legitimate claims that become imbued with moral meaning and significance and targeted at the perpetrators of the unjust actions. An example of diagnostic framing would be: "That chemical company has polluted our drinking water and caused our children to get leukemia." Thus an aggrieved group uses diagnostic framing to signal that an injustice has been done to them (Gamson, Fireman, and Rytina 1982; Goffman 1974). Second, "prognostic" framing goes a step further to propose strategies and tactics for dealing with the target and rectifying the grievance (Snow and Benford 1988). For example, "The government should make them pay every penny it takes to clean up our water." Finally, "motivational" framing is used by movement leaders as a rallying cry to mobilize support for the cause. This is accomplished through the use of "vocabularies of motive" that justify movement participation and legitimate noncompliance with institutional norms. "If we don't challenge these big companies, no one will, and our children will continue to be sick." Social movement activists have also been shown to adopt specific rhetoric to crystallize adherents' views about social injustice or entitlement, for example, by imputing intentionality to others' actions (e.g., referring to a corporation's attempts to "poison" us) (Gamson and Meyer 1996, Ibarra and Kitsuse 1993). The rhetoric used in these frames stirs people up, attributes blame to others, and mobilizes supporters for the social movement who then adopt a "collective action" frame to redress the wrongs. The framing both inspires action taking and provides a basis for justifying it (Snow and Benford 1992).

A critical step in the mobilization process is "frame alignment." This occurs when individuals realize that their frames match those of social movement members (Snow et al. 1986). This step involves commitment by the individual to the ideological assumptions, values, and norms of the social movement group. By voicing one's commitment, an individual member effectively assumes a new identity constructed in accord with the movement and, especially important, in opposition to existing institutional norms and values of those they deem responsible for their plight (Gamson 1992, Tajfel and Turner 1985). We further discuss the role of identity later in the chapter.

The role of framing in promoting social movement activism has been demonstrated in many environmental arenas, including the nuclear disarmament movement (Benford 1993), the movement for "environmental justice" in the United States (Taylor 2000), the growth of regional populism in Italy (Diani 1996), as well as others. For example, Taylor (2000) has made a convincing case that environmental justice framing mobilized people of color to join the environmental movement during the 1980s and '90s. Framing environmental issues as social justice issues, comparing them to other labor and human rights issues, and connecting them to the urban environments where they live and work enabled people of color to identify with the environmental movement, albeit via their own distinct brand of environmentalism.

Also noteworthy is the possibility of frame conflicts among movement members. For example, during the early 1980s some members of the nuclear disarmament movement expressed much more radical views than others (Benford 1993). Similarly, the advent of the environmental justice movement initially introduced consternation among mainstream environmentalists in the United States, until the Environmental Protection Agency (EPA) took several steps to legitimize the movement's activities (Taylor 2000). Similar differences in strategy became the basis for conflict among environmental groups concerned about "green marketing" campaigns‡ in Canada (Westley and Vrendenburg 1991).

Need for a More Systematic Frame Analysis

Researchers studying social movements have made significant progress in demonstrating a relationship between framing and conflict dynamics. How-

‡ Green marketing refers to the development and distribution of environmentally friendly products such as detergents without phosphates or water soluble packaging materials. The conflicts developed over whether products really met the test of being environmentally friendly or not.

ever, there has been no comprehensive, systematic analysis of differences in frames among all the key parties in major environmental disputes. In fact, most researchers write as if all stakeholders hold the same frames about environmental issues, rather than acknowledging that framing is a complex process in which disputants may hold multiple (Benford 1997) or even contradictory frames. As some scholars have noted, frames are not static entities, but can be revised or transformed under certain circumstances (LaBianca, Gray, and Brass 2000; Mather and Yngvesson 1980–81; Putnam and Holmer 1992). And, while this premise undergirds the practice of third parties who mediate environmental disputes (cf. Lam, Rifkin, and Townley 1989, Moore 1986), evidence of reframing has largely been anecdotal. For example, in a conflict over homelessness in Massachusetts, the three major contending parties (advocates for the homeless, local charitable and nonprofit organizations, and members of the state government) each started with different and largely exclusive frames about the problem. But eventually, as the disputants learned about the powerful role that crack cocaine played in the problem, each began to adopt a reframed perspective that included elements of all three perspectives: a social welfare frame, a market frame, and a social control frame (Schön and Rein 1994). More systematic research analyses of frame changes (e.g., analyzing the parties' communications) are few (cf. Feyerherm 1995, for a notable exception). This analysis of communications, called discourse analysis, allows researchers to identify frames by studying transcripts of conversations and analyzing the perspective being used by a speaker (Potter and Wetherall 1987). Finally, an understanding of which frames or combinations of frames contribute to perpetuating intractable conflicts is also needed.

We seek to remedy these deficiencies. We utilize a discourse analytic approach to examine transcripts of interviews with stakeholders in the eight intractable conflicts. While our data will show that environmental disputants use a wide repertoire of frames (see Wiethoff et al. 1999), in this book we concentrate on three generic frames that were prevalent in all of our cases: identity frames, characterization frames, and conflict management frames. These three frames helped to shape the dynamics in each of our cases. Additionally, in some cases, other types of generic frames were also salient and critical to the dynamics of a particular conflict. These included views of social control, risk, whole story, power, and loss versus gain frames. Though less central to this book, these five types of frames are also explained briefly later in this chapter.

Frames Analyzed in Our Cases

Identity Frames

The concept of identity focuses on how individuals answer the question, Who am I? (Hoare 1994, 25). Individuals may answer this question in a variety of ways, depending on their membership in social groups and who they understand themselves to be. In general, people think of themselves as belonging to certain social categories that have given characteristics (Hogg, Terry, and White 1995), for instance, an "environmentalist" or a "rancher" or a "New Yorker." Similarly, Tajfel and Turner (1985) view social identity as the self-image that is created via social category membership. These social categories, or group characteristics, then become part of the definition of whom that individual is (i.e., a part of the person's self-identity) (Hogg, Terry, and White 1995). Identity, then, is iterative: shaping and being shaped by the individual's social and cultural experiences and memberships (Hoare 1994).

Identities of social groups are constructed through social comparison processes with other groups and often in opposition to the identity of another group (Gamson 1992, 1997; Snow and Benford 1992; Tajfel and Turner 1985). By comparing our group with others, we usually pay attention to the differences between the groups and the similarities within our own group. Group members tend to see each other in a positive light, while conceiving of other groups in a less favorable light (Tajfel and Turner 1985). This kind of comparison allows members of the in-group to solidify their own identity and conclude that they are superior to other groups. Thus groups develop reflexive frames that depict the way disputants feel about themselves and projective identity frames that carry disputants' characterizations of others in the conflict.

Why are identities so important in understanding environmental disputes? Conflict almost inevitably arises when people's identities are threatened (Rothman 1997) because such identity challenges call into question the beliefs and values that undergird who people believe they are. Identity challenges call into question the legitimacy of how a group has defined itself and even its very right to exist (Kelman 1999). This type of conflict can be particularly difficult to overcome because people become extremely defensive when the essential beliefs and values that define who they are are questioned or threatened. They are not willing to compromise on these issues. In the extreme, to do so would produce anomie—a lack of purpose, identity, or ethical values. Additionally, during this framing process, people typically externalize responsibility for negative events to others whose identities oppose their own. This process of externalization, or blaming the other, fuels the conflict (Sherif 1958). When parties are invalidating each other's identities, the potential for escalation is high (Northrup 1989).

In addition to identities based on demographic characteristics (e.g., race, gender, and ethnicity), individuals may form salient identities around four other aspects of their lives: a location (e.g., where they are from or where they live or work), their role (e.g., as a carpenter or social reformer), the institutions with which they associate (e.g., a federal government employee), or their interests (e.g., whether they support or oppose capital punishment) (Kusel et al 1996).

Often a strong relationship forms between an individual's identity and the beliefs of the community to which that person belongs (Roland 1994). Our analysis revealed that the disputants in our cases derived aspects of their identities from all of these sources. For example, place-based identity statements concern "who I am" in relation to my geographic location or community. We often associate speech, behavior, and dress, as well as beliefs, with place-based identities. For example, when we see someone with a cowboy hat and boots, we think of Texans, or we link a fast-paced, frenetic lifestyle with New Yorkers. An example of a place-based identity frame from a stakeholder who lives close to Voyageurs National Park is illustrative:

> I moved up here specifically to enjoy the area. If it wasn't for Rainy Lake, and . . . being able to get in my boat, from my front and my back yard, and navigate the most beautiful scenery in the world, right here, I would have never moved up here. And the day they take that away from me, I'll tell you, that'll be a sad day.

Identities based on roles usually reflect characteristics or behaviors that people in those roles typically engage in. Over time these roles become socially constructed and imbued with values, and may pose constraints on those holding such roles. For example, the role of "stay-at-home mom" has traditionally been applied to mothers who weren't employed outside the home and who remained at home to care for their children. However, since the electronic age has made it possible for people to conduct their work at home, the frame of "stay-at-home" mom may soon be an anachronism.

Institutional identities derive from affiliation with a particular organization and its mission or values and can be at the root of policy controversies (Schön and Rein 1994). For example, government employees who work for two different federal agencies—the U.S. Forest Service and the U.S. Fish and Wildlife Service—often find that their institutional identities clash because the mission of the former is to manage national forests, including determining when and where timber harvests can occur, while the latter is concerned about protection of endangered species that might be adversely affected by logging. When individuals wear the mantle of their agency or organization, they likely will display institutional identity frames.

Finally, an interest-based identity statement reflects shared concerns about particular issues, causes, or values that may be reflective of a special interest group. A citizen who has campaigned doggedly for environmental conservation might make the following interest-based identity statement:

> I'm deeply committed to preservation of the earth and all its species. I've devoted my life to this cause.

Which of the various identities an individual holds will become salient at any given time is determined, in part, by the strength of that identity for the individual as well as by situational factors (Luthanen and Crocker 1991, Stryker 1968). When individuals join a social movement, their commitment to a particular identity will likely be bolstered by their interactions with other activists (McAdam and Paulsen 1993, McCall and Simmons 1978). Thus identity strength and identity salience may be crucial factors in heightening a dispute's intractability because they narrow their range of acceptable alternatives (McAdam and Paulsen 1993, 146). The more people perceive a direct threat to an identity to which they are strongly committed, the more likely they are to resist compromise proposals.

In some of our cases, place-based identities figured more prominently in the conflict than other types of identity. Identities were also constructed around interests and institutions. In general, identities tend to remain immutable over time—a factor that can feed intractability. However, in a few of the cases, some redefinition of identities has taken place as the conflict has evolved, and with revisions in disputants' self-perceptions have come opportunities to resolve dispute episodes.

Characterization Frames

Characterization frames mirror identity frames in that they are statements made by individuals about how they understand someone *else* to be; that is, Who are *they?* Characterization frames arise from the attributions of blame and causality that we make about our experiences and about what others have done to shape our experiences. We are all prone to what is called the fundamental attribution error—that is, we tend to blame others, or situational factors, for our fate, rather than blaming ourselves (Ross 1977). On the other hand, when we evaluate others' behavior on similar issues, we attribute the failing to them, rather than to external factors. Also, we do not consider whether we have contributed to their problems.

As noted in the previous section, to define oneself as a member of a group, one must commit to adopting the values and behavior espoused by that group, at least to some degree. That is, we accept a group identity (Taylor and Moghaddam 1994). This group identity influences what members of a given group should believe as well as how they should behave (Ashforth and Mael 1989; Hogg, Terry, and White 1995). Once individuals establish their identities and group memberships, they perceive themselves as similar to or different from members of other groups and often evaluate those other groups negatively (Hogg, Terry, and White 1995, Tajfel and Turner 1985). The more an individual's social identity is framed as a group identity, the greater will be the motivation to denigrate members of other groups to which the person doesn't belong (Tajfel and Turner 1979). Thus identity and group membership may create strongly perceived differences or similarities among in-group members and lead to discrimination and prejudices (Tajfel and Turner 1985) as well as conflict (Rothman 1997) toward out-group members.

Thus, to identify characterization frames, we looked for comments that expressed perceptions of another group or its members, specifically comments that helped answer the question, How do I see others in the conflict? These characterizations can be either positive or negative. For example, government employees could be referred to as "power nuts" or people from a particular town as "jerks." In most of our cases, derogatory characterization frames were frequently voiced about the other parties. Moreover, like identity frames, these characterization frames seemed to reflect strongly ingrained beliefs or judgments by the individuals who uttered them.

Conflict Management Frames

This category of frames deals with disputants' preferences for how the conflict should be managed or dealt with. Early work by Sheppard, Blumenfield-Jones, and Roth identified four frames that informal third parties use to deal with disputes. Depending on which of these frames the parties selected, they would use different strategies to deal with the dispute. For example, parties who held a "stop" frame would actively work to get the parties to set aside their differences. On the other hand, if they held a "negotiation" frame, they would prefer that the parties sought resolution by conversing with each other. This perspective on frames is helpful for predicting whether and how an individual disputant may become involved in a conflict, but we determined that it did not offer the full range of conflict resolution options available to participants in environmental and public policy conflicts. Instead, we found that Keltner's (1994) "struggle spectrum" provided a wider range of options for our classification of conflict management frames. Keltner proposed a continuum of six aspects of struggle that ranged from discussion at one end to fighting at the other. We adapted Keltner's model to refine the number of options within both the discussion and the negotiation categories.

We coded our data for nine types of conflict management preference frames, including an "other" category for frames that did not align with any of the other eight frame types. Like Keltner's classification our categories ranged along a spectrum from the least active (avoidance, passivity) to the most active (struggle, sabotage, and violence). See Table 1.1 for the complete list.

When disputants have different conflict management frames, it is usually harder for them to find a way to resolve the dispute that all find acceptable.

Table 1.1. Conflict Management Frames

Frame Type	*Definition*	*Example*
Avoidance/passivity	Statements that give a preference for doing nothing, letting the matter rest, inertia, no action.	
Fact-finding	Recommendations for investigation, collecting more information, getting scientific facts, conducting research on the problem. A broad category that means conduct a study or any type of research or investigation.	But I think you need to know that we have presented the facts of this incineration project, the actual data we've collected. We have been very forthcoming and open with the entire community.
Joint problem solving	Statements that prefer community or joint action, common ground, mediation, collaboration, conciliation, and collective processes. Two subcategories exist:	
	Consensus—All parties participate in any decision taken.	*Consensus*—I'd really prefer to get everyone to sit down and talk this thing out. We're all reasonable people.

(*continued*)

Table 1.1. *Continued*

Frame Type	*Definition*	*Example*
	Authority decides after consultation—Agencies gather input from stakeholders but make final decision themselves.	*Authority decides after consultation*—The Community Advisory Committee will make recommendations to the agency, but in the end the agency will make the final decision.*
Authority decides based on expertise	Local authorities, agencies, or institutions or boards make the decision because they have the technical knowledge and expertise.	As a matter of fact there are fights within the Environmental Protection Agency over some of these issues and then somebody has to decide. You know. It's just like anything else. In the end, you have to weigh the pros and cons and all of the points of view.
Adjudication	Statements that imply that a third party should decide, such as an arbitrator, the courts, judges, or judicial authority.	The only chance we have . . . is the courts. And there are some of us that feel that the only way the issues are going to be resolved is through litigation.
Appeal to political action	Recommendation to handle the problem through enacting or abolishing laws and regulations. Addressing the conflict through lobbying, referendums, supporting candidates, and legislative actions. Appeals to state or federal agencies to enact, change, or abolish laws.	We used to write letters to everyone and now we know whom to target. We know who has the power. The power starts at congressperson and ends at president. They're the only ones who are going to make any difference for us at this point. We don't waste our time very much any more with (name of State Rep.).
Appeal to market economy	Negotiation of water rights, market solutions, economic and system changes.	We should develop an incentive system that would encourage some users to sell their water to others.
Struggle, sabotage, and violence	Statements that refer to continued fighting, civil disobedience, force, etc.	If necessary, we will engage in civil disobedience to get our point across.

Frame Type	*Definition*	*Example*
Other conflict management modes	Statements that recommend decisions based on "common sense," all other approaches that do not fit into the categories above.	This conflict would have been solved years ago if they would just have used common sense.

*Federal agencies in the United States are required to comply with the Federal Advisory Committee Act that outlines a specific set of procedures for using consensus-based processes. An Authority Decides Based on Consultation process enables them to consider citizen input without violating the provisions of the act because nonagency personnel do not actually make the final decision.

For example, if one group prefers joint problem solving while another prefers adjudication, it may be difficult for them to sit down to negotiate a resolution. If both prefer adjudication, however, or appeal to political action, the conflict is likely to escalate with each side claiming temporary victory until the courts or legislative bodies reverse an earlier decision.

Whole Story Frames

We found that often our interviewees would provide encapsulated summaries of what they believed the conflict they were engaged in was about. For example, in the Voyageurs' case, one disputant suggested, "This dispute is mainly about how the National Park Service is managing the park," whereas another concluded that the conflict was basically about value differences. We call these whole story frames because they provide a concise summary of the basis for the conflict. These frames are often denoted with phrases such as, "It all boils down to" or "Essentially the problem is" or "In a nutshell." Our use of the term, "whole story frames," is both similar to and different from that introduced by Schön and Rein (1994), who used it to refer to the process of wholesale transportation of a story from one situation to another, where it may or may not be directly applicable. The difference in our use of the term lies in the fact that we are not concerned with the process of "reflective transfer,"§ but rather in the process by which the essence of an experience is captured in a succinct format, a *whole story frame,* which then informs or guides a disputant's behavior in a conflict.

§ By "reflective transfer" Schön and Rein mean "the process by which patterns detected in one situation are carried over as projective models to other situations where they are used to generate new causal inferences and are subjected to new, situation-specific tests of internal validity" (1994, 204).

	low **Interdependence** high	
high **Ownership**	Individualist	Egalitarian
low	Fatalist	Hierarchist

Figure 1.1. Social Control Frames

Social Control Frames

The set of four frames referred to as social control frames closely parallels the original delineation by Dake (1991, 1992) and Wildavsky and Dake (1990). Social control frames represent individual views about how decisions regarding social issues should be made. The distinctions are derived from two separate dimensions: (1) the degree to which people should be dependent on others (particularly on experts) for decisions and (2) the degree of ownership over the decisions (e.g., collective or individual ownership). See Figure 1.1 for the four types of social control that are possible when these two dimensions are placed on a matrix.

Fatalists (low ownership, low interdependence) believe they have no control over anything. Because of this they are resigned to tight controls on their behavior by others and rationalize any isolation they may experience.** Individualists (high ownership, low interdependence) believe that they know best how society should be governed and prefer individual freedom to bid and bargain as they choose. Egalitarians (high ownership, high interdependence) prefer that a group or community exerts control over any conflicts that arise. This frame is concerned with equality and a desire to minimize differences between individuals. Egalitarians prefer that everyone have voice in the process. Finally, hierarchists (low ownership, high interdependence) prefer control by experts. They expect a stratified society with clear social boundaries and, therefore, see the control of the situation from the "top" down. They also show a clear respect for authority, comply with regulations, and expect the same from others.

For egalitarian and hierarchical views of control, we found that people in our cases also made a distinction between local and nonlocal control, and some preferred local while others preferred nonlocal. "Local" refers to community-, regional-, and state-level control, and "national" refers to federal, national, or global decision control. As a result, for the egalitarian and hierarchist frames we

** Wildavsky and Dake (1990) found few examples of this category and dropped it from their subsequent analyses. We also did not find any examples of fatalists, but this is not surprising, since it is unlikely that these people would be actively engaged in environmental conflicts. Still, we cannot rule out their existence.

distinguished local perspectives from nonlocal perspectives. In the Quincy Library case, for example, after a local consensus had been reached, other stakeholders who had not participated in the decision sought to elevate the dispute to a federal level where it eventually was voted on in the Congress. So it moved from an egalitarian local to an egalitarian nonlocal form of social control. In contrast, a hierarchist nonlocal view of social control would argue for the importance of federal agency expertise to protect a natural resource (e.g., in the Edwards case when the U.S. Fish and Wildlife Service intervened to protect endangered species) or to prevent air or water pollution (e.g., involvement of the U.S. EPA in Superfund site cleanups).

Power Frames

In our case studies, we used a "grounded approach" (Glaser and Strauss 1967) to identify power frames; that is, we allowed the frame categories to emerge from the way various stakeholders talked about power in each dispute. Nine categories of power frames were eventually identified and are listed with examples in Table 1.2.

Table 1.2. Power Frames

Frame Type	*Definition*	*Example*
Authority/positional	Actual ability to make decisions on the basis of formal role assignment, job title/description, or organizational position.	I mean he had the power because he was the ranking member of the transportation committee. He had the power to basically just push through whatever he wanted.
Resources	Have power because of resources (e.g., time, support staff, money, etc.) that others do not possess.	It all comes down to the golden rule again. Those who got the gold make the rules.
Expertise	Possess relevant or unique knowledge and experience that others do not have.	He is influential because he knows a lot about the technical issues in the case.
Personal	An individual's interpersonal style grants credibility and power in interaction (e.g., charisma, competent communication skills, negotiation experience, etc.).	I think that if we would have had somebody like Dave from the beginning it probably would have been really good because Dave is a very powerful person and has a lot of capability.

(continued)

Table 1.2. *Continued*

Frame Type	*Definition*	*Example*
Coalitional/relational	Power comes from membership in and/or affiliation with a particular group of people who support that individual's perspective.	They know how to rally the numbers just like the National Rifle Association can put their people, whether it's right or wrong, you know what I mean, they know how to rally their people.
Sympathy/vulnerability	Power comes from the victim role because the victims' situation is likely to be supported by others on an emotional level (e.g., children, endangered species).	They've used it to get their way, and after a while they either just did not come back to the table or they would come back and just be angry and mad for the rest of the day, like a small child would be, because they didn't get their way.
Force/threat	Power comes from coercion, or from threatening coercive action, from a party's threat to use their Best Alternative to a Negotiated Agreement (BATNA) (e.g., to sue another).	When the government came in to possess the land . . . there were some threats and some intimidations that were made.
Moral/righteous	Have power because position is on the "moral high ground" or believe themselves to be ethically or morally "right."	He's usually not in big trouble when he runs for reelection. But, if he took on the moral high ground, as it were, he stands a terrible risk of really pissing off people who have very deeply held beliefs.
Voice	Have power because they have a forum in which to be heard, a "voice at the table" in this dispute. Power comes from participation, from having the ability to be a spokesperson and/or communicate one's own views.	Whatever type of board is set up, I want a seat at the table.

Risk Frames

A major source of conflict in some environmental disputes stems from the differences in how the parties view the type and level of risk associated with an environmental hazard. As we noted earlier, government agencies and lay populations often view these risks differently (Elliott 1988). In ascertaining the risks associated with various solutions to environmental problems, stakeholder groups use cost–benefit analyses (i.e., they weigh the advantages or disadvantages of a particular solution, such as pros and cons of constructing a new power plant or trying a new process for cleaning up hazardous waste). In making such determinations of the costs and benefits of a new facility or a toxic cleanup, government agencies often use contingent valuation analysis to determine public acceptance of a risk (Mitchell and Carson 1989). These methods attempt to quantify and weigh all of the possible consequences and then make trade-offs to come up with a final determination of the best approach to select. Consider the case of cleanup at Three Mile Island mentioned earlier. In determining how best to clean up the radioactive krypton gas that remained in the reactor after the accident, the EPA generated three possible solutions. One of these was to cryogenically freeze the krypton to liquefy it, and then keep it bottled up on the island. While this solution may have produced the least possible exposure to radiation for the surrounding community, it was prohibitively expensive and posed a risk of future exposure if the bottles ever leaked. Instead, the EPA chose to slowly vent the krypton to the atmosphere taking into account wind and weather patterns to ensure that only very low levels of radiation were released while the krypton dissipated into the upper atmosphere. Although agency officials assured the public that radiation exposure during the venting was safe, not all residents were comfortable with the EPA's assessment. Thus, their frames about the level of risk differed from those of the EPA (Gricar and Baratta 1983).

Gain versus Loss

One perspective on risk that is common to environmental disputes is whether the parties see actions taken by others as creating a loss or a gain for themselves or for others. It is quite likely that environmental disputants see a particular action as resulting in a personal loss or gain. This determination will be affected, in part, by the "reference point" they select for evaluating the decision's likely consequences. For example, government agents may view cleanup of hazardous material to be a gain for a community because compliance with federal standards for exposure to that material has been achieved. In contrast, community members may view the decision as a loss because they believe that, even when the standards are observed, some residents will still be exposed to health hazards. As noted earlier, whether a dispute is framed as a loss or a gain has been shown to affect the degree of risk a decision maker will accept (Tversky and Kahneman 1981). Examples of gain–loss framing in environmental disputes are also evident in how people frame social dilemmas (McCusker and Carnevale 1995).

Reframing

We have mentioned briefly that reframing occurs when disputants change their frames; that is, when they develop a new way of interpreting or understanding the issues in the dispute or a new way of appraising one or more of the other parties in the conflict.[††] In order to reframe one's understanding of a conflict, some degree of perspective taking is required. Perspective taking involves standing back, observing, and reflecting on the fact that there is more than one way to view the issues. Reframing "depends on the ability of at least some of the actors to inquire into the intentions and meanings of other actors involved with them in the controversy" (Schön and Rein 1994, 171). As long as parties believe that their own view is the only one possible to understand the issues in dispute, they cannot reframe. But once they begin to realize that one's frame depends on one's own vantage point, this realization makes reframing possible. Reframing depends on the ability to entertain a perspective other than one's own, to weigh the relative merits of each perspective, and to select the most preferable one.

Since reframing requires perspective taking, it is often difficult for parties to reframe without the help of a neutral third party or someone who does not have a direct stake in the conflict. Descriptions of the role of mediators, for example, explicitly describe their role as one of framing the issues for the parties and helping the parties to reframe the issues in a way that encourages resolution (Lam, Rifkin, and Townley 1989; Moore 1986). Disputants typically use positional language to present their frames, stating what their preferred outcomes are. By listening closely for the parties' underlying interests (their underlying needs), mediators attempt to reformulate and re-present to the parties an interpretation of the conflict that incorporates both (or all) parties' interests.

[††] See Putnam and Holmer (1992) for a comparison of several theoretical approaches to framing and reframing.

Several techniques for reaching integrative solutions in negotiations involve reframing of the issues or the alternatives (Lewicki, Saunders, and Minton 1999). For example, logrolling involves reframing the negotiation around each party's most preferred outcome. Finding a bridge solution allows the other party a lot of influence over deciding what the problem is and making sure that any problems they have with implementing the agreement are addressed. Reframing can also be used in response to another's negative tactics—by interpreting the tactic in a different light or directly renegotiating the rules of the game being played (Lewicki, Saunders, and Minton 1999). For example, when the negotiator for a manufacturing company was labeled a "polluter" by an environmentalist, the former could reframe that negative characterization in this way, "None of us are interested in polluting our town's drinking water, but we are interested in reaching agreement about appropriate tests to measure water quality. What are your specific objections to the tests we have proposed?" This comment deflects the personal attack and reframes the conversation in terms of the problem both parties are trying to solve.

Let's consider an example of reframing a conflict between a state highway department and a rapidly growing township. To accommodate an expected increase in traffic, the highway department would like to build a road through a park in the township. The township, however, is not eager to give up its park. It appears that the parties are deadlocked—each holding firm to its position—to build or not build the road. More detailed inquiry, it turns out, reveals that the highway department wants to purchase the land for the highway now to save money; they don't intend to build the road until sometime in the future when an increase in population warrants it. The township, on the other hand, wants to ensure that there is green space for its citizens, but it is not wedded to the particular location of the current park. The conflict can be reframed by one of the parties or by a mediator who realizes that it is possible to satisfy both parties' interests rather than one party having to give in to the other's wishes. The mediator might suggest the following reframing: How can the state acquire the land now that it needs for the future highway and still allow the city to have a park? By reframing the problem in this way, a constructive solution can emerge. Let the highway department purchase the land now, but keep it as a park until the city (using the money from the purchase) can construct a park somewhere else. Then the road can be constructed through the old park. Although in this example the reframing produced an agreement that satisfies both parties, reframing does not necessarily guarantee that the conflict will be resolved.

Several techniques for reframing have been identified by Moore (1986).

These techniques include: (1) shifting from specific interests to more general ones, (2) narrowing the issues or breaking them into smaller parts, (3) translating disputes over values into interests, (4) identifying superordinate (or overarching) goals (Sherif et al. 1961), and (5) agreeing to disagree. By shifting to more general interests, a more inclusive agenda is created for the disputants, presumably one that enables each to envision how their particular concerns can be satisfied within a constellation of solutions that satisfy others' interests too. This was illustrated in the reframing of the highway/park conflict above. Reframing can also accomplish a narrowing of the issues that enables the parties to craft solutions to part of the conflict at a time and possibly to trade off these outcomes to partially satisfy each party. The third approach to reframing, translating values into interests, is likely to be more difficult because disputants in value-based conflicts usually feel considerable attachment to their values. Still, if the reframing preserves the integrity of their values, it could be successful. For example, in a dispute over salmon fishing, Native Americans held strong beliefs that the spawning grounds of the salmon were sacred places. This was reframed into an interest stated as "protecting the spawning grounds of the salmon." The fourth approach to reframing involves finding a higher-level goal to which all parties can subscribe. For example, a conflict within a family over which activities to include in their vacation can be reframed to emphasize the importance of spending time together no matter what activity they choose. The final option for reframing is to acknowledge that there is no easy resolution, and the parties must respect each other's right to hold distinct and opposing viewpoints. While this reframing does not lead to resolution of the issues, it may result in reduced tension and prevent escalation of the conflict.

Conclusion

This chapter has introduced the concepts of frames and framing and established their importance in environmental disputes. We have shown how frames are used by all of us to make sense of our surroundings and experiences. And, although framing is not unique to environmental conflicts (or to conflicts generally), we have identified certain kinds of frames that are prevalent in environmental conflicts that make them especially intractable or resistant to resolution. In the next chapter we identify the dimensions of intractable conflict and consider their role in environmental conflicts in particular.

Chapter 2

Intractability: Definitions, Dimensions, and Distinctions

Linda L. Putnam and Julia M. Wondolleck

The Hatfields and McCoys feuded for many years. It never mattered what the issue was, nor what the law said. They despised each other, it was as simple as that. They fought whenever an opportunity arose to do so. All that mattered in this conflict was who was involved—the parties—not the issue or the social system within which it resided. Their conflict was rooted in the fundamental nature of the relationship between these families (Donnelly 1972).

Unlike the Hatfields and McCoys, the parties engaged in the long-standing conflict over abortion are not fundamentally opposed to each other. In fact, while some are complete strangers, others are good friends, and even members of the same family. Abortion is an issue that divides people who agree on all other matters. It is an issue that persists regardless of changes in the law and regulations. With abortion it does not matter what the law says; and it does not matter who is involved. The source of the conflict is the issue itself, one that contains fundamental but opposing values that trigger conflict, regardless of the social system or the nature of the relationships between the parties (Tribe 1992).

The conflict over global warming—its reach, implications, and potential responses—has been intensifying for over a decade. Panels of esteemed scientists, candidates for high political office, industrial associations, environmental organizations, and schoolchildren ponder, debate, and propose solutions that some people embrace while others quickly dismiss them. An environmental problem of this scope and complexity that requires dramatic changes in economic systems, social patterns, and human behavior has not arisen before. Developing a credible and acceptable problem definition and generating approaches to resolving it are elusive. Resolution requires concurrence across nations, cultures, economies, and organizations for which no prescribed path for decision making exists (Gray 1999). Unlike the Hatfields and McCoys, this conflict is not rooted in the nature of the relationships between these parties. Unlike abortion, global warming is not an issue about which people are in fundamental disagreement. The ambiguity within the social system about how to proceed perpetuates this conflict. No policies, procedures, institutions, or authorities have jurisdiction to deal with the full scope of an issue like global warming. In this vacuum, the conflict continues to rage.

The Vietnam conflict began as a war against French colonialism and evolved into a civil war between North and South Vietnam. It quickly escalated beyond the country's borders, drawing in other nations with objectives that differed from those of the Vietnamese. Vietnam became a theater in which conflict between capitalist and communist systems were played out, often symbolically. It erupted through social unrest in the United States, eventually dividing this nation. Over time, political institutions became committed to perpetuating the dispute for reasons unrelated to the original conflict. Civil strife between North and South Vietnam eventually had little to do with the perpetuation of this conflict. While relationships between the parties, issues, and social systems were initially an important force driving the controversy, over time the conflict became rooted in itself and its own escalatory processes.

The conflicts involving the Hatfields and McCoys, abortion, global warming, and the Vietnam War are all intractable. But they are not the same. At a surface level, all intractable conflicts look alike. That is, they engage adversaries in vivid and volatile interactions, involve strategic behaviors that are often confusing, frustrate the parties involved, and exist in a seemingly irresolvable stalemate. In effect, they seem hopeless (Pruitt and Olczak 1995). However, while they may look similar at first glance, deeper analysis suggests important distinctions for examination. Conflicts may be rooted in the parties, the issues, the social systems, and the conflict processes. These distinctions may shed some light on the roots or sources of intractability and, moreover, potential paths to tractability.

This chapter aims to make sense of the murky waters of intractability. The theoretical literature has largely focused on identifying overarching characteristics of intractable conflicts or providing case analyses of intractability (Azar 1990; Coleman 2000; Kriesberg, Northrup, and Thorson 1989). This literature is largely descriptive about the nature and dynamics of intractable conflicts. In contrast, this chapter highlights the variations as well as the commonalities among intractable conflicts and sets forth a continuum on which to understand the movement and patterns of intractable disputes. What causes these variations? What do these variations imply about different approaches for enhancing tractability? What do these patterns say about the links between intractability and framing? This chapter constructs an organizing framework to aid in understanding the factors that contribute to and distinguish among intractable conflicts and to link these factors to conflict framing.

Definitions

Intractable conflicts are messy. They are hard to pin down, manage, and analyze and extremely difficult to resolve. They are intense, frustrating, and complex, with no readily conceivable solutions. As one author put it, intractable conflicts are "stubborn" (Thorson 1989). Webster defines intractability as "hard to manage; unruly or stubborn; hard to work, manipulate, cure, [and] treat." In contrast, Webster defines tractable as "easily led, taught, or managed; docile; manageable; [and] governable."

Although hard to manage, intractability does not imply that a conflict is not resolvable. Intractability is a dynamic process in that perceptions of conflicts may shift over time and vacillate between tractability and intractability. Hence, intractability is not a label that we attach to a conflict in a static way. Rather, intractability is a perceptual issue in that different stakeholders often see the possibility of resolution differently at any given moment in time (Hunter 1989). Perceiving and labeling a conflict as intractable, however, can function as a self-fulfilling prophecy in that the parties act accordingly and treat it as irresolvable (Rubin, Pruitt, and Kim 1994). Resolution, in this sense, does not mean that the conflict is solved; rather, it refers to the ability of the stakeholders to reach some mutually acceptable decisions and move forward to address the central problems raised in the dispute.

Even though the terms "conflict" and "dispute" are used interchangeably throughout the literature, important distinctions separate the two processes. "Conflict" refers to the fundamental and underlying incompatibilities that divide parties while a "dispute" is an episode that becomes actualized in specific issues and events. Underlying incompatibilities, however, infuse the nature of dispute episodes. For example, numerous dispute episodes occurred in the history of the conflict between the Hatfields and McCoys, and although each episode was resolved in its own way—by the sheriff's intervention, by the parties choosing to go separate ways, or by a family member getting shot—the underlying conflict between the families always remained.

Similarly, the abortion conflict erupts in individual court cases, protests, and clinic bombings; thus, each dispute episode comes and goes. However, the broad underlying conflict about "what constitutes life" and "killing embryos" remains. This dynamic of dispute episodes and underlying conflicts is illustrated throughout the cases in this volume. Reducing intractability requires that the fundamental nature of a conflict be altered in a manner that dramatically changes the situation and moves the conflict to a point of resolution. Moreover, resolution of a dispute episode, whether through negotiation, litigation, or legislation, does not in itself make the underlying conflict tractable, although it may help move a conflict in a more tractable direction.

Three aspects of intractability will be explored in this chapter. First, we describe two primary characteristics of intractability—"long-standing" and "eluding resolution." We contend that all conflicts that fit the category of intractability are long-term and continually elude resolution. But, second, intractable conflicts also differ in important ways and we explore these differences through dimensions of divisiveness, intensity, pervasiveness, and complexity. These dimensions function as variables to distinguish among intractable disputes. For example, the conflict between the Hatfields and McCoys was highly divisive but not necessarily pervasive nor complex, while the Vietnam conflict was not only complex and divisive but also very intense. Finally, this chapter explores the sources that lead to intractability and distinguishes among the conflicts described at the beginning of this chapter. That is, we explore how parties, issues, social systems, and processes shape the underlying conflicts and make them difficult to resolve.

Primary Characteristics of Intractability

Phrases like "protracted," "long-term," and "mired in controversy" are often used to describe intractable disputes. For this book, we define intractability as those conflicts that are long-standing and elude resolution. "Long-standing" refers to conflicts that have an extensive past, a turbulent present, and a murky future. Historically, they have persisted over a long period of time and are expected to continue. Their persistence leads them to recycle over time in that they may subside through one episode and seem resolved, but then resurface and intensify when circumstances call for a resurgence of the conflict (Coleman 2000).

This persistence is an outgrowth of the characteristic that they elude resolution. Intractable conflicts are typified by repeated and unsuccessful interventions. One reason for this inability to reach resolution is that many interventions, such as negotiation and mediation, often result in impasse; or in the case of litigation, they only address partial issues that lead to unexpected consequences and further escalation. A second reason why intractable conflicts elude resolution is that settlements parties have reached fail to hold; that is, other disputants challenge or appeal the decisions. Burgess and Burgess (1996) point out that these decisions or actions in a dispute episode function as Band-Aids thrown over a gaping wound—they just don't hold. Thus negotiated agreements are ignored, adjudicated settlements are appealed, and legislative actions are challenged. A third reason why intractable disputes elude resolution is that the perceived costs of resolving them are too great and outweigh the perceived costs of continuing the conflict. Whether political, economic, or personal, settling the conflict involves more sacrifice than continuing it does. In effect, intractable conflicts are ones "riddled with long-standing tensions that defy resolution."

These definitions refer to the state of a conflict at a point in time: it is long-standing and eludes resolution. Intractability, however, is not a static concept in which a conflict remains stuck indefinitely. Internal processes and external events contribute to the variability of it; thus intractability is best represented on a continuum, with problem solving and common goals at the far left end of the spectrum and intractability at the far right (see Fig. 2.1).

Tractable disputes, defined as conflicts characterized by divergent interests and incompatible goals, appear in the middle of the continuum. These disputes have integrative potential and incentives for resolution. Hence, the perceived costs of continuing tractable conflicts are relatively high and the costs of settling are relatively low. Moreover, the individual and institutional stakeholders find ways to resolve the conflict without threatening their core identities or values.

Intractable conflicts seem to vary along this continuum between the far right side of the spectrum and the middle of the scale—depending on the circumstances and the efforts to address issues in the conflict. In effect, intractable conflicts are dynamic and can move in a different direction based on changes in the events and underlying causes (Thorson 1989). Conflicts are evolutionary in that a controversy may begin as problem solving in which parties see common interests, but end up as intractable based on changes in the situation. Moreover, different aspects of a dispute episode may be more or less tractable along this continuum. For example, a dispute may contain issues of environmental justice that are becoming more tractable while issues of structures or institutional systems become more intractable.

Problem Solving	**Tractable Disputes**	**Intractability**
Common Ground	Integrative Potential	Eludes Resolution

Figure 2.1. Continuum of Intractability

Dimensions of Variation in Intractability

Even though all intractable conflicts are long-standing and elude resolution, they vary in other ways that affect their dynamics at a point in time. The dimensions along which intractable conflicts vary include divisiveness, intensity, pervasiveness, and complexity. At any point, an intractable conflict may be more or less divisive, intense, pervasive, or complex than other intractable conflicts or than itself at another time.

Divisiveness

Intractable conflicts vary in their level of divisiveness; that is, the extent to which the conflict engages and divides people. Highly divisive conflicts increase intractability by backing parties into corners in which they find it difficult to escape without losing face. Conflicts exhibiting a high degree of polarization, multiple types of polarization, and distinct in-group and out-group identifications also typify the degree to which a dispute is divisive (Burgess and Burgess 1996, Dahrendorf 1959). For instance, when ties to a particular place or ethnicity correspond to class, religion, and regional differences, crosscutting ties will be difficult to construct and disputes will be hard to manage (Kriesberg 1989, Smyth 1994). Moreover, when disputants segregate based on this divisiveness, the lack of contact between the parties can foster intractability through reinforcing negative stereotypes and leading to breakdowns in communication (Fisher and Keashly 1990). The more divisive a dispute, the more likely it is to move toward the intractability end of the continuum (Coleman 2000).

Intensity

Intensity centers on the level of emotionality, involvement, and commitment that typifies a conflict. Intense conflicts have moments in which they are boiling or nearly erupting, potentially "blinding" parties and triggering different understandings of what is at issue. They are seen as unruly because intensity often leads to crisis episodes in which stakeholders escalate their commitments to positions.

Pervasiveness

The spread of conflict as it infuses social and private lives of individuals defines its pervasiveness. As conflicts become more intractable, they permeate cultural, educational, political, and social institutions that have a stake in various disputes (Coleman 2000). The number of stakeholders also increases as a conflict engulfs a community. In addition, highly intractable conflicts consume the human experience, affecting every aspect of a person's life. Specifically, a stakeholder committed to protecting the endangered species dedicates her work to this cause and sees all aspects of her life imbued with this controversy. Thus the conflict can consume the lives of disputants as well as spread to multiple stakeholders.

Complexity

The fourth dimension along which intractable conflicts vary is complexity. Complexity is linked to the number and interwoven nature of issues and parties in the conflict, the levels or the layers of social systems in which disputes reside, and the difficulties of locating arenas in which to address a conflict. In highly intractable situations, the number and interconnectedness of issues escalates. Issues "snowball [and] bits and pieces of other issues accumulate into a large, unmanageable mass" (Lewicki, Saunders, and Minton 1999, 420). The issues not only grow in number and scope, they also become intertwined so that it is difficult to tease out subparts and sort out stakeholders' concerns. The information needed to address these interwoven issues is also tedious, difficult, and often contradictory.

Intractable conflicts often involve large numbers of parties because they cross societal levels (Kriesberg 1989). Dispute episodes in these conflicts infuse interpersonal, intragroup, intergroup, organizational, interorganizational, and sometimes international levels. No single level or institution can effectively manage all the issues and parties in the conflict. Thus complexity stems from a widespread and interwoven maze of issues and parties who have no clear institution or social system to regulate the full scope of the conflict.

Overall, divisiveness, intensity, pervasiveness, and complexity are different dimensions in which intractable disputes vary. They also signal when a particular dispute is eluding resolution, thus becoming long-standing. Although any one of these features is not necessarily a defining element of intractability, all of them in tandem increase the potential that dispute episodes will evolve in an intractable way.

Sources of Intractability

In examining the concept of intractability, we have identified two essential characteristics—long-standing and eluding resolution. Thus, all intractable conflicts exhibit these characteristics. However, they differ from one another in many ways. One way is through the dimensions that vary over time and across conflicts. Thus some intractable conflicts are more divisive, intense, pervasive, and complex than are others. Moreover, dispute episodes linked to these conflicts may elude resolution through several of these dimensions, but not all of them.

A second way in which intractable conflicts differ from each other is through sources of the underlying nature of the conflict. Sources refer to factors that contribute to making the conflict intractable. The literature on intractable conflicts provides a cornucopia of reasons for their existence, such as moral differences, incompatibility in fundamental values, and struggles over power and political dominance (Burgess and Burgess 1996, Pruitt and Olczak 1995). Yet many conflicts with these features are nonetheless resolved, either through court rulings, legislative mandates, decisions of arbitrators, or negotiations among the parties, while others are not. Next we review four factors that form the genesis of and dominate the way disputes evolve into intractable conflicts.

While all disputes are an amalgam of parties embattled over issues in distinct social systems, not all conflicts have the same genesis (Kriesberg 1998). Embedded within a conflict's genesis are clues as to the source of its intractability. Discerning this source can provide insights into why it is intractable and can reveal potential strategies for making it more tractable. A comparison of the different types of intractable conflicts highlights dissimilar explanations of causes and particular strategies for intervention.

Parties or Adversaries

Some conflicts exist because of fundamental tensions between the adversaries. Like the Hatfields and McCoys—or any number of long-standing ethnic conflicts across the globe—these conflicts are defined by the nature of the relationships between the feuding individuals and groups. While specific issues and contexts provide fuel for these conflicts, addressing the issues will do little to diminish the fundamental tension that exists between the parties, and hence the conflict persists. Issues of identity often lie at the core of intractable conflicts that are rooted in parties. In fact, Lederach (1997) contends that nearly two-thirds of the world's highly intense armed conflicts stem from identity-related disputes, and Coleman (2000) concludes that identity-based disputes are more susceptible to intractable situations than are conflicts rooted in other causes. Identity, however, unfolds in a myriad of ways, including (a) ideologies of the parties, (b) group membership, (c) relational power, and (d) organization of the parties.

Ideologies

Differences in ideologies among the parties contribute to intractability through highlighting discrepant fundamental beliefs and values between individuals (Frohock 1989). Ideology frames the way that individuals see a particular situation, often revealing disparate perceptions of reality (Hunter 1989). Moreover, ideology infuses forms of reasoning and attitudes and thus surfaces in different ways that people think and solve problems. Although ideology is commonly aligned with ethnic and racial conflicts, Hunter (1989, 26) concludes that "many of the most intractable conflicts between environmentalists and prodevelopment [parties] stem from the ontological [and ideological] differences, which affect perceptions of the problems, values, and beliefs."

Group Membership

Group identity of the parties is also linked to intractability through the way membership, societal values, and cultural experiences shape self-image (Tajfel and Turner 1985). Strong beliefs in social causes contribute to the intensity and divisiveness of a conflict solidifying group membership and merging self with social identity. When identities are intertwined with shared ideologies, the stakes in a conflict are much greater and the costs of reaching a resolution are much higher than for conflicts not rooted in group membership. In effect, if group identity is prominent in the emotional lives of individuals, it provides a motivational force for pursuing the conflict (Smyth 1994).

Intractable conflicts also occur when the opportunity structures favor one group over the other, contributing to polarization and divisiveness (Azar 1990). Parties that suffer from denial of their group identity, threats to membership, and an absence of voice become self-declared victims. These social injustices, then, are tied to concerns for dignity and control over one's life. Thus failure to address group identity concerns explains why agreements reached during many intractable conflicts are often ineffective and fleeting (Coleman 2000). Smyth (1994) contends that negotiated deals are possible in intractable ethnic, religious, and territorial conflicts, but only after issues relating to group identity have been addressed.

Relational Power

Connected to ideology and group membership are concerns about relational power and political dominance among groups. Power struggles, also called "pecking-order conflicts," contribute to intractability through enhancing divisiveness and longevity (Burgess and Burgess 1996). Thus a struggle for control often ensues when there is a threat to or objection about the power relationships between parties (Smyth 1994). The more powerful parties in a conflict often maintain their power base by drawing from group differences in access to resources. For instance, disputes between developers and neighborhood residents, particularly in lower-income communities, often involve developers exercising their power in a community in which their economic control is questioned. Divisiveness is also evident in the imbalance of power between the parties, particularly when the more powerful groups exploit and intimidate the less powerful one (Coleman 2000). Power imbalances among parties that extend for long periods of time also contribute to the long-standing nature of intractable conflicts.

Organization of the Parties

Some intractable conflicts rooted in relationships between the parties persist because of the way groups are organized. Kriesberg (1998, 211) notes that adversaries "vary in the degree to which they are clearly bounded and internally differentiated." Clearly bounded units are groups that are publicly recognized and have members who do not overlap with other conflicting units. They comprise members and authorities that are organized around an explicit guiding mission. For example, persons, states, and organizations are clearly bounded compared to social classes, ethnic groups, and supporters of different environmental policies. Bounded groups with defined purposes are better able to deal with their differences more constructively than are diffuse and unorganized adversaries. Bounded groups assume specialized roles, especially ones tied to conflict relations with other units. In contrast, parties who are not clearly bounded or highly differentiated handle conflict differently. Because they are not organized in the classic sense, the parties are seen as diffuse—lacking in roles, structures, and clearly defined missions (see Table 2.1).

In effect, parties contribute to the intractability of a conflict through vesting their identities in the outcome of the dispute, especially identities rooted in ideology and group membership, power differences, and organization of social groups. When the salient underlying source of the dispute is the parties,

Table 2.1. Sources of Intractable Conflicts

	More Tractable	More Intractable
Parties	*Bounded*	*Diffuse*
	Well-organized	Unorganized
	Clearly Defined Members Roles and Mission	Loose Collective Members Roles and Mission
		Lacking Structure
Issues	*Consensual*	*Dissensual*
	Agreement on Values	Fundamental Value Differences
	Disagreement on Allocation	
Social System	*Prescribed*	*Ambiguous*
	Well-defined Structures	Ill-defined Structures
	Clear Procedures and Rules	Uncertainty in Procedures
	Legitimate Authority	Absence of Clear Authority
Conflict Process	*De-escalated*	*Escalated*
	Contained and Focused	Growth in Parties, Issues, and Costs
	Commitment to Resolving Issues	Polarization and Segregation
	Conflict Cycles Broken Up	Conflict Spirals

Source: Adapted from L. Kriesberg, *Constructive Conflicts: From Escalation to Resolution*. Lanham, Md.: Rowan and Littlefield, 1998.

conflicts can go on for generations, crossing multiple issues and subsystems, and re-creating identity concerns. In the environmental area, intractable struggles between Native American land rights and rapid population development illustrate identity concerns through threats to ideology, challenges to group membership, and the unbounded or diffuse nature of these cultural units.

Other examples of conflicts in which intractability is rooted in the parties or nature of the relationship include the Hatfields and McCoys, the Israelis and Palestinians, or any number of centuries-old ethnic conflicts. These situations persist as intractable disputes regardless of fluctuations in issues and changes in the social system. For rational or irrational reasons, these parties are fundamentally in conflict with each other—the conflict has become a core element of their identity. Threats to identity, as Northrup (1989, 76) suggests, "are not likely to be readily changed from within."

Issues in the Dispute

For some conflicts, the major source of controversy lies in the issues or in diametrically opposed values and beliefs that underlie specific issues. For instance, topics like abortion, nuclear power, or human rights trigger conflicts in which the parties and contexts are less central than the issue itself. Research suggests that disputes rooted in value and moral differences, high-stake distributional issues, and threats to health and human safety contribute to the intractability of a conflict (Burgess and Burgess 1996, Burton 1987, Coleman 2000, Kriesberg 1998).

Value Issues

Controversies that stem from fundamental moral, religious, or personal values often surface as irreconcilable, particularly when disputants label the other parties' values as evil or wrong. The conflict, then, centers on the correctness of the moral issues rather than on the parties' needs and interests. In this case, issues become dissensual in that both parties believe that neither can force the other one to comply (Kriesberg 1989, 1998). In consensual issues, parties agree with what is valued but disagree on its allocation; thus the parties fight about interests. Dissensual issues, on the other hand, trigger conflicts that revolve around fundamental value differences that are not easily changed or reconciled; at least one side insists that the other one adopt its belief system (see Table 2.1). Most conflicts have elements of both consensual and dissensual issues. In fact, some disputes may emerge through one party treating the issues as consensual and the other party defining them as dissensual.

In addition to concerns about consensus, value issues contribute to intractability through a complex layer of latent and manifest sub-issues (Coleman 2000). The layered nature of religious, economic, cultural, and social equality concerns are interwoven in complex ways that affect the conduct of both parties. These layered issues create what Burgess and Burgess (1996, 308) call conflict overlays; that is, multiple issues that get "laid over" the core issues, thus making it difficult to decipher the core issues and understand their full impact in the conflict. For example, activists who protest the building of a nuclear power plant may oppose this action through desires to protect the environment, to save their communities, and to avoid hazards to personal health. These goals tie back to economic concerns, scarcity of energy, and the tacit beliefs in progress and social development. Add the element of location in a historic community in which extended families are rooted in the soil, and this overlay of values creates a complex layer of societal, identity, and interest-based issues that make moral conflicts intense, long-standing, and hard to manage.

High-Stake Distributional Issues

Issues centered on high-stake distributional claims also lie at the source of a number of intractable conflicts. This type of resource-related dispute leads to circumstances in which the cost of settling is higher than the cost of fighting; hence, the conflict develops into an irreconcilable win–lose dilemma in which parties make public pronouncements of their untenable positions and their aims to defeat the opposition. These public proclamations intensify commitment strategies that work against concession making (Lewicki, Saunders, and Minton 1999). Moreover, if the stakes are high, the parties may turn to power plays and employ threat, pressure, and other force before they accept defeat. Power plays, then, become interwoven with distributional issues to escalate the conflict and contribute to notions of rightness and wrongness, good and evil.

Threats to Health and Human Safety

Disputes rooted in risk and human safety issues also underlie the emergence of intractable conflicts. For example, environmental disputes on toxic waste, nuclear power, and pollution are issue-based conflicts imbedded in concerns for health and human safety. In their zeal to protect the public welfare, stakeholders often engage in "bidding wars" or one-upmanship regarding who has the greatest concern for human safety (Burgess and Burgess 1996). Proposals to address these concerns have "unintended and often adverse consequences" as disputants become mired in anticipating uncertainties, controlling for potential consequences, and uncovering relevant facts. An extreme version of this syndrome known as "analysis-paralysis" stifles the disputants in appeals for yet "another study of the problem" (Burgess and Burgess 1996).

Thus value issues, high-stake distributional issues, and issues rooted in risk and human safety contribute to the potential development of intractability. These issues shape the intense and long-standing nature of the conflict through their dissensus and disagreement on allocations, regardless of the parties or the social system. In other words, the same parties in the same conditions would likely be in full agreement on other issues, but when deep-rooted moral values or health and safety issues surface, the conflict moves toward intractability. The parties construe resolution as requiring value concessions that are fundamentally untenable and even reprehensible to them.

Social System or Context of the Conflict

The source of some intractable conflict is not the issues or the parties in a dispute, but the context or social system within which the disputes reside. If the social system lacks rules for how to address particular issues, conflicts over these issues will likely be protracted. If disputants disagree about the legitimacy of an existing institution, conflict can arise over institutional turf and sovereign rights. Similarly, if the context is overprescribed with too many rules, conflicts can be triggered. When structures within the social system are ambiguous, decision-making authority and procedures are often unclear, and stakeholders lack legitimacy of representation. To this end, Kriesberg (1998, 212) contends: "The social systems within which adversaries contend vary in the degree to which they have institutionalized rules for managing conflicts and in the content of those rules." Prescribed social systems have formal or informal rules for handling a dispute. In ambiguous systems, in contrast, rules for individual conduct in conflicts are in flux or are not well developed. In effect, some systems have policies and procedures that are quite well defined, whereas other systems lack rules and procedures for managing a dispute or facing challenges to legitimacy and sovereignty (see Table 2.1).

Ambiguous Social Systems

A system with prescribed dispute resolution procedures, whether formal or informal, is more likely to develop in a tractable manner than one in which no institution has the authority to regulate conflicts. Specifically, conflicts among multiple stakeholders often lack prescribed rules because the existing procedures do not extend to activists, citizen groups, international boundaries, or nonbureaucratic organizations. The problem of global warming, as noted earlier in this chapter, spans nations, cultures, economies, and political agencies, with no clearly defined institution designated as the arbitrator or convener. Ambiguity in social structures also contributes to power struggles among adversaries as they sort out who has or should have control (Smyth 1994). These social systems are also characterized by concerns about the legitimacy of adversaries and about the authority to represent stakeholders. Without official sanction, parties in a conflict often lack the authority to interpret and implement decisions. Basically, in many intractable disputes, parties lack a clear and well-developed institutionalized means for managing the conflict (Burgess and Burgess 1996).

Challenges to Social Systems

Moreover, context becomes the source of intractability when the legitimacy and sovereignty of existing institutions are challenged and when rapid social and political changes throw prescribed policies into flux (Kriesberg 1989). For example, ethnic appeals for self-determination and accusations of imperialism illustrate types of intractable conflicts in which disputants have challenged the legitimacy of extant social systems (Smyth 1994). Often, the very institutions that regulate the conflict are the targets of contention. Thus the parties have no agreed framework in which to manage these disputes. In addition to direct challenges, changes in events can alter social structures, leading to ambiguity or conflicts with policies and procedures (Coleman 2000). Challenges to institutions surface when issues arise that are regarded as "new territory" for society to cover. In effect, challenges to existing authority, lack of institutional clarity in handling disputes, and rapidly changing social structures are sources of conflicts that can contribute to intractability.

Overprescribed Social Systems

Intractability can also occur when a social system is overprescribed. Overprescribed social structures constrain autonomy and self-determination, are encumbered with strict and often contradictory rules, or are stymied by layers of restrictive bureaucracy. For example, the early colonists and the king of England battled for many years. Regardless of the issues addressed, the colonists despised the intrusion of England on their freedom, and England despised the colonists' quest for independence. The social system that prescribed and constrained their interactions was the source of their friction. Hence, when disputes become institutionalized in overprescribed ways, they can become intractable (Kriesberg 1998).

Clearly, social systems impinge on the intractability of a conflict through their ambiguity, direct challenges to authority, or overprescription of rules and procedures. As Thorson (1989, 2) points out, "The interaction between intractable conflicts and the [social systems] in which they occur is highly consequential for any attempts at transforming or resolving them."

Conflict Processes

A fourth and final source of intractability occurs within the conflict itself when cycles of escalation, conflict spirals, and destructive patterns make movement toward tractability difficult. The process that perpetuates a conflict is linked to escalation in which the parties' issues, costs, and commitments to winning increase. For example, although the Vietnam conflict was initially rooted in divergent issues, it eventually escalated and became a conflict with a multitude of concerns that were unrelated to the original dispute. Strategies that focused on the initial issues were no longer feasible paths to resolution. In like manner, a water dispute in the Southwest might grow from concerns over resource allocation to defense of private property rights, to protection of endangered species, and, as the costs continue to escalate, to the eventual disillusion of agrarian communities.

Thus, as the conflict grows over time, the stakes become higher and the moral commitments become deeper. Additional parties become involved, and the conflict spreads to a public level. This escalation produces a conflict spiral in which skirmishes cycle in and out of enactment, become dormant at some points, and then resurface to intensify the controversy. In a conflict spiral, the circular causality of motivations, cognitions, affect, and behavior feeds escalation and perpetuates the conflict (Deutsch 1973). Conflict spirals often develop into destructive processes that shift the focus of the dispute from substantive interests to annihilation of the other party. Thus escalation evolves through stages characterized by discussion, polarization, segregation, and destruction (Fisher and Keashley 1990).

Discussion

The beginnings of a dispute may grow out of problems that are usually resolved through discussion. As the conflict escalates, the mixture of objective and subjective features of the dispute becomes imbalanced and the subjective elements take on greater importance (Coleman 2000). That is, what parties see, feel, and express as subjective elements become more important than the objective circumstances or the events.

Polarization

The second stage of escalation, polarization, occurs when parties cast the conflict in bipolar terms, which forces participants to choose sides (Burgess and Burgess 1996). Social–psychological processes that fuel escalation include negative stereotypes, evaluation of evidence in favor of one's own side, extreme commitment to a preferred course of action, dehumanizing the other party, and treating the opponent as an enemy (Pruitt, Parker, and

Mikolic 1997, Rubin, Pruitt, and Kim 1994). These processes are tied to self-fulfilling prophecies in that the way parties live out a conflict reinforces their own polarizations and perpetuates negative stereotypes of the other party. For instance, in the Vietnam War negative stereotypes of the Vietnamese led to dehumanizing both soldiers and civilians, evaluating evidence in favor of winning the war, and escalating military and monetary commitment to this aim. In an environmental dispute about water rights, stakeholders might polarize into upstream and downstream users, evaluate evidence about water distribution in favor of one group, and eventually treat the other stakeholders as enemies.

Segregation

The third phase, segregation, ties back to the way parties misinterpret what opponents say, overreact to positions, and eventually decrease or cease interactions. In this stage, the parties put forth extreme and unyielding positions, overreact by treating their opponents as wrong, and finally segregate themselves from other disputants through minimal or nonexistent communication. In multiparty disputes, segregation is evident when parties refuse to appear at the table or withdraw representatives from attending public forums and debates.

Destruction

Segregation feeds into destruction, the fourth stage, in which explosive cycles of provocation and counterprovocation replace substantive debate with a desire to win, to hurt, or even to inflict harm on the other parties (Burgess and Burgess 1996). Thus escalation becomes cyclical and self-perpetuating over time. Even if the parties, issues, and social systems of the dispute change, conflict escalation becomes normative and takes on "a life of its own" (Folger, Poole, and Stutman 1997). Destructive processes develop through the parties' subjective experiences, their expectations and self-fulfilling prophecies, their actions toward each other, and the group norms that become rooted in the social system (Coleman 2000).

In summary, the literature suggests that four sources contribute to intractability of conflicts: parties, issues, social systems, and conflict processes. The relationship among disputants often fuels intractability through disparate ideologies, strong and diverse group memberships, power struggles, and diffuse organization of stakeholders. Issues and issue dissensus become a source of intractability when they are rooted in values and moral standards, involve high-stake distributional concerns, and deal with threats to health and human safety. Social systems that are ill-defined, contested by parties, or in flux also contribute to intractability in that parties have no acceptable institution or authority to oversee the dispute. Finally, escalation of a dispute becomes a source of intractability through creating conflict spirals that perpetuate adversity, polarize disputants, segregate parties, and sometimes lead to violence and destruction.

Overall, intractability occurs when the parties are diffuse; the issues are dissensual; the social system is ambiguous, contested, or in flux; and conflict processes have escalated. Tractable conflicts, in contrast, are more likely to be bounded, consensual, prescribed, and de-escalating (see Table 2.1). Although Table 2.1 presents these factors in discrete categories, the four sources overlap. Group identities often become intertwined with ideologies and value issues. The Israeli and Palestinian conflict, while strongly linked to parties as the primary source of the conflict, is also tied to the ideologies and the religious and cultural value differences that define group membership.

Moreover, bounded and diffuse parties are linked to prescribed and ambiguous social systems. Diffuse parties often challenge bureaucratic and prescribed rules as being ineffectual or inadequate for their needs. Activists in environmental conflicts raise issues publicly and confront power structures in opposing a nuclear waste dump or the building of a reservoir. Hence, as a source of intractable conflict, their freedom as a diffuse group (parties) allows them to challenge the legitimacy of social structures in ways that can shift power relationships (social systems). Finally, the parties, issues, and social systems feed into the escalation or de-escalation of a conflict; and, in turn, the conflict processes perpetuate whatever contributes to the development of an intractable dispute. For instance, if the ideologies of the parties lie at the core of intractability, escalation perpetuates the salience and divisiveness of the rightness or wrongness of these positions.

Even though the four sources overlap, one may be more central in defining a conflict and accounting for its perpetuation. In particular, the prototypical dispute between environmentalists and developers over the location of a new shopping mall is rooted in a historic set of fundamental differences between the parties. In contrast, conflicts about nuclear power and population growth underscore the health and human safety issues or high-stake distributional nature of these controversies. Irrespective of the source, the dynamics and interplay of these four become self-reinforcing and reflect back on the conflict, contributing to its intensity, endurance, and difficulty to move in a tractable direction.

Intractability and Conflict Framing

Framing is an overarching feature of a conflict that feeds into intractability in a reflexive way. That is, when disputants frame a conflict, they define what a dispute is about and how it should be settled. Frames can therefore directly contribute to perceptions of intractability. For example, if disputants frame a conflict as rooted in value dissensus or the illegitimacy of a given social system, this conflict will likely be viewed as intractable. The more disputants frame a conflict as intense and eluding resolution, the more framing feeds into polarization and other conflict processes that perpetuate intractability. Thus the overall relationship between framing and intractability is reflexive in that framing both contributes to and signals the development of intractability.

Intractability is reinforced when the parties to a dispute frame each other and the issues in divergent ways. When identities are framed as primary, characterizations are negative, and issues are opposing, the dynamic that is set in motion is quite divisive. Shifts in framing that prompt shared identities, positive characterizations, and commonalities are unifying and can diminish intractability. The challenge, of course, is that these shifts in framing are not easily triggered. Using the framework depicted in Table 2.1, if the parties are diffuse, what types of identity frames can aid in unifying and bonding them? If the issues are dissensual, what patterns of framing can help transform them into a consensual state? If there is ambiguity in the social system, how could changes in social control frames help parties reach agreements on social structures? If the conflict processes have escalated, how could changes in conflict management frames aid in de-escalating these dynamics?

This section discusses the relationship between framing and intractability in ways that highlight these different sources of conflict. First, we explore the way that framing triggers intractability. Then, we examine how framing signals the development of intractability. Next we reverse this relationship to question how intractability influences particular types of framing. Finally, we address frame changes and, in particular, the way shifts in framing can move a conflict to a more tractable state.

Framing Triggers Intractability

Both identity and characterization frames are salient in the roles that parties play in conflicts and have a central role in triggering intractability. Discrepant value issues and group ideologies grow out of identity framing and link back to social categories and comparison among groups. A high ratio of negative characterization frames to positive ones disconfirms the other person's identity and contributes to intractability through assessing blame and promoting polarization. For conflicts rooted in parties, the negation of the opponent is often central to one's own identity (Kelman 1985). Thus a positive identity frame of one's own group becomes merged with a negative characterization of the other party. For example, if environmentalists believe that their own identities and fundamental interests are concomitant with the negative framing of developers, then environmentalists cannot alter their negative frames of the other without jeopardizing their own identities. Thus tight links between identity and negative characterization frames influence intractability through heightening intensity and divisiveness.

Mismatches between different parties' patterns of framing may also trigger intractability. Since framing is a way of labeling what a problem is, mismatches in frames are tantamount to issue dissensus or different definitions of the dispute. Thus differences in framing can be a source of what is valued, what is good or evil, and what is reconcilable in a conflict.

Framing Signals Intractability

Framing may signal that a conflict is moving in an intractable direction. In particular, two types of framing serve as indicators of intractability: views of social control and conflict management frames. Since intractability is likely to occur when social systems are unclear or overprescribed and institutions that manage disputes lack authority or legitimacy, the way that disputants frame social control directly relates to how they see the social system. For example, stakeholders who hold strong egalitarian frames may see social structures as more ambiguous than those who prefer hierarchical or individualistic approaches to regulation and decision making.

This mismatch in framing may signal the development of intractability or stakeholder challenges to the legitimacy of the current social system. Specifically, in the Quincy Library case mismatches in egalitarian and hierarchical views of social control split along the lines of local versus federal authority, creating considerable uncertainty in how to proceed or move forward in managing the conflict. Mismatches in framing, then, can reveal how stakeholders regard current rules and social institutions and when they see regulation and dispute management systems as ambiguous, unclear, or in flux. In general, mismatches in institutional framing and perceptions of social control often signal the way a conflict is becoming intractable.

Second, the framing of modes of conflict management also indicates the way a conflict is moving toward intractability. Specifically, reliance on conflict management frames associated with avoidance/passivity, adjudication, and struggle/sabotage often leads to conflict spirals that perpetuate cycles of escalation. An avoidance cycle signals escalation through unresolved issues that resurface and through promoting segregation of disputants (Folger, Poole, and Stutman 1997). Use of avoidance frames in highly intense conflicts delays confrontation and heightens the intensity of the next conflict episode, thus contributing to the potential of a long-standing conflict. Preferences for adjudication and struggle/sabotage as modes of conflict management reinforce win–lose orientations that foster threats, pressure, and force. In this case, the way parties mimic or match each other's frames both signals and contributes to intractability through a pattern of one-upmanship. In particular, court battles in the Edwards Aquifer case in Chapter 5 illustrate how framing signals intractability as parties saw no other alternative than to fight each other in state and federal judicial systems. These suits, countersuits, and court appeals clearly escalated the dispute and reinforced its intractability.

Intractability Influences Framing

As a reflexive process, intractability influences framing through the way it shapes future actions, justifies actions taken, and mobilizes others to act. Intractability feeds into crisis episodes that perpetuate struggle and continual challenges to negotiated settlements. Intractability influences identity and characterization frames by rooting them in polarization, stereotypes, and in-group/out-group definitions of the other party. Thus conflict processes that promote intractability shape identity frames that justify continued escalation and future actions. The Voyageurs National Park case in Chapter 4 provides an example of the way intractability reflects back on identity frames. As parties saw the dispute as intractable, they framed the park service and the locals in ways that fostered distinct in-groups and out-groups with well-defined polarized positions. Thus intractability intensified the framing of parties as the source of the conflict.

To summarize, framing and intractability are reflexively linked; that is, framing shapes perceptions of intractability and intractability influences framing. Framing triggers intractability through the use of identity and characterization frames to negate other parties, to accentuate value dissensus, and to promote polarization. Moreover, mismatches in frame type and importance can also trigger intractability through leading parties to act on different definitions of the problem. Framing also signals intractability in the way that views of social control reveal different preferences for hierarchical, egalitarian, and individualistic social systems. Mismatches in types of social control frames can indicate when a system is ambiguous or in flux. Conflict management frames also signal intractability through frequent preferences for avoidance, adjudication, and struggle/sabotage frames. These frames feed into conflict cycles that perpetuate escalation of the dispute. Finally, intractability influences framing through perpetuating the use of particular identity frames that promote in-group/out-group alignment and polarization among stakeholders.

Frame Changes and Intractability

Because framing and intractability are reflexively intertwined, changes in one should have an impact on the other. But specifically, how do changes in framing affect intractability? Moving an intractable dispute toward tractability is difficult because the patterns that perpetuate conflict spirals, escalation, and deep-seated moral issues are rooted in the very nature of the conflict. Reframing issues, pursuing superordinate goals, and finding integrative win–win alternatives only scratch the surface in many of these complex disputes. To alter intractability, frame changes must address the intensity, long-standing nature, and way in which a conflict eludes resolution. Three approaches to frame changes offer the potential to alter the direction of intractable conflicts; namely, internal shifts, responses to external changes, and links between framing and transformation.

Internal Shifts

Internal shifts or changes within the conflict itself occur when parties abandon their patterns of escalation and lower their costs for settling the dispute. Ripeness, as an initial step to de-escalation, targets important obstacles amenable to change and aims to diminish opposing forces resistant to change. Ways to change opposing forces include decreasing rage, enhancing trust, and developing skills for managing conflict effectively (Pruitt and Olczak 1995). Framing and reframing can target these subjective elements that perpetuate conflict cycles and redirect the focus of a dispute. For example, parties in a dispute over individual property rights might reframe their nonnegotiable position of "no regulation of their water or land" to "our community must control any regulation of water on private property." This shift from a rights frame to a social control frame also de-stabilizes the source of intractability by moving it from an entrenched high-stakes distributional issue to negotiation of control in the social systems. Hence, this moment of internal shift in framing offers an opportunity to uproot intractability and relocate the conflict in another, less intractable, sphere.

Responses to External Changes

In like manner, responses to external forces can lead to frame changes that move a conflict toward tractability. External conditions such as an economic crisis or a drought can create a catastrophic moment in which disputants alter their frames or reach consensus on previously mismatched frames as they realize a common hazard or common enemy. These conditions introduce a hurting stalemate, a shock to the system, or an impending disaster that awakens the parties to their intractability (Zartman and Aurik 1991). For example, the threat of federal intervention into a regional environmental dispute often jars stakeholders into shifting their frames and reorienting the direction of the dispute. In this case, frame changes are responses to external crises or conditions that alert disputants to the potential harms of intractability.

Framing and Transformation

Finally, framing may help transform the fundamental nature of a conflict. Transformations are major changes in the parties, social system, or nature of the dispute (Putnam 1994). They function at both microlevel interactions and macrolevel conflict dynamics. Transformations are brought about through in-depth and lengthy interventions facilitated by three processes: dialogue, sustainable reconciliation, and transcendent discourse (Littlejohn and Domenici 2001, Pearce and Littlejohn 1997). Dialogue focuses on exploring differences through understanding the interpretations that parties bring to and present in the conflict, whereas sustainable reconciliation centers on forgiveness, acknowledging past wrongs, and reuniting relationships. Interventionists have employed dialogue to help local communities deal with intractable conflicts on abortion rights and urban planning (Littlejohn and Domenici 2001). Through dialogue sessions, parties gain an appreciation for each other's backgrounds, build common bonds through sharing new values, and approach their moral issues from a different angle.

Sustainable reconciliation works from personal suffering to build forgiveness and mutual recognition of loss and remorse. Applied to ethnic disputes, it has centered on changing characterization and identity frames that perpetuate intractability. Through forming new identity frames, parties are able to reconcile relationships and build new patterns of interaction. Transcendent discourse aims to uncover the assumptions about knowledge, being, and values that lie beneath the conflict. It is a type of discourse in which parties are trained to transcend their frames and sources of intractability to compare different value systems and expose each side's limitations (Pearce and Littlejohn 1997). Transcendent discourse also addresses identity frames to alter sources of intractability rooted in parties, issues, and social systems. It employs techniques that help parties compare, contrast, and extend value and social systems. For example, Pearce and Littlejohn (1997) relied on transcendent discourse to mediate multiparty disputes on animal rights and academic freedom on college campuses.

In summary, these processes work through making changes in identity and characterization frames that help parties acknowledge their roles in perpetuating intractability and help them develop new interpretations of the conflict. To this end, parties need radical shifts in characterization frames to strengthen relationships and alter patterns of accusations and negative evaluations of the other party. Changes in power and trust frames are crucial for reconciling relationships and developing fundamentally different forms of interaction among the parties. Both dialogue and transcendent discourse center on frame changes that step out of and look beyond values that keep parties entrenched. In effect, transforming an intractable dispute hinges on changing identity, characterization, and conflict management frames that facilitate connections and move conflict toward tractability.

Summary and Conclusion

Intractable disputes are part of the conflict landscape that permeates environmental debates. Whether it is a hazardous waste dump in a particular neighborhood, the cost of regulating and cleaning up pollution, or the ownership and management of private property next to public lands, environmental disputes have the potential to develop into intractable conflicts. Intractability, as defined in this chapter, is both a process and a descriptor of a conflict. It is perceptual in that different parties may see the conflict in different ways and yet it is a descriptor of the way that a conflict has evolved.

Intractability is defined through two characteristics—long-standing (the way a conflict subsides and resurfaces over a long period of time); and eluding resolution (the way repeated interventions and agreements become fleeting, ignored, and challenged). In addition to these characteristics, highly intractable disputes are likely to be intense, divisive, pervasive, and complex—dimensions that vary across conflicts and make them stubborn and hard to manage.

This chapter has explored the way intractability stems from four different sources of conflict—parties, issues, social systems, and processes. These sources are closely tied to conflict framing through the way that frames trigger and signal intractability, the way intractability influences framing, and the links between frame changes and intractability.

Identity and characterization frames trigger and signal intractability in the ways they are tied to differences in ideologies and group membership of the parties. Views of social control are frames that arise from and signal intractability in diffuse parties and ambiguous, contested social systems. Issues cast as irreconcilable, dissensual, and deeply moral contribute to intractability through interest-based identity frames. Conflict management frames reflect and signal intractability through the way avoidance, adjudication, and struggle/sabotage lead to escalation.

This chapter further suggests that frame changes can promote tractability. Although altering any one frame may not change the direction of a conflict, radical changes in the frames attached to the overall definition of the dispute can lead to transformation. These changes may occur through internal frame shifts, frame changes in response to external circumstances, and long-term interventions that occur through dialogue, sustainable reconciliation, and transcendent discourse.

Overall, intractable disputes have become more commonplace in society (Pruitt and Olczak 1995). This type of conflict, although typically used to describe entrenched ethnic disputes, also depicts environmental, family, and many societal conflicts. Framing provides a way to understand how parties, issues, social systems, and conflict processes both contribute to and reflect intractability. Framing is also a key to the way disputes and relationships can be fundamentally transformed to move a conflict in a tractable direction.

Part I

Natural Resources Cases

Chapter 3

When Irresolvable Becomes Resolvable: The Quincy Library Group Conflict

Todd A. Bryan and Julia M. Wondolleck

In some cases, changing frames results in new ways of viewing problems and new ways of working collaboratively to resolve conflicts. Often, however, such changes reveal tensions in other areas and lead to new and unanticipated conflicts. The Quincy Library Group (QLG) is such a case. The Quincy case, in our view, demonstrates how changing frames can create opportunities or "space" for collaborative action on the part of disputing parties. For action to occur, however, critical individuals in the dispute must be willing to step across the boundaries of the conflict and into the space created. As we will see, the QLG members crossed interest-based boundaries to talk with traditional enemies in the controversial "timber wars" that have plagued the northwestern United States for three decades. Altering the way the timber wars were framed by traditional enemies at the local level played a significant role in how the conflict was transformed. As mentioned, the Quincy case also demonstrates how frame changes can reveal new tensions and new conflicts. As they began collaborating, QLG members suddenly propelled themselves into the national spotlight as their homegrown forest management plan caught the attention of Congress and the national environmental community. Few could have anticipated the intense conflict that was generated by their action. A decade after QLG formed and transformed its local version of the timber wars, the controversy over what they did remains.

The Quincy Case

The QLG formed in the fall of 1992 out of the efforts of an unlikely team of partners: Plumas County supervisor Bill Coates, a Republican who had historically supported the timber industry; Tom Nelson, a forester with Sierra Pacific Industries (SPI), California's largest timber company; and Michael Jackson, a local environmental attorney and member of the Friends of Plumas Wilderness, an environmental organization based in Quincy, California. The three men were all concerned about effects on the local economy of sharp declines in timber harvests on the Plumas National Forest, which virtually surrounds the town of Quincy. QLG started when Coates and Nelson approached Jackson with an idea—to resurrect a forest plan that a coalition of local and regional environmentalists had put forward in 1986. Rejected then as a blue-sky idea that could cripple the local economy, the plan had begun to look like the only hope for saving the battered timber industry and local economy. So Coates, Nelson, and Jackson assembled a group of their peers from within the Quincy community that included, among others, representatives from local timber and business interests, environmental activists, county supervisors, and local citizens. Jackson also phoned his activist friends in Sacramento and San Francisco and invited them. Some had worked on the environmentalists' 1986 plan. But Sacramento was a three-hour drive from Quincy on a good day and San Francisco was about five. Attending regular and intense meetings to further develop the plan would be difficult. Moreover, it was questionable whether the plan was a priority when compared with other environmental battles.

The group of mostly locals agreed to meet on neutral ground at the Plumas County Library, some only half-joking that meeting in a library would prevent them from raising their voices. The beginning was difficult. But as Nelson noted, he and Jackson and Coates could agree on a lot of things, among them that they all wanted community stability and that all were convinced the U.S. Forest Service could not provide it. Eventually, as trust among the participants grew, they were able to agree to a "Community Stability Proposal" (QLG 1993) that reflected the environmentalists' original plan and called for old-growth forest protection, selective logging, and riparian buffer protection while nearly restoring traditional timber harvest levels on the Plumas, Lassen, and a portion of the Tahoe National Forests.

The Timber Wars—the Context for the Conflict

The QLG emerged within a larger political, social, and economic context that influenced livelihoods, social status, and political power within natural resource–dependent communities in the Northwest. The original conflict heightened in the 1980s under the Reagan administration, whose officials favored extractive uses of natural resources and presided over policies that increased timber harvests throughout the Northwest (Hirt 1994). At the same time, many rural communities in the Northwest were experiencing an in-migration of more liberal urban professionals (Duane 1998). While this migration began a trend that would start to tip the balance of power in the direction of nonextractive uses of national forests, during most of the 1980s extractive users outnumbered nonextractive users greatly. At the time, environmentalists had very little power at the local level and instead depended on national environmental organizations, and, to a greater extent, the courts. Environmentalists and many professionals within the Forest Service also believed that timber harvest levels were both unsustainable and ecologically disastrous. Even R. Max Peterson, chief of the Forest Service from 1979 to 1987, acknowledged in 1989 that, "Anybody—on the back of an envelope—could have figured out that the rate of harvest cannot be sustained" (Hirt 1994, 272). **[1]***

The reaction of local environmentalists to the increased harvests during the Reagan years was to flood the Forest Service with appeals of federal timber sales and inundate the courts with lawsuits. Quincy attorney Michael Jackson was in the thick of the efforts to slow the harvest. "The environmental community wasn't going to be intimidated," recalled Jackson, "so we were filing appeals on every sale" (*High Country News,* 1997). **[2]**

The main battlefield for the conflict was the Forest Service's formal planning process. The National Forest Management Act of 1976 (NFMA) required each national forest to develop a comprehensive plan to guide its decision making. The Forest Service released a draft plan for the Plumas National Forest in January 1986. The agency had attempted to strike a balance between timber interests and environmentalists by setting an annual target of 265 million board feet of timber to be harvested, primarily through clear-cutting (the average harvest at the time was in the range of 200 million board feet annually). A timber industry coalition, Plumas County, and the Friends of Plumas Wilderness each submitted alternatives to the Forest Service plan. The timber industry and Plumas County alternatives sought dramatically increased harvest levels, in the range of 318 million board feet per year. The Friends of Plumas Wilderness alternative proposed a lower annual harvest—247 million board feet per year—less than the agency's proposed plan but still more than average harvests. In addition, the Friends' plan proposed setting aside significant old-growth, roadless, and riparian areas. Most importantly, it banned clear-cutting, choosing instead selective logging practices designed to leave larger trees while

*In subsequent chapters, this quote will be referenced as "Quincy 1," and subsequent quotes from this chapter as "Quincy 2," "Quincy 3," etc.

harvesting smaller trees that contributed most to disease and the danger of catastrophic fire. The Friends' plan attempted to find common ground between timber and environmental interests. "None of us is opposed to logging," said Michael Yost of the Friends of Plumas Wilderness. "If done carefully, a great deal of this forest can provide timber for the economic benefit of these communities that depend on the forest" (*Chico News and Review,* 1986). **[3]**

But timber interests were skeptical of the Friends' plan and the group's motives. They were also distrustful of the Forest Service, which was faced with the new challenge of balancing emerging environmental and recreational values with traditional extractive values. Fearing a dramatic change in policy direction, a coalition of conservative citizens from Plumas and neighboring Sierra County opposed the Forest Service and Friends' plans on the grounds that they overemphasized nontimber values such as recreation and conservation. "The Forest Service now has de-emphasized the production of forest products in favor of the preservation policies of a vocal minority," a group member decried. "Jobs are being sacrificed for visual constraints and non-motorized semi-private recreation areas" (*Feather River Bulletin,* 1986). **[4]** Another member from Quincy lamented, "It's getting to the point of absurdity. One has to be realistic and if a stand is not made, our communities and our jobs are going to disappear. The working person in Plumas and Sierra counties is going to be listed on the endangered species list" (*Feather River Bulletin,*1986). **[5]**

As part of the planning process, the Forest Service held public meetings throughout the region. According to a *Sacramento Bee* newspaper report,

> The timber industry amassed logging trucks, backhoes and forest workers on the streets of this mountain town Tuesday in a show of force to support maximum harvests on the Plumas National Forest. Speakers wearing wide suspenders and hard hats dominated the hearing, attended by more than 300 people. (*Sacramento Bee,* 1986) **[6]**

One after another, timber industry supporters attacked the Forest Service's proposed plan (environmentalists stayed away for fear of violence). An SPI official warned the Forest Service that they were ignoring the needs of the local logging community: "We who live here, work here, pay taxes here, and die here should be able to get the government's ear. We're part of the forest and our lives are at stake" (*Feather River Bulletin,*1986). **[7]**

As news of the Forest Service plan spread throughout the region, negative reaction to it only increased. No one, it appeared, was happy with the agency's apparent compromise. In a newspaper article dated September 14, 1988, County Supervisor Coates warned of a pending appeal:

> As a county we asked for 315 million board feet of timber a year. We got 265.5 million. We and all the counties in northeastern California opposed set-aside lands for the spotted owl. We got more than 100,000 acres. The regional forester has ignored our requests and I think we ought to take a hard look at an appeal ourselves. Up here we have some very real concerns about the job base. With the amount of litigation we see coming at us like a wave and the amount of federal budget cuts we see coming at us like a wave, we're being told that 265.5 million board feet is OK for us to survive. It's only OK if we're skillful and very lucky" (*Feather River Bulletin,* 1988). **[8]**

Not surprising, the Forest Service selected its own plan. But the agency also recognized the Friends' plan as the "environmentally preferred alternative" and touted it for providing "community stability" better than the other options, including its own. The Forest Service did not choose the Friends' plan, however, because its selective logging practices were less efficient than clear-cutting, the agency's preferred method of harvest.

Unhappy with the Forest Service's compromise, the Friends of Plumas Wilderness and twelve other groups formally appealed the Plumas Forest plan. While the appeals joined hundreds of other national forest plans in a cumbersome Washington, D.C., review process, the Forest Service initiated timber harvesting under its plan. Even as it did so, however, it was clear that change was on the horizon. The northern spotted owl, a cousin of the California spotted owl, was proposed for listing as a federally threatened species under the Endangered Species Act (ESA) in 1989 (it was officially listed in June 1990), after more than five years of intense public debate (Yaffee 1994). This event accelerated the decline in the timber industry in the Pacific Northwest. And, although the northern spotted owl would not affect the Plumas Forest, it suggested that similar declines in California spotted owl populations would eventually threaten local timber production. In fact, the U.S. Fish and Wildlife Service was already looking into such a listing throughout the Sierra Nevada Range

In February 1989, local loggers began a grassroots effort to fight back with what became known as the Yellow Ribbon Coalition. The coalition was an attempt by local timber workers to draw attention to Forest Service policies they claimed were causing the timber shortages. Yellow ribbons, flying from supporters' property and vehicles, were a symbol of community solidarity with the timber industry. A local newspaper ad described the campaign under the headline "Why We Fly Yellow Ribbons":

> The Yellow Ribbon is silent, but it radiates a power for change, a power to save our Timber Industry, our communities and our natural-resources lifestyle. A lifestyle that embodies all of the values that have made our Nation the greatest Nation on Earth. When we pass a car or truck that is also flying Yellow Ribbons, a bond is formed that cannot be severed by words or deeds of preservationist adversaries. Our Timber Industry, our homes, our families and our communities are at risk. We are united. (*Feather River Bulletin,* 1990) **[9]**

The Yellow Ribbon Coalition garnered considerable support throughout Plumas County and soon yellow ribbons were flying from vehicles across the region, and in other parts of California and the West. The coalition also organized a logger rally and truck convoy through Northern California. Festooned with banners, the first convoy of sixty-one logging trucks left Quincy on Labor Day 1989 and was joined by others along the way to the state capital in Sacramento. A September 1989 *Sacramento Bee* article reported:

> More than 100 loggers met at dawn in Quincy to proclaim themselves the true forest environmentalists in a daylong parade of lumber trucks from Plumas County to the state Capital. "I'm a fourth generation logger in Plumas County and damn proud of it," said a sign on a logging truck. . . . Many log-truck drivers complained that their jobs are being threatened by the spotted owl. (*Feather River Bulletin,* 1989) **[10]**

Jim Kirkland, an independent log-truck driver, argued that the forest plan threatened the fundamental rights of local workers. "This rally is about the spotted owl and my rights—people's rights to work. If we don't stop the spotted owl deal, you're not even going to be working" (*Feather River Bulletin,* 1989). **[11]** Lou Haberstat, an independent log-truck driver from Eugene, Oregon, blamed environmentalists for the threats. "It's not really the bird that's the problem. It's the environmentalists not wanting anyone in the woods. They don't want to see progress" (*Feather River Bulletin,* 1989). **[12]**

In their travels, loggers were also becoming aware of the growing public sentiment against the practice of clear-cutting. They also began to realize that the blame for clear-cutting was falling directly on them. Signs that distanced loggers from Forest Service clear-cutting policies began to emerge. "Forest Service management today is terrible forestry," said one local logger. "They're cutting our future" (*Sacramento Bee,* 1993). **[13]** Mac McCutcheon, a logger from Quincy, told a reporter:

> Clear-cutting is as much of a problem for the logger as the spotted owl. Most loggers are for selective cutting. With proper selective cutting, we'll always have a timber industry and we'll always have our jobs. With clear-cutting we get erosion and brush fields. (*Feather River Bulletin,* 1989) **[14]**

Donna McElroy elaborated:

> I'm tired of loggers getting blamed for what's going on in the woods. In every news report you see, the logger—the working man—takes the blame for clear-cutting. (*Sacramento Bee,* 1990) **[15]**

But McElroy and other loggers continued to use the rallies to hammer the environmental community, which they ultimately blamed for the situation:

> If these radical environmentalists have their way we are going to have the cleanest depression this world's ever seen. If we didn't have the timber industry, there would be no town here, and that's a fact. (*Sacramento Bee,* 1990) **[16]**

McElroy later reflected a growing frustration with the Forest Service:

> I blame everything on the Forest Service. They sit on the middle of the fence. Whoever it looks like is going to win, they drop down on that side of the fence. We care about what goes on in the woods, but we don't set policies. The Forest Service does. And I'm not just concerned about loggers. I'm concerned about the communities too. I love Plumas County, and I hate what's happening to it. (*Chico News and Review,* 1991) **[17]**

Ironically, environmentalists shared much of the frustration with the Forest Service. The agency's attempts to balance competing values were not satisfying anyone, it seemed. Attorney Michael Jackson told a reporter:

> If you ask me if there is any real change going on with the Forest Service, I will tell you that there is not. I don't think they are doing anything other than propaganda. (*Chico News and Review,* 1991) **[18]**

Clearly, the Forest Service was in flux. While an extractive use philosophy still pervaded the agency throughout the 1980s, it was beginning to recognize that public values were changing. Greg McClarren of the Deschutes National Forest in Central Oregon summed up the agency's dilemma this way:

> Our values are slowly catching up with the public's perception of multiple use. There are some fundamental changes coming in the way our forests are managed. We're on the cutting edge, but we are leading from somewhere in the middle. Timber people say the Forest Service is too liberal; conservationists say our head is in the sand—and to some extent it is, because of our strong traditions in timber management. (*Chico News and Review,* 1986) **[19]**

The reaction to these changes was extremely disruptive to the region, however. Acts of vandalism and threats to community members began to surface in July 1988 when a heavily spiked board was found buried across a steep logging road. In August 1988, a Quincy publisher received a false bomb threat intended for the Sierra Pacific mill. Threats to environmentalists occurred as well. Michael Jackson reported receiving death threats, including a phone message that was tape-recorded on his answering machine. He also received a well-placed bullet hole in his office window.

In a 1989 letter appearing in the *Feather River Bulletin,* Jackson decried the vandalism and threats. He also attempted to reach out to loggers. Jackson referred to a recent letter to the editor by Donna McElroy, commenting, "I was more encouraged by reading that letter than anything I have seen or heard in the last ten years in this county" (*Feather River Bulletin,* 1989). **[20]** Jackson empathized with loggers' frustration with Forest Service policies and suggested that they had more in common than they realized.

> The Plumas County environmental community has been preparing for the forest planning process for over ten years. . . . We know what is wrong with present Forest Service activities and we know how to fix it. We know how to do that while preserving all of the local timber industry jobs and potentially increasing them. We also know that the logging community has answers to some of our common problems which we may not have considered. We know that for a complete solution to our common goals we need the wisdom of the people who have worked in the woods for the four generations that we have been logging Plumas County. (*High Country News,* 1997) **[21]**

Jackson also suggested that environmentalists and loggers had a common love of the forest and a common foe in the Forest Service and large timber companies:

> We believe that we are all honest people who want to continue our way of life. We believe that we all love the area in which we live. We believe that we all enjoy beautiful views, hunting and fishing, and living in a rural area. We believe that we are being misled by the Forest Service and by large timber, which controls the Forest Service, into believing that we are enemies when we are not. (*Feather River Bulletin,* 1989) **[22]**

Jackson and the McElroys attended a Board of Supervisors meeting in September 1989, in which a resolution condemning acts of violence was unanimously approved. The resolution "calls upon members of our community to cooperate and continue positive discussions on the future of the forest and the stability of our rural quality of life" (Plumas County Board of Supervisors, Sept. 19, 1989). **[23]**

While Jackson's editorial and the county's resolution pointed the way toward a collaborative solution, the timing was not yet right for change. The Plumas Forest Plan was in appeal, the forest plan on the Lassen National Forest to the north had not yet been released, and the Forest Service had taken no drastic action on declining California spotted owl populations. Moreover, the forests were still producing enough timber in 1989 and 1990 to keep the rural economy buzzing. All of that was about to change, however.

In July 1991, the Forest Service temporarily suspended all timber sales and harvests in areas containing California spotted owls. A Forest Service spokesperson described the suspension as part of a larger move toward a "landscape approach" to managing national forests. The logging community, needless to say, was not pleased with this latest threat, and feared that the Forest Service was caving in to environmental concerns, which they perceived as minority special interests. An industry spokesperson told a reporter:

> Until John Q Public stands up and says what he wants, the Forest Service responds to that vocal minority—that 1 percent of the public that wants to lock everything up for owls and wandering minstrels. (*Chico News and Review,* 1991) **[24]**

While approximately 200 million board feet were harvested on the Plumas Forest each year in 1989, 1990, and 1991, the 1992 harvest dropped to 112 million board feet. The Forest Service estimated that the Plumas Forest would produce only 114 million board feet in 1993 and projected further declines to 60 million board feet for 1994 and only 45 to 50 million board feet per year beyond that.

Similar declines were projected on the Lassen National Forest. While the initial draft Lassen Forest plan targeted an annual harvest of 154 million board feet (from a high of 178 million board feet in the mid-1980s), the Forest Service's estimates suggested that the revised plan, once completed, would slowly decrease the harvest from approximately 133 million board feet in 1991 to 120 million in 1993. The agency hinted that reductions would continue and that spotted owl habitat would have to be preserved if an ESA listing was to be prevented. When the plan was finally released in August 1992, however, the target had dropped to 96 million board feet.

County officials took Lassen Forest officials to task for "caving in" to special interest groups. "We sense that the Forest Service is losing its will to fight," Bill Coates told officials. "We're counting on you guys to start making a stand for these communities. They're counting on you and we're counting on you, and we expect you to fight" (*Feather River Bulletin,* 1992). **[25]** Lassen forest supervisor Leonard Atencio cited a shift in national priorities, which had forced a change in the agency's traditional emphasis on timber:

> Internally [the agency] is in a lot of chaos. As a country we are not sure we want to continue with our way of life or start protecting our environment. For the Forest Service it isn't a choice. Based on the laws we are required to follow, we are not given a choice of protecting animal species or communities. (*Feather River Bulletin,* 1992) **[26]**

In September 1992, Lassen County Supervisors held a special meeting at the county fairgrounds to hear public comment on the plan. Susan Baremore, from a third-generation logging family, reflected the growing desperation in the local logging community. "This plan will effectively exterminate an entire culture of families like ours. We're not going to allow our families to be torn apart without a fight" (*Sacramento Bee,* 1992). **[27]** The meeting ended with the unanimous adoption of a resolution condemning the Forest Service and demanding that the agency postpone adoption of the plan until it could adequately review local economic and social impacts.

The Emergence of the Quincy Library Group

It was becoming apparent to both environmentalists and logging advocates that their administrative appeals to the Plumas Forest plan were going to fail.

The Friends of Plumas Wilderness contemplated a court action to force the Forest Service to adopt its alternate plan, which the agency had already recognized. Bill Coates and Tom Nelson saw no reasonable legal recourse for their appeals. They also recalled the Friends' promise that under its plan the forest could support old-growth and spotted owl habitat protection while nearly restoring traditional harvest levels. So Coates and Nelson approached Jackson with the idea to dust off the Friends' plan. Jackson was eager to meet but did not mince words: "The timber industry came to us on their knees. We let them up to do the right thing" (*California Wild,* 1998). **[28]** Fortunately, SPI's philosophy made it easier to talk. According to Nelson, "[T]he company's position has always been go talk to your adversaries as long as you can keep your wits about you, because you may not be at odds on all points. If you can find some common ground, it is a good business practice" (Nelson, March 4, 1999). **[29]**

Coates, Nelson, and Jackson agreed that the concepts in the Friends' plan appeared sound. With initial agreement the three brought in other community members to help develop the concepts. The focus of the group's discussions, according to a report released at the meeting, was "to develop a plan that would promote the objectives of forest health, ecological integrity, adequate timber supply, and local economic stability" (*Feather River Bulletin,* 1993). **[30]** The group also started meeting at the county library, where it could accommodate a larger group, demonstrate openness, and, some say, keep them from raising their voices.

In July 1993, Coates and Jackson reported their progress to the larger community at a town meeting. The *Feather River Bulletin* covered the meeting of about 150 citizens and Forest Service employees:

> After two hours of discussion on the bipartisan proposal, a straw poll show of hands was called for. Only four people disapproved. It could be the beginning of the end of a long struggle over forest use in the Sierra and a harbinger of the Sierra's future. (*Feather River Bulletin,* 1993) **[31]**

The *Chico News and Review* boldly declared a "Truce in the FOREST WARS":

> No one who knows the combative attorney and the politician who hates to lose would be shocked if they suddenly exchanged fisticuffs. Instead, Jackson and Coates surrender their 15-year owls-versus-jobs fight to stand together and embrace a proposal to save

> their community and the national forests that surround it. (*Chico News and Review,* 1993) **[32]**

The group's report contained a list of basic points they could all agree upon, general strategies for accomplishing their goals, and an image of what they called a desired future condition, "an all-age, multi-storied, fire resistant forest approximating pre-white-man conditions" (*Feather River Bulletin,* 1993). **[33]** With broad community support, the "Library Group," as they referred to themselves, pushed forward. The group soon developed a five-year conceptual plan for the Plumas and Lassen National Forests and the Sierraville District of the Tahoe National Forest, a total of 2.5 million acres of federal land. Coates commented in 1993: "None of us has ever done this before, and I'm sure we'll make mistakes. But the work we've done so far represents a four-letter word—hope. We haven't had a lot of that in the past" (*Sacramento Bee,* 1993). **[34]** Coates was more confident of the group by the summer of 1994. "It has gone a long way toward unifying people," he noted. "Before the project, each camp had its own restaurant. It's not like that any more" (*California County,* 1994). **[35]**

Jackson, who had been involved in numerous national battles as an environmental attorney, had his own reasons for getting involved:

> I've taken part in listing almost every salmon on the West Coast. But I can't fix the salmon problem with the law. They're in too much trouble. I need the help of everyone. It's the same with logging. I need my neighbors. If the logger who drives the Cat in the woods won't help me, then the tractor will go through the stream, no matter how many rules there are. (*High Country News,* 1997) **[36]**

But Jackson had other reasons as well. "These are my neighbors," he told a reporter. "My heart doesn't bleed for Sierra Pacific Industries, but bleeds for the folks getting $12 an hour who don't have alternatives for work" (*Sacramento Bee,* 1993). **[37]** In a September 1993 letter to a timber industry newsletter, Jackson elaborated:

> We sat down, and worked it out. In doing so, we began rediscovering our sense of community. The conversations, both formal and informal, that have occurred as a result of the efforts of the QLG have been very positive. They have made us realize how dysfunctional a community we were before, always fighting each other, instead of trying to move forward on common goals. The social experiment of working together as neighbors is perhaps as impor-

> tant, or may be more important, than the forestry experiment we are now proposing. (*Timber,* 1993) **[38]**

While the majority of Friends of Plumas Wilderness members decided to join QLG, not everyone connected to the group could live with the plan. For the most part, however, local environmentalists supported the group. Outside environmentalists, however, were growing wary of the emerging coalition. They viewed the forests more as national assets and made little connection between the forests and local communities. According to David Edelson of the Natural Resources Defense Council: "We're talking about public land. All citizens have a stake in how it is managed" (*Sacramento Bee,* 1993). **[39]** Nor did they all trust SPI. In fact, some outside environmentalists characterized SPI's Tom Nelson as a "snake in the Garden of Eden: smart, charming and lethal" (*American Forests,* 1995). **[40]**

QLG also gained early attention and support from California political leaders including liberal Democratic senator Barbara Boxer and conservative Republican congressman Wally Herger. "This is not easy," Boxer told the group after a 1993 visit. "And you did it. It is a myth that we can't be for a sound economy and also for a strong environment" (*Feather River Bulletin,* 1993). **[41]** The group approached Boxer to gain support for the plan in Washington and to secure funding for the plan's implementation. Boxer pledged to support the plan in Washington and concluded, "Here's what I want to leave you with. I think it's exciting. I think it's a model" (*Feather River Bulletin,* 1993). **[42]** Congressman Herger also praised the group but used his praise as an opportunity to criticize the Clinton administration:

> Unwilling to sit idly by while distant forces decide the fate of our mountain communities, local leaders and activists from across the ideological and political spectrum have been quietly meeting together in a constructive effort to find common ground. (*Timber,* 1993) **[43]**

In spite of their efforts, QLG members and supporters in Congress could not, with minor exceptions, get the Forest Service to implement its plan. A year passed, then two, with little action other than verbal support from the agency. Michael Jackson described the group's frustration with the Forest Service: "They say that they're all for this plan, but we're still waiting for them to do something—anything" (*American Forests,*1995). **[44]**

The official response from the Forest Service was positive. Outgoing regional forester Ronald Stewart commented, "We don't have anything else like this, but we're committed to making it work as long as it meets our legal needs and the needs of the scientific community" (*American Forests,* 1995). **[45]** And incoming regional forester Lynn Sprague wrote in a letter to Coates: "I am very supportive of this kind of community interest and involvement and very much want to see some successes" (*American Forests,* 1995). **[46]** Plumas forest supervisor Wayne Thornton remarked at a public hearing in 1993:

> Something really unique and special has gone on here. All sides are applying equal pressure to the Forest Service, but they're singing from the same song sheet, and that's music to my ears. (*Sacramento Bee,* 1993) **[47]**

Publicly, Forest Service officials applauded the community for moving beyond gridlock, even though they were skeptical of their ability to work together and doubted that it could find the $39 million to implement the group's plan. But not all in the Forest Service were as committed. One reporter wrote, "Some employees are as frustrated with their agency as community group members and have welcomed the opportunity for real change in forest management. Others resent the intrusion of what they consider non-professional outsiders" (*American Forests,* 1995). **[48]** One forest supervisor dismissed QLG's efforts in an internal memo, commenting, "This group does not have all the answers, and they don't have the expertise they claim" (*American Forests,* 1995). **[49]**

In March 1994, the group sent forty-two members to Washington, D.C. While there, they visited Forest Service chief Jack Ward Thomas and the offices of 110 members of Congress, whom they considered key funding votes for the upcoming budget year (Brooks 1994). The group received favorable reports from Congress but got little response from the Forest Service. "We can't get (officials of) the Plumas National Forest to do anything but talk," reported Michael Jackson. "They ought to change their name to the U.S. Lip Service. I'm hoping its only local ineptness. But if it's not, owls versus jobs was never the problem" (*Sacramento Bee,* 1994). **[50]** An April 1994 *Sacramento Bee* article began: "Plumas County's storybook tale of environmentalists and loggers working side-by-side to save their community now has a purported villain: the U.S. Forest Service." The article reported that the agency had, so far, failed to fund the QLG plan, even though it was implementing some of QLG's recommendations on the ground. A spokesperson called it an irony. "The very things that led the Quincy Library Group to meet in the first place are the very things that are limiting our ability to respond." Another added: "We're killing ourselves trying to find ways to do something, but we have to obey the law" (*Sacramento Bee,* 1994). **[51]**

QLG waited two more years for the Forest Service to act. A few experiments were forthcoming along with a modest amount of money from the U.S. Department of Agriculture. With growing frustration, QLG began to see Congress, and federal legislation, as its only hope for action. QLG biologist Linda Blum viewed legislation as necessary to get the Forest Service to take the plan seriously: "This is to get them off the dime—to do this work and do it right" (*Sacramento Bee,* 1996). **[52]** So in late 1996, Congressman Wally Herger (R-CA) quickly translated the QLG plan into legislative language and began ushering a bill through Congress.

The QLG bill was first introduced in the fall of 1996 but saw no congressional action until early 1997 when conservative western Republicans began to rally around it. The bill's popularity was a wake-up call to environmentalists, who suddenly became more interested in finding an "administrative" solution that would allow the Forest Service to carry out a scaled-down version of the plan. Environmentalists, it appeared, had more problems with the legislation than with the actual plan. As the director of the Klamath Forest Alliance remarked:

> For many years we have believed that a consensus on management of public forests is needed and that such a consensus can only come about as a result of on-the-ground efforts involving local, regional and national interests. We also believe that among so-called "partnership" efforts the QLG is the only one that has demonstrated real potential. Unfortunately, the bill you sent cannot be accepted. (Pace 1996) **[53]**

Hopeful that he could find such a consensus, Undersecretary of Agriculture Jim Lyons set up a series of negotiations between QLG and outside environmentalists. Within weeks the negotiations produced a tentative agreement that had Lyons' office supporting federal legislation if administrative action did not produce the desired results. However, while environmentalists could agree in principle to the plan, they ultimately could not agree to any form of legislation. They wrote to Lyons: "We do not want to sign an agreement that commits USDA to supporting federal legislation to implement the QLG agreement, under any circumstances" (Blumberg et al. 1997). **[54]** Concerned that environmentalists would balk once legislation was taken off the table, QLG terminated the negotiations and went back to Congress.

In the Republican-controlled House, the Herger bill quickly moved forward, but with a distinct pro-logging flavor. House Democrats charged that the bill was a Republican "hijacking" of the QLG plan and did not reflect the group's hard-fought consensus (*High Country News,* 1997). **[55]** It took Congressman George Miller (D-CA) and a Clinton administration veto threat to get the bill on track. After a relatively quick, albeit rancorous, debate, it passed the House by a 429–1 vote. The bill then moved on to the Senate where it became mired in even more controversy.

While environmentalists were opposed to the bill from the beginning, they dramatically escalated their attacks once it cleared the House. A Sierra Club "Action Alert" now called the improved bill "The most dangerous forest legislation since the infamous 'salvage rider'" (Action Alert, Oct. 3, 1997). **[56]** The Alert also charged that the bill "abdicated [forest management decisions] to a small number of local interests" (Action Alert, Oct. 3, 1997). **[57]** Louis Blumberg, assistant regional director for The Wilderness Society, charged that the bill was not a "public consensus" because it failed to win support of the national and regional environmental community. "What's collaborative about lobbying Congress to pass a law?" asked Blumberg. "You want consensus? What about the opposition of 140 environmental groups? Now that's a consensus" (Louis Blumberg, pers. comm., March 1, 1999). **[58]** While environmentalists are in favor of "local involvement," Blumberg wrote, they are opposed to "local control. Just because one group of local people comes to an agreement over how they would like the land managed, does not automatically mean that the agreement is good. Our national forests belong to all Americans." (Blumberg, pers. comm., March 1, 1999). **[59]**

Carl Pope, executive director of the Sierra Club, wrote a letter to the editor of the *San Francisco Chronicle* attacking Congress and the consensus process:

> They love consensus. They are eager to embrace a win–win solution that makes everyone happy and no one mad. It gives the appearance of an ideal pact between the timber industry and environmentalists. . . . It sounds too good to be true. It is. A look beneath the gloss reveals no consensus at all. A few stakeholders developed this misguided plan by pushing out dissenters and ignoring issues that did not fit the easy solution. (*San Francisco Chronicle,* 1997) **[60]**

A September 1998 issue of the Sierra Club newsletter, *The Planet,* began referring to QLG "environmentalists" in quotation marks (*The Planet,* 1997). **[61]** As the criticisms intensified, QLG members began defending themselves from assaults to their plan and their reputations. Michael Jackson believed that the Senate bill was now "the best it has ever been" (Jackson 1997). **[62]** He acknowledged the diverse opinions that existed regarding QLG and used the opportunity provided by a Senate hearing to strike back:

> The people of the Library Group have been exalted for "putting aside differences" and panned for being "self-serving sell-outs mesmerized by bright lights and smooth tongues." Our opponents offer nothing to you but more of the same—the status quo of endless fighting, divisiveness, and hatred. No real improvement for the environment. No new recruits interested in a long-term balance between the economy and the environment that sustains us all. (Jackson 1997) **[63]**

Jackson referred to the opposition as either "right-wing people who believe this is a left-wing plot to weaken the moral fiber of loggers and who support the cutting of more trees" or a "small left-wing environmental contingent that believes the plan is too kind to loggers," and characterized them as "wing-nuts," who were "holding the center together" (*California County,* 1994). **[64]** National environmental groups fired back, characterizing the QLG and its plan as "the Ginsu knife of forest management" (American Lands Alliance Press Release, Oct. 18, 1999). **[65]** QLG was also being characterized by outside environmentalists as another of many "special interest groups" (*High Country News,* 1997). **[66]** Jackson also made sure that Congress knew that Blumberg and other environmentalists had participated in the development of the Friends of Plumas Wilderness plan back in 1986. "They think they can get a better deal now that the timber industry is on its knees," said Jackson. "They're mad at us because we're going to let it up to do the right thing" (*High Country News,* 1997). **[67]**

But environmentalists only intensified their attacks. A Sierra Club Action Alert called the bill a "Trojan horse" that "masquerades as 'community input' but in reality [is] a hoax designed to eliminate existing controls in the laws that protect national forests." It claimed that the bill was a "fraud" containing "lots of talk about protecting communities . . . and protecting roadless areas," but is "really about getting the cut out—the final cut" (Action Alert, Oct. 3, 1997). **[68]**

As Congress was recessing, radical environmentalists even began attacking their moderate counterparts for not doing more to fight the bill. A full-page ad appeared in the *San Francisco Bay Guardian,* slamming Senator Boxer for cosponsoring the bill and Sierra Club executive director Carl Pope for endorsing Boxer's run for Senate reelection. The ad, titled "If a Tree Falls in the Forest and a Democrat Is Holding the Chainsaw, Will Carl Pope Make a Sound?" claimed that Pope and the Sierra Club were "strangely quiet about [the] century's worst forest legislation." The ad called for Pope to resign, stating that, "Pope's inability to say 'No' to Boxer on an issue of this magnitude is proof that his loyalty to the Democratic Party comes before his loyalty to protecting our natural heritage" (*San Francisco Bay Guardian,* 1997). **[69]** Boxer was characterized by one activist as a "servile, obsequious greenwasher" (*San Francisco Bay Guardian,* 1997). **[70]**

Boxer received so much pressure from environmentalists that she withdrew her support. Boxer then put a Senate "courtesy hold" on the bill in 1998 that essentially prevented it from being debated on the Senate floor. Eventually, Senator Dianne Feinstein, the bill's Senate cosponsor, attached the bill to the 1998 appropriations bill where it became law. It was signed shortly after by President Clinton.

The Herger–Feinstein Quincy Library Group Forest Recovery Act of 1998 (HFQLG), a five-year pilot project, underwent an environmental impact analysis in 1999. The Forest Service released a Record of Decision (ROD) on the analysis in August of that year (USFS 1999). The ROD upheld the QLG plan but with the addition of "mitigation" measures that declared all "suitable" California spotted owl habitat off-limits to logging pending the findings of a Sierra Nevada–wide analysis of the owl's status. QLG appealed the Record of Decision. The Sierra Nevada Ecosystem Framework, the regional owl study, was completed in January 2001 (USFS 2001). And, although the Framework used the most recent scientific information to assess the potential impacts of timber harvests on the spotted owl, it did not overturn the HFQLG mitigation requirements. At this writing, the Framework is being reviewed by a team of Forest Service resource managers to determine whether it can better accommodate the HFQLG Act. Congressman Herger, opposed to the framework, vowed to support "any effort to undo this rushed judgment . . . including legislative, regulatory relief or legal efforts" (*San Francisco Chronicle,* 2001). **[71]**

Analysis—the Reframing of an Intractable Conflict

The QLG effort is but one component of a broader conflict over management of national forests in the United States. This broader conflict has been brewing since the establishment of the national forest reserves in 1891. Its intensity has heightened, however, since the 1960s and 1970s when new environmental laws and national policy directives such as the Wilderness Act, National Environmental Policy Act (NEPA), and ESA began elevating the status of recreational, aesthetic, and conservation values in public land management. These laws and policies have challenged a half-century dominance of resource extractive uses. Consequently, a classic environmental conflict erupted, pitting development and preservation interests in a high-stakes and divisive political battle.

The QLG conflict suggests how changing identity, characterization, and conflict management frames might foster collaboration in the face of an intractable conflict. It also demonstrates the significant role that the changing political and social context plays in influencing frames and strategic behavior. In the Quincy case, a common concern for community played a role in triggering a more unifying and solution-seeking language by those at the local level. The Quincy case also demonstrates how the resolution of a dispute on one level can create conflict on another level, causing new frames to emerge, joining former adversaries, and pitting former collaborators against each other. The Quincy case appears to demonstrate that the changing context was necessary for the frames to change. It suggests that intervenors need to be aware of context changes and subsequent perceptions within environmental disputes. It might also suggest that intractable disputes are those wherein the context is either constant, its changes are not readily perceived by the disputants, or its changes are not acted on in ways that allow or foster resolution.

Identity and Characterization Frames—the Timber Wars

The timber wars of the 1980s were punctuated by stark "interest-based" arguments that reinforced "us versus them" identities. Most of the statements captured in the case during this period demonstrate the deep division among factions over forest management. Interest-based identity frames evoked by outspoken members of the logging community during this period include "the working person," **[5]** "working man," **[15]** "loggers," **[11, 14, 15, 17]** and "our natural resources lifestyle" **[9]** to name a few. All of these identity frames are inclusive of certain "communities of interest" based on a common vocation and values (Kusel et al. 1996). At the same time, they are exclusive of others. When a logger proclaims, for example, "I'm a fourth-generation logger in Plumas County and damn proud of it," **[10]** he is evoking a common identity with a heritage of loggers who have lived and worked in the forests for four generations—an identity that is now threatened. He is simultaneously distinguishing himself and those like him from dissimilar identities.

Statements containing the proverbial "we" have the same effect. The "we" to whom loggers are referring during this period are usually members of their communities of interest, or who share similar values and beliefs. **[8, 9, 11, 17, 25]** The statement, "We who live here, work here, pay taxes here, and die here . . . ," **[7]** when stated at a logger rally by an official of a large timber company, is intended to be inclusive only of community members with similar interests, values, and beliefs. It is worth noting that local citizens opposed to massive logging during this period also lived there, worked there, and paid taxes there. But the statement, when taken in the context of the timber wars, is obviously not intended to be inclusive of the broader "community of place" (Kusel et al. 1996). The "we" in the statement therefore captures only a community of like interests and serves to preserve the existing divisions and perpetuate the conflict, thus maintaining its intractability.

Environmentalists also used interest-based identity frames to talk about themselves and others, as in Michael Jackson's statement that "the environmental community wasn't going to be intimidated so we were filing appeals on every sale." **[2]** The community Jackson is identifying with is a community of similar interests and values. The environmental community is Jackson's most salient identity during the timber wars of the 1980s. Even though he and other local environmentalists live in a rural community, far from their cohorts in Sacramento and San Francisco, they identify themselves more strongly with those interests. Moreover, the "environmental community" in Jackson's statement reveals an identity with both national and local interests, which were aligned during the timber wars. Place-related identity frames occurred during the timber wars as well, but were usually thinly disguised calls to recognize only that part of the community that shared a particular belief about forest management, and to discount other beliefs. References to "our community" **[5, 9]** are thus "code" for interest-based arguments. The following "Yellow Ribbon" statement conveys an inclusive place-based identity and concern for "our communities" but, taken in context, excludes community members who may not share the same set of interests, values, and beliefs. It therefore supports an interest-based argument and serves to perpetuate the conflict: "The Yellow Ribbon is silent, but it radiates a power for change, a power to save our Timber Industry, our communities and our natural-resources lifestyle." **[9]**

We could argue that the place-based identity claimed here is placed between the "bookends" of an identity with the "Timber Industry" and "our natural-resources lifestyle" and is therefore an interest-based identity in disguise. The statement, "We who live here, work here, pay taxes here, and die here . . ." **[7]** has the same effect. The statement focuses almost entirely on interests—live, work, pay taxes, and die—but uses an identity with place—"here"—to convey them. The statement sounds very inclusive but actually discounts those who do not support the interest-based pro-timber message behind the statement. The statement also directly implies that people outside that community—the national interest—should have a limited voice in forest management.

Place-related identity frames came from environmentalists as well. Like the logging community, place-related frames evoked by environmentalists during the early stages of the timber wars contained predominantly interest-based messages. The following statement offers a subtle example: "None of us is opposed to logging. If done carefully, a great deal of this forest can provide timber for the economic benefit of these communities that depend on the forest." **[3]** In the statement, "us" refers to the local environmental community and specifically the Friends of Plumas Wilderness. The statement recognizes the diverse forest-related interests at stake in the community and evokes an identity with place but more as a "background" element. In the foreground are competing interests for forest use, and an attempt by environmentalists to reconcile them with an alternative plan.

As mentioned in the case, local environmentalists wanted to keep attention on their forest plan, which they believed was good for the logging community as well as the environment. They did this by consistently focusing on common interest–based and place-based ties to the broader community and its values. Michael Jackson's statement is perhaps the best example of the attempt by local environmentalists to reframe the conflict:

> We believe that we are all honest people who want to continue our way of life. We believe that we all love the area in which we live. We believe that we all enjoy beautiful views, hunting and fishing, and living in a rural area. **[22]**

The "we" in Jackson's statement is both an interest- and place-based identity. The first "we" in each sentence refers to Jackson's interest-based identity with the local environmental community. The second "we" refers to the broad place-related community as a whole. Jackson's statement offers a very different identity frame than those used by the local logging community and is intended to bridge the ongoing conflict by evoking common ties to the broader community, rather than perpetuate it by reinforcing narrow interest-based distinctions. Jackson and other local environmentalists were unsuccessful in reframing the local at that time however. In 1989, when this statement was made, timber harvests were relatively high and loggers were optimistic that they could win the war. Environmentalists' attempts to reframe the conflict fell on deaf ears.

The Forest Service used institutional identity frames throughout the conflict. Forest Service officials consistently refer to themselves in their institutional role as forest managers and consistently use "we" as the institution itself, **[19, 26, 45]** as in the statement, "We're killing ourselves trying to find ways to do something, but we have to obey the law." **[51]** The statement also suggests that the Forest Service does not see itself as part of QLG. This is not surprising given the evolution of the group and the common belief among its members that the Forest Service was part of the problem.

Characterization frames are often evoked in the same breath as identity frames and in some cases are inseparable. Negative characterization frames are often part of an intractable conflict and are used to discredit or discount adversaries by portraying them in a negative light. During the timber wars, loggers characterized environmentalists as a "vocal minority" **[4, 24]** and "wandering minstrels," **[24]** thus challenging their claims to legitimacy. The following characterization statement implies that the vocal minority does not represent the broad public, who could not possibly agree with the policies being advocated: "Until John Q. Public stands up and says what he wants, the Forest Service responds to that vocal minority—that 1 percent of the public that wants to lock everything up for owls and wandering minstrels." **[24]**

Local environmentalists were also portrayed as extreme "preservationists" **[9]** and "radicals" **[16]** who were "against progress," **[12]** even though they had proposed a forest plan that targeted significantly more timber than had been harvested in recent years. The message being conveyed was that environmentalists were unconcerned with community economic stability or the well-being of their neighbors, and cared infinitely more about owls than about people. Like identity frames, negative characterization frames were intentional attempts to discount, discredit, and de-legitimize the interest-based arguments that environmentalists were making toward forest management. Like identity frames, negative characterization frames served to perpetuate the conflict and reinforce its intractability.

As already mentioned, local environmentalists saved their negative attacks for the Forest Service and timber industry, as in Jackson's statement that "we are being misled by the Forest Service and by large timber, which controls the Forest Service, into believing that we are enemies when we are not." **[22]** Jackson's statement was apparently designed to drive a wedge between the local logging community and the Forest Service and timber industry, which environmentalists believed were in cahoots to maximize efficiency at the expense of local communities and the environment. While the strategy appears to have eventually worked, especially with the Forest Service, it appears to have led to an intractable conflict of another kind, and one that still persists.

In contrast, local environmentalists often characterized the local logging community in positive terms, even though they were vilified in return. Jackson and other local environmentalists commonly referred to local loggers as their "neighbors." **[36, 37, 38]** Jackson also granted them legitimacy, for example, when he wrote, "We know that for a complete solution to our common goals we need the wisdom of the people who have worked in the woods for the four generations that we have been logging Plumas County." **[21]** While negative characterization frames helped fuel the conflict and perpetuated its intractability, positive characterizations at the local level may have kept the timber wars from erupting into violence. They did not, by themselves, cause the conflict to move from an intractable to a more tractable conflict, but they appear to have played a role in moving in that direction.

Identity and Characterization Frames Shift

By the fall of 1992, the future appeared so bleak throughout the northern Sierras that even local environmentalists were concerned. The timber wars, it appeared to some, had a winner and a loser. The timber industry had lost. Many also believed that timber-dependent communities had lost as well. When Bill Coates and Tom Nelson visited Michael Jackson, it was akin to surrender. Environmentalists were winning, but at what cost? Mills were closing, unemployment was around 20 percent, schools were suffering, forests were succumbing to insect infestations, and at least a few local environmentalists feared that desperation would trigger arson attacks on the forests, since dead trees would likely be harvested. Conditions were ripe for something to happen.

Common threads began to emerge. First, while the battle was principally between loggers and environmentalists, both factions began to blame the Forest Service for their situation. In the preceding years, Forest Service policies had achieved neither community prosperity nor forest protection. Second, and more importantly, members of each faction began to see that "community stability and forest health" **[30]** constituted a common place-based "super-ordinate goal" (Sherif 1958) that reframed their narrow interest-based "owls vs. jobs" **[10, 32, 50]** arguments. Local environmentalists expressed concern about their unemployed neighbors, and loggers expressed concern about forest destruction through clear-cutting.

For its part, the Forest Service was "missing in action," hamstrung by its planning process and its forest plan. The Forest Service was still caught in a "false choice" of sorts that the community was beginning to shed—that it had to choose between owls and jobs. Community stability and forest health were not yet on its radar. As one forest supervisor lamented:

> Internally [the agency] is in a lot of chaos. As a country we are not sure we want to continue with our way of life or start protecting our environment. For the Forest Service it isn't a choice. Based on the laws we are required to follow, we are not given a choice of protecting animal species or communities. **[26]**

In spite of the Forest Service's inaction, or perhaps because of it, the inclusive message by the Friends of Plumas Wilderness began to take hold within the community and provided a space for the emergence of QLG. As QLG evolved, place-related identity frames became more salient and inclusive—"us" and "them" changed to "we" and "our" based on a common identity with place. Michael Jackson reflected on the transformation:

> We sat down, and worked it out. In doing so, we began rediscovering our sense of community. The social experiment of working together as neighbors is perhaps as important, or may be more important, than the forestry experiment we are now proposing. **[38]**

The ability to reframe the conflict from "owls vs. jobs" to "community stability and forest health" appears to have been made possible through a common, place-related identity that became salient among the principal parties—local loggers and environmentalists. Moreover, although the local environmental community maintained a consistent and inclusive message, the message was not accepted by the logging community until two of its trusted advocates, Coates and Nelson, adopted it. While the conditions were ripe for something to happen, it took Coates and Nelson to step into the breach. It also took a third individual, Jackson, a trusted member of the environmental community, to be open to their offer.

Place-related identities did not appear to overshadow institutional and interest-based identities among Forest Service officials or "outside" environmentalists. As mentioned, the Forest Service maintained a consistent institutional identity throughout the conflict and did not see itself as a member of QLG. No one broke rank publicly even though QLG members reported Forest Service employees secretly cheering them on. Even the forest supervisor's paternal comments suggest that whatever has gone on is occurring outside of the institutional framework of the agency: "Something really unique and special has gone on here. All sides are applying equal pressure to the Forest Service, but they're singing from the same song sheet, and that's music to my ears." **[47]**

So-called "outside" environmentalists, for their part, continued to frame the conflict in stark interest-based dimensions, and began to view QLG environmentalists as sellouts for deliberating with the timber industry. Others argued that QLG environmentalists had been co-opted by slick industry negotiators. Some outside environmentalists, we recall, characterized Tom Nelson as a "snake in the Garden of Eden." **[40]** Moreover, outside environmentalists viewed the forests as national assets with little connection to local communities. David Edelson's statement subtly makes this point. "We're talking about public land. All citizens have a stake in how it is managed." **[39]**

Negative characterizations only intensified once legislation was imminent. Jackson referred to the opposition as "wing-nuts." **[64]** National environmental groups fired back, characterizing the QLG plan as "the Ginsu knife of forest management." **[65]** The Sierra Club questioned the legitimacy of QLG "environmentalists" when it began using quotation marks when referring to them. **[61]** QLG members began defending themselves from assaults on their plan and their reputations. Jackson, who strongly identified with the environmental community during the timber wars, now referred to them as "our opponents." **[63]** For Jackson and other local environmentalists, "we" was now their community. Then, at the height of the tension, the most radical environmentalists began attacking one of the moderates for placing his political party loyalty before his loyalty to "protecting our natural heritage." **[69]**

As the attacks escalated, the conflict only became more intractable. Passage of the HFQLG Act diffused some of the tension around the legislation but did not end the conflict. Stark interest-based arguments reemerged during the environmental review. In spite of the outcome, Jackson is optimistic about the future of the community: "The social experiment of working together as neighbors is perhaps as important, or may be more important, than the forestry experiment we are now proposing." **[38]**

Conflict Management Frames

Conflict management frames in the QLG case tend to shift with power and with dynamic conditions. During the timber wars, for example, environmentalists generally believed that legal appeals of timber sales were their best resource for protecting forests. Jackson's statement that, "The environmental community wasn't going to be intimidated so we were filing appeals on every sale" **[2]** indicates their chosen conflict management strategy at the time. When communities began to suffer, some looked for more cooperative approaches, first by negotiating with timber interests and then through community-based collaboration. As mentioned, local environmentalists had more substantive reasons for changing strategies as well. Again we turn to Michael Jackson:

> I've taken part in listing almost every salmon on the West Coast. But I can't fix the salmon problem with the law. They're in too much trouble. I need the help of everyone. It's the same with logging. I need my neighbors. **[36]**

Others, however, continued to believe in and pursue adjudicative and regulatory approaches that were available under federal environmental laws and regulations. After all, they were successful in slowing logging in the past. Louis Blumberg of The Wilderness Society argued that existing procedures under NEPA provided adequate public involvement and that while he was in favor of "local involvement," he was opposed to "local control," which, he argued, "abdicated [decisions] to a small number of local interests." **[59]**

Likewise, when the timber industry was in power in the 1980s, existing regulatory and adjudicative approaches to conflict management were preferred. It was only when environmentalists were solidly winning legal battles that some in industry began looking for alternative approaches. For the timber industry, negotiating with local environmentalists was a strategic decision, as in Tom Nelson's statement that, "the company's position has always been go talk to your adversaries. . . . If you can find some common ground, it is a good business practice." **[29]**

On one level, the formation of the QLG appears to mark a joining of individuals who believed in negotiation and common-ground approaches, and a splitting off of individuals who preferred adjudicative and regulatory approaches. Ironically, the roles seem to flip when QLG decides to take its plan to Congress. Suddenly, QLG was opting for the adversarial win–lose arena of federal lobbying and legislation, where it had more power, while environmentalists began advocating for an administrative solution brought about by negotiation. **[53]** This shift in conflict management frames also appears to be strategic. QLG member Linda Blum argued that legislation was not QLG's preferred approach but was necessary to get the Forest Service to take its plan seriously, "to get them off the dime—to do this work and do it right." **[52]** QLG had already been wooed by many in Congress and knew that it was eager to help. But outside environmentalists were opposed to federal legislation because of the concern that it might set a precedent for locally controlled forest management and/or congressional meddling, neither of which looked appealing with the current Congress. They also knew that Congress was salivating over QLG, especially Republicans who, as we recall, were eager to find an environmentally friendly cause.

The irony of a community-based collaborative group initiating federal legislation was not lost on environmentalists. Nor was the irony of the reaction among environmentalists against the plan lost on QLG. As The Wilderness Society's Louis Blumberg remarked, "What's collaborative about lobbying Congress to pass a law? You want consensus? What about the opposition of 140 environmental groups? Now that's a consensus." **[58]** QLG's response might be something like, "What about the consensus of 429 U.S. congresspersons? Now that's consensus." Interestingly, people involved in the conflict were apparently able to easily change conflict management frames depending on the need, and depending on which strategy gave them greater standing or power. As the political and economic context shifted around them, they were able to adapt and find a suitable strategy.

The QLG conflict continues today. It involves many of the same parties and issues, but is being played out once again back in California where the three national forests are struggling with ways to harmonize the HFQLG legislative mandate with the Sierra Nevada Forest Plan Amendment. Senator Feinstein and Congressman Herger expressed deep disappointment in the new forest plan. Herger vowed to support "any effort to undo this rushed judgment . . . including legislative, regulatory relief or legal efforts." **[71]** Regardless, the brief interlude of collaboration in the midst of this intractable conflict, and the evolving language of the parties as they stepped through the various phases, provides insights into critical precursors to resolvability in the face of what otherwise appears intractable.

Note on Sources

The information in this paper was derived from newspaper and magazine articles, press releases, newsletters, action alerts, and correspondence and from interviews with community residents, activists, business leaders, environmentalists, civic leaders, and public officials. Newspaper and magazines articles were collected from the *Sacramento Bee, Feather River Bulletin, Chico News and Review, High Country News, California Wild, American Forests, San Francisco Chronicle,* and *San Francisco Bay Guardian.* The time span covers 15 years from the 1980s forward.

Chapter 4

Freeze Framing: The Timeless Dialogue of Intractability Surrounding Voyageurs National Park

Barbara Gray

When the French Voyageurs* first traveled the steely blue waters of what is now Voyageurs National Park transporting furs and trade goods, they had no idea that this series of big lakes that afford such calm and tranquility would eventually be the site of bitter battles between the federal government and people who now reside on the lake's shores. But since 1891, when the idea of creating a national park in the area was first conceived, park advocates and opponents have engaged in protracted wrangling over whether there should be a park and who should control it. Over 110 years later, these battles continue.

Voyageurs National Park on Minnesota's northern border with Canada consists of one large lake and portions of three others, a number of small inland lakes, and a peninsula of land that separates three of the large lakes. There are several gateways to the park including Ash River, Crane Lake, Kabetogama, and the main entrance near International Falls (see Fig. 4.1). Because Voyageurs is largely a water-based park, its enabling legislation specifically allowed for "the appropriate use" by different means of access. Practically this has meant that, unlike most other national parks, fishing and the use of motorized boats and snowmobiles are permitted. Prior to becoming a park, the land and water were used for logging operations, for hunting and fishing, and for private cottages and camps.

The case that follows traces the history of the park from that initial proposal to the present, focusing particularly on the last 40 years. The case data are

---

* The term "Voyageur" means "traveler," but in northern Minnesota it refers to a canoeman in the fur trade (Nute 1969, 6) who ventured into the park's lakes around 1688.

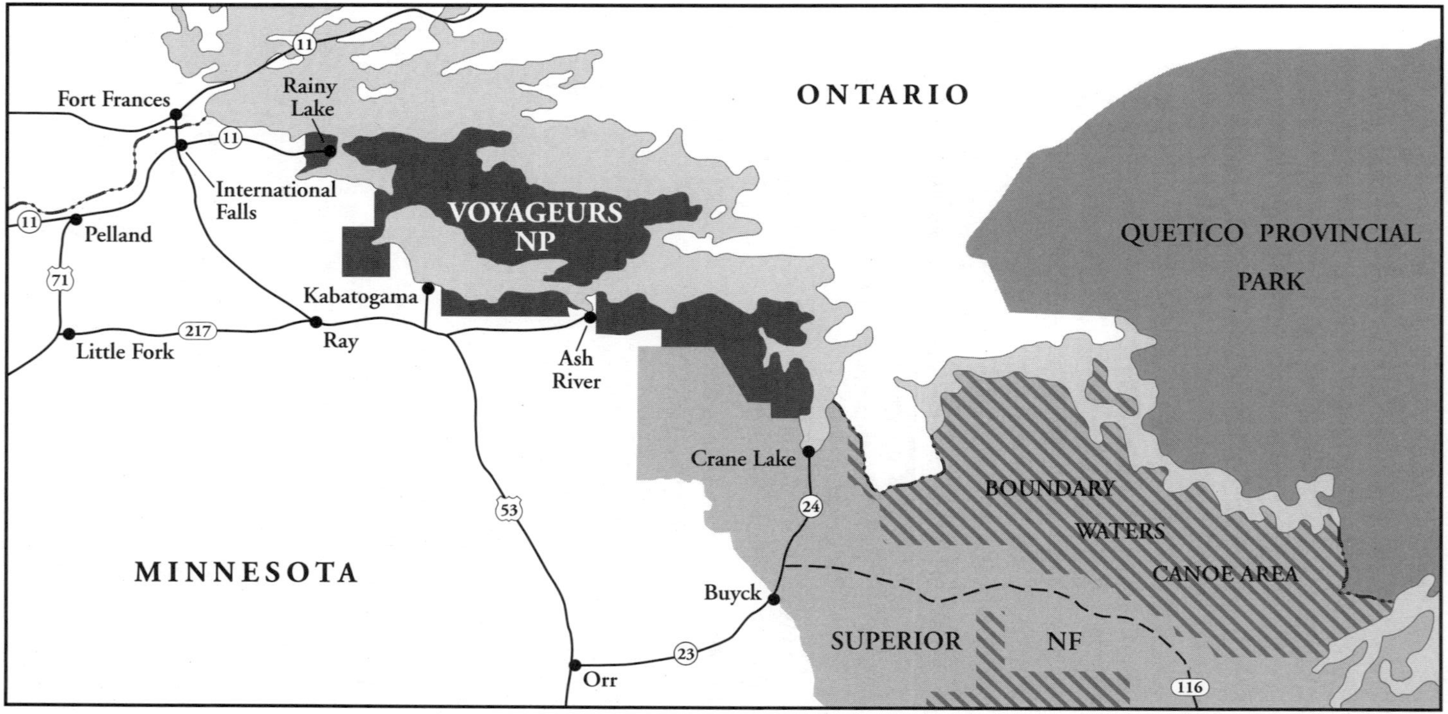

Figure 4.1. Map of Boundary Waters

drawn from archival records, media coverage, and interviews. Interviews were conducted with 47 stakeholders of the park, including state and federal natural resource managers, environmentalists, park opponents, local businesspeople, and federal, state, and local elected officials.

Overview

The original proposal for a northern Minnesota national park was made by the Minnesota legislature in 1891 one month after the U.S. Congress enacted the Forest Reserve Act, authorizing the use of public land for forest reserves. Timber interests and local politicians from northern Minnesota mounted immediate opposition to this proposal. They feared loss of private lands to federal control and viewed the proposal as interference by Twin Cities residents "with the established resource utilization practices in northeastern Minnesota" (Witzig 2000, 3). **[1]**[†] This resentment was expressed pointedly in a Duluth newspaper, "Our people are tired of outsiders misrepresenting these northern lands as useful only as the hunting and playground of a few nabobs who have more money than brains" (*Duluth News Tribune,* 1990, 19). **[2]**

Numerous other attempts by conservationists and timber advocates to gain control of portions of what is now parkland were undertaken over the next sixty years. It wasn't until 1971 that Congress passed legislation creating the park. The intervening years witnessed a firestorm of controversy over the proposed park—controversy that continues to this day.

Once the enabling legislation was passed and funds were allocated, objections by local people to creation of the park turned to how the land had reportedly been acquired from local landowners who had private landholdings within the new park's boundaries, restrictions on the kind of activities that were prohibited within the park boundaries, and preferences for local, as opposed to federal, control of the park. Purchase of the land by the federal government left a bitter taste in the mouths of many—some of whom challenged the acquisition values in court and received higher payments for their properties than did others who accepted the government's offer without contest or elected a provision for fixed-term use and occupancy.[‡]

[†] In subsequent chapters, this quote will be referenced as "Voyageurs 1," and subsequent quotes from this chapter as "Voyageurs 2," "Voyageurs 3," etc.

‡ Use and occupancy prescribes a fixed term of residence, after which the land ownership transfers to the National Park Service.

By the early 1980s, once the park had acquired sufficient lands, a temporary period of cooperation ensued during which the park and the local community undertook construction of some of the park's current facilities. Resistance to the park has taken many forms over the years, and, despite these cooperative initiatives, resistance festered. Once the park had acquired about 90 percent of its land area, protests turned to other issues, particularly frequent contests over decisions made by park officials about usage versus protection of natural resources. For example, conflict erupted over evaluation of parts of the park for wilderness status and decisions to close a few lake bays to protect gray wolf habitat.[§] Concerted efforts by state and federal environmental groups to urge wilderness designation for the park's peninsula have contributed to the conflict's escalation. Many motorized users of the park (e.g., boaters, snowmobilers, houseboat owners) fear that such designation will result in the loss of all motorized access to the park.

Environmentalists, on the other hand, support the wilderness designation arguing that it will ensure preservation of the resources for future generations. Contests between these two groups over decisions made by park officials about usage versus protection of natural resources have been frequent.

During the 1990s the controversy over recreational versus wilderness use surfaced several times. The closing of some lake bays to investigate the impact of snowmobiling on wildlife infuriated many motorized users. A compromise proposal failed to carry the day, and numerous federal court decisions also failed to end the controversy. In 1995 locally led efforts to decommission the park during the summer of 1995 heightened the tension dramatically. After this contest proved unsuccessful and at the urging of Minnesota's Democratic senator, Paul Wellstone, concerted efforts were made to settle the Voyageur's controversy through mediation in 1996–97. A panel of eighteen people representing the various interests in the conflict met for almost a year and a half. However, even with the assistance of a federal mediator, the mediation concluded without any agreements despite multiple drafts of a compromise between wilderness and motorized advocates. From 1998 to 2000, at the request of local officials, the park undertook a General Management Plan (GMP) process to establish guidelines for its next fifteen

---

[§] A provision that the parkland be evaluated for wilderness status was included in the park's enabling legislation.

to twenty years. Although this process included several opportunities for public input, the draft plan offered by the park was once again challenged by local residents.

The last forty years of the park's history can be divided into six phases:

1. The fight for authorizing and enabling legislation
2. Resisting the land acquisition and federal control
3. The (somewhat) peaceful period
4. The wilderness wars
5. The mediation that failed
6. Planning for the future: the GMP process

The key issues and the protagonists in each phase of the conflict are outlined in Table 4.1. One critical organization at the heart of much of the controversy was a state-level oversight commission called the Citizens Council for Voyageurs National Park (Citizens Council) charged by the Minnesota legislature in 1975 to serve as a source of community input to park management. The Citizens Council was composed of legislators, citizens from Koochiching and St. Louis Counties (that house the park), and other Minnesota citizens appointed by the governor. Another key group, the Voyageurs Region National Park Association (VRNPA), was formed to help promote the park before its official designation as a federal park and has continued to the present to champion the environmental side of the conflict. We now take a more in-depth look at each of the phases in the park's history.

Phase 1: The Fight for Authorizing and Enabling Legislation

After the initial proposal for a national park in 1891, numerous attempts to gain control of what would eventually be parkland were made. In 1925, the Minnesota and Ontario Paper Company (M and O; later acquired by Boise Cascade) proposed a series of dams that would substantially raise water levels. In 1928, conservationists urged that the area be designated an International Peace Memorial Forest. The suggestion (first made in 1937) that some Superior National Forest land be shifted to National Park Service (NPS) control met with continued resistance by the U.S. Forest Service (USFS) over the years. Meanwhile, the Forest Service's 1944 attempt to purchase land on the Kabetogama Peninsula was rebuffed by Minnesota's governor. Some of this land was later purchased by M and O Paper for its logging operations. Despite this, some individuals persisted in advocating national

Table 4.1. Key Issues and Protagonists in Voyageurs National Park Dispute

Conflict Phase	*Time Period*	*Key Events*	*Key Issues*	*Key Players*
The fight for enabling legislation	1898–1975	1. Authorizing legislation passed in 1971 2. Enabling legislation passed	1. Who controlled the area in 1975 2. Whether Voyageurs would be a national recreation area or national park 3. Whether the park would bring economic benefit to the area	Gov. Elmer Andersen Sigurd Olson Congressman John Blatnik VNPA Boise Cascade Jeno Paulucci
Resisting the land acquisition and federal control	1975–1981	1. Acquisition of private land for the park 2. Protests by Vic Davis 3. Battles over Black Bay	1. Hunting and trapping within Black Bay and its inclusion within or exclusion from the park 2. Contests over land acquisition values	Vic Davis Citizens Council for Voyageurs National Park Supt. Myrl Brooks
The (somewhat) peaceful period	1981–1986	1. Cooperation in building the park's infrastructure 2. Removal of Black Bay 3. Environmentalists file lawsuit	1. Hunting and trapping within Black Bay 2. Opposition to Bay closures	Supt. Russell Barry Citizens Council Minnesota DNR VRNPA Don Parmeter, ex. dir., Citizens Council

The wilderness wars	1987–1995	1. Closing of bays to protect gray wolf habitat 2. MNUSA files lawsuit 3. Legislative oversight hearings	1. Whether the park is permitted to limit snowmobiling to protect wildlife habitat 2. Whether Voyageurs will continue as a national park	Supt. Ben Clary Supt. Barbara West begins State Sen. Bob Lessard Cong. Jim Oberstar
The mediation that failed	1996–1998	1. Sen. Wellstone proposes mediation 2. Mediation panel begins work with FMCS as mediators 3. No agreement reached 4. Political decision on BWCA	1. The extent of snowmobiling on Kabetogama Peninsula 2. The extent of other uses such as houseboats and floatplanes	Supt. Barbara West FMCa Brian O'Neill Jeff Mausoff Jan Takaichi Rep. Irv Anderson Citizens Council
Planning for the future	1999–2001	1. General Management Plan process begins 2. Funds for Citizens Council suspended 3. VUFP committee meets 4. Draft plan rejected by county commissioners	1. How to determine number of park visitors 2. Which of three alternative plans should be adopted (e.g., whether to regulate camping, houseboating, etc.) 3. Role of VUFP group	Supt. Barbara West VUFP consultation group Koochiching County commissioners St. Louis County commissioners

BWCA, Boundary Waters Canoe Area; DNR, Department of Natural Resources; FMCS, Federal Mediation Conciiation Service; MNUSA, Minnesota United Snowmobilers Association; VRNPA, Voyageurs Region National Park Association; VUFP committee, Visitors' Use and Facilities Plan committee.

park designation for the Kabetogama area as well as adjacent areas already controlled by the USFS.**

Throughout the 1960s, during (and after) his term as Republican governor of Minnesota, Elmer L. Andersen championed the idea of a national park in Minnesota. In 1961 the NPS authorized advanced studies of Kabetogama–Rainy Lake region for national park status, but local opposition to the proposed park grew between 1961 and the fall of 1964 when the first public hearings were held. Local opposition was fueled, in part, by the NPS delay in releasing information about the proposed park to the local citizens, many of whom were historically wary of federal land management (Witzig 2000). For example, in 1964, a Republican candidate for Congress from Duluth asserted that the proposed park was "another example of expanding government control, once again taking away the right and freedom of individuals to truly make decisions regarding their lives and livelihoods in their own backyards" (*Duluth News Tribune,* Sept. 23, 1964). **[3]** Several factors contributed to this delay and ratcheted up opposition to the NPS: (1) struggles between NPS and the USFS over the land, (2) a recommended increase in the no-cut zone†† within the Boundary Waters Canoe Area (Witzig 2000), (3) acquisition of M and O Paper by Boise Cascade Corp., and (4) economic opposition to the park.

Struggles with the U.S. Forest Service

Some of the land that park proponents wanted to include within the park lay to the south and east of the Kabetogama Peninsula and included three lakes (Namakan, Sandpoint, and Crane) that were then under Forest Service control. The NPS had hoped to gain approval for a joint study of the suitability of the area as part of the national park proposal. However, the USFS had remained intransigent, leaving the NPS to propose a much smaller park in 1961. This controversy was part of a larger conflict nationwide between the USFS and NPS over control of federal land. In 1962, to ensure its hold over this area, the supervisor of the Superior National Forest urged the USFS to

** These advocates included U. W. "Judge" Hella (director, Minnesota State Parks), Wayne Judy (secretary, International Falls Chamber of Commerce), Conrad Wirth (director, National Park Service), Evan Haynes (chief, NPS Recreation Resources Planning Unit), Sigurd Olson (a noted naturalist and writer, who originally supported USFS control of the area), and Gov. Elmer L. Andersen. Others preferred creation of a state park.

†† The no-cut zone refers to areas where logging was prohibited.

establish an aggressive development plan for the forest (Neff 1962). Meanwhile, the NPS continued to request that a joint study of the area be conducted (U.S. Dept. of the Interior 1964).

Purchase of M and O by Boise Cascade

Another factor that impeded public disclosure of the park's plans for Voyageurs was the takeover of M and O Paper by the Boise Cascade Company. Since M and O had considerable landholdings on the Kabetogama Peninsula, transfer of them to the federal government (in exchange for other state forest land) was essential for the park's creation. Prior to 1964, M and O had agreed to this plan, but when Boise acquired M and O in January 1965, they began to resist a park on the Kabetogama site (Witzig 2000). Their stance on these issues clearly had local influence since they were a major employer in the area.

Proximity to the Boundary Waters Canoe Area

Another reason for the early and strong (as well as protracted) opposition to Voyageurs stems from the park's proximity to the Boundary Waters Canoe Area (BWCA) south and east of the park. Substantially different in geographic features from Voyageurs with its large lakes and often rough waters, the BWCA consists of a series of small lakes interlinked by land portages. The area had been part of the Superior National Forest since 1909, and by 1965 consisted of several areas on which logging was prohibited. To local timber interests the Voyageurs proposal was just one more incursion into their shrinking resource base. Comparisons between the two areas have continually been invoked, initially as arguments against national park status and later to prevent wilderness designation for Kabetogama since, in 1978, the BWCA was designated a wilderness area and most motorized use there was prohibited. The comparisons are propelled by fears that Voyageurs, like the BWCA, will be designated a wilderness area—a continuing mantra of many park opponents, as these two quotes separated by 35 years in time illustrate:

> In the Boundary Waters roadless wilderness area, Northeast Minnesota already provides vast expanses of territory for the canoe and sleeping bag enthusiasts and enough is enough without giving up more large tracts to this class of more rugged vacationists. (Paulucci 1964) **[4]**

> Although this park [Voyageurs] was not intended to be BWCA West, we are losing all the allowable local uses one by one. (Woods 1999) **[5]**

Many residents of northern Minnesota deeply resented removal of motors from the Boundary Waters, and bitter fights over it have also continued to this day.

Early Economic Opposition to the Park

In addition to other reasons for opposing the park, local citizens feared that it would change their way of life and cause economic problems for the area. Despite the possibility that the park would draw new visitors to the area and improve the local economy, a 1964 statement attributed to the president of the Northeast Minnesota Organization for Economic Education articulates this basis for resistance to the park.

> This effort on the part of NPS bureaucrats strikes at the very roots of our striving to upbuild our resort and visitor industry, . . . We must stop usurpation of our economic rights by these government agencies who would damage rather than serve the best interest of Northeastern Minnesota with this proposed Voyageurs National Park that would take additional lands from Minnesota and would mean even less business and commerce and fewer jobs than this area has now (Paulucci 1964). **[6]**

Park opponents feared that the park would "damage the area's economy and drive tourists to Canada and curtail timber production" in the area (*Duluth News Tribune,* June 19, 1965) posing a real threat to resorts in particular. **[7]** Concerns were also expressed about reduced tax revenue for the two counties in which the park would be located. Others were more optimistic about the economic potential of the park. For example, in a letter to Jeno Paulucci, Congressman John Blatnik predicted the park could be a "boon to the entire region" (Minnesota Historical Society 1964). **[8]** An economic study from the University of Minnesota at Duluth supported this view and countered predictions about loss of taxes (Witzig 2000). Still, laments about the area's currently depressed economy are frequently attributed to the park. Not only do detractors express bitter disappointment that such resources have not materialized, they also blame the park for what they perceive to be their loss. In the words of one businessperson,

> There are still a lot of hard feelings amongst some individuals that, you know, who are still just angry . . . that the park was even created and in some respects, because they were right, because the things they feared back then have come to pass. The economic boom did not materialize and so, we're left with an economy that is, you know, sort of stagnant, in fact it is stagnant and predicted to be declining. **[9]**

On the other hand, someone in the recreation business expressed an opposite view about the park's economic contribution to the area.

> If you ask almost any resorter up there privately, "Are you better off with the park or without it?" they will say they are better off with the park. **[10]**

A third person recounted a conversation he had with a resort owner near the park about the possibility of promoting the park.

> [T]hey don't really look at the park as an asset. . . . It certainly could be if they used it, if they promoted it. And, in fact, some of them do promote it in word, but they don't philosophically. . . . I was talking with one of the owners of the resorts on Rainy about winter time activities. He was talking about . . . if they close down these bays and they close down more of the snowmobiles, then I'll be out of business, I said, "Well, what about cross-country skiers?" [He replied] "I don't want those damn cross-country skiers. They're a bunch of hippies. They're no good. They don't spend any money." He doesn't know modern cross-country skiers, obviously. **[11]**

A similar characterization of environmentalists "as 'extremists' and 'yuppies' with foreign cars and one pair of overalls and a $20 bill, neither of which they change when they come to visit" was offered by state senator Douglas Johnson in a newspaper article (Dawson 1995). **[12]**

Passage of the Authorizing and Enabling Legislation

Legislation creating Voyageurs National Park was passed by Congress on January 8, 1971. But it still required four more years of concerted effort by Sigurd Olson, Gov. Elmer L. Andersen, and Rep. John Blatnik, in whose congressional district the proposed park was located, before Congress authorized funds for enabling land acquisition to begin. Blatnik supported the formation of the park despite persistent opposition from groups in the Crane Lake and International Falls areas in particular. Part of the delay also stemmed from resistance to the park within the Minnesota legislature. The secretary of the interior was prohibited from establishing the park until the State of Minnesota donated the land to the secretary.[‡‡] Focused battles over what state lands should be included in the park lasted several years. During this time a vocal champion of the park was the Voyageurs National Park Association (VNPA), a statewide group of environmentalists formed in 1965 to continue the work (both within Minnesota and nationally) of promoting the idea of a national park.

Phase 2: Resisting the Land Acquisition and Federal Control

The authorization of funds for Voyageurs in 1975 enabled the U.S. government to begin acquiring land for the park. Initially landowners were given several options, which included selling to the park at a value determined as "fair market value" by a government appraiser, selling but reserving the right to occupy and use the premises up to 25 years or until their death, making a counteroffer, or going to federal district court if no agreement was reached. Some landowners sold quickly accepting the government's offer without contest, whereas others chose the occupancy and use option. Still others challenged the acquisition values in court, claiming that the government had grossly underpriced the land. Some have even characterized the NPS actions as "Gestapo tactics." **[13]** In 1978, a federal court jury awarded a local attorney 3.5 times the appraised value of his property. Other successful legal challenges followed in the next year. By October 1979, the park had acquired 318 of the 343 cabins and all but 7,500 of the total acres of designated parkland. But because the court decisions raised the overall costs of land, additional funds were needed to purchase the remaining acreage.

Protest of the park's land acquisition efforts became personalized when a Canadian citizen, Vic Davis, purchased land designated for inclusion within the park and erected a 25 ft., 2300 lb. fiberglass replica of a gun-toting Voyageur in a strategically visible spot to the park. To further foil the NPS, Davis subdivided his property into 1-square-foot parcels that he sold for $19.95 each to

---

‡‡ This language appears in Section 160A (16USC 1602).

over 2000 buyers, thereby complicating the NPS acquisition efforts substantially.

During this same contentious period, a local hunter named Carl Brown was cited for duck hunting in the Black Bay area of the park and found guilty by a federal magistrate. Brown appealed his conviction claiming that the State of Minnesota had not ceded rights to the waters within Voyageurs National Park. Brown's conviction was upheld by the district court, and eventually by the appeals court in 1977. Despite this, some park opponents, like Brown, believed that litigation was their only option for dealing with the conflict.

> The only chance we have . . . is the courts. And there's some of us that feel that the only way the issues are gonna be resolved is through litigation. 'Cause you get into the political area and Washington and the Congress, and, if a bill ever does get through . . . there's member of Congress on the Senate side that said they'd filibuster it . . . to killl it. And if it does get passed, they've got assurances that Clinton will veto it. So, you know, where can you go? **[14]**

In response to the court decisions in the *Brown* case, a state legislator from northern Minnesota, Tom Baak, introduced a bill into the Minnesota House that directed the state constitutional officers to defend the state's jurisdiction over the navigable waters, land, streambeds, and lake beds. The bill claimed, in effect, that the State of Minnesota had never ceded control of the waters in the park to the federal government. Despite testimony by the Minnesota attorney general's office that the bill would have no effect, it passed anyway, paving the way for additional lawsuits on this issue. This contest over control of the lakes in the park represents another attempt by some northern Minnesotans to wrest control of the park from the federal government, as this quote suggests,

> See one of the reasons that right now this is our last hope is if we can hold that water under state control. It isn't that the state isn't gonna manage the water . . . with the intent of the national park in mind. . . . It's just that we can be assured that, at least, we have a chance to be involved in the legislative process. On a state level we can play the politics. I mean if there's some rules and regulations that would come about on the water at least we have an opportunity to be involved in the process. **[15]**

Another claim levied by those who oppose the park's management is that the park has failed to deliver on several promises that were made to the local people—citing a lack of correspondence between the park's plans and the community's expectations. In addition to economic gain, another promise that opponents frequently cited was the park's failure to develop a Visitors' Use and Facilities Plan (VUFP), a requirement inserted in boundary adjustment legislation in 1983. The current superintendent explained that, although the requirement existed, Congress had not allocated any funds to enable such a plan to be developed until 1998 when it released funds for Voyageurs General Management Plan (see below).

Despite the provision in Voyageurs' enabing legislation for "appropriate use," disagreements about this issue have evoked bitter debate. While the option to create Voyageurs as a national recreation area (in which hunting would have been permitted) had initially been favored by some, it was rejected by Congress in favor of national park status, which clearly prohibits hunting. While the land acquisition battles were raging, controversy arose over the Minnesota Department of Natural Resources' 1979 decision to allow hunting on the 7700 acres of parkland still in private hands. The NPS objected to this decision. Since deer and duck hunting had been popular uses of the land before the park existed, many local people resented the NPS's efforts to keep the ban in place, even though no other national park permits hunting. As one park user explains, logging and family recreation were intimately linked to the culture of the area.

> The history of what they did there compared to what they can do or can't do there now is one of the big problems . . . there are still people alive who hunted. There are still people who worked logging jobs up there. They got their livelihood from the area. . . . And a lot of those folks have some real animosity towards the park and what it did to change their way of life. **[16]**

A proposal by Rep. James Oberstar, a Democrat from the area containing the park, to return an area called Black Bay to the state, was introduced into Congress in the fall of 1978 but was removed from legislation before it passed. The issue didn't die, however, and resurfaced again later.

Phase 3: The (Somewhat) Peaceful Period

Once the majority of land acquisition was completed, the park and the community experienced a qualitatively different relationship for a short time during the mid-1980s. According to one current opponent,

> There actually were some good times in there between 1983 and 1986 when we actually lobbied for development money for the visitors center, roads, and some things, you know, and that was very successful. Then we had some park management that was receptive to that and appreciated the fact that we did a lot of things that the Park Service in Washington can't do. They can't lobby. . . . Frankly, I thought the thing had been fixed . . . relationships were pretty positive, the statute had been revised§§ to the extent that the people felt it needed to be revised and the biggest issues got resolved. Well, it looked like they were going to get resolved. (1998) **[17]**

During this period work was undertaken to plan the park's development including identification of campsites, trails, and visitors' facilities. The Citizens Council and the park worked together to garner additional resources for building access roads, refurbishing the landmark Kettle Falls Hotel, and constructing the Rainy Lake Visitor Center, completed in 1987. According to then superintendent Russell Berry Jr.:

> The relationship has warmed up as the park's plans have become more developed and people have become more knowledgeable about what a national park is. (*Daily Journal,* Feb. 26, 1988) **[18]**

While this period was marked by cooperation around construction projects, the conflict had not completely subsided. Old objections to the park periodically resurfaced, new skirmishes were fought, and seeds were sewn for subsequent battles. For example, the issue of Black Bay heated up again in 1981 when a delegation of state and federal legislators from Minnesota urged a U.S. Senate subcommittee to remove the area from the park. Both the NPS director, Russell Dickenson, and Don Parmeter, executive director of the Citizens Council and a local opponent of the park, argued that the transfer would alleviate the tension around the park. Dickenson commented, "[T]he issue . . . detracts from the spirit of local and state cooperation which we are seeking to maintain at Voyageurs National Park" (McConagha 1981). **[19]** A St. Paul newspaper editorial in 1982 agreed,

---

§§ Reference is made to the 1983 change in the enabling legislation that removed Black Bay from the park.

> Much of the dispute surrounding the creation of Voyageurs could have been avoided if area residents' wishes had been taken into consideration when the parklands were acquired. Black Bay was not essential to the park, and the closing of one of the state's best duck hunting areas was regarded by northern Minnesotans as a slap in the face. (*St. Paul Pioneer Press,* October 3, 1982) **[20]**

Environmentalists eventually agreed to the land transfer with provisions that allowed hunting of waterfowl but prohibited all trapping. The compromise deal crafted in Congress was passed in September 1982 and signed into law by President Reagan in January 1983. At the time, Minnesota's Republican senator predicted this action would "help bring to an end the longstanding controversy among residents of northern Minnesota, the state government, and the Department of Interior" (McConagha 1982). **[21]**

While it appears that it did help to usher in a more peaceful period in the park's history, the conflict over Black Bay and management of the park writ large was still not over. Following the 1983 congressional action transferring Black Bay to the state, when the Minnesota Department of Natural Resources issued its rules for the area, they included both hunting for waterfowl and trapping. The park superintendent, Russell Berry Jr., opposed the trapping provision, but in September 1984 Interior Secretary James Watt ruled in favor of it. However, in March 1984 a coalition of nine environmental groups (including the VRNPA, the National Audubon Society, the Sierra Club, and Defenders of Wildlife) filed a federal lawsuit against the NPS charging that protected species (wolves and bald eagles) might accidentally be caught. The suit was settled in the environmentalists' favor in 1985.

During this period Vic Davis also continued his protests against land acquisition for the park during the 1980s. He continued to buy up land in the park and propose development on it; he ended up in condemnation proceedings in court.*** With funds from his earlier skirmish with the park, Davis purchased a second Voyageur statue, Big Louie, which he erected across the bay from the site of the new visitors center so that it was fully visible during the groundbreaking ceremony in 1985. Later, on the night before the new visitors center was dedicated, Davis clear-cut the same land and painted the rocks on it red. Earlier, he had threatened to develop condominiums on this land. In 1987 a federal jury awarded Davis $1.37 million for the 122-acre tract (which he had purchased in 1981 for $200,000). The case remained unresolved, however, and

*** Condemnation means the property is legally appropriated for public use.

the threats of condominium construction continued when the Justice Department refused to pay Davis what the jury awarded. Finally, in 1991, the government struck a deal with Davis to purchase the land for $1.2 million.

Phase 4: The Wilderness Wars: The Battle over Wolves and Eagles and the Park Itself

Voyageurs' enabling legislation required that the NPS study the suitability of the park for wilderness designation. This fueled yet another aspect of the Voyageurs controversy—whether snowmobiling would continue to be permitted on the Kabetogama Peninsula (a jut of land between two of the park's primary lakes). In 1979 the NPS had prohibited use of snowmobiles in all national parks except on automobile roads and frozen lake surfaces,[†††] but the decision about whether off-road snowmobiling would be waived for a 26-mile Chain of Lakes trail, which ran the length of the peninsula, remained under consideration by the NPS director.[‡‡‡] In 1980, the park issued a draft environmental impact statement (EIS) stating that the Kabetogama Peninsula met the qualifications for wilderness designation except for the Chain of Lakes trail, and for motorboat and floatplane access to certain of the peninsula's interior lakes.

While the park views the decision to allow snowmobiling on the Chain of Lakes trail as a compromise, some local citizens still strongly object to what they perceive as a reduction in recreational opportunities compared with what they had before the area became a national park. They contend that, over the years, the park has continually chipped away at their recreational freedom, and this is the basis for their hostility. In the words of one park opponent,

> They're telling us we can't use this area as a playground, as a recreational area because they want to manage it as a wilderness void—basically void of motorized vehicles, and most human activity. People are not going to stand still for that. It's pure and simple, it's not being hostile toward the government, it's a reality. (1998) **[22]**

Local opponents view wilderness designation as an axe waiting to fall and contend that wilderness designation is "not appropriate for Voyageurs and never was intended by Congress" (*St. Paul Pioneer Press,* June 3, 1992), a remark

[†††] This prohibition implemented executive orders by Presidents Nixon and Carter.

[‡‡‡] It was not decided until the early 1990s when it was allowed by a policy waiver from the director of the NPS.

echoed in several of our interviews in 1998–99. **[23]** The NPS counters that it was mandated by statute to evaluate wilderness suitability for the park. Further, the current superintendent notes,

> The NPS is charged with the responsibility to promote and regulate the use of parks. Regulation of users is absolutely at the core of what we do; that is why national parks are different from other places—use is regulated. We try to do it fairly and reasonably and in pursuit of public purposes. Perhaps this aspect of national parks was not emphasized in the debates about the park, but it has been part of the mandate of the National Park Service since 1916. (Barbara West, personal communication, Nov. 2000) **[24]**

Environmentalists have actively lobbied for wilderness status for all of the Kabetogama Peninsula, and at least one vocal environmentalist argues that public support for the protection of such lands is growing.

> There is a force of history, I think, that is going to result as wild land and wild creatures get scarcer and scarcer, and there's less, low cost places where people can have high-quality outdoor vacations. Those places are going to become more of a concern to most American citizens and uses of those resources that are noisy and vexatious and are harmful are going to become less and less prevalent, and that's the way the world is moving. **[25]**

An elected official explained the reasoning for the intensity of local reaction to the park,

> What they [referring to environmentalists] don't understand is that every time they push that agenda further and further, they are taking away from the culture of the people who live here. . . . The people that live here are just constantly seeing our federal government chip away and chip away at the lifestyles and the culture, the kind of recreation that people here like to do. See, the thing that you have to remember about this area is it is predominantly blue collar jobs. People work a lot in the outside, basically all of which is physical labor. They work very hard and when they have an opportunity to recreate on the weekends they don't want it to be some kind of marathon that they have to run, because they run that all week anyway. . . . They don't want it to be a big, rigorous experience, because their entire life is rigorous. Living here when it's 40 below and the wind chill is 100 below, its tough, especially

> when you do a lot of your work outside, in the mines and in these paper mills or at the logging jobs. **[26]**

Intensity also describes the commitment of the environmentalists to the park and its preservation.

> We consider ourselves . . . a supporter of the park service, encouraging them to manage the park based on the way the park was established originally. We see ourselves as being responsible for the creation of the park. We were . . . the coalition of interest groups that worked hard in the '60s to establish the park, . . . and with the understanding of what people were looking for in a national park, we have a responsibility to continue that work. . . . We work with the Park Service mostly in a very positive vein, but, at times, not positive when the Park Service recommends alternatives, for example, that do not match up with how we believe that the park is supposed to be managed. (1998) **[27]**

Interestingly, many park opponents also consider themselves caretakers of the parklands. "It's been like that for hundreds of years, and . . . the locals have been pretty good stewards of the area. The only reason why it is like that right now is because the local people have taken care of it for many years." **[28]**

In early 1990, resistance to the park's actions came from the environmentalists who filed a lawsuit enjoining the NPS from allowing snowmobiling until the park completed a statutorily required wilderness recommendation. In April 1991, a federal judge required the NPS to comply within one year with a ten-year-old directive to evaluate which parts of the park should remain wilderness but he did not enjoin snowmobiling. During the next couple of years, former governor Elmer L. Andersen and Milton Knoll, chair of the Citizens Council, floated compromise proposals, but these were rejected either by the VRNPA or the Citizens Council itself. Tensions between the Citizens Council and the VRNPA are captured in this comment by an environmentalist who referred to the Citizens Council as "a political boondoggle that wastes its time trying to impose local control—and a multiple-use philosophy over a federal agency that isn't about to bend to the pressure" (Myers 1997). **[29]**

Meanwhile, in June 1992, the park staff submitted a wilderness plan to Interior Department secretary Manuel Lujan who forwarded it to the Office of Management and Budget (OMB), over objections from environmentalists. The plan found that 92 percent of the parkland met the wilderness criteria, and proposed snowmobiling on an 11-mile corridor through the peninsula, on 16 miles of portages, and on 84,000 acres of lake surface. According to Jennifer Hunt, executive director of the VRNPA,

> The Park Service is on the right track by recommending official wilderness protection for Voyageurs. But we feel the Park Service has twisted the intent of Congress to protect the last traces of wilderness in the United States by caving in to the demands of lobbyists for the motorized industry (*St. Paul Pioneer Press,* June 3, 1992) **[30]**

Neither OMB nor President Bush acted on the proposal. In 1993, OMB returned it to the Department of the Interior.

Also in 1992, after required consultation with the U.S. Fish and Wildlife Service (USFWS) (under section 7 of the Endangered Species Act), the park's superintendent, Ben Clary, was instructed to close seventeen lake bays within the park to minimize harm, harassment, and taking of gray wolves (West 1997). This time a lawsuit was filed by Minnesota United Snowmobilers Association (MNUSA) who objected to the bay closures. Subsequently, a federal appeals court concluded that the park was free to take the action it had, but, in the meantime, the conflict intensified. The park's next superintendent, Barbara West, who took over from Clary in 1995, observed, "The seventeen closed bays were fairly minor in the scheme of things," especially in light of what happened over the next several months." **[31]**

West's arrival could not have come at a more contentious time. Just prior to her arrival, in January 1995 a Republican majority took control of Congress for the first time since the park was authorized, and leadership of the House Subcommittee on Park, Forest, and Public Lands shifted from Bruce Vento, a Democrat from Minnesota, to James Hansen, a Republican from Utah. This power shift opened the door for a March 1995 proposal from two Minnesota politicians, Senator Rod Grams (R) and state legislator Robert Lessard (D), that the park be decommissioned. Lessard testified before a Senate subcommittee that Voyageurs should be reclassified as a national recreation area to encourage more economic development in northern Minnesota and that three portages in the BWCA should be reopened for truck traffic. A BWCA wilderness supporter characterized Lessard's testimony as "a blitzkrieg attack against our precious national parks, wildlife refuges and wildernesses" (*St. Paul Pioneer Press,* March 3, 1995). **[32]** The shift in congressional control also enabled Congressman James Oberstar (D), whose district includes both Voyageurs and BWCA, to introduce legislation proposing to wrest control of the park from the NPS and give it to a local management council. The controversy heated up and came to a boiling point when a joint U.S. House–Senate subcommittee conducted oversight hearings in International Falls in August and again in October 1995 in the Twin Cities.

At the hearings, attended by some members of Minnesota's congressional contingent as well as the general public, opponents and proponents of the park revisited many of the old issues and rekindled old animosities. For example, allegations were again made that the park had had a negative economic impact on the area. Countering that view was a paid ad sponsored by the Save Our Park movement that charged that the effort to declassify the park was inspired by "a radical, county supremacy movement" that was using local citizens "as pawns for big business interests" (*Daily Journal,* 1995). **[33]** The following accusations toward an environmentalist by a member of a motorized user group, the Greater Northern Coalition, were captured in media coverage of the first hearings, "You're an elitist and you're selfish," **[34]** to which the environmentalist replied, "Look in the mirror, buddy" (*St. Paul Pioneer Press,* Aug. 19, 1995). **[35]** A retort in a letter to the editor accused wise-use proponent Bob Lessard of spewing out "poison" and characterized his followers as a "constituency of selfish self-interest groups" (*St. Paul Pioneer Press,* March 14, 1995). **[36]** Another reader defending the national parks labeled the locals as "crybabies" and "spoiled brats" who couldn't get what they wanted (*St. Paul Pioneer Press,* March 21, 1995). **[37]** Interestingly, in 1964, the secretary of the Koochiching County Planning and Zoning Commission had referred to "people in the South and East" parts of the state as also having "a selfish interest" (*Daily Journal,* Dec. 1, 1964). **[38]**

In an effort to resolve the issue, in 1996 Congressman Oberstar modified his legislation urging that the park remain a national park, but that a joint management council be created to give local people more control over the park's management. The council was to have eleven members including some local legislators, some appointees, and a representative from the Department of the Interior. Despite local criticism of Voyageurs during the hearings, Congress did not change its designation, and the management council proposal was never enacted.

The park was dealt a setback on the issue of bay closings in January 1996 when U.S. district court judge James Rosenbaum ordered all bays to be reopened except those within a specified distance of bald eagle nests. The judge ruled that NPS and USFWS studies had provided insufficient evidence for the closures.[§§§] MNUSA claimed the judge's decision as a victory insisting

§§§ This ruling was eventually overturned by the Eighth Circuit Court of Appeals in 1999.

that the closures had been arbitrary and unfair. In light of the judge's ruling, during the winter of 1996 Superintendent West requested voluntary compliance with the closing of eleven bays to all human use. This action infuriated many local residents, who criticized the park's scientific approach and characterized their actions as naïve and stupid.

Part 5: The Mediation That Failed

During 1996–97 concerted efforts were made to settle the Voyageurs controversy through mediation. Minnesota senator Paul Wellstone, a Democrat, proposed that stakeholders in the Voyageurs dispute, and in another over reopening portages in the BWCA, try to resolve their differences through mediation. Wellstone selected the Federal Mediation and Conciliation Service in Minneapolis to mediate. For Voyageurs, a panel of eighteen people representing the various interests in the dispute met for almost a year and a half, but eventually concluded the mediation without any agreements, despite a proposed agreement between wilderness and motorized advocates over what activities would be permitted on the Kabetogama Peninsula.

Many opposed to the mediation charged that Wellstone's proposals for mediation of the Voyageurs and the BWCA conflicts were a political maneuver that allowed him to avoid taking a stand on these issues during a critical election year (1996). They argued that taking a pro-environment stand in northern Minnesota might have cost Wellstone needed support. Wellstone maintained that it was simply wise to seek a Minnesota solution, and that mediation was a viable alternative to the years of bickering. Wellstone's aide, Lisa Patni, explained the senator's views about mediation in this way,

> If everyone is reasonable . . . we will solve this together. Let's talk it out and come up with a solution that can work. He was also praised with coming up with this by people from across the spectrum, Republicans as well as Democrats and Independents—that this is really a good way of coming up with a solution. **[39]**

Wellstone won the election, but, when both mediations eventually failed to reach agreement, the issues were thrust back into the political arena. Finally, a political deal over the BWCA portages was struck between Congressmen Oberstar (from northern Minnesota) and Vento (from the Twin Cities), but nothing about Voyageurs was part of that agreement.

Others contend that the mediation never could have succeeded because local opposition to it doomed it from the onset. When the mediation panel offered the seventh version of a compromise plan for Kabetogama Peninsula, Rep. Irv Anderson, longtime member and original promoter of the Citizens Council, claimed the mediation panel was doomed to failure, insisting, "People who live around the park will get nothing more from mediation except further compromising, giving up even more of what they once had" (Myers 1997). **[40]** Some critics assert that the Citizens Council's ultimate rejection of the compromise was engineered by Anderson. Superintendent West, who describes herself as "someone who always wanted to be a park superintendent," was a bit more circumspect. **[41]** She had high hopes for the mediation, initially, but reflected afterward, "I thought that it was possible to get past this," but she conceded in the end that it was not. **[42]** Still, she, and others, concluded that the mediation had afforded a chance to educate people about the park's mission and that some animosities had been set aside, as one observer of the mediation process described.

> I always looked at [name] as someone who I should be opposed to. And through the process, I looked at him as someone who was representing a group of people who are pretty reasonable . . . who were pretty close to my own views. And there were other examples where the bulk of the members sort of developed a bond that we were committed to trying to get resolved these long-standing battles. **[43]**

Part 6: Planning for the Future: The GMP Process

In 1998, after Senator Grams pushed for funding for a Visitors' Use and Facilities Plan (VUFP) for the park, Congress allocated funds for Voyageurs to develop a General Management Plan (GMP). The GMP involves a three- to four-year process of developing alternatives for the next fifteen to twenty years of the park's management. The GMP process, begun during the summer of 1998, provided several opportunities for public input into the plan (during initial scoping meetings and in reaction to the draft and final plans). In May 1999 three management alternatives for future development of the park were outlined for public consideration: (1) make no change, (2) increase resource protection, (3) emphasize visitor experience. The GMP process also enabled the park to convene an ad hoc group of about forty diverse stakeholders to provide input for the VUFP. Critics had chided the park for its failure to prepare a VUFP—a requirement written into boundary change legislation for the park in 1983—for which no funds had been authorized until the GMP. The decision to include the VUFP as part of the GMP was one agreement the mediation panel did reach. Convened in fall 1999, the VUFP committee commented on details related to park facilities and use, such as the number of campsites, visitor use and promotion of the park, entry fees, and possible limits on houseboats and floatplanes. Transcripts of these sessions and interviews taken during the scoping meetings showed that many old issues resurfaced in these dialogues. At times it was difficult for the VUFP group members to get past what some referred to as the broken promises of the past. In addition, because the VUFP committee as a group had no formal recommendation power,**** some members seemed angered and confused about its role and whether the NPS would implement suggestions made by the group as a whole or by individual members. Therefore, a critical test of whether the planning process would quiet the long-standing dispute was the extent to which park opponents believed the park staff were open to their views and addressed them in the draft final plan. The NPS insisted they needed to balance the VUF Committee's ideas with other input received throughout the GMP and with their own professional assessment of the park's natural, historical, and cultural resources. One natural resource employee explained the NPS's role this way:

> I think there needs to be . . . if there's a way to have local input, but at the same time realizing that there's special managers that are here to manage the parks, Voyageurs in particular. That they take their input, but that they don't cede their authority over to the locals. **[44]**

Despite efforts by the Voyageurs National Park staff to conduct the GMP in a constructive fashion, some nonparticipating VUFP group designees criticized the process. When the draft GMP was released in June 2000, it recommended that the park adopt a combination of all three alternatives. But the commissioners of Koochiching and St. Louis Counties spearheaded local resistance, charging that the community had not had time to react to the provisions of the plan.

> "There was a feeling among the public that they had not really been invited" to comment on the visitors' use and facilities plan that accompanied the park's general management plan. (Mike Foresman, *Timberjay,* Sept. 30, 2000, 6) **[45]**

**** The VUFP Committee was not a Federal Advisory Committee and did not have authority to make consensus recommendations to the NPS.

After listening to varied opinions of the VUFP group members, the park had concluded it lacked sufficient data on specific visitor use for many of its facilities. Thus, in the draft plan, most decisions about whether to assess user fees and issue permits for use were deferred until a permit system could be implemented (except limitations on the number of houseboats) to better understand visitor use patterns and their impacts. Opponents maintain considerable skepticism about any scientifically based decisions the park takes as these words from longtime opponent Don Parmeter convey, "The plan lacks a scientific basis for the proposed action. This is typical of NPS plans, because the agency's management of areas is based on philosophy, not on science" (Parmeter 2000). **[46]** Failure of the draft final plan to definitively settle use issues seems to have reopened old wounds. Note the similarity between the comments of two International Falls elected officials, one in 1986, and another describing the VUFP consultation process in 1999:

> It's imperative for the Park Service to finalize a commitment they made eight years ago for an on-land snowmobile trail. (Boswell 1986). **[47]**

> When we sat down for the initial meeting, we were told that all those controversial issues were off the table. Certainly the county representing the citizens here wanted to look at the more controversial issues and hopefully get some closure or agreement on them. Certainly that failed in mediation. **[48]**

Park opponents want assurances that the NPS's future decisions about use will not eliminate the kinds of uses they have traditionally enjoyed. In the words of another elected official,

> My fears are pretty much that . . . the multiple uses of the park will be reduced to more and more nonmotorized usage. . . . This goal that it has to be a wilderness experience, it never was really promoted as a wilderness park. . . . It was never really sold and never really developed as a park that would guarantee wilderness. And, I guess that it does appear that it will become a wilderness park. **[49]**

Analysis

The Voyageurs conflict can clearly be classified as an intractable one based on longevity alone. Episodes of the conflict have flared up repeatedly since Governor Andersen's championing of a national park in the 1960s. The dispute episodes between the park and its opponents or between opponents and environmentalists have been intense and bitter, and negative feelings, particularly in the International Falls community, refuse to die, even though some of the early players have passed on. The conflict has remained unresolved for almost forty years. In addition to its longevity, this conflict is intractable because it defies resolution. While the conflict's intensity rose at many key points in the park's history, there were also occasional short periods of relative peace. Looking historically, however, it appears that it is the dialogue itself that has become entrenched and resistant to change—even though some of the substantive issues in the conflict, such as land acquisitions, have been settled merely by the force of time. We now examine the root of the intractability of this conflict and show how it is bound up in dialogue between the park and its opponents that has become frozen in time.

Identity Frames

Three core issues are at the root of this conflict: (1) economic control over the natural resources of the area, (2) political control over land use, and (3) different values associated with how the land should be used. Identity frames are derived from this third issue. Strong and conflicting identity frames undergird the conflict and its perpetuation (Rothman 1997). As Northrup (1989) notes, threats to identity often generate entrenchment and escalation of conflict. Our preliminary analysis reveals that disputants use both reflexive identity frames—to describe themselves—and projective ones—to characterize other disputants. Both are prominent features of the Voyageurs conflict and repeatedly feed on each other.

Specifically, the formation of the park challenged the core identity of many local residents of the area whose livelihood and well-being were intricately enmeshed with the parklands and their use and with an orientation to resource extraction that has characterized northern Minnesota for over a century. The reflexive frames of park opponents are epitomized in **[16, 20, and 26]**. At a fundamental level some residents have perceived the park as a threat to their way of life and to their autonomy to determine how the lands that make up the park will be used. These threats were both real (e.g., some prime hunting and logging areas are no longer available for those activities) and symbolic; and today the distinction between what is real and what is symbolic remains difficult to disentangle in the dialogue surrounding the park. Stories demonizing the park (and the federal government) as monoliths of evil abound in the interviews with opponents **[3, 6, 13, and 16]**. While some who originally opposed the park no longer view it in this light, strong identity-based resistance remains in the International Falls area. With Boise Cascade as the primary employer in this community, place-based identities have become entangled with those based on roles and interests tied to resource extraction and freedom. At a fundamental level, what are perceived to be at stake are their livelihood and a way of life characteristic of the area for 100 years. Threats to this fused identity are expressed in a report summarizing the GMP for the Koochiching County Commissioners:

> Being known as a logging/paper processing community and having to grapple with the change of identity that is inherent to a park-supporting community is difficult and painful. (Parkinson 2000) **[50]**

Although early concerns that the park would "damage the area's economy and drive tourists to Canada and curtail timber production" in the area (*Duluth News Tribune,* June 19, 1965) **[51]** and pose a real threat to resorts, in particular, have not materialized, the area did not realize substantial economic gain over the last 25 years either. The resource extraction identity is fueled by the absence of many voices that reflect alternative perspectives in the area. Additionally, the community itself has not proactively sought, and even appears unwelcoming of, economic revenue from recreationalists who reflect different identities than their own. Perpetuation of this fused identity is further bolstered by self-conceptions of stewardship over the park area reflected in **[28]**. Individually, people believe that historically they have cared for the resources of the park. Consequently, many opponents adopt multiple, and seemingly contradictory, identities, both as "stewards" as well as "victims" of the park. Schooled in jobs that are close to the land, they are reluctant to acknowledge the possibility that systematic, science-based management techniques are superior to their idiosyncratic observations and experience, as evidenced by **[46]**.

Examples of other disputants wrapping themselves in identity banners related to the land abound in the case. For example, the strong commitment of natural resource managers to the institutional identity of the NPS is revealed in **[24]** and in the current superintendent's life goal of becoming a park superintendent **[41]**. These natural resource managers' identities feel intense loyalty to the organization and express dedication to the mission of their organization—consistent with the image of NPS staff described by Hartzog (1988, 79): "Park people are intensely committed to their mission, hard-working, strong-willed and fiercely independent." **[52]**

Environmentalists' identities are no less prominent. As **[30]** demonstrates, environmentalists have assumed role-based identities as defenders of the park and its resources. While this role often aligns them with the NPS, they too have enacted this identity through litigation when they believed the park's resources were in jeopardy. In combination, over the years these identities have made it difficult for players on all sides of the dispute not to feel that their way of life and personal values were on trial during the conflict. Cloaked in their identities and bolstered by their group or institutional affiliations, the parties have not been able to forge a common identity based on love of the park areas and promotion of the gateway areas for use by all of the park's constituents.

Characterization Frames

The entrenched nature of the dialogue is evidenced by the characterization frames that parties use to describe their opponents and the almost myth-like status that certain stories about the conflict have attained through repetition over the years. While a variety of people have identified themselves as environmentalists, their opponents dub them "yuppies" **[12]**, "hippies," **[11]** and "nabobs." **[2]** In return, some environmentalists label park opponents, "pawns for big business" and "radical supremacists." **[33]** Other characterizations, such as depictions of the park's land acquisition efforts as "Gestapo tactics," **[13]** a politician's action as a "bleitskrieg attack," **[32]** residents of International Falls as jerks, and mutual charges of selfishness, **[34–38]** while equally colorful, have tended to sharpen the battle line, solidify the camps, and prevent people from the kind of civil discourse that leads to understanding and joint problem solving rather than name-calling and stalemate.

Interestingly, at times the park has been framed as the "bad guy" by both wise-use proponents and environmentalists. The park was viewed as siding with both sides at different points in the conflict. They were challenged by the environmentalists over the Black Bay compromise, and again in the late 1980s when provisions for some snowmobile trails on Kabetogama Peninsula were approved. They were also the target of wise-use proponents throughout the park's history—particularly when restrictions on hunting, trapping, snowmobiling, or other motorized uses were levied.

Perhaps the most telltale, but not surprising, observation is that negative characterizations were used liberally by all parties in the conflict. Characterizations about the park and its supporters and detractors ran rampant especially during the push for enabling legislation and again during the efforts to decommission the park in 1994 and 1995. Not only did these stereotypes ratchet up the conflict at these times, they also keep it alive despite possibilities for mutual understanding and compromise. Interestingly, when the nature of the conversation among some of the key players was shifted during the mediation efforts, some parties came to see the others in a new light—as real human beings with legitimate concerns. This kind of sensitivity is demonstrated in **[43]**—one of the few efforts we heard in which parties sought to examine how their own behavior had perpetuated the conflict and admit the validity of others' experiences over the years. For example, charging that the local citizens are "pawns for big business interests" **[33]** doesn't acknowledge the fact that many park opponents have depended on timber for their livelihood and that continued economic viability for the area will require everyone in the area to pull together to find alternative economic resources. Nor does it allow that the park, if promoted actively, could provide a source of revenue to sustain the community. Similarly, calling environmentalists "hippies" and deriding their desires for solitude and protection of the resources seems contrary to the very spirit of stewardship that park opponents themselves espouse and which their own families once enjoyed in the area.

Conflict Management and Social Control Frames

A particularly interesting aspect of this case lies in the conflict management frames adopted by the disputants. Opponents of the park preferred more adjudication and appeal to political action frames than either natural resource managers or environmentalists, although environmentalists did use some adjudication frames, and natural resource managers did use appeals to political action at times. Natural resource managers, however, preferred fact-finding conflict management frames, but these were not commonly preferred by either environmentalists or park opponents. In fact, the latter routinely disparaged fact-finding actions undertaken by the park. While litigation was prevalent in the early history of the park and litigation and protest continue as the preferred strategies of some opponents, **[14]** the inability of the parties to agree on alternatives to litigation is critical to the conflict's intractability. This is particularly important since joint problem-solving frames were used most often by all parties in describing the conflict. While all parties espoused joint problem solving, debate among them hinged on the question of whether problem-solving efforts should be locally or nationally constituted, and this question has been used to undermine conciliatory efforts such as the mediation. On this issue, the debate takes on political overtones pitting local versus state interests within Democratic politics in Minnesota. These differences are rooted in the social control frames that the parties held. The most vocal opponents of the park, for example, held individualistic social control frames, claiming the park deprived them of their freedom. **[3, 6]** This distinguished them from either the environmentalists or the natural resource managers to whom we talked. The latter tended to hold more hierarchist, nonlocal social control frames—indicative of their beliefs that decisions about the park belonged to experts who reflected a national perspective on the issues. **[44]** It also shaped their views about what joint problem solving might look like—since they envisioned advisory rather than fully participatory forums for settling the issues. And the failure of the parties to agree on a legitimate forum for resolution of the dispute has certainly contributed to the illusiveness of any agreement. Also of interest is that no local or state elective officials (with the exception of the former governor) have come forward to champion a resolution of the conflict. As long as the local participants fail to acknowledge that national parks have national constituents and the NPS remains impervious to the local identity issues and no local leaders are willing to display the necessary leadership, the uneasy tension between local and national preferences for resolving the conflict is likely to divide the parties. Whether the current GMP process can offer a lasting solution remains an open question.

The Sources of Intractability in Voyageurs

We can see all four of the sources of intractability in the Voyageurs conflict: issues, parties, the larger social system, and the processes of interaction among the stakeholders. Additionally, the groups of parties remain remarkably constant (e.g., the VRNPA and the Citizens Council have existed for over 35 and 25 years, respectively[††††]), and some of the same players (e.g., Don Parmeter, Irv Anderson, Carl Brown), who have been long-standing park opponents, are still active players in the dynamics. While the NPS staff have changed, the identities projected onto them have shifted only slightly with different superintendents. Interestingly, the issues, even those that have essentially been settled (such as land acquisition and whether there should be hunting in the park) do not die. In recent testimony before the Koochiching County Commissioners on the park's GMP, references are still

†††† The Citizens Council ceased to exist when the state legislature stopped funding it in 2000.

made to how residents perceived they were treated at the time. The dynamics of Voyageurs are also inextricably caught up in a larger societal dialogue over environmental politics and the use of federal land—a dialogue that shifts with changes in political power in Washington, periodically giving rise to challenges to the very mandate to have a park in northern Minnesota at all. When new dispute episodes arise, they are inevitably tied to the national-level dialogue. Finally, the interaction process among the players has become habitual and rigidified and even mythologized—as if stakeholders are reading prescribed scripts that have been prepared for them—reenacting the conflict each year almost as if it were a Passion Play. This mythologizing and the repetitive dynamics among the Voyageurs actors are considered further in the following text.

The Development of Myths

The mythologizing that has occurred around certain individuals and events, many of which occurred 20 to 25 years ago, has created a kind of permanence about the Voyageurs conflict that is difficult to disrupt. The fact that in 2000 these people and events still loom larger than life in the accounts of the conflict portrayed to us by informants suggests they have acquired a kind of mythical status in the history of Voyageurs. The events and the individuals involved in them were portrayed to us as if they happened yesterday instead of ten, twenty, or even thirty years ago. Each side tells stories of the Davis protests, the Brown escapades, and park decisions to ban live bait and dogs from the park, or the mediation as tales with the force of truth—rather than with the kind of nuanced detail that would more accurately convey what actually happened. The protagonists in these tales are all wrapped in their respective identity banners—Vic Davis and Carl Brown, who fought the park through protest and litigation; Superintendents Myrl Brooks, Russell Barry, and Barbara West who all exude strong institutional identities associated with the NPS and are victims of the projective identities others ascribe to the park; and state and federal legislators Irv Anderson and Bob Lessard, Representatives Blatnik and Oberstar, and Senators Wellstone and Grams whose interest-based identities cast them as players in a larger political game. These identities are portrayed as either good or evil depending on who is telling the tale. The repetitious telling of these mythological tales keeps the conflict alive and socializes youth or newcomers to stereotypical impressions of one side or the other.

Freeze Framing

In addition to mythologizing, the Voyageurs conflict appears to be suspended in time. Although much about society has changed in the last 35 years, the conflict remains impervious to these developments. Evidence of this suspension is found in local and state newspaper coverage of the conflict. Stories from the early 1970s are hauntingly similar to those in the late 1990s, and comments in our interviews parallel those reflected in early news coverage of the dispute despite the periodic recognition that opportunities to get past the conflict existed. For example, the 1964 assertion that the federal government was usurping the freedom of local people **[3]** was echoed by an interviewee in 1998, and again in a letter to the *Daily Journal* in the fall of 2000. The words used in these quotes are virtually the same. The 1964 charge claimed that the park was "once again taking away the right and freedom of individuals to truly make decisions regarding their lives and livelihoods in their own backyards." **[3]** The 1998 quote described the need for leaders to "make sure that people's freedoms are protected and not stripped away from them." **[53]** The echo in 2000 asserted, "This is all part of the process of 'incrementalism' used by the park service which will . . . slowly erode personal freedoms. . . . Then locals will be forced to move on due to . . . an economy that can't survive" (McHarg 2000). **[54]** As is evident from these remarks, the political issues surrounding Voyageurs are rooted in a deep mistrust of the federal government and are clearly perpetuated through the stories and myths that are told.

Still another theme continually repeated by park opponents is the failure of the park service to keep its commitments. This was evidenced over and over again in opponents' comments about the park's management by the NPS. This argument suggests that the original language in the legislation creating Voyageurs and the intent of the U.S. Congress that passed the legislation can be deciphered without interpretation—a point argued at various times in the dispute by environmentalists, park service employees, and wise-use proponents when it was convenient to do so.

Language linking the park to economic decline of the area (particularly International Falls) was being used by opponents in the mid-1960s when the park was still only a proposal. Citizen complaints made in 1964 that the government was usurping their economic rights **[6]** were echoed in the 1995 hearings by local citizens in International Falls who complained that the park was the source of the communities' economic woes. Virtually the same language was used again in the 1999 interview with a local businessperson **[9]** and again in 2000 in the McHarg quote just cited. **[54]** While the parties have changed, the discourse is identical.

Even the characterizations of parties remain virtually unchanged over the years. The 1964 characterizations by an elected official from Koochiching County of people from the Twin Cities and other areas of the state as "selfish" (*Daily Journal,* Dec. 1, 1964) **[53]** were echoed in reverse thirty-one years later by opponents of the wise-use movement when they accused state senator Bob Lessard and his "constituency of selfish self-interest groups" as spewing out "poison." **[36]** Characterizations levied at environmentalists were equally unflattering, suggesting that they were "extremists" and "yuppies with foreign cars" who never spend money when they visit the park (Dawson 1995). **[12]** This kind of stereotyping permeates the atmosphere surrounding the park, and we researchers also fell prey to it when we were mistaken for environmentalists while conducting interviews in a small town near the park because we had license plates from the Twin Cities on our rental car. Other characterizations asserting childish behavior can also be found spanning history. A local newspaper's description in 2000 of the reaction to the draft GMP characterizes the opponents as paranoid, and their retributory attack on the park as "childish" (*Timberjay,* Sept. 30, 2000, 7). **[55]** This parallels another **[37]** calling local residents "crybabies" and "spoiled brats" who "couldn't get what they wanted." The use of such stereotypes repeatedly throughout the public discourse of this conflict is antithetical to its resolution.

In the International Falls community, in particular, where the park is headquartered, the conflict seems frozen in time. In terms of framing, it is as if the parties are caught in a freeze frame that never thaws, despite the passage of thirty-some years. While many of the players have changed over the years, the core issues in the conflict continue to be played out as variations on a theme. According to Superintendent West,

> Nowhere else has a park had the constant . . . opposition as Voyageurs gets from this community. Nobody ever moves here. They don't get past that hatred. There's always another issue. And, if there isn't, they create one. (Myers 1997) **[56]**

Conclusions

Several conclusions can be drawn from the way the conflict over Voyageurs has been framed: (1) Identities (of local residents, environmentalists, and park employees) play a powerful role in the intractability of this conflict. (2) The use of negative characterization frames has run rampant in the dispute and has perpetuated mistrust and intractability. (3) Selective listening and rumor-mongering have exacerbated already frayed relations among key stakeholder groups. (4) Preferences for different conflict management frames (or the same conflict management frames at different levels—e.g., local vs. federal) have made it impossible for the parties to agree on an appropriate and legitimate forum for resolution of the dispute. (5) The GMP process and, in particular, the VUFP consultation committee had the potential to create such a forum, but, despite the park staff's efforts to listen to community input, some residents either did not see how it was incorporated into the plan (and thus remained suspicious of the park's intentions) or elected to keep the conflict going for other reasons. Failure to reach closure on the use issues appears to have precipitated a rejection of the draft final plan by the Koochiching County commissioners. (6) Opportunities for joint promotion of the park and the communities surrounding it are being lost because of the controversy, but these could serve as a focal point for joint collaboration if local leaders (in the gateway cities) were willing to champion these efforts. (7) Intractability is being fed by mythologizing of key players and events, a reliving of past issues and concerns, and an unwillingness of the parties to focus on the future rather than the past.

Some close to the conflict have suggested that the park could do more to reach out to the community. Still, unless someone steps up to this assignment or there is an external unifying event that gives all the Voyageurs stakeholders reason to join forces, there is little room to predict a quick end to this conflict. Superintendent West's hindsight on the mediation may best sum it up,

> Because so much of the difficulties with Voyageurs are mired in "the past" and I thought it was a point we could take off from this point forward and be honest and straightforward . . . and you could get rid of the baggage of the past that it might work. And I overestimated our abilities, and I underestimated the power of history. **[57]**

One can speculate that, unless the dialogue among the parties is consciously changed, the freeze frame will continue creating a dark shadow over the crystal clear waters of the park.

Note on Sources

The information in this chapter was derived from newspaper articles and from interviews with community residents, activists, business leaders, environmentalists, civic leaders, and public officials. Newspaper articles were collected from the *Star Tribune* (Minneapolis), *St. Paul Pioneer Press, Daily Journal* (International Falls), *Duluth News Tribune,* and the *Timberjay* (Ely, Minn.) over the period 1964–2000. Other archival sources include books, park records, documents provided by interviewees, a mediation report, correspondence, and transcripts of meetings of the Visitors' Use and Facilities Plan Consultation Group.

Chapter 5

The Edwards Aquifer Dispute: Shifting Frames in a Protracted Conflict

Linda L. Putnam and Tarla Peterson

The Edwards Aquifer in the south-central region of Texas is an underground water formation that has been the source of controversy for over fifty years and a source of life since the beginning of recorded history in the region. The controversy centers on its limited physical structure, multiple users, potential contamination, and potential loss of endangered species. To complicate these issues even further, both agricultural and urban communities have relied completely on the Edwards to supply their water needs. Moreover the water in the Edwards is historically considered as private property. Since the early 1980s, however, even this legal definition has been in flux. Thus the parties in this dispute disagree not only on the amount and mode of water allocation, but also on its ownership and governance.

Management of the Edwards Aquifer provides an excellent example of how competition among multiple users of a limited, renewable, common-pool resource can generate fierce and protracted disputes within and between communities (Blomquist 1992; Ostrom 1990; Ostrom, Gardner, and Walker 1994). There are four key issues in this dispute: (1) the management of a scarce environmental resource limited by physical structure and used by many interdependent stakeholders, (2) concerns for property rights, (3) the regulation and distribution of water, and (4) the effects of water shortage both on the endangered species that live within the aquifer's associated springs and on the quality of the aquifer's freshwater zones. Feuds between private property rights and protection of the common good underlie decades of disagreements about the management of this irreplaceable water resource, especially the years from 1980 to 1997—the major focus of this case description.

The Edwards Aquifer

The Edwards Aquifer is a unique underground limestone formation that stretches south of Austin to 100 miles west of San Antonio, Texas. As an underground formation, it has well-defined boundaries, occurring in a band 5 to 30 miles wide and stretching 176 miles through portions of six counties (Harden 1986). Holding approximately 40 million acre-feet of recoverable water, the Edwards Aquifer is exceptionally large and characterized by excellent water quality. The aquifer replenishes itself from runoff over a large catchment area in the Hill Country of south-central Texas. The water flowing downhill from the Hill Country crosses an area of exposed Edwards limestone, known as the recharge zone. Much of the water disappears from the surface and flows down into the aquifer.

The pressure levels of the confined water in the Edwards Aquifer are exceptionally responsive to rainfall and drought. If the water declines due to drought or overpumping, the aquifer level drops and the springs cease to flow. Although the Edwards has an average rate of 75 percent recharge from surface water through an extensive network of faults and fractures, the recharge is highly variable and unpredictable (Votteler 1998). From 1934 to 1997, the average recharge to the aquifer was 676,000 acre-feet per year, with annual pumping from the aquifer averaging close to 500,000 acre-feet (Harden 1986, U.S. Geological Survey 1998); hence, in major drought years, the pumping easily exceeds the recharge, particularly when users compensate for the absence of rainfall by pumping additional amounts of water from their wells.

A confounding problem for the aquifer is a steady increase in the number of users. The aquifer has been the sole source of water for San Antonio, the third-largest city in Texas and the ninth-largest city in the United States. In addition, numerous towns in the eastern communities depend on the aquifer for economic survival. These residents rely on the aquifer for a thriving tourism and recreational business. Communities in the western counties draw from the Edwards to support farming and irrigation. More specifically, from 1950 to 1980, irrigators were the fastest-growing users of the aquifer in volume increase of water withdrawn (Votteler 1998). Even with improvements in irrigation techniques, the western counties in the region have steadily increased the number of wells dug and the overall rate of consumption from the aquifer until recently (Texas Water Development Board 1996).

The growth of municipalities, including military bases, shopping malls, and housing developments in the San Antonio and Austin regions, also impacts both the quantity of pumping and the quality of the water. In the southern portion of the Edwards, a "bad water line" separates the usable groundwater from the highly saline water. There is evidence that current withdrawal rates from the

Edwards, particularly in drought years, might lead to an intrusion of bad water into the freshwater zone and degrade the water quality (Perez 1986, Votteler 1998). The "bad water line" is near the Comal and San Marcos Springs, an area that supports the habitat of seven species listed as endangered by the U.S. Fish and Wildlife Service (USFWS).* As a result of the unique ecosystem in the rivers that originate from these springs, excessive pumping alters the aquatic environment, decreases the flow of surface water downstream, and potentially leads to harming a member of or the habitat of an endangered species, or to jeopardizing the survival of the entire species (Votteler 1998).

As noted earlier, the dispute over the Edwards Aquifer crosses the divide between private property and common property resources. Technically, groundwater in the state of Texas is derived from the English common law of "absolute ownership." The rule of absolute ownership states that landowners have the right to take for use or sale all the water they can capture from below their land, unless the pumping harms other users, contaminates the wells of others, wastes artesian water, or causes surface injury to adjacent property (Getches 1990, Kaiser 1987). Common property resources, in contrast, are ones in which many users can tap into and pump the water. Since these resources are not owned or controlled by a single party or agent, they are often exploited on a first-come, first-serve basis, unless restrictions are developed to regulate access to and distribution of the water. The Edwards Aquifer crosses both of these terrains in that the aquifer is an underground water system and private property, and at the same time, it is a common property resource with multiple users. More specifically, the multiple users cluster into eight broad-based groups of stakeholders that cross local, regional, state, and federal levels: environmentalists, industry and developers, farmers and irrigators, citizen activists, governmental officials and policy makers, water agencies, judicial authorities, and media (see Table 5.1).

Since this conflict covers such an extended period of time, the analysis is grouped into five key events that characterize potential turning points in the conflict: (1) the demise of the Edwards Underground Water District, (2) mediation and the threat of federal intervention, (3) legislation to declare the Edwards Aquifer an underground river, (4) the Sierra Club's lawsuits against violations of the Endangered Species Act and the establishment of the Edwards Aquifer Authority (EAA), and (5) the EAA actions from 1997 to 2000 (Votteler 1998; Wolff 1997, 65–77, 369–395).

---

* The seven endangered species are the fountain darter, the Texas blind salamander, the Comal Springs riffle beetle, the Comal Springs dryopid beetle, the Peck's cave amphipod, the San Marcos gambusia, and Texas wild rice.

Table 5.1. Key Agencies and Stakeholders Involved in the Edwards Aquifer Dispute

Local Organizations	*Regional Organizations*	*State Organizations*	*Federal Agencies*
San Antonio Water System	Edwards Underground Water District	Texas Legislature	U.S. Fish and Wildlife Service
Living Waters Artesian Springs, Ltd.	Edwards Aquifer Authority	Texas Natural Resources Conservation Commission	U.S. Secretary of Interior
Barton Springs Water District	The Guadalupe-Blanco River Authority	Texas Farm Bureau	U.S. Department of Agriculture
Bexar Metropolitan Water District		Texas Water Commission	U.S. Fifth Circuit Court of Appeals
Medina-Uvalde Water District		Texas Supreme Court	U.S. Justice Department
		Texas Water Development Board	U.S. Department of Defense
		Texas Justice Foundation	U.S. Geological Survey

Key Events in the Edwards Aquifer Dispute

The Edwards Underground Water District

The major crisis over the Edwards Aquifer began in the 1950s when a severe drought caused the aquifer to fall below safe levels. In response to this crisis, the Texas legislature established the Edwards Underground Water District (EUWD) in 1957 to protect and conserve water in the region. Even though the District consisted of representatives from the five major counties linked to the aquifer, it lacked the authority to limit pumping or even to require people to register their wells (Wolff 1997). In the words of one environmentalist and one farmer/irrigator, respectively:

> The EUWD did not have the regulatory authority that even some other groundwater districts had to be able to manage withdrawal of water from the aquifer. They had many conflicting interests—political interests in San Antonio, agricultural interests in Uvalde and Medina, and springs interests in Hays and Comal counties—

> and no overall mechanism to reach any conclusions about how the aquifer should be managed. So it was pretty chaotic. **[1]**†
>
> My favorite description of the EUWD is The Gutless Wonder. They were out there to conserve and protect, but they had no power and no rule-making authority. It was like a Magnavox TV—great big beautiful tube that gets a good picture, but you look behind it and there's not a whole lot in there. **[2]**

In the years between 1970 and 1984, several events occurred that caused people to consider some regulation for the aquifer. First, the EUWD built four small recharge dams over the aquifer to conserve water. During this same period, irrigation in the farming region increased dramatically; the City of San Antonio rejected a plan to purchase water from the Canyon Reservoir; and pumping of water from the Edwards averaged over 500,000 acre-feet per year. In 1984 during a brief drought, the flow at Comal and San Marcos Springs reached critical levels.

Thus, in the mid-1980s, stakeholders took several measures to respond to the drought. For example, the City of San Antonio instituted a voluntary water-rationing plan (*San Antonio Express-News,* June 25, 1988) and Mayor Henry Cisneros along with the EUWD chair, Bobby Hasslocher, appointed a regional ad hoc task force to develop a water plan that would regulate aquifer use throughout the region. One member of the task force described the group's growing awareness of the Edwards' limits.

> There were five of us from the City Council (San Antonio), five from the eastern interests and six from the western interests, and five people from the springs. We met once a week in the fall of 1987. It was the first of many, many negotiations as we began to consider the severity of the Edwards Aquifer issue. **[3]**

In 1987, after five years of negotiating, the committee reached consensus on a policy that would manage pumping from the Edwards so that the annual volume of water taken did not exceed the average rainfall and stream percolation.‡ They also agreed that the entire region should pay for the development of additional water sources, including a plan for reuse of wastewater and the

† In subsequent chapters, this quote will be referenced as "Edwards 1," and subsequent quotes from this chapter as "Edwards 2," "Edwards 3," etc.

development of new reservoirs and lakes (*San Antonio Light,* July 29, 1988; Wolff 1997).

In keeping with the recommendation, the San Antonio City Council approved the regional water plan and voted to construct the Applewhite reservoir on the Medina River in south Bexar County (*Austin-American Statesman,* July 24, 1988). They sought support for the reservoir and the water plan among the farmers and ranchers in the western counties and promised that they would not implement pumping limits—if the farmers would not add irrigation wells. Three local and regional water agencies also approved the Regional Water Management Plan (Jensen 1988). Finally, with a split vote of 8 to 6, the EUWD approved the plan (*San Antonio Light,* July 29, 1988), with all six no votes coming from representatives of the western counties. Despite these dissenting votes, the Regional Water Management Plan was forwarded to the Texas legislature for approval (*San Antonio Light,* July 29, 1988; Wolff 1997).

The failure of the five-year negotiated Regional Water Management Plan became a major controversy in that a rough draft of the completed plan had passed with an 11 yes, 0 no, 2 abstain vote. The ad hoc regional committee had brought together stakeholders who represented many different interests in this dispute. "For the last year, Cisneros had prodded the farmers in the west, spring flow advocates in the east, and local politicians in Bexar county" to hammer out a "delicate, technical, and intricate 212-page document" that San Antonio mayor Cisneros termed, "the finest example of consensus building" (*San Antonio Light,* July 29, 1988), yet there was no agreement. **[4]**

In the meantime, the farmers and ranchers in the western counties circulated a petition requesting that their representatives withdraw from the EUWD and that the western regions develop their own underground water boards. The president of the Southwestern Property Rights Association claimed that the proposed Regional Water Resources Plan was very costly and favored the more populated counties (e.g., Hays, Comal, and Bexar) over the interests of rural users in Medina and Uvalde. Even a state senator noted that urban areas had a greater need for a drought management plan than did rural communities. The conflict became more heated as farmers based their position on private property rights. According to a San Antonio government official:

‡ Stream percolation refers to the recharge of the Edwards from surface streams in the western part of the aquifer. Many surface streams cross over the aquifer and recharge it rather than flowing downstream (Jensen 1988, 2).

> The farmers were unyielding in their belief that it is their right to pump water from underneath their own land. This "property right principle" held an almost sacred status in the western counties. We tried compromise, but it did not work and may never work. **[5]**

Indeed, former governor Dolph Brisco was noted as saying:

> I urged fellow Uvalde citizens and residents of adjoining Medina County to secede from the EUWD to protect their rights to pump unlimited amounts of water from the Edwards Aquifer for irrigation. **[6]**

A San Antonio consultant described it this way:

> A lot of them [irrigators] see it [the aquifer] the way they see gun control—you can have my water when you peel my cold, dead hand off my pump. It's that level of emotion. **[7]**

After securing 1000 signatures on a petition, the western counties pulled out of the EUWD in January 1989. According to the chairman of the EUWD:

> The eastern counties forced Uvalde farmers to raise funds to fight proposed legislation that would erase their right to drill wells on their own land and pump unlimited amounts of water from the Aquifer. **[8]**

In response, San Antonio, the EUWD, eastern municipalities, and the major water agencies Guadalupe-Blanco River Authority (GBRA), and San Antonio River Authority (SARA) formed a coalition to urge the legislature to allocate groundwater as part of the Regional Water Resources Plan. Additionally, the EUWD approved a special drought management plan for regulating springflow during rainfall shortage.

But in May 1989, the legislature reached an impasse. "Scuttled by intense infighting over a proposed Regional Water Resources Plan, the legislature adjourned without acting on an aquifer bill" (*San Antonio Light,* May 28, 1989). **[9]** In frustration with the process, the lieutenant governor and the Speaker of the House established a legislative committee composed of both House and Senate members to study the aquifer.

The outcome was described by one San Marcos/New Braunfels government official:

> Yea, we made an agreement on how we'd divide the Edwards up. We made a contract and that's the pen that I signed it with and then they [the legislature] didn't honor it. We fought for approval of the plan, but the rural interests that dominated the legislature defeated it. Now the plan and the EUWD were destroyed. However, the farmers were right about one thing—we would be in the courts for years to come. **[10]**

The conflict escalated when, in June 1989, the EUWD pulled its bank deposits from the Uvalde State Bank. In response, Uvalde and Medina Counties created their own underground water districts, which were later declared illegal (Wolff 1997). Stakeholders began to polarize—pointing fingers, blaming the other parties, and escalating the conflict through heated attacks. The general manager of the EUWD "charged that San Antonio is downplaying the problem in order to preserve its lucrative tourist industry and not scare away corporate relocations" (*San Antonio Light,* June 28, 1990). **[11]**

The media cast the conflict as a war between urban and rural factions, with the rural communities blaming the urbanites for poor planning and the urban constituents chiding the rural stakeholders as demanding, unrealistic, and refusing to compromise (*Dallas Morning News,* August 19, 1990). The media portrayed the conflict as a "fight for water rights" (*San Antonio Express-News,* June 30, 1990), "feuding interests" (*San Antonio Light,* June 28, 1990), "latest shots in the regional water battle" (*San Antonio Express-News,* June 30, 1990), and "a face off" (*San Antonio Express-News,* May 6, 1991). **[12]**

Mediation and the Threat of Federal Intervention

Fearing prolonged court battles, the chairman of the Texas Water Commission (TWC) met with different stakeholders to negotiate a "miracle agreement" on the Edwards allocation strategy (*San Antonio Express-News,* July 1, 1990). He proposed a plan to replace the EUWD with countywide districts overseen by a regional board. When these negotiations ended in stalemate in June 1990, the Joint Legislative Committee on the Edwards Aquifer hired a professional mediator who facilitated private discussions among the major aquifer users through the fall and winter months of 1991 (*San Antonio Light,* March 9, 1991). Although these talks engendered a better understanding among the parties, they ended in March 1991 with no agreement.

During this time, other events in the Edwards' saga occurred. A drought in the summer of 1990 forced the City of San Antonio to enact an emergency action plan and, in December 1990, the City Water Board began construction on the Applewhite Reservoir. Mayor Henry Cisneros's initiative and the role of San Antonio in adopting an emergency action plan was a major turning point in this dispute. However, in a hotly contested election on May 4, 1991, the citizens of San Antonio voted to abandon this project. Texas's highest-ranking water official commented, "San Antonio's decision to abandon the Applewhite reservoir has blown the city's credibility in resolving an Edwards Aquifer water dispute" (*San Antonio Express-News,* May 6, 1991). **[13]**

Amidst these happenings, a catfish farmer provided a vivid illustration of the consequences of "the rule of capture" approach to managing the aquifer. Living Waters Artesian Springs Ltd. catfish farm began operations southwest of San Antonio in September 1990, pumping an estimated 40 million gallons of aquifer water per day and discharging it into the Medina River. "On an annual basis, this usage equaled approximately 25 percent of the City of San Antonio's total pumpage" (Votteler 1998, 855). **[14]** In October 1991, EUWD and the TWC filed suits in the state district court to shut down the catfish farm for violations of wastewater discharge regulations; and in 1992, the courts prevented the catfish farmer from resuming operations. Adding a layer of complexity to the dispute, in February and April 1990, respectively, the Guadalupe-Blanco River Authority and the Sierra Club delivered separate notices warning the U.S. Department of the Interior of possible violations of the Endangered Species Act. As a last effort to achieve a compromise among the stakeholders, Austin's mayor, Bruce Todd, intervened in October 1991 to facilitate negotiations. Although these efforts failed to produce a regional solution for managing the aquifer, they created more mechanisms for negotiation and mediation in this dispute.

The Edwards Aquifer as an Underground River

In desperation, the Texas attorney general declared that the TWC (later to become the Texas Natural Resources Conservation Commission) had authority for regulating groundwater in the state. And in February 1992, the TWC released a concept paper for managing the Edwards Aquifer, instituted emergency rules for drought periods, and declared the aquifer an underground river subject to state regulation. TWC issued this action to protect the springflows and the endangered species. While stakeholders in Uvalde and Medina Counties reacted negatively to this declaration, residents of Hayes and Comal Counties were jubilant about TWC's action. Moreover, Bexar, Uvalde, and Medina Counties, previously seen as arch enemies in this dispute, now joined forces in opposition to the TWC strategy, and, in the view of some stakeholders, pitting east against west and downstream against upstream users. The words of a Uvalde County judge epitomized the conflict, "This just indicates that the people downstream are more important than the people upstream. . . . I don't think this is good news for anybody" (*San Antonio Express-News,* April 16, 1992). **[15]**

San Antonio and Austin residents were "stunned," "surprised," and "alarmed" by the actions of TWC. "Shockwaves from Wednesday's decision continue to rock the state from city hall, to Austin, to a West Texas federal judge" (*San Antonio Light,* April 17, 1992). **[16]** While most agencies questioned the legality of TWC's action and its power to make this decision, the Texas Farm Bureau sued to obtain a restraining order against TWC, and state legislators expressed concern that property values might drop because property was being taken without compensation (*San Antonio Light,* April 17, 1992).

Uvalde and Medina Counties scheduled meetings to plan a counteroffensive, vowed to raise taxes to fight a legal battle, and hired a lawyer to fight the TWC's declaration. Agricultural officials believed that a "seizure" of the Edwards represented a statewide coup to control all the natural resources. They threatened to join with San Antonio and file a suit against TWC to preserve the property rights and local economies of their communities. According to the Medina Underground Water District, "TWC's action is ridiculous. They're just grabbing straws. The end result will be lawsuits" (*San Antonio Express-News,* April 16, 1992). **[17]**

This action brought immediate responses from the water consumers in the region. Lawmakers vowed to pass legislation reversing the TWC's takeover of the Edwards Aquifer and threatened "to force a water plan down the throats of environmentalists" (*San Antonio Express-News,* May 6, 1991). **[18]** An irrigation farmer was quoted in the media as exclaiming, "I would expect action such as this from Hitler and Stalin, but not the Texas Water Commission" (*San Antonio Express-News,* May 6, 1991). **[19]** The state representatives and other legislative committee members "faced off against [the] TWC Chairman . . . in a raucous five-hour hearing . . . called to review the commission's takeover of the aquifer on grounds it is an underground river subject to state regulation" (*San Antonio Express-News,* May 6, 1991). **[20]** To counter this opposition, the TWC held hearings in May 1992 in San Antonio, Uvalde, and Austin about its recent rulings.

From these hearings, TWC struck a deal that guaranteed San Antonio rights to the Edwards while allowing the state to control the 'underground river.' The Medina County Underground Water Conservation District (MCUWCD) reacted by insisting that the TWC has no authority over their county's water. As the president of MCUWCD commented, "We have filed as an intervener in the farm bureau suit as the only governmental agency authorized by the Texas legislature to conserve and regulate the use of water [in Medina County]" (*San Antonio Express-News,* August 5, 1992). **[21]**

Although Medina County acknowledged that rules and regulations were needed for the aquifer, it challenged the TWC's plan and solution. In Uvalde, a landowner and his sister, supported by the Uvalde County Water Conservation Association and the Uvalde Bar Association, filed a lawsuit in the Thirty-eighth District Court challenging TWC. The battle of the lawsuits against the TWC ended in September 1992 when an Austin district court and a state court invalidated the TWC's declaration of the Edwards as an underground river.

The Sierra Club, the Endangered Species Act, and the Edwards Aquifer Authority

Sierra Club v. Lujan

The federal government became a party in this dispute when the Sierra Club filed a suit with the U.S. District Court in May 1991, claiming that the U.S. Fish and Wildlife Service (USFWS) and the Department of the Interior failed to protect the endangered species that lived in the San Marcos and Comal Springs. They alleged that the USFWS allowed overpumping of the aquifer, causing the endangered fountain darter fish to die when the springs almost went dry in 1984, 1989, and 1990. The plaintiffs requested that the court determine the minimum springflows needed to sustain the fountain darter and implement a plan to limit aquifer pumping to guarantee that flow (*San Antonio Express-News,* November 20, 1992). When the suit went to trial in November 1992, four parties joined the side of the Sierra Club while six parties, including the City of San Antonio, united on the federal government's side. As described by a lawyer for the plaintiffs,

> The case grew into a fairly large controversy with multiple parties on both sides who were probably the folks you are thinking of as the stakeholders. It was enough of a dramatic event to finally get people's attention. **[22]**

> On the defendant side, San Antonio claimed that the Sierra Club's demands would cost the city's economy "billions of dollars in reduced spending and thousands of lost jobs." (*San Antonio Express-News,* November 20, 1992) **[23]**

On January 30, 1993, U.S. District Judge Lucius Bunton III ruled in favor of the plaintiffs and directed the USFWS to set standards for minimum acceptable flows; the state was instructed to enact a plan to regulate pumping and guarantee springflows. San Antonio appealed this ruling to the Fifth U.S. Circuit Court of Appeals, but an appellate court dismissed this appeal, claiming the city was not directly affected by Bunton's ruling. The USFWS also appealed Bunton's ruling, but they withdrew their appeal negotiating a settlement with the Sierra Club to determine the springflow requirements for avoiding "taking" and "jeopardy" of the listed species in the Comal and San Marcos Springs.[§]

The Edwards Aquifer Authority (EAA)

Throughout the Sierra Club suit, stakeholders continually challenged the establishment of a regional authority to regulate the aquifer. Although they agreed that the aquifer needed to be managed, stakeholders differed as to how regulation should occur. In 1993, after marathon bargaining sessions and pouring over dozens of pieces of legislation, a senator from Victoria spearheaded a compromise proposal in the Senate "among the feuding parties in the Edwards Aquifer war" (*San Antonio Express-News,* April 28, 1993). **[24]** The agreement, however, lacked the blessing of the irrigators or the Texas Farm Bureau, as evidenced by statements from the president of the Uvalde County Underground Water Conservation Association:

> This is absolutely a violation of people's constitutional rights to own property. (*San Antonio Express-News,* April 28, 1993) **[25]**

and the Texas Farm Bureau, Public Affairs Office:

> Under this plan the western counties take it in the neck. They are going to lose their water. (*San Antonio Express-News,* April 29, 1993) **[26]**

---

§ The term "take" means to harass, harm, pursue, hunt, shoot, wound, kill, trap, capture, or collect (or attempt to engage in any such conduct) of any species declared endangered or threatened. "Jeopardy" refers to threatening the continued existence of any endangered or threatened species or leading to destruction or adverse modification of the habitat of such species (*Endangered Species Act of 1973*).

Farmers would support a drought plan to limit pumping, but they opposed a permanent cap on pumping and marketing provisions for buying and selling water rights. As stated by the president of the Uvalde County Water Conservation Association, "You start buying water rights up and you are going to kill the economy" (*San Antonio Express-News,* April 29, 1993). **[27]** The Natural Resources Committee of the Texas Senate voted 8 to 3 to approve the compromise bill, and the Senate approved the measure on a nonrecord voice vote.

A representative from San Antonio took the Senate bill and worked with legislators to get it through the 150-member House of Representatives. It passed the House after four hours of debate and went to a joint committee to hammer out a final agreement in a marathon session that ended at 4:30 A.M. on Friday, before Judge Bunton's Monday deadline. The many compromises led the Sierra Club to question the ability of the created EAA to protect the endangered species, particularly under the House version of the bill (*Austin-American Statesman,* May 25, 1993).

The bill, which was passed and signed into law on May 31, 1993, created the EAA as a nine-member appointed board to limit pumping and manage the aquifer in the six-county region. It also abolished the EUWD and granted the EAA the power to regulate and enforce pumping limits among all well owners and the power to issue annual water rights based on historic claim. Under the new legislation, pumping limits could not surpass 450,000 acre-feet of water annually through 2007. Subsequent withdrawals were reduced to 400,000 acre-feet by 2008. The EAA would be collecting pumping fees to finance its endeavors and would begin operations with $10.2 million in reserves from the defunct EUWD (*San Antonio Express-News,* August 24, 1993).

But before the new EAA members could be sworn into office, the Mexican American Legal Defense and Educational Fund (MALDEF) filed a claim with the U.S. Justice Department contending that the bill violated the Voters Rights Act by switching from an elected to an appointed board. The Justice Department requested a lengthy list of documentation, including the composition of the EUWD. On November 19, 1993, the U.S. Justice Department rejected the new state plan as a violation of the Voters Rights Act, thus leading to further delays in state management of the aquifer situation (*San Antonio Express-News,* November 20, 1993).

The Justice Department's intervention triggered a rash of actions that fueled additional battles. The secretary of state and the governor sent a letter to the Justice Department on December 30, 1993, suggesting that the EAA and the EUWD could coexist—EAA as the appointed regulatory body and

EUWD as the elected educational agency. The letter was attacked by the western counties as "underhanded" and "a back room deal in which the EUWD would serve as a token agency to meet the act's one person, one vote provision." **[28]** The chairman of the Uvalde County Underground Water District described it thus:

> This letter to the Justice Department is just another case of San Antonio going to Austin with their money and we all know that money talks. We are going to fight this thing. We are going to develop our own response to the state's action and send it to Washington. (*Uvalde* (Texas) *Leader News,* January 6, 1994) **[29]**

Thus the western counties, which opposed the compromise bill that established the EAA, sided with MALDEF against the state. The EUWD, who was fighting for their existence, also sided with the Justice Department. As the chair of the EUWD remarked, "We decided to get involved to protect voting rights and to be at the table in case there is to be any kind of proffered settlement" (*San Antonio Express-News,* March 30, 1994). **[30]** After the Justice Department denied the request for the coexistence of the EAA and the EUWD, the state filed a suit objecting to the Justice Department ruling. Both the governor and the mayor of San Antonio blasted MALDEF actions, claiming they were "vicious" and "insane" and could result in loss of federal funds and the closure of military bases. But the attorney for MALDEF retorted that state officials were also at fault for wanting an appointed board that they could control (*San Antonio Express-News,* April 24, 1994).

In another retort, a San Antonio councilwoman branded the governor and the mayor as "divisive . . . in a multicultural community that ordinarily prides itself on exhibiting racial harmony" (*San Antonio Express-News,* April 28, 1994). **[31]** Although the mayor claimed he understood the desire for an elected board, he contended that the political reality of the one person, one vote meant that Bexar County would be in control of the EAA with virtually no representation from the eastern and western counties. In response to the mayor's justification, Representative Rodriguez pointed out that the state had forty-four water boards and all but two of them (including the EAA) had elected members. Growing weary of the verbal volleys, Representative Romo called for a cooling of tempers and the realization that both sides were blaming the people who were not at fault for this problem (*San Antonio Express-News,* April 28, 1994).

In another tumultuous session of the legislature, the aquifer bill passed with just twenty-four hours remaining in the session on May 28, 1995. In the House, the bill was rescued when the San Antonio mayor and a councilman broke up a deadlock between two San Antonio representatives who disagreed on the number of elected EAA members. The Senate approved a fifteen-member EAA board elected from single-member districts in the region. The legislature, however, killed a separate bill that established deadlines for the EAA to impose pumping limits during drought conditions—an action that would bring the courts right back into the middle of the fight (*Austin-American Statesman,* May 29, 1995). Senate Bill 1477 as signed by Governor Bush on May 31, 1995, established an elected EAA board composed of seven members from Bexar County, four from the western counties, and four from the eastern counties. Two nonvoting members, one appointed by the Medina and Uvalde county commissioners and one representing the downstream users, would also serve on the board (*San Antonio Express-News,* May 30, 1995).

Again, before the board could be sworn in on August 28, 1995, a state district judge, in response to arguments from Medina attorneys, issued a temporary restraining injunction that forbade EAA operations until the issue of constitutionality of the board was addressed. On November 29, 1995, the state district judge ruled that the law that created the EAA was illegally retroactive and violated landowners' constitutional rights to draw as much water from beneath their land as they need. The state, the EAA, and San Antonio appealed this decision to the Texas Supreme Court with the argument that the constitution allowed regulation to protect broad public interests. The issues are aptly reflected in the words of an attorney for the EAA:

> The "us against them" mentality has won the day, but we are confident that the Texas Supreme Court will tell us that we have the capability under the constitution to manage and safeguard our natural resources. **[32]**

and the attorney for the Medina County Underground Water Conservation District:

> It's people's property. You can't take it without due process or compensation. (*San Antonio Express-News,* October 28, 1995) **[33]**

Judge Bunton reacted by noting that on two separate occasions the legislature had passed bills that were challenged, and now the state was back to square one. The senator who coauthored the bill remarked, "that's how politically charged this issue is. You have to get it to the Texas Supreme Court to make a decision of what's good for the entire state" (*San Antonio Express-News,* October 28, 1995). **[34]**

On June 28, 1996, the Texas Supreme Court ruled unanimously (9–0) that the EAA was a constitutional entity. Supreme Court justice Abbott noted that the court centered on whether the law is constitutional on its face not whether it is unconstitutional when applied to a particular landowner. Reactions to the Supreme Court decision varied. In the words of the Medina District general manager,

> The Supreme Court left the door open for individual . . . suits. I think they [EAA] are going to have to proceed with caution." (*San Antonio Express-News,* June 29, 1996) **[35]**

And in the opinion of the EAA attorney,

> This decision creates a big table for everyone to sit down at and work out their problems politically through compromise and consensus building instead of . . . running off to various courts seeking judicial interventions. (*San Antonio Express-News,* June 29, 1996) **[36]**

The attorney for San Antonio Water System (SAWS) was also positive:

> This act provides the basis for the development of a market for water rights and a market for conservation incentives. (*San Antonio Express-News,* June 30, 1996) **[37]**

One of the EAA's first actions in July 1996 was to produce, in less than two weeks, a drought management plan that all counties could accept. The EAA held three hearings throughout the state on whether current drought conditions posed an imminent peril to public health, safety, or welfare. Although there was no question that the region faced a drought of epic severity, demonstrating the potential peril to public health was difficult. The western counties opposed any plan to adopt emergency rules that would limit pumping. Thus, in a decision that split along regional lines, the EAA voted 7 to 6 not to implement emergency rules. They drafted proposed rules that would be modified over thirty days and then voted on the rules (*San Antonio Express-News,* August 1, 1996).

Sierra Club v. Babbitt

With the EAA in limbo during 1994–95, the Sierra Club requested that Judge Bunton appoint a water monitor to gather, summarize, and evaluate aquifer data; present monthly reports; and advise the court as to whether plans for regulating pumping complied with the Endangered Species Act. Judge Bunton agreed and ordered the City of San Antonio, the State of Texas, and the USFWS to share equally in paying the $125 per hour salary of the monitor and warned them that if they failed to protect the aquifer-fed springs, he would impose new measures to enforce his 1993 ruling (*San Antonio Express-News,* March 2, 1994).

On April 15, 1994, the Sierra Club asked Judge Bunton to declare an aquifer emergency and to draw up a plan to limit pumping, which the judge would impose in place of state legislation to protect aquifer species. The Club also proposed to expand its original 1991 lawsuit to include the City of San Antonio, the Department of Defense, and other municipal, agricultural, industrial, and domestic users. Lawyers for the utilities and other water users, who had fought the Sierra Club in its suit, characterized the motion as an "environmental scorched-earth policy" (*San Antonio Express-News,* April 16, 1994). **[38]** Should the plan become stalled, the Sierra Club also requested that the judge order an immediate halt on federal funds for home loans, highway construction, transportation projects, and agriculture programs. The Sierra Club also asked the U.S. Department of Defense Base Realignment and Closure Commission to consult with the Environmental Protection Agency and the USFWS on possible violations of the Endangered Species Act and to consider closure of several military bases if violations have occurred (*San Antonio Express-News,* April 16, 1994). One San Antonio attorney expressed dismay:

> This is an unfortunate effort to derail Senate Bill 1477. It's the nuclear option. **[39]**

And in the words of a Uvalde attorney,

> They're calling for no new wells, no more lawn watering and no more irrigated agriculture all for a little fish that you can grow in a hatchery without too much trouble. (*San Antonio Express-News,* April 16, 1994) **[40]**

San Antonio leaders, including the mayor, responded with a "verbal firestorm":

> The Club's actions are a vicious attack on the city's [San Antonio's] economy, creating a potential loss of as many as 150,000 jobs. (*San Antonio Express-News,* April 30, 1994) **[41]**

But the Sierra Club's state director retorted:

> We did not attempt to do a basic economic analysis and identify the ripple effects on the area . . . we wanted to jolt people out of their denial. . . . We characterized the base closures as an option of last resort. It was not our preferred legal option. (*San Antonio Express-News,* April 30, 1994) **[42]**

And on May 5, 1994, Judge Bunton ruled against the Sierra Club's request. The plaintiffs then filed an amended suit dropping the additional defendants, but persisting in a plea for a management plan to limit pumping.

In response to these actions, three water agencies, the EUWD, the Medina, and the Uvalde Underground Water Conservation Districts, signed an agreement on May 24, 1994, to renew talks on a regional water management plan and to formulate proposed legislation to support this plan. The *Texas Weekly* pointed out the irony of this agreement; that is, two of these water districts contributed to the problem in the first place through blackballing the original 1988 regional management plan, which they now agreed to support with modifications in October 1994. Moreover, the EUWD, officially abolished through Senate Bill 1477, "is not only acting like it is going to live forever," but it attempted to hire a lobbyist to assure its continued existence (*Texas Weekly,* June 6, 1994). **[43]**

However, in the summer of 1994, flow at Comal Springs decreased substantially and the Sierra Club again filed a request for an emergency plan to reduce pumping from the aquifer. This time Judge Bunton ordered the monitor to prepare an Emergency Withdrawal Reduction Plan (EWRP) to educate the public as well as to develop staged reductions of pumping to maintain springflows at Comal above 150 cubic feet per second (Votteler 1998). With the onset of heavy rains in the fall of 1994, the court had no need to implement the emergency withdrawal plan, but the plan served as a warning that federal control of the aquifer was imminent.

Later in August 1994 the citizens of San Antonio voted against completion of the Applewhite Reservoir for the second time. This action capped a series of defeated efforts to develop alternative water sources for the city of San Antonio. Hence, both the Sierra Club and the court-appointed monitor intervened to assist San Antonio in reducing its reliance on the aquifer. Sierra Club representatives engaged in informal talks with San Antonio leaders about reusing wastewater, developing surface water alternatives such as a pipeline to the Guadalupe River, and other measures to reduce reliance on the aquifer. Their proposal, however, "put the group on a collision course" with citizen activists who claimed San Antonio did not need additional surface water if it used recharge dams and springflow augmentation** (*San Antonio Express-News,* August 24, 1994).

To extend these deliberations, the court asked the monitor to convene eleven panels throughout the Guadalupe River region to discuss the available water supply, hear presentations on methods to conserve water, and explore alternatives for new water sources for the region. The panels, consisting of the monitor as chair and professional staff members from nine major water districts in the region, collected information to develop a habitat conservation plan released in June 1995 and aimed at "conservation and reuse of existing water supplies and the introduction of 250,000 to 350,000 acre-feet of additional water supplies to the region" (Votteler 1998, 863). **[44]**

Thus, from March to June 1995, several proposals were put on the table—a revised Emergency Withdrawal Reduction Plan produced for the court in anticipation of a drought; a brief concerning the ability of the court to implement the monitor's plan; a letter of intent by five water purveyors to transport 15,000 acre-feet of Guadalupe River water to the military bases in San Antonio; and a lawyer's panel plan, developed by attorneys of stakeholders with suggestions for maintaining the springflow above 150 cubic feet per second through a 10 percent reduction in water consumption by municipalities.

While these proposals were still under consideration, *Sierra Club* v. *Babbitt* was resolved in February 1996 when the Fifth Circuit Court of Appeals ordered Bunton to end the litigation; Bunton and the water monitor were blocked from taking control of the aquifer; the USFWS published a recovery plan for the endangered species; and the U.S. District Court stood poised to take control of the aquifer if the EAA was declared unconstitutional. Despite the difficulty in determining who should be in control of the aquifer, this litigation established limits on the rule of capture and affirmed that the aquifer would be regulated—by either the EAA or the federal government.

SIERRA CLUB V. GLICKMAN

On April 28, 1995, the Sierra Club filed a second complaint in the U.S. District Court against Secretary Dan Glickman and the U.S. Department of Agriculture (USDA) for a three-count violation of the Agricultural and Water Policy Coordination Act and the Endangered Species Act. This suit, officially filed

---

**Springflow augmentation is supplementing and artificially maintaining springflow levels by pumping water into the aquifer by various means; for example, injecting water directly into the aquifer through deep wells and underground retention dams (*San Antonio Express-News,* September 2, 1994).

in September 1995, contended that the USDA had fostered adverse environmental impacts stemming from irrigation, had failed to develop programs to conserve water and protect the endangered species, and had subsidized irrigation from the aquifer without consulting with the USFWS. The suit requested a halt in the use of federal tax dollars for grants, loans, and below-cost insurance to irrigators, claiming that these programs led to increased pumping from the aquifer. Reactions to the lawsuit varied; the Texas attorney general had this to say:

> [It is] a misguided and extremist effort by the Sierra Club that could harm farmers and ranchers in Central Texas. I favor environmental protection but I oppose the Sierra Club's ultimate objective: the prohibition of all federally funded projects over the Edwards Aquifer. (*Austin-American Statesman,* May 11, 1996) **[45]**

An Austin attorney for the plaintiffs retorted:

> That statement is purely false. The lawsuit is targeted at the U.S. Department of Agriculture and programs that may harm the aquifer's environment. (*Austin American-Statesman,* May 11, 1996) **[46]**

In May 1996, the Fifth District Court of Appeals reversed Bunton's decision that barred the State of Texas and the Texas Farm Bureau from intervening in this lawsuit, and on July 2, 1996, Judge Bunton ruled in favor of the Sierra Club and ordered the USDA to (1) develop and implement a program for preserving natural resources and protecting fish and wildlife through land conservation and utilization, (2) implement an intra-agency program to protect waters from contamination, and (3) consult with the USFWS in developing a program to conserve endangered species in the aquifer. But this judgment was appealed and the U.S. Fifth Circuit Court of Appeals granted a stay on October 23, 1996.

SIERRA CLUB V. SAN ANTONIO

When the springflows reached critical levels and the USFWS did not take action to reduce pumping, the Sierra Club filed a class-action suit on June 10, 1996, alleging that pumpers were causing a taking of the seven federally protected species of fish, salamanders, and rice by reducing aquifer springflows that formed the habitat for the species. The suit was filed against all aquifer pumpers, "as many as one thousand individuals, organizations, and corporations" including municipal, commercial, domestic, and agricultural users (Votteler 1998,

869). **[47]** The USFWS admitted that Comal Springs was down 40 percent of its normal flow, but their field supervisor for ecological services contended:

> We're going to spend every dollar we have trying to work with you to find solutions rather than being in court. That's very expensive and I don't think anyone gains in that. (*San Antonio Express-News,* June 1, 1996) **[48]**

The attorney for the Sierra Club's Lone Star Chapter responded that the USFWS was not doing their job:

> We definitely think the U.S. Fish and Wildlife Service should be doing that. It's the federal agency that's supposed to be protecting the species. They're just bowing to politics despite their responsibility. (*San Antonio Express-News,*, June 1, 1996) **[49]**

In July 1996, the flow at both Comal and San Marcos Springs fell below levels necessary to maintain the habitat and survival of the listed species, and the Sierra Club asked Judge Bunton to grant a temporary restraining order and to limit pumpers to 1.2 times their winter average use. The restraining order targeted everyone except agriculture, since these users would not require water for irrigation after July (*Tyler* [Texas] *Morning Telegraph,* July 12, 1996). According to the state director of the Sierra Club,

> What is at stake here is not simply the survival of several endangered species . . . but the protection of a resource, the Edwards Aquifer, which is critical not only to the environment but also to the well-being of over two million people. (*Dallas Morning News,* June 12, 1996) **[50]**

This view was countered by the general counsel for San Antonio Water System one of the defendants in the lawsuit:

> We're in the third stage of a very mandatory program that has drastically curtailed discretionary water use. . . . We've done everything a city can reasonably do consistent with preserving the health, safety, and welfare of the people. . . . We can't just turn the valve down by 50 percent and have water in the lines to take care of human needs and put out fires. (*Dallas Morning News,* June 12, 1996) **[51]**

Judge Bunton withheld ruling on the Sierra Club suit until the new Edwards Aquifer Authority met to consider emergency pumping limits (*San

Antonio Express-News, July 18, 1996). One day after the EAA failed to declare a drought emergency, Judge Bunton denied the Sierra Club request, but he appointed two water masters and gave them ten days to develop a drought management plan. They proposed the 1996 Emergency Withdrawal Reduction Plan that consisted of staged reductions triggered by declines in springflows. Judge Bunton, hoping that the restrictions would be voluntary and would allow municipalities flexibility in achieving the required limits, asserted:

> I am convinced there is an emergency. . . . I don't think we can sit here and twiddle our thumbs and not do anything. (*Austin-American Statesman,* August 2, 1996) **[52]**
>
> Let's don't blow it like we did 40 years ago when God tried to call this to our attention, and we tended to ignore it. We can't go on like this. We're not going to have any surface water available. (*San Antonio Express-News,* July 26, 1996) **[53]**

On August 23, 1996, when no agencies had intervened to reduce aquifer pumping, Judge Bunton set a deadline of October 1 to activate the 1996 EWRP and to implement a reduction on pumping restrictions that would remain in effect until the EAA put into operation a critical management plan. In response, lawmakers from San Antonio challenged the constitutionality of Judge Bunton's proposed plan (*San Antonio Express-News,* August 22, 1996) and filed an appeal in the Fifth U.S. Circuit Court of Appeals in New Orleans on August 27. The mayor of San Antonio was in attendance:

> My presence here is a statement that this is not just a legal, technical issue. This is a community issue. Our citizens are just frustrated with what they are going through. . . . [Bunton's] requirements for aquifer pumping limits would cause extraordinary and irreparable harm to the city and its inhabitants. (*San Antonio Express-News,* August 27, 1996) **[54]**

Moreover, the Texas attorney general petitioned Bunton to allow the State of Texas to intervene on behalf of the defendants, alleging the State had a right to safeguard the interests of four water and wildlife agencies. Bunton granted the State's motion to intervene in its capacity as a pumper through a prison in Hondo, but he denied the State permission to intervene on behalf of the four agencies.

On September 10, 1996, the Fifth Circuit Court of Appeals stayed Judge Bunton's August 23 order until a hearing was held on December 2. The following April after the crisis had passed, the Fifth Circuit Court of Appeals vacated Judge Bunton's order, reasoning that the federal court should have abstained from becoming involved in a matter that the state regulatory agency, the EAA, should handle. In response, the Sierra Club appealed the Fifth Circuit Court's decision to the U.S. Supreme Court, stating the EAA had done nothing to limit aquifer withdrawals; but on January 26, 1998, the Supreme Court denied the Sierra Club's appeal, letting the Fifth Circuit Court's ruling stand.

Although the Sierra Club state director was disappointed that the EAA was postponing action to deal with an immediate crisis, several EAA members felt that declaring an emergency with no action to support it would provide ammunition for the plaintiffs in the *Sierra Club* v. *San Antonio* suit. The drought ended through heavy spring rains and the Fifth Circuit Court ruled that Bunton should have abstained from acting on a matter that fell under the EAA's jurisdiction.

The Edwards Aquifer Authority—1997–2000

Amidst continual filing of lawsuits, the EAA took several actions in 1997 and 1998 that paved the way for eventual adoption of permitting and regulatory rules. They approved a critical period management plan to develop stages for water conservation aimed at slowing the decline of springflow in times of drought. They also implemented the Agriculture Water Conservation Loan Program to help farmers purchase water-saving irrigation equipment and approved the Irrigation Suspension Program, aimed at reducing irrigation in drought periods by paying farmers not to irrigate (*San Antonio Express-News,* July 20, 1997). Other actions included drilling wells in San Antonio's recharge zones to document pollution and check water quality on a continual basis, developing a Precipitation Enhancement Program to increase rainfall over the EAA recharge region, approving a habitat conservation plan, and establishing the Authority Groundwater Trust to provide access for the selling and leasing of water rights.

Also, the EAA spent three years conducting surveys and making site visits for field verifications of water permit applications, and by February 2001, they issued 1084 municipal, industrial, and irrigation permits based on historical use and 383 initial permits to new users (EAA 2001). Of major importance, in October 2000 the EAA received final approval of the Texas Administrative Codes for assessing aquifer management fees and issuing permits for withdrawal. They also successfully managed a drought period in the summer of

2000 through enacting emergency drought management rules when flow levels at Comal Springs dropped below 150 cubic feet per second. Overall, the EAA has asserted its authority and moved forward amidst continual opposition.

This opposition included several court suits that challenged the EAA's actions and decision-making process. In 1997, Wells charged that the EAA engaged in acts that caused harm to plaintiffs and violated the enabling statute. In 1998, the Sierra Club and the Environmental Defense Fund notified EAA and USFWS of their intent to sue for violations of the Endangered Species Act, and the Travis County Court invalidated the EAA permit rules and their drought management plan. These suits were dropped when further actions were taken by the EAA. Also, in 1998, the catfish farmer challenged the EAA to proportionally reduce each applicant's permitted groundwater withdrawal amount and petitioned the courts to delay issuing groundwater withdrawal permits. This action was also overturned. One case that has continued through the appeal process to the Texas Supreme Court is *Braggs* v. *EAA,* filed in July 1998 as an objection to the EAA denial of a well withdraw permit. Although a district court issued a temporary injunction preventing the EAA from proceeding with the well permitting process, this decision was overturned at the State Court of Appeals in January 2000. After Braggs appealed the overturned decision, the Texas Supreme Court ruled that the judgment of the State Court of Appeals stood, but Braggs filed a motion for a rehearing in December 2000.

Although the EAA continues to wrestle with how to allocate water effectively, it has made major strides in issuing permits and regulating the aquifer. Based on historic use, the current regulatory policy as established in Senate Bill 1477 suffers from problems in penalizing stakeholders who conserved water versus those who were heavy users in the past. This policy has led to criticism of the law and the EAA. Overall, the Edwards Aquifer Authority has forged important inroads in establishing agency jurisdiction and claims for legitimacy. Its credibility continues to be challenged through objections to actions that it takes, but the EAA has brought optimism that this conflict is now manageable through negotiation with a legitimate decision-making body.

Analysis of Conflict Frames and Intractability

As a conflict mired in controversy and riddled with long-standing tensions, the Edwards Aquifer could be classified as an intractable dispute. It fit the primary characteristics of long-standing and eluding resolution. The central questions in the conflict namely, whether the aquifer should be regulated and if so, how and by whom—continued to elude resolution through challenges to decisions, interventions that failed to reach agreements, and court cases that were later appealed. The conflict escalated through rulings that provoked extreme reactions, such as the TWC's declaration of the Edwards as an underground river and the Sierra Club's filing of multiple endangered species suits. **[15, 18, 19, 23, 25, 26]**

Framing also played a critical role in perpetuating this conflict. In particular, identity frames rooted in interests, place, and institutions triggered polarization, particularly between rural and urban stakeholders. **[5, 10]** Negative characterization frames contributed to intractability through reinforcing stereotypes and shifting blame among stakeholders. Conflict management frames both triggered and reflected intractability through recurring court battles that led to conflict spirals and win–lose struggles. Thus identity, characterization, and conflict management frames intensified stakeholder commitment to positions and increased the costs of reaching a settlement.

Identity Frames

Identity frames refer to the way stakeholders describe their own roles in the conflict; that is, who they are and what is important or central about their roles in the dispute. The three most dominant kinds of identity frames in this dispute were those based on interests, place, and institutional affiliation. The early stages of this dispute were dominated by interest-based frames as depicted in defending the sacred principle of private property rights, preserving the springflows and endangered species, and protecting local economies. **[5, 11]** These identity frames surfaced when farmers and irrigators pulled out of the EUWD, claiming that pumping limits were like gun control—"a violation of basic rights"—and when the municipalities defended their rights to protect their citizens. **[6, 7, 8]** Any efforts to limit pumping would threaten "the right to drill wells on private lands" or "would cause extraordinary and irreparable harm to the cities and their inhabitants." **[8, 54]** Disputants, then, defined their roles in this conflict through defending and justifying their interest-based claims.

Place-based frames became prominent after the western counties withdrew from the EUWD and the media depicted the conflict "as a war between rural and urban factions." **[12]** Place identities continued to typify stakeholder frames during the period in which the TWC declared the Edwards an underground river. Eastern counties were pitted against western residents, and upstream users against downstream users. **[15]** Thus place-based identities were associated not simply with a city or a community, but with a region of the aquifer that delineated stakeholders by their type of water use. Characteristic of this pattern, stakeholders interpreted their own roles in this conflict in terms of in-group and out-group membership. For example, a Uvalde judge commented, "[The EUWD action] just indicates that the people downstream are more important than the people upstream." **[15]** Strong in-group and out-group identities also fueled stakeholders' intense characterizations of each other during this period and throughout the conflict.

During the struggle over which agency had the authority to regulate the aquifer, identities shifted to institutional domains. For example, in opposition to the TWC's ruling, the Medina Underground Water District claimed they were "the only governmental agency authorized to conserve and regulate the use of Edwards water [in their area]." **[21]** Challenges to institutional authority were evident in the restraining orders and lawsuits against the TWC, failed actions of the EUWD, and face-offs in the legislative committees. These challenges over institutional identity culminated with a series of Sierra Club suits in which the U.S. Government became a stakeholder in the conflict through claims against the USFWS, the secretary of the Department of the Interior, and the U.S. Department of Agriculture. These challenges were institutionally based in that they called for the legitimacy of a state-appointed authority to permit, regulate, and oversee both the withdrawal limits and the springflow levels of the aquifer. Both the EUWD and the TWC lacked the legal authority to implement permitting and regulating practices. **[1, 2, 17, 20]**

In this stage, institutional identities shifted to the federal agencies and the courts with the main controversy between state and federal jurisdiction rather than between regional and local water districts. Judge Bunton of the U.S. Fifth District Court ruled on a continuous stream of lawsuits filed by the Sierra Club, appointed a water monitor to advise the courts, and responded to requests for emergency plans to reduce pumping, actions usually not taken by the courts. As the San Antonio mayor noted, "If you consider that [Judge Bunton] is ordering up a plan that he can impose on us, to me that's a federal takeover" (*San Antonio Express-News,* June 5, 1994). **[55]** In its institutional role as the watchdog of the endangered species, the Sierra Club called for a "prohibition of all federally funded projects over the Edwards Aquifer" unless action was taken to reduce pumping. **[46, 47]** Institutional roles, then, typically cast as a watchdog, protector of resources, or ruler, remained the dominant identity frame for the latter stages of this conflict—with stakeholders focusing on the salience of their own agencies, constituents, or organizations in this dispute.

Stakeholders viewed the different jurisdictions of federal, state, regional, and local authorities as a central frame for their own identities in this conflict. Even though most stakeholders saw the legislature and the EAA as the primary regulatory bodies, they defined the conflict from their own institutional position. That is, in the latter days of the dispute, when stakeholders were asked to characterize what this conflict was about, they responded with a strong institutional bias—"it's about who can regulate and limit pumping from the aquifer." **[50, 53]**

Ironically, the one agency that had the constitutional power to regulate the aquifer, the EAA, did not project a strong or consistent institutional image. Many of the EAA members spoke in the voice of their constituents rather than as the central regulatory agency empowered to manage the aquifer. Born out of legislative strife and amidst lawsuits, the EAA's identity was defined through temporary restraining orders, questions of illegality, and split votes on major actions. In the early years of the EAA, some members assumed a parochial perspective of their role. As one member commented in an interview, "It's a difficult process because of all the lawsuits, getting our rules kicked out, and complying with property issues. That's been a setback for us." **[56]** The EAA overcame its early years of split decisions and has moved slowly to a state of consensual action, but the agency continues to struggle with its image in the public arena.

Characterization Frames

Characterization was the most frequently used frame in this dispute. Differentiated as positive or negative, depending on the language that stakeholders used to describe other disputants, characterization frames focused on the labels that disputants used and potential stereotypes they held of other groups. In the early stages of the conflict, characterization frames were stereotyped into polarized categories; for example, urban versus rural, environmentalist versus property rights, regulators versus antiregulators. This polarized image of stakeholders is evident in the comments of the director of the Medina Water District who noted, "urban areas have a greater need for drought management than do rural communities" (*San Antonio Light,* May 28, 1989). **[57]**

These polarizations were eventually transformed into characterization frames rooted in challenges to authority and legitimacy of various agencies. For the most part, stakeholders unilaterally saw the EUWD as "The Gutless Wonder," paralyzed by conflicting political interests and void of regulatory power. **[2]** The EAA, in contrast, garnered some positive characterizations as evidenced in remarks such as, "a step in the right direction," and "changing how the public thinks about water." **[58]** These comments, however, were balanced by negative characterizations that centered on internal conflicts within the group, its slowness to act, and its lack of impact. Remarks such as "The EAA has not been very aggressive in managing the Aquifer; it's too little, too late; the permitting is done too softly" illustrated these perceptions. **[59]**

Environmentalists were another group of stakeholders that were cast both positively and negatively. Because they took action to protect water quality and quantity, most stakeholders supported the basic interests of this group. However, on the issue of the endangered species, other stakeholders criticized the motives of the Sierra Club and their readiness to file a suit without even warning the other parties. One stakeholder observed, "the Sierra Club uses the endangered species as a lightning rod for leverage and clout." **[60]** The U.S. Fish and Wildlife Service had no prior contact with the Sierra Club before they received the official notification of the lawsuit. As an agency official noted, "It caught us by surprise and made us feel backed into a corner." **[61]**

For the most part, stakeholders characterized the City of San Antonio as well as irrigators and farmers with negative images. The City of San Antonio surfaced as a power broker that had "an insatiable appetite for water and growth." **[62]** They surfaced as the "bully who didn't like the rules and expected all of us to change them." **[63]** One farmer noted, "San Antonio was the one that wanted the bill [Senate Bill 1477] in the first place. Now they got it, they are not pleased with it." **[64]** Further, a rancher noted that "SA folks value water differently. There is so much waste in the city. We worship and cherish it because we rely on it for a living." **[65]** In effect, San Antonio emerged as the villain in this dispute—they are large, use the most water for drinking and recreation, and appear to other stakeholders as unwilling to seek out alternative water sources and were not doing enough to reduce their consumption.

Ironically, the irrigators and farmers were also seen as "using a great deal more water than necessary," not using it efficiently, and "wanting cheap water." **[66]** The municipalities and the City of San Antonio believe that the farmers have "lucked out" in their allocation. As one stakeholder depicted, "the pigs get fat and the hogs get slaughtered." **[67]** From their perspective, the agricultural community is the primary beneficiary of Senate Bill 1477. In effect, environmentalists, some government officials, and smaller municipalities blame both San Antonio and the farmers/irrigators for being "greedy," "misusing the water," and "being indifferent to other stakeholders." **[68]**

Conflict Management Frames

Conflict management frames reflect how the conflict has been managed in the past or refer to how it should be managed in the future. Most disputants described the Edwards case as being managed through adjudication, appeal to political action, and appeal to the market economy. However, early stages of the dispute revealed processes aligned with consensus recommendation and joint problem solving, exemplified by the five-year negotiated Regional Water Management Plan that reached consensus followed by resistance. Several rounds of mediation ensued as the chairman of the TWC sought to negotiate "a miracle agreement." These mediations, however, engendered a better understanding among the parties and introduced and refined many ideas and mechanisms that were eventually incorporated into Senate Bill 1477, but they failed to produce any agreements.

But after the TWC declaration of the aquifer as an underground river, litigation dominated the conflict scene, including suits by the Sierra Club, the catfish farmer, and other farmers and irrigators. For the environmentalists, litigation provided a benchmark or a way of setting aquifer levels and withdrawal amounts at a specified acre-foot; for citizens, adjudication was a reactionary tactic—used to obtain "voice" or to recover rights lost through previous rulings. Adjudication also served to legitimate state and federal agencies as well as environmentalists and water districts. Continual suits at the district, state, and federal levels led to the eventual acceptance of a state-appointed regional authority to oversee the aquifer. Without these actions, the battle between local groundwater agencies versus state regulation would likely have continued.

The Sierra Club's federal suits helped legitimate the EAA through edicts ordering the USFWS to set groundwater limits and through requiring the state to regulate the aquifer. Thus appeals to political action became dominant in response to heated court battles over federal and state jurisdiction. Stakeholders, who at one time fought the existence of any regulatory agency, appealed to the legislature to take control and develop a viable water management plan, "to keep the federal government from taking over the aquifer." **[69]**

Intractability and Conflict Framing

All three types of frames (identity, characterization, and conflict management) are intertwined with the intractability of the Edwards conflict. In particular, statements about the degree to which the conflict was "irresolvable," "tied up in litigation," or "escalating out of control" influenced the direction that a particular episode took. **[10, 12, 24, 39]** Stakeholders, at times, seemed resigned to the long-standing nature and hopelessness of the conflict. Highlighting the complexity of the situation, one stakeholder referred to the conflict as total chaos surrounding the governance of water and through "fighting a jillion fights" about water rights. **[70]**

Other stakeholders pointed out how polarized and divisive the conflict was with a variety of oppositional tensions—urban versus rural, humans versus endangered species, and regulators versus individual rights. **[15, 32]** Negative characterization frames reinforced this divisiveness through backing disputants into corners. In particular, the withdrawal of the western counties from the EUWD, the TWC's declaration of the Edwards as an underground river, and the Sierra Club suits had the effect of backing different parties into corners in an effort to control the direction of the conflict. The parties backed into corners, however, varied across these events, and coalitions among stakeholders seemed fluid and transitory. For example, San Antonio sided with the western counties of Medina and Uvalde in opposing the TWC declaration that the Edwards Aquifer was an underground river. **[20]** This alliance on this issue broke the schism between the rural and urban polarization that dominated the episode of the demise of the EUWD. Both of these issues were important in understanding how this conflict eventually moved to a more tractable level. Finally, the conflict became pervasive as evidenced in the interest and place identity frames of disputants. Disputants equated their inevitable right to groundwater as central to their identities. **[5, 6, 8]** Activists within both the cities and the rural districts put their reputations on the line "to fight for their rights," and leaders of governmental agencies lost their jobs in the struggle for their institutional legitimacy and the common good. **[25]**

Value issues and ill-defined social systems were the central factors that contributed to intractability in the Edwards conflict. Framing reinforced the prevalence of these causes and made it difficult to address the underlying problems. In the early conflict stages, identity frames underscored the salience of fundamental rights, ones protected by law and by precedent cases that ruled in favor of this law. These interest-based frames were linked to personal values, such as the common good, protection of endangered species, economic viability, and preservation of communities, that created a web of latent and manifest issues. Each episode in this conflict highlighted dissensus on value issues and interest-based frames that mismatched and clashed with institutional identities. Namely, protection of individual property rights mismatched and clashed with the goal of governmental agencies to regulate the allocation of water.

Once the conflict shifted from interest-based identity frames to institutional frames the social system in which the conflict was managed became salient. The social system for the Edwards conflict was clearly ambiguous with no agency or governmental body authorized to arbitrate groundwater disputes for this entire region. The EUWD could conserve and protect, but had no decision-making authority; **[1, 2]** local groundwater districts could oversee disputes in their domain, but the structure for handling regionwide groundwater issues was ill-defined. **[21]** Extant water agencies were often unclear as to their jurisdiction over the Edwards and when the TWC acted aggressively to force the state's hand, they were accused of "overstepping their boundaries." **[17, 18]** Hence, institutional frames that stemmed from ambiguous social systems perpetuated intractability, even after a number of disputants accepted the fact that the Edwards would have to be regulated. This problem was compounded by marked social changes in the region, including rapid population growth, increased irrigation, and a fast-growing tourism industry. Thus a sense of urgency, driven by rapid growth and the resurgence of periodic droughts, accentuated the ambiguity in the social system and led to power struggles among stakeholders and institutions.

Conflict management frames both perpetuated intractability and facilitated ways of de-escalating the conflict. Although beginning with efforts at joint problem solving, the early dispute quickly moved to adjudication when stakeholders challenged each other's rights and legitimacy in making decisions about the aquifer. **[3, 4, 10]** Explosive cycles of provocation and counter-provocation by the farmers and irrigators, the City of San Antonio, the Sierra Club, and even the governor contributed to this escalation. **[16, 19, 27, 34]** Once the conflict reached a state of escalating spirals, it was hard to break without force and threats of federal intervention.

The conflict management frame of authority decides based on expertise has moved into the forefront in addressing current Edwards issues. Stakeholders, for the most part, abide by the EAA's rules for assessing aquifer management fees and for issuing permits. Legal challenges to the EAA actions have diminished and the conflict has all appearances of moving in a tractable direction. Stakeholder implementation of the EAA's Emergency Drought Management Rules in the summer of 2000 serves as further evidence that parties in this conflict can work with the EAA.

Conclusion

Although only time will tell, the Edwards Aquifer conflict has de-escalated and has the potential to empower disputants through the buying, selling, and leasing of water permits. As one stakeholder remarked, "They'll either have to go and buy additional ground water rights from permit holders, or they will have to abide by the limits that the EAA has set." **[71]** Overall, most stakeholders feel that the EAA legislation will work, but "it has got to follow the law. If there is no enforcement, the law is not worth the paper it is written on." **[72]** Clearly, this market economy stage could mark a new beginning for a once highly intractable conflict.

Note on Sources

The information in this chapter was derived from newspaper articles and from interviews with seventy stakeholders, including farmers, irrigators, elected and appointed government officials, environmentalists, citizen activists, water agency officials, industrial leaders, developers, judicial authorities, and media reporters. Newspaper articles were collected from the *San Antonio Express-News, San Antonio Light, Austin-American Statesman, Tyler* (Texas) *Morning Telegraph, Uvalde* (Texas) *Leader News, Dallas Morning News,* and *Texas Weekly*. Interviews were conducted in 1999–2000 and newspaper articles covered the time span of 1988–2000.

Chapter 6

Comparing Natural Resource Cases

Barbara Gray, Tarla Peterson,
Linda L. Putnam, and Todd A. Bryan

In this chapter we begin by comparing and contrasting how participants in the three natural resource conflicts frame these disputes, focusing on identity, characterization, conflict management, and social control frames. Secondly, we summarize the theoretical and practical implications of these analyses by examining the relationship between frame changes and the disputes' intractability.

Identity Frames

One important frame type that played a significant role in all three of the natural resource conflicts we studied was the identity frame. Across the three cases, we found that three types of identity frames, in particular, were significant: place-based, interest-based, and institution-based identities. That is, stakeholders identified themselves to varying degrees with interests, places, and institutions pertinent to the conflict. The configuration of these different identities and their intensities directly contributed to the degree of intractability of these conflicts. When strong identity frames were present that sharpened distinctions among disputants, this generally exacerbated the conflict among them, whereas the development of a common identity created opportunities to reduce the conflict.

Place-Based Identity

At least some stakeholders in each case formed significant identities based on place. This kind of identification may have been the strongest in the Quincy Library case. During the "timber wars" the identities of both the environmental and the logging community protagonists had centered on the interests they represented. Local environmentalists expressed a strong identity with others of like interests—those protecting the forest—and fought practices such as clear-cutting, the harvesting of old-growth trees, and timber harvest volumes that they believed were unsustainable. Members of the logging community also identified with a community of like interests—those making a living from timber products—and supported maximum levels of timber harvests that included clear-cutting and old-growth harvesting. Thus each group represented what Kusel et al. (1996) call communities of interest. The environmentalists' community of interests included other local environmentalists as well as environmentalists from other natural resource–dependent communities in Northern California and Oregon, and environmentalists from urban centers in Sacramento and San Francisco. They fought side by side in the timber wars. The loggers' community of interests included other loggers as well as timber industry representatives and supporting businesses from throughout the Northwest, who together formed the environmentalists' opponents during the timber wars. During the time covered by this analysis, however, for environmentalists and loggers in the town of Quincy, these polarized identities began to give way to a shared identity based on identification with their local town and its preservation as a viable Sierra community. This place-based identity, which became salient when the community began to show significant signs of distress from the downturn in the community's timber economy, served as a powerful unifying force that gradually overshadowed the divisive interest-based identities that had previously served to keep local environmentalists and loggers at odds with one another. The warring factions discovered, at the local level, what Kusel et al. (1996) call a common community of place. As place-based identities moved into the foreground, however, local environmentalists and loggers found themselves at odds with their respective communities of interest. This was particularly acute among local environmentalists who were challenged and vilified by their mostly nonlocal peers for collaborating with the enemy. The division between local and nonlocal environmentalists, or more accurately, community-based and interest-based environmentalists, led to one of the more divisive battles ever to take place within the national environmental community.

Identity frames also figured prominently in the Voyageurs case. Throughout the time of this analysis, members of each of the three principal stakeholder groups in the case (wise-use proponents, environmentalists, and National Park Service employees) continued to maintain strong interest-based identities that overlapped considerably with place-based identities. Environmentalists adopted the mantle of "protectors" of the park. They viewed it as their responsibility to safeguard the park and ensure its continuance. Many of them had an affinity for the specific resources within the boundaries of Voyageurs National Park, and they took pride in the fact that Voyageurs was a Minnesota park. Their place-based identity, however, is not limited to Voyageurs; rather they describe themselves as champions for all future wilderness protection. And while the environmentalists in the Voyageurs case were not all from the Twin Cities, others projected onto them the identity of being from "the South" and therefore not true stakeholders of the park.

Strong placed-based identities were exhibited by some of the Voyageurs disputants who had roots in International Falls, or whose families had homes or cabins on Rainy Lake (the largest of the park's lakes). These stakeholders had a strong place-based identity with the cultural and economic history of northern Minnesota. They aligned themselves with the resource extraction culture of the region, with its connotations of hardworking, rugged, outdoorsy people on whose labor the prosperity of the rest of the nation depended. Consistent with this identity, they assumed the right to enjoy the natural resources of the region once the workday was over. Additionally, they viewed the growing number of environmental protections such as limitations on logging and motorized recreation as unreasonable regulations that posed a direct threat to their personal lifestyle and to the future economic welfare of the region. The National Park, which symbolized and enacted those regulations, thus presented a threat to both their economic interests and to the place they identified as their community.

Place-based identity was not as strong in the Edwards case as it was in the Quincy Library and Voyageurs disputes. Place became a way of aligning stakeholders through regions and locations. For example, San Antonio residents identified with the needs of their city and the concerns of an urban region. In a similar way, residents of San Marcos and New Braunfels strongly identified with the natural beauty of their region and the preservation of the springs fed by the aquifer. Clearly, the residents of the western counties of Medina and Uvalde reflected the strongest place-based identities in the Edwards case. United through the desire to preserve their lifestyle and agrarian communities, place-based identity merged with interest-based concerns to shape their hard-line approaches to managing the Edwards dispute.

Interest-Based Identity

The interest-based identities of the wise-use proponents in the Voyageurs dispute reflected a strong orientation to individual freedom to use the land as one chooses. While they believed this freedom should be inalienable, they also feared these rights would be jeopardized by the presence of the national park system. This frame is similar to the interest-based identities of the ranchers and irrigators in the Edwards dispute, who construed their right to water as "god-given" and saw intervention by regulatory agencies as infringing upon these rights. In efforts to protect their local economies, defend their rights to drill on their private property, and take a stand against more centralized regulation, they withdrew their participation from the Edwards Underground Water District and their support of the Regional Water Management Plan. Similarly, some of the most vocal opponents of Voyageurs refused to participate in the VUFP Committee. While the shared place-based identities of the Quincy disputants motivated them to search for a joint solution to save their community, the Voyageurs disputants have never developed a joint place-based identity. That is they have never allowed their common love for the natural resources of the park to transcend their conflicting, interest-based identities. As a result, there has never been a strong enough platform to sustain, or even initiate, joint problem solving among the disputants. Similarly, disputants' place-based identities in the Edwards case never converged around the aquifer as a region of joint concern, but instead served to polarize the conflict between rural and urban or upstream and downstream users. In the absence of claiming a "common place," disputants also lacked common ground and common interests on which to accept any outcome of joint problem-solving efforts.

Institution-Based Identity

In all three of our cases, employees from federal agencies also exhibited distinct identity frames largely rooted in the institutional identities of their particular agencies. For example, in the Voyageurs case, National Park Service employees defined their identities two ways. In addition to serving as guardians of the nation's natural resources, their mission was to fulfill congressional intent or the Interior Department's directives—serving as a kind of conduit or spokespersons for the intentions of those who drafted these directives. Furthermore, when faced with challenges, they frequently tended to retreat into their institutional identity. According to the current park superintendent,

> The NPS is charged with the responsibility to promote the use of parks. Regulation of users is absolutely at the core of what we do; that is why national parks are different from other places—use is regulated. We try to do it fairly and reasonably and in pursuit of public purposes. Perhaps this aspect of national parks was not emphasized

> in the debates about the park, but it has been part of the mandate of the National Park Service since 1916. **[Voyageurs 24]**

The U.S. Fish and Wildlife Service (USFWS) manifested a similar institutional identity frame in the Edwards case. One of the Service's most unique mandates is the conservation and protection of endangered species. However, despite the fact that biologists had documented that current pumping practices threatened essential habitat for endangered species, the USFWS did not become involved in the Edwards Aquifer conflict until the Sierra Club sued them for failure to discharge their institutional responsibilities. From the time of the Sierra Club's first successful lawsuit against the USFWS (*Sierra Club* v. *Lujan,* 93), the USFWS's identity became publicly linked with the Sierra Club's identity, aligned around an agreement regarding the institutional responsibility of the USFWS with respect to endangered species. Both in personal interviews conducted for this analysis and in the media, USFWS personnel consistently stressed that any action they took was motivated exclusively by that institutional mandate of protection.

In the Quincy case, U.S. Forest Service (USFS) personnel also identified themselves as representatives of their institution. However, because the USFS was going through fundamental changes regarding its institutional mandate, this identity was less clear. While a timber production philosophy still pervaded the Forest Service throughout the 1980s, the agency was beginning to recognize that public values, as well as its own, were changing:

> Our values are slowly catching up with the public's perception of multiple use. There are some fundamental changes coming in the way our forests are managed. We're on the cutting edge, but we are leading from somewhere in the middle. Timber people say the Forest Service is too liberal; conservationists say our head is in the sand—and to some extent it is, because of our strong traditions in timber management. **[Quincy 19]**

Another official saw the agency's confused identity and mandate as loosely tied to changing public sentiments toward natural resources:

> Internally [the agency] is in a lot of chaos. As a country we are not sure we want to continue with our way of life or start protecting our environment. **[Quincy 26]**

As a result, Forest Service personnel experienced less unanimity with respect to their institutional identity and its attendant responsibilities than did disputants representing federal agencies involved in the Voyageurs and Edwards cases. While they clearly identified with the Forest Service as an institution, they were less sure what this identity meant and what the Forest Service was supposed to do. This uncertainty appears to have contributed to the resolution of the timber wars at the local level by creating a vacuum that local environmentalists and loggers, acting as problem-solvers, stepped in to fill. Bill Coates, Tom Nelson, and Michael Jackson all agreed that the agency was not adequately addressing any of their needs. As Jackson noted, "We sat down and we worked it out." **[Quincy 38]**

Characterization Frames

Another dominant frame in these three cases was the frequent use of characterizations. By and large, characterizations stakeholders used to describe each other were negative—conforming to stereotypical depictions of enemies typical of polarized conflicts generally (Sherif et al. 1961). In the Edwards and Voyageurs cases, enmity was diffused among multiple parties, whereas in Quincy the Forest Service emerged as a common enemy for both the local loggers and the environmentalists. Both sides agreed that the Forest Service and its clear-cutting policies were damaging the forest, albeit for different reasons. For the other stakeholders in Quincy, the USFS represented the bureaucrats who promoted policies that hampered both economic prosperity and forest protection. In the Quincy case, having a common enemy served as a way of bringing local loggers and environmentalists together against the bureaucrats in an "us" against "them" defense of the homegrown forest management plan.

No common enemy surfaced to bond stakeholders with different interests in the Voyageurs dispute. All stakeholders were cast in polarized ways and each aimed their characterizations at one or more other parties, rather than at a common enemy. Although various groups objected to the park's actions at various points in time, the reasons for their objections differed substantially from one another. Thus both environmentalists and residents who identified with resource extraction industries, such as mining and logging, periodically characterized the Park Service negatively, though they did so for different reasons. As a consequence, dissatisfaction with the NPS never emerged as a common enemy to unify opposing factions as it did toward the Forest Service in Quincy. Instead, coalitions of groups formed on each side of the conflict (e.g., local residents, houseboat owners, some resort owners, and elected officials on one side and environmentalists, outfitters, and other resort owners on the other) that served to entrench the conflict.

Enmity in the Edwards case was both diffuse and shifting. In the early stages of the dispute, no common enemies existed, and the conflict was characterized through polarized interest frames of urban versus rural or regulators versus antiregulators. As a catalyst in the dispute, the Texas Water Commission (TWC) emerged as a common enemy, uniting some stakeholders but not others and shifting the dominant polarization away from rural and urban interests. San Antonio and the western counties united to oppose TWC's declaration of the Edwards as an underground river while residents in the springs area favored this declaration. When the environmentalists moved to center stage, the Sierra Club and federal courts became common enemies for some stakeholders (e.g., farmers, ranchers, and irrigators), but champions for others—hence, again no single common enemy surfaced. Eventually, however, the common enemy that united many stakeholders was a potential one—the threat of federal takeover of the aquifer. The strong intervention of Judge Bunton through issuing rulings on lawsuits, mandating court-appointed water masters, and issuing restraining orders signaled that this threat of federal takeover was real.

Other commonalities in negative characterizations center on the way particular stakeholder groups were cast across disputes. For example, environmentalists in all three disputes were portrayed through negative images such as "preservationists" and "wandering minstrels" who were "against progress" in Quincy; as "ecoterrorists," "hippies," and "highly political and well-organized" in Voyageurs; and as "using the Endangered Species Act as a lightning rod for leverage and clout" **[Edwards 60]** in Edwards. No matter which natural resource dispute we examined, we found that other stakeholders framed environmentalists as overly zealous about protection of the environment and its species. In the Quincy dispute, the loggers' characterizations of local environmentalists changed, but these positive characterizations were reserved only for those environmentalists within QLG. Members of the national environmental movement were still cast as "opponents" who were perpetuating conflicts to appease their membership and offered nothing but "more of the same" **[Quincy 63]**—the status quo of endless fighting, divisiveness, and hatred. Local environmentalists, on the other hand, were seen as approachable members of the Quincy community.

Another common characterization that surfaced in all three disputes was the derogatory image projected onto governmental agencies. In the Voyageurs dispute, the park became "another example of expanding government control, once again taking away the right and freedom of individuals." **[Voyageurs 3]** In Edwards, the characterization of governmental agencies reflected a struggle between local, state, and national levels with the state intervening on behalf of some stakeholders by declaring, "the state has a right to safeguard the interests of its four water and wildlife agencies." **[Edwards 73]** Yet, state agencies were criticized for being "a Gutless Wonder" (EUWD), **[Edwards 2]** "overstepping their boundaries" (TWC), **[Edwards 17, 18]** torn between stakeholder positions and characterized "by intense infighting" (Texas legislature). **[Edwards 9]** In the Quincy case, many residents characterized the Forest Service as an "inept" bureaucracy that "sits on the middle of the fence" **[Quincy 17]** and has not achieved either forest health or community stability. The agency's slowness to react to the QLG plan also earned it the title of "U.S. Lip Service." **[Quincy 50]**

Although positive characterization frames were rare in all three cases, they did appear occasionally. However, the three disputes differed in how these positive frames operated. In the Quincy case, local environmentalists maintained consistently positive characterizations of the logging community throughout the conflict and often referred to them as "our logging friends" or "our neighbors" even while they were being vilified by the loggers in return. Although many citizens continued to blame the logging community for clear-cutting and other damaging forestry practices, local environmentalists knew that these practices were not supported by the logging community. Local environmentalists also claimed that both environmentalists and loggers shared a common love of the forest, an aesthetic appreciation for its beauty, and a loyalty to the community in which they lived. They characterized the Forest Service as an institution that had misled them into seeing each other as enemies. Thus the positive characterization frames stemmed from a construction of the Forest Service as the common enemy and a common identification of a superordinate goal of community stability and forest health.

In contrast, disputants in the Edwards Aquifer case used positive characterizations only to soften negative images and to resist further polarization. Acknowledgments that, though they were extremists, environmentalists still had a laudable goal of protecting both the quality and quantity of water that was needed by humans living in the region broke the pattern of polarization that pitted human rights against protection of the endangered species. In like manner, positive characterizations of the Edwards Aquifer Authority (EAA) as "a step in the right direction" and "clearly changing how the public thinks about water" **[Edwards 58]** limited the polarization between stakeholders who favored regulation and those who opposed any limits on their right to pump from the aquifer. In effect, even though negative frames dominated characterization in the Edwards case, cautiously positive frames contributed to frame shifts, and they broke patterns of polarization that could have further escalated the conflict. Such acknowledgment of common interests was conspicuously absent or, at best, only given lip service among the Voyageurs disputants.

In the Voyageurs case, few positive characterization frames were evidenced except that some voices of conciliation surfaced during and after the mediation. Senator Wellstone attempted to set a positive and hopeful tenor by proposing the mediation. Additionally, as a result of the mediation, a few stakeholders came to appreciate each other's perspectives and revise their negative characterizations of each other. Specifically, some environmentalists and some proponents of motorized use began to see each other differently and agreed to respectfully, and even playfully, disagree on their issues in subsequent interactions. However these shifts were not sufficient to produce an actual mediated solution. Almost immediately, other constituents in their groups overpowered the moderate voices, and the historically negative characterizations prevailed. Curiously, the mutually held positive characterizations of the park's natural resources and the need to ensure their availability to future generations have never been acknowledged as shared interests of all the stakeholders, nor was a common place-based identity served as a unifying force, as in Quincy.

In effect, positive characterization frames served three different functions in each of these disputes. First, in Quincy, they facilitated the management of superordinate goals and solidification around a common enemy; second, in Edwards, they balanced polarized positions that could otherwise have further solidified and escalated the conflict; and, finally, in Voyageurs, their brief emergence hinted at the possibility of conciliation.

The Evolution of Conflict Management Frames

The fact that stakeholders in natural resource disputes often hold very different preferences for what strategies should be used to resolve the conflict is a major factor contributing to the intractability of these conflicts. In the Voyageurs case, litigation was prevalent in the early history of the park, and litigation and protest continue as the preferred strategies of some opponents. Moreover, the inability of the parties to agree on alternatives to litigation was also critical to the conflict's intractability. During interviews conducted for this research, most informants claimed a commonality in their preference for joint problem solving as a conflict management frame. However, debate over whether problem-solving efforts should be locally or nationally constituted undermined all efforts to develop joint problem-solving venues. Moreover, the debate took on harsh political overtones pitting local versus state interests within Minnesota politics. These differing conflict management frames (or the same conflict management frames at different levels—e.g., local vs. federal) made it impossible for the parties to agree on an appropriate and legitimate forum for resolution of the dispute. As a result, joint problem-solving efforts (such as the mediation and the PVUF Committee) did not have the necessary legitimacy and were not sustainable.

Although concerted efforts were made to settle the Voyageurs controversy through mediation during 1996–97, the mediation was fraught with conflict from its inception. While ostensibly they agreed to try mediation, there is some evidence to suggest that not all who were represented at the table believed that the process was the best way to resolve the conflict, and they acted accordingly during the mediation. Additionally, both sides framed the potential outcomes of the mediation as additional losses for themselves. Motorized users feared loss of all motorized access to the park while environmentalists feared that nothing short of wilderness designation would ensure preservation of the resources for future generations. Although the mediation panel members met for one and a half years with federal mediators and worked through several drafts of a compromise proposal for the Kabetogama Peninsula, in the end, no agreement was reached on the major issue.

While it is likely that the mediation effort did represent a major shift in conflict management frames for some stakeholders in the Voyageurs case, others contended that the proposal for mediation was politically motivated by a senator eager to ensure reelection and unwilling to take a stand that might jeopardize that end. Thus, despite the fact that some people framed both mediations as joint problem solving, other observers framed them as political maneuvering and questioned the sincerity of all parties to mediate in good faith. Ultimately, neither the Voyageurs nor the adjacent Boundary Waters Canoe Area (BWCA) mediation panel was able to reach agreement. Some believe local political opposition to the Voyageurs mediation was instrumental in its failure. For example, when the mediation panel offered the fifth version of a compromise plan for the Kabetogama Peninsula, Rep. Irv Anderson, founder of the Citizens Council, characterized it negatively, proclaiming that "the people who live around the park will get nothing more from mediation except further compromising, giving up even more of what they once had" **[Voyageurs 40]**. In the end, the BWCA issue was settled through a political deal between Congressmen Oberstar and Vento, but no decisions were reached about snowmobiling versus wilderness protection for the Kabetogama Peninsula in Voyageurs.

Subsequently, the General Management Plan (GMP) process, and, in particular, the VUFP Committee, can be construed as attempts at joint problem solving by the park because they created constructive forums for stakeholders to air concerns about the park and give input on how it would be managed in the future. However, because many residents had not considered the park to be acting in good faith (e.g., following through on its previous promises to the community), several members of the community were suspicious about these invitations by the park to sit down at the table. While the park staff framed the VUFP group as offering input for the park's consideration (joint problem solving–consensus recommendation), and they believed they had made good faith efforts to hear the concerns of the committee's members, dissatisfaction with the VUFP consultation process arose because some stakeholders framed the VUFP process as joint problem solving–full participation believing that the park should implement whatever the VUFP group agreed to. However the park viewed it as advisory at best, contending that it could not privilege this small group of stakeholders with making decisions for the park's entire constituency that included national level interests. Unsatisfied, local government representatives charged the park with failing to meet its obligations in the GMP process and, once again, appealed to Washington to override the park's proposals in the draft plan.

Curiously, opportunities for joint promotion of the park and the communities surrounding it were lost in the controversy. They might have served as focal points for joint collaboration if local leaders had been willing to champion these efforts. And despite recommendations by the researchers that the community redirect the dialogue toward collective efforts to improve the social and economic well-being of their community, this intervention was quickly overshadowed by the community's negative reaction to the draft GMP, which set off yet another cycle of political protest that once again strained the relationship between the park and its stakeholders.

In the Quincy case, on the other hand, we begin to see the potential for frame change. The shift of conflict management frames in Quincy appears to coincide with the transformation from an emphasis on interest-based identity to an emphasis on place-based identity. With the local economy in disarray, local disputants began reframing the conflict as something they might be able to manage, if they could "cooperate and continue positive discussions on the future of the forest and the stability of our rural quality of life." **[Quincy 23]** The group also agreed to meet at the public library, partially to encourage civility. As trust among the participants grew, they agreed to an integrative Community Stability Proposal (CSP) that was intended to "promote the objectives of forest health, ecological integrity, adequate timber supply, and local economic stability." **[Quincy 30]**

For the QLG, a conflict management frame of joint problem solving was instrumental in enabling participants to reframe the dispute as tractable. Joint problem solving satisfied both strategic and ethical concerns of people who perceived a threat to the very survival of the community they cared about deeply. For members of the timber industry, cooperating with local environmentalists was consistent with both their individual and their business interests in assuring continued timber harvests, as well as their concerns for Quincy as a location for their operations and home to their workers. As it had become increasingly unlikely that the Forest Service would continue providing the industry with ready access to timber, community consensus (but notably without the Forest Service participation) presented a favorable alternative. Although participating in joint problem solving with the "timber industry" ran contrary to environmentalists' interest-based identities, their place-based identity frames as "neighbors" and "friends" assumed greater salience as they witnessed local hardships, making engaging in joint problem solving with fellow citizens seem like not only the best approach but the most compassionate. Moreover, local environmentalists were keenly interested in testing their forest plan and were handed an opportunity to do just that when industry advocates came to them "on their knees." Cooperative interaction among previously avowed enemies thus became a reality—albeit one that omitted a key institutional stakeholder—the Forest Service—whom they continued to view as their common enemy.

As stated in the case analysis, however, cooperation was achieved only at the local level, within the community of place. Conflict management frames in the Quincy dispute took on a different tone when the group decided to pursue federal legislation. In the new more adversarial arena of Washington politics, the conflict swung sharply back toward intractability. As new players entered the conflict with a new set of issues (national environmental groups and their Washington lobbyists as well as a politically divided Congress) the QLG, while maintaining a joint problem-solving frame at home, shifted to a conflict management frame that emphasized appeals to political action at the national level.

Ironically, the QLG's switch to a political strategy brought them squarely up against the national environmental community, which had used a consistent conflict management frame throughout all phases of the QLG conflict: pursue administrative and regulatory strategies that would force the agency to decide in their favor. Yet when the QLG adopted this same conflict management frame, the national environmental community argued that neither Congress nor community-based collaborative groups should be the entities making these decisions; it was solely the agency's responsibility. But QLG saw Congress as its only hope, and source of power, given that the Forest Service, in four years, had not adopted its plan. Unfortunately, the local disputants' consensus that the Forest Service was their common enemy put them at odds with the agency from the start and left them with an adversarial political strategy (approaching Congress) to gain the agency's compliance. The QLG further argued that it was not trying to force the agency to adopt the plan but only to fairly and objectively "consider" it.

For the QLG, adopting a political action frame was also ironic because it meant relinquishing control to a higher power by placing its local plan, and hopes, under the high-powered microscope of federal policy-making and into the hands of distant politicians. If passed as law, the QLG plan would go through a lengthy environmental impact analysis that would entail the further close scrutiny of public review. Although the process was fraught with uncertainty, the QLG was optimistic about the outcome because the plan had received very strong support and encouragement from both aisles of Congress.

Environmentalists, on the other hand, argued that the QLG's strategy amounted to local control (to which it objected) since QLG bypassed the Forest Service's administrative procedures when it went to Congress. Going to Congress was, to them, tantamount to forcing the Forest Service to adopt the QLG plan. Since the national environmental community consistently relied on the political action process to achieve its goals, their opposition to the QLG's use of the same conflict management strategy was both ironic and hypocritical. As such, conflict management frames that one would expect to find operating within both the environmental community and QLG had flip-flopped as political contexts and power bases shifted around them.

The Edwards Aquifer conflict reveals additional complexities associated with the development and use of conflict management frames within natural resource conflicts. As stated in the case analysis, most disputants in the Edwards case could not envision conflict management through any frames other than adjudication, appeal to political action, and appeal to the market economy.

Ever since the original ruling declaring the aquifer an underground river, litigation was the preferred frame for conflict management in this dispute, including lawsuits brought by the Sierra Club, the catfish farmer, and the farmers and irrigators. For the environmentalists, litigation provided a relatively predictable means for achieving their goals. For other water users, adjudication was their reaction to the lawsuits filed by the Sierra Club. Rather than questioning the conflict management frame proffered by the environmentalists, other parties simply accepted adjudication as the dominant conflict management frame for the issue.

Unlike the Voyageurs case, most of those interviewed voiced a straightforward preference for adjudication as the means for resolving disputes. Some claimed that in the ideal world they would prefer joint problem solving, but they discounted its reliability as a means for resolving issues related to the Edwards case. In fact, joint problem solving eventually came to be viewed as a failure because agreements previously reached through this approach had been rejected by one or more stakeholder groups and had been challenged in the courts. However, several parties noted that, despite the failure to achieve resolution, these procedures had: (a) engendered a more complex understanding of the biophysical processes at work in the aquifer; (b) introduced the large-scale problems of overpumping to a broad spectrum of the public; and (c) refined most of the ideas, principles, and mechanisms later incorporated into new Texas groundwater law. Thus, despite these ultimate effects on groundwater legislation, there was no agreement as to what constituted an appropriate resolution of the Edwards conflict. In fact, following these early joint problem-solving attempts, there was strong agreement that adjudication was the preferred frame for conflict management until this approach led to stalemate once court settlements began to be appealed and routinely challenged.

Now that the EAA has the legal authority to regulate the aquifer, the emergence of conflict management frames other than litigation has provided possibilities for disputants to reshape the conflict toward greater tractability. Appeal to political action, authority decides based on expertise, and appeal to market solutions have emerged as viable conflict management frames. Stakeholders who at one time fought the existence of any regulatory agency appealed to the legislature to take control, develop a viable water management plan, and keep the federal government out of the dispute. As one of the San Antonio activists explained, "I mean, these are political decisions about who gets water and who doesn't. I guess the elected representatives from the people who use the water is [*sic*] probably the best as opposed to getting a state agency like the Water Development Board or something trying to adjudicate who gets water and how much." **[Edwards 74]** This stakeholder, it seems, had come to terms with letting the political process be the arbiter of disputes over the Edwards. In addition, stakeholders eventually followed the mandate that the EAA should make decisions on the aquifer, based on their expertise. Early days of challenging the EAA legitimacy subsided, as evidenced by a reduction in lawsuits and adherence to regulatory practices. Through developing a Critical Period Management Plan, receiving Texas code approval for issuing permits, and managing a difficult drought period, the EAA established agency jurisdiction to regulate the aquifer, and stakeholders adopted a conflict management frame of authority decides based on expertise.

Additionally, the water contained in the Edwards Aquifer, while remaining fundamentally connected to historical concepts of private property rights, is increasingly framed as an economic interest that can be traded among reasonable parties. Markets, according to some parties to this dispute, help avoid escalation because people realize "that markets are being created and that water is available and it's not going to be outrageously expensive, it's not like you're going to be left out. It's there, if you want to go pay for it . . . so I think a lot of people are buying into it more." **[Edwards 74]** The EAA has supported this frame through establishing the Authority Groundwater Trust to pave the way for selling and leasing of water rights. Although there is no guarantee that this reframing of the conflict management strategies will lead to greater tractability, the new frames provide all parties with more flexibility, and open the possibility for joint problem solving to become a dominant conflict-management frame. Market-based mechanisms (such as permitting) might also hold some promise for Voyageurs, if opponents would realize that their economic interest could be served by this approach.

In all three cases, fear played a significant role in both the choice of conflict management frames and how they were lived out. In each case, however, the parties responded differently to the danger they sensed. Residents of the region around Voyageurs National Park have responded to the perceived threat to their communities by closing ranks against any currently opposing factions. In this process, they discourage any flexibility in how the conflict might be managed. The members of the QLG responded to the perceived threat to their community by building a structure that both expected and rewarded cooperative action among previously opposing factions. Coates, one of the founders of the QLG, noted that small towns were already endangered and this action was going to wipe them out. In the Edwards Aquifer case, disputants have responded reactively. Whether the crisis is brought on by lack of rain or by a judge's decree, water users react in predictably defensive ways. They have brought countersuits, dug deeper wells, and vilified their opponents. However, they also have begun to weigh and discuss trade-offs between their rights to the resource in question (water) and the money they can make by selling it to other parties.

All three cases suggest that conflict management frames that focus on litigation, protest, and sabotage tend to escalate the conflict and deepen intractability. The Quincy case suggests that if parties reframe their conflict management preferences to focus on coalition building among the stakeholders, the dispute moves toward tractability. It also suggests that conflict management frames are not fixed and can shift with changing contextual features, such as shifts in social and economic conditions that produce hardship and result in greater compassion toward fellow humans, or shifts in power and influence that change the odds of one party prevailing by using a particular strategy. For example, the Edwards case indicates that shifts in conflict management frames due to federal threats, continual droughts, and population growth in the region can move conflict management frames from litigation to political action to authority decides based on expertise. Together, the cases also suggest that some conflict management arenas, like the arena of political action, are knowingly adversarial and, as such, provide few opportunities for joint problem solving and collaboration. Thus their continued use is more prone to perpetuating intractability.

The Evolution of Social Control Frames

The social control framing was also critical in all three cases. The most common social control frame centered on opposition to the federal government from local participants. We have already seen that representatives of federal agencies were characterized negatively by many of the other participants. These negative characterizations are indicative of differences between these stakeholders' expectations about how social control should be exercised and the expectations of federal agents. Despite this, opposition to federal control was framed differently among the three cases. For example, local opponents of Voyageurs National Park viewed the National Park Service staff as incompetent because the former's expectations about how the park should be managed differed from those of the Park Service staff. Similarly, Quincy residents, whether or not they joined the QLG, characterized the USFS negatively because the Forest Service did not manage timber harvesting in the manner these stakeholders believed to be best. The fear that the federal courts and eventually the USFWS would take control of the Edwards Aquifer led parties who were otherwise opposed to any regulation of use of natural resources to support a regional management authority.

Interestingly, all three disputes—Quincy, Voyageurs, and Edwards—began as local and regional disputes that grew into national-level contests. The Quincy conflict evolved from a local to a national dispute when the QLG took its forest plan to Congress. It was elevated again when national environmental organizations pressed the Forest Service to protect the California spotted owl on a regional basis, thus transferring decision making from the national forest, where QLG held greater power, to the regional forester and to the courts, where environmentalists believed they held more power. Likewise, the Edwards dispute began as a conflict among differing regional interests; as it escalated, it expanded into lawsuits in which organizations such as the Sierra Club sought to protect endangered species by raising the issue of pumping from the Edwards Aquifer from the regional to the federal level. In Voyageurs, local conflict over whether a national park should be proposed broadened in scope when these proposals threatened Forest Service landholdings. Thus, at some point in all three conflicts, disputes that began as local or regional tussles were elevated to a national level of debate.

The Voyageurs case follows the pattern of those with primarily local interests preferring either individualist or egalitarian social control (at the local level), and those with primarily national interests preferring more hierarchist social control. Individualists (1) repeatedly told of how the National Park Service continually made ill-considered decisions and (2) insisted that they knew better how to manage the park's resources. National Park Service personnel, on the other hand, emphasize that their decisions are made in accordance with legal mandates, professional knowledge, and a systemic view of how to manage the resource. As one Park Service employee explained,

> What we try to explain to people is the fact that we're trying to manage systems, not necessarily individual species. But, when you have a layer of legalities such as the Threatened/Endangered Species Act, you need to manage that accordingly too. But they say the wolf population is increasing in the state and why should we be concerned about just a few animals, and our point is, we got [*sic*] 95% of the frozen lake surface available to the public, and we're just trying to restrict activity in a few small areas. You know, we should have the legal authority and proper justification for managing that. So it's issues like that . . . what the value of the park is for the nation as a whole as opposed to just the value of your recreational experiences. **[Voyageurs 58]**

The Quincy case illustrates a fairly straightforward polarization in social control frames. Those who wanted management decisions to be made at the local level demonstrated strong preferences for the egalitarian, nonlocal social control frames, whereas those who wanted decisions made at the national level demonstrated equally strong preferences for the hierarchist, nonlocal frame. Additionally, although it played an important role in both the Voyageurs and the Edwards cases, individualistic social control did not appear to be fundamentally important in Quincy.

As was mentioned previously, those who decided to work out this conflict at the community level strategically chose to meet in a library, with the hope that this would encourage civility among members. The choice to label itself as a "library group" further emphasizes the egalitarian frame, and the decision to rely on the idealized image of American democracy. When organizers assembled a group of stakeholders from within the Quincy community, it included representatives from local timber interests and environmental groups, as well as county supervisors and local citizens. Rather than determine membership or manage the group with exclusionary rules such as requirements of technical expertise or official status, members relied on self-policing. The QLG's egalitarian approach to social control provided the mutually agreed upon mutual coercion advocated by Garrett Hardin (1968) as the only way out of the dilemma faced when trying to manage a commonly held natural resource.

Not all parties in the Quincy case preferred egalitarian social control. Those who did not think local residents should make decisions regarding management of the forest favored a hierarchist management frame. From their perspective, members of the QLG had no business developing a management plan because they lacked both the necessary technical expertise and political legitimacy at the national level. For example, when the QLG presented its plan to the Forest Service, service personnel did not take it seriously, claiming that the QLG possessed neither the expertise nor the authority. In Washington, D.C., environmentalists decried the process as well, arguing that local judgments would fail to account for both the broader spatial and temporal scales and the national interests that were at stake. Their arguments followed the same pattern as those of the Forest Service, emphasizing that local groups such as the QLG lacked the technical expertise necessary to make wise decisions regarding natural resource management, sentiments echoed by national-level environmental groups who also argued that the formal authority for such decisions resided at the national level, and within administrative and public involvement processes that environmentalists had fought for during the 1960s and '70s.* Thus, ironically in the 1990s, both QLG and national environmentalists view themselves as acting on behalf of the people; QLG by wresting

---

*The National Environmental Policy Act (NEPA), the National Forest Management Act (NFMA), and the Federal Land Policy and Management Act (FLPMA) gave concerned citizens a greater role in natural resource decisions. Environmentalists at that time were part of the larger movement driven by egalitarian and social justice motives that sought to wrest power away from the "military industrial complex" and distribute it more equally to "the people" (Gottlieb 1993).

power away from the Forest Service and powerful environmental interests in Washington and empowering the local community, and the national environmental organizations by wresting power away from a local community they assumed was fronting for the largest timber company in California and generally empowering the citizens of the United States. Both strategies contain egalitarian roots even though superficially the frames appear to be different. While conflict management frames seem to shift with changing conditions, egalitarian frames seem to remain constant, even though the disputants enact them at different levels in the conflict.

In the Edwards case many of the participants preferred egalitarian forms of social control. An informant who was the mayor of San Antonio during part of this conflict explained that he supported the EAA,

> because it gives us control as locally as it can be and still be a regional authority. The state has the state to worry about, the federal government has the federal, the U.S. to worry about. The EAA has only the aquifer region to worry about. And then to work with other regions, but my preference is local control, and that's as local as you can get for a regional area. **[Edwards 75]**

From his perspective, the most valuable service provided by the EAA was local management of a community resource. He viewed the Edwards Aquifer as a commonly shared resource that should be managed for the good of the community, and by the community that relied on it, and, in this case, community meant "regional." Along with many of the participants in this dispute, he was increasingly leaning toward this egalitarian frame, rather than toward either an individualist or a hierarchist frame. Although many disputants shared this view, others understood social control either individualistically or hierarchically.

Many of those involved in the Edwards dispute exhibited a strong preference for individualistic social control. From their perspective, water from the Edwards Aquifer was private property, and in the ideal society, individuals should be free to do as they wish with their property. They viewed any attempts at management as a breach of their fundamental rights. They viewed any regulation of their right to pump water from the aquifer in the same "way they s[aw] gun control—you can have my water when you peel my cold, dead hand off my pump." **[Edwards 7]** This view has withstood decades of attempts to change water management in Texas, and is maintained today. In 1993, the president of the Uvalde County Underground Water Conservation Association opposed the establishment of any regional authority because it would be "absolutely a violation of people's constitutional rights to own property." **[Edwards 25]** And the attorney for the Medina County Underground Water Conservation District echoed his sentiment, proclaiming, "It's people's property. You can't take it without due process or compensation." **[Edwards 33]** Another stakeholder explained to us that, "I don't support it [the EAA] because I'm a property rights, I'm a constitutionalist person." **[Edwards 76]** Yet another explained that she "would not support a moratorium [on development in the aquifer's recharge zone] because that's a violation of property rights." **[Edwards 77]** For these parties to the dispute, no option other than completely individualistic behavior was legitimate, and to suggest otherwise was outrageous.

Finally, many parties to the Edwards dispute expressed a hierarchist view of social control. They argued that technical expertise and legal authority were required for participating in decisions about the aquifer. The Sierra Club, which is the most visible environmentalist presence in this dispute, repeatedly states its preference for decisions to be made by disinterested technical experts. Further, they turned to those with legal authority (such as Judge Bunton) to ensure that the decisions based on biological and geological information were implemented.

Observed Links between Frames and Intractability

These case analyses suggest that making the intractable tractable requires frame shifts, and this often triggered by significant internal and external events. Internal events refer to changes within or between the stakeholders themselves, whereas external events occur in the broader context in which the conflict is embedded. For example, they may be changes in the economy, political power, or natural environment. A frame change requires an event that stimulates at least one individual to view a conflict in a different way. For example, if a key individual party, for whatever reason, begins talking or acting in a different manner, public sentiments and agency priorities may shift, or a federal law may change the legal options available to parties. Parties may reassess their no agreement alternatives differently in light of new information. They may reach a "hurting stalemate" (Zartman and Aurik 1991) and conclude that an agreement would be preferable to stalemate.

Internal Events

The statement that individuals can and do make a difference is trite but true. In all three cases, we found that champions (individuals who enable new processes/actions) and blockers (individuals who stifle new processes/actions) played important roles. Individual parties to a conflict, through their language and actions, can affect how others see or frame a situation. People who express hope, offer vision, capture commonalities, or simply provide an opportunity for dialogue enable those involved to interact in a different way, perhaps shattering stereotypes or misunderstandings, and function as champions for conflict resolution. Conversely, individuals who cut off conversation, who stifle creativity, who cement the status quo, or who heighten animosity through provocative and divisive language and behavior function as blockers. Thus any party to a dispute can enable other parties to reframe the conflict as more tractable, or can encourage other parties to cement their frames, creating polarization and making a conflict more intractable.

In each case, key individuals said or did things that stimulated shifts in the frames of others. In the Quincy case, Bill Coates, a Republican who had historically supported the timber industry; Tom Nelson, a forester with Sierra Pacific Industries; and Michael Jackson, an environmental attorney, reached across years of acrimonious battles to form the QLG. Michael Jackson had seen a glimmer of hope in a letter from a female member of a logging family: "I was more encouraged by reading that letter than anything I have seen or heard in the last ten years in this county," wrote Jackson. **[Quincy 20]** Her words triggered a reframing response from him in which he acknowledged the necessity of including the logging perspective in any solution. "We know that for a complete solution to our common goals we need the wisdom of the people who have worked in the woods for the four generations that we have been logging Plumas County." **[Quincy 21]** His words, in turn, prompted Coates to approach Jackson three years later.

In the Edwards case, a San Antonio mayor took the role of champion. His predecessor had flagrantly attacked rural areas, making inflammatory comments on a regular basis. He argued that San Antonio had no need to conserve, regulate, or look for alternative water sources. The new mayor used his office to publicize a changed San Antonio attitude, one that would incorporate water conservation and water reuse. One after another, he listed decisions taken to place San Antonio in a more cooperative position relative to other water users: "We're buying water rights from Edwards land holders, we're buying Canyon Lake water, we've got a deal working for some water up near Bastrop, so we've got lots of possibilities out there." **[Edwards 78]**

In both the Edwards and Quincy cases, their champions helped other disputants to reframe negative characterizations and to consider alternative modes of conflict management and social control. A superordinate goal became apparent to at least some parties, who realized that the conflict was causing people to lose sight of something that was of greater concern to them. In the Edwards case, a San Antonio mayor tried to reframe the conflict as a dispute among equally reasonable people, one that could be worked out to everyone's advantage. He justified his optimism that the conflict was becoming more tractable as follows:

> The public has been brought in to actually work on our water problems and solutions and that's helped make things go smoother. The city just adopted a water plan last fall with almost no commotion, which is unusual in San Antonio, and that's largely a result of the most inclusive planning process that we've used in the last couple years, that recognizes that there are lots of opinions out there and gives everybody an opportunity to express them. **[Edwards 79]**

In the Quincy case, a recognition that the conflict was tearing apart the community, a consequence that none of the parties desired, caused local environmentalists to renew their focus on their own forest plan, which reframed the stark "jobs-versus-owls" debate into a more integrated superordinate goal of "community stability and forest health." By consistently conveying this message and carefully avoiding attacking the local logging community, local environmentalists created conditions favorable to a frame change. They also kept the pressure on the Forest Service and timber industry by filing appeals on objectionable timber sales. However, local environmentalists could not by themselves change the frame. It took Bill Coates and Tom Nelson to initiate the local frame change.

In Voyageurs, there were few, if any, champions except perhaps Governor Andersen and Milton Knoll (who tried to arrange a compromise), and Senator Wellstone (who recommended mediation). But no one was able to inspire sufficient frame revision by others to overcome the forces that kept the conflict alive.

Blockers' actions in all three of our natural resource cases worked against frame revision. Voyageurs National Park was subject to charismatic blockers from its inception. As described in Chapter 4, when the National Park Service was attempting to acquire land for the park, Vic Davis purchased land within the park boundaries, upon which he had a 25 ft., 2300 lb. fiberglass replica of an armed Voyageur erected in a strategically visible spot. He sustained the confrontation by subdividing his property into 1-square-foot parcels, each of which he attempted to sell to private individuals. During the 1980s, Davis continued to purchase land designated as part of the park, and propose development on it. He purchased a second Voyageur statue, known by local residents as Big Louie, which he erected in a location near the visitors center in 1985. Davis continued to plague the NPS with development threats and lawsuits until it struck a deal to purchase his land in 1991.

Others in Voyageurs have been described as playing blocking roles. Local resident Carl Brown was cited for hunting within the park. Although Brown was found guilty and was unsuccessful in his subsequent appeals, he became a kind of "cause celebre." The resulting publicity from his cases served to highlight the polarization between many northern Minnesotans and the park. Anderson, who was instrumental in founding the controversial Citizens Council, also blocked attempts to reframe the dispute. Although he was not a member of the mediation panel, some parties to the dispute credit him with orchestrating the Council's rejection of the mediation agreement.

Kay Turner, a stakeholder whose family has owned land above the Edwards Aquifer for generations, has put all of her resources into blocking movement in the Edwards dispute. She insists she is "not a hothead, not a loose cannon," **[Edwards 80]** but simply an honest and dedicated individualist who is holding the line for freedom. She enthusiastically described events she had staged. For example, "I got my friends to dress up like Colombo in their raincoats and we took crime tape and roped off City Hall. And we called it the Theft of the Century. . . . When they tried to arrest me the night before, and my friend says, 'do you want to get arrested?' And I said, 'well what time is it?' And I said, 'well too late for news coverage, so let's wait until in the morning.'" **[Edwards 81]** Turner does not always describe her involvement as an adventure. At times she portrays herself as a sacrificial figure, explaining that she "took a huge hit. So, you can't feel sorry for yourself. You just have to kind of say, 'hmm . . . that hurt, but if I survive this, I'll be stronger.'" **[Edwards 82]** Whether the topic of conversation is endangered species, water conservation measures, or the emerging water markets, her answer is the same, "Kay Turner has not bought in." When she surveyed the community groups involved in efforts at joint problem solving, she recalled commenting, "I don't want anybody hurt, but what's it going to take to make people fight?" **[Edwards 83]**

Other blockers that surfaced in the Edwards case included an outspoken farmer from one of the western counties who opposed the first Regional Water Resources Plan and a former governor who continually supported the stand for private property rights. The former governor, who was the biggest landowner and irrigator in Uvalde, led the campaign against the regional plan and for withdrawal from the Edwards Underground Water District (EUWD).

Both made public statements regarding "fighting for your water," "opposing compromise," and "revolting against aquifer regulation" (Wolff, 1997). **[Edwards 12]**

Another blocker in the Edwards case arose serendipitously. After the Texas Legislature passed a law in 1993 creating a nine-member appointed EAA Board, the Mexican American Legal Defense and Educational Fund (MALDEF) blocked implementation of it through filing a claim that the bill violated the Voters Rights Act. Although motivated by concerns for racial parity, the governor of Texas and the mayor of San Antonio clearly viewed MALDEF as blockers who fostered a three-year delay in enacting essential legislation.

Many stakeholders in the Edwards dispute viewed environmentalists and particularly the Sierra Club as blockers. Armed with a legal brigade, the Sierra Club filed multiple suits in rapid succession to invoke restraining orders; investigate realignment of military bases; and stop the infusion of federal support for home loans, highway construction, and agriculture programs. Some stakeholders viewed these actions as the "nuclear attack" on Senate Bill 1477 while others saw the Sierra Club as a necessary catalyst for taking state action to regulate the aquifer.

Blockers in the Quincy case primarily included the outside environmentalists who decided not to join QLG. These included Louis Blumberg of The Wilderness Society, who, along with David Edelson of the Sacramento office of the Natural Resources Defense Council and Steve Evans of the Sacramento-based Friends of the River, helped organize the massive campaign against QLG that eventually got Senator Boxer to withdraw her support of the legislation. Attacks over the wisdom of federal legislation turned into a personal vendetta between Blumberg and Jackson, who once had been friends, but who had often sparred with each other at regional debates.

Federal legislation attracted a whole new list of environmentalist blockers from throughout the country, including the American Lands Alliance based in Washington, D.C., and the Center for Biodiversity based in Tucson. A small handful of local blockers, including two former members of the QLG, have continued to follow the QLG's activities after deciding that they could be stronger forest advocates outside of the group. Another local opponent was suspected of using QLG meetings to gather information that would later be used in a lawsuit. This suspicion caused QLG to hold closed executive meetings for a short period of time.

Blockers are also found in the Forest Service, although the institution itself, and not individual officials or employees, is seen as blocking the QLG plan.

This appears to be one of the more maddening elements of QLG's relationship with the agency—the agency, through its representatives, appears to support the group's proposal yet the agency itself is slow to act on the plan. Thus there is no "face" to the inertia the group experiences.

Senator Barbara Boxer can also be considered a blocker in the Quincy case because of her efforts to block the QLG bill from a full Senate hearing. Boxer placed a courtesy hold on the bill, which essentially kept the Senate from debating, amending, and voting on it. Senator Dianne Feinstein finally succeeded in attaching the bill to the Senate appropriations bill where it passed and was signed by President Clinton.

Frame shifts also occur when new parties enter into the conflict, introducing new issues and objectives. When the QLG bill was being considered in Congress, national environmental groups took issue with it, introducing community-based collaboration as the core issue needing debate. Sudden attacks like this put others on the defensive, and the frames on all sides take a dramatic shift. The Edwards dispute escalated from a regional issue to the national level when the Sierra Club began bringing lawsuits against various parties. Efforts to catapult Voyageurs to a federal level (during the 1995 oversight hearings and again in 2000 by the Koochiching County Commissioners), however, did not prove sufficient to produce frame shifts in either direction. The mediation, however, as we have seen earlier, did enable some parties to alter their conflict management and characterization frames with regard to some of their arch enemies.

External Events

Natural resource conflicts are enmeshed in a larger political, socioeconomic, and ecological context that affects the framing process. It is clear from our cases that the contextual features of the three natural resources cases we studied also played a role in how the conflicts evolved, how they are framed, and how stakeholders manage them.

The QLG is embedded in a national political and public policy context that shifts dramatically over time, creating vastly different forest management policies that affect economic conditions in the communities and, ultimately, how stakeholders respond to the changing conditions. In fact, the QLG developed its plan to provide "community stability and forest health" **[Quincy 30]** in a region that was reeling from boom and bust local economies and forest conditions characterized by catastrophic fire danger, declines in endangered species, destruction of riparian habitat, and the loss of old-growth forests. QLG's plan, we recall, grew out of a plan developed by environmentalists in 1986 in response to the Forest Service's planning process on the Plumas National Forest. The environmentalists' plan was developed during the Reagan administration, when forest protection was a low priority within federal land management policy. It was also a relatively low priority within local communities, like Quincy, that were dominated by commodity-based industries and controlled by political leaders that supported such industries. In this context, the environmentalists' plan was soundly rebuffed, not only by the Forest Service but also by community leaders.

But that was then. By 1990 the political and policy context had shifted dramatically. Environmentalists had succeeded in crippling the timber industry by appealing timber harvests on the national forests throughout the West, and the northern spotted owl had been listed by the USFWS as a federally endangered species. The timber economies in many small towns in the Northwest had almost completely collapsed with lumber mill closures appearing almost weekly. In addition, national public sentiment was gradually shifting toward forest protection and recreational and aesthetic uses of the national forests. Following President Ronald Reagan, President George Bush had declared himself the "environmental president" and had not challenged existing environmental laws such as the Endangered Species Act. President Bill Clinton's election in 1992 did not necessarily usher in a change in national environmental policy; however, it reflected the contextual changes that had been occurring up to that point. QLG, formed in 1992, was, in many ways, a response to that change.

In the Edwards Aquifer case, contextual shifts occurring in weather patterns created either abundant water supplies or drought conditions that affected how intensely stakeholders pursued remedies. In addition, rapid urban and suburban growth, the identification of federally endangered species, the declining role of agriculture, and changing statewide water policies and authorities have increased conflicts over use of the aquifer and affected the dynamics of water allocation and use. The rapid growth of San Antonio and the heightened demand for development in the region intensified the need to regulate the aquifer before permanent damage occurred to either the quality or the quantity of water. The existence and use of the Endangered Species Act to address environmental concerns around the nation provided a social and political context for the Edwards Aquifer dispute. It raised concerns about the ecosystem and collaboration among users that led to redefining and repositioning stakeholders. Downstream users, who had never been major players in the early years, became central to the conflict and important in developing policies for regulation. In many ways, the clout that the Sierra Club brought to the dispute stemmed from the changing social and economic context, including the decline of military bases around the country, increased attention to conservation and reuse of extant water resources, and maintaining the habitat and survival of endangered species.

The impact of external factors on the dispute over Voyageurs is less obvious than in either of the other two cases. Nonetheless, some effects can be seen. National- and state-level environmental policies emphasizing greater environmental protection over the last thirty years have gradually reduced the acreage available for timber harvesting in the state. This shift, while not directly affecting the main issues in the Voyageurs case, does contribute to the general sense of loss experienced by residents of northern Minnesota—the loss of life as they once knew it. International Falls, in particular, like many rural towns across the United States, has experienced the attendant loss of jobs and a declining population (10 percent between 1990 and 2000). The park becomes an easy scapegoat for these changes because of the federal presence and because the values of the NPS closely align with the more general national-level trends. Changes in wilderness policy with respect to the BWCA have also reverberated in the dialogue over Voyageurs because of the proximity of the two areas. Nor has the conflict been immune to shifts in the political landscape, nationally and within Minnesota. Were it not for a shift in the makeup of Congress in early 1995, for example, the oversight hearings most likely would not have taken place. Additionally, the park's frequent adversary, the Citizens Council, fell prey to Governor Jesse Ventura's cost-cutting measures when he took office in early 2000, and had to close its doors. Thus the contextual effects on the Voyageurs conflict have acted as a pendulum—advantaging one side or the other in the conflict for a time, but they have not been precipitous enough to effect the kind of "hurting stalemate" (Zartman and Aurik 1991) that could bring both sides to the negotiating table. This may offer one explanation for why frames have remained relatively constant over the life of that case.

Frame Changes as They Relate to Context

The contextual features of natural resource cases can influence the framing process in numerous ways. For the most part, contextual shifts appear to create opportunities for frames to shift, although they do not always produce frame shifts. In the Quincy case, for example, the steep decline in the timber economy between 1989 and 1992 appears to have enabled an identity-based frame change that prompted opposing community members to come together in response to a threat to the community's social and economic well-being. As we have discussed, common place-based identities emerged, became salient, and appear to have overshadowed interest-based and institutional identities. When environmentalists spoke of "we" in the early stages of the case, they were usually referring to the environmental community. As the QLG developed, however, "we" shifted from a community of interests to a community or place—"we" became "our neighbors." This shifting identity frame enabled community members to view themselves as a "superordinate" group, of sorts, with a "superordinate" goal (Sherif et al. 1961).

Local environmentalists in Quincy had been trying to reframe the conflict from one of starkly opposed interests—jobs versus owls—to something more inclusive and integrated—community stability and forest health. In fact, their message appeared consistently in local environmental literature since their 1986 plan. Throughout this period, however, environmentalists were in a clear minority, and their message was ignored. The contextual conditions favored commodity-based industries leaving political and community leaders relatively unresponsive to environmental concerns. Once the context began to shift, however, community well-being began to decline, and environmentalists' power grew. At this point some members of the timber industry and local community began to view the plan as a beacon of hope in an otherwise bleak future. As such, the contextual shifts enabled revised framing to emerge.

One wonders, however, what, if any, contextual factors could unite the participants around a superordinate goal in the Voyageurs case. Just how serious an economic downturn would it take, for example, to motivate the parties to set aside their differences and jointly promote the park for all users—an activity that could benefit the park but also boost the economy of the entire region. Or, on the positive side, when might their common love of the natural beauty of the park geography outweigh past animosity toward the park so that the locals and the environmentalists could set in motion plans to assure these resources remain for the recreation and solitude of future generations?

Natural Resource Conflicts as Zero-Sum Games

In our three natural resource cases, the conflicts have been framed as "zero-sum" contests: if resources are used in one particular way, this precludes others from using them for the same or other purposes. This is most apparent in the Edwards case because it is a common pool resource that can literally dry up if too many users indiscriminately siphon off water for their own use. Additionally, the Edwards Aquifer case deals with a natural resource that is central to human survival. The shortage of potable water represents the most immediate threat to human life on earth. Although water is technically a renewable natural resource, human demands have long outstripped regeneration capacity. And shortages become even more salient during times of drought.

In Quincy and Voyageurs the contests are also framed as zero-sum battles between those wanting to consume or use resources and those wanting to preserve them, but neither the scarcity of the resources nor the consequences of the scarcity are as apparent as is the depletion of the water supply. Thus, in the Edwards case, the impacts of one disputant's action on another are direct. If one water user sinks a deeper well, his/her neighbors may have to choose whether to lose the ability to pump from their wells, or to invest in deeper wells themselves. Whereas, in the Quincy and Voyageurs cases, the impacts may be more subtle, they are nonetheless consequential and are also constructed as zero-sum games.

Forests are a shrinking resource worldwide. Whether the wood product in question is firewood for basic cooking or an artistically designed entertainment center, the supply has fallen far behind the insatiable demands of a growing human population. Similarly, the remaining wilderness area within the United States is shrinking, succumbing to increased demands for new development and recreational opportunities. While proponents and opponents of resource consumption differ in their predictions about the limits of such consumption, the battles are pitched such that one's gain is another's loss. For example, depletion of forests creates hazards for other natural resources, the species of wildlife that inhabit the forests. Efforts to preserve the resource pose other kinds of threats, however, to the occupational well-being of loggers and the economic viability of the communities sustained by the wood products industry. Thus, the well-being of loggers is pitted against the well-being of owls and, by extension, the biodiversity of the planet.

In Voyageurs the zero-sum contest is essentially between those who want to use and those who want to preserve wilderness lands. With increases in population and in leisure time, and shrinkage in greenspace through urban expansion, competition among recreationalists for the remaining undeveloped areas is keen. Although the park does not interfere with basic human survival needs, the Voyageurs conflict represents a battle for how that remaining undeveloped land will be governed and used and who will get to claim it for their preferred use. Some uses are framed to curtail others. Viewed from this perspective, the dispute remains intractable, for the resource is limited, while demands placed on it are ever increasing. Unless parties can successfully reframe the dispute (as an area that all stakeholders want to protect for future generations' recreation and solitude), it seems destined to continue.

Constructing natural resource disputes as zero-sum games contributes to their intractability. As we have seen in both the Quincy and Edwards cases, however, reframing has shifted the focus from zero-sum to more integrative interpretations. By reframing the conflict, parties have begun to find some workable solutions. The QLG's forest plan enables both logging and conservation. Additionally, contextual advances (with respect to milling technology) now enable the processing of smaller diameter timber and thus enhance conservation efforts. As San Antonio develops water reuse programs that enable the city to reduce the amount of water it "wastes," downstream users lose the flow of freshwater. Shrimp farmers and environmentalists concerned with endangered turtles see both conservation efforts and water markets differently than do San Antonio's mayor or farmers who have decided to sell their water rights. The more water that is captured before flowing south to the Gulf of Mexico, the less water is available to perform essential ecological functions downstream. Thus, while natural resource conflicts do often pose fundamental constraints that cause them to be framed as zero-sum contests, reframing that reveals possibilities for integrative outcomes may indeed be possible and should be assiduously explored in these cases.

Conclusion

As has already been stated, all three cases include general hostility toward the federal government, yet each group of people framed that hostility differently. The Voyageurs case is dominated by interest-based identities and extremely negative characterization of all other parties. It presents a saga of failed attempts to wrest control from the current enemy. Polarization, violence, and escalation characterize its dominant conflict management frames. Threats to critical identities of various stakeholders continue to fuel the conflict, and stakeholders battle over hierarchist or individualistic frames for social control, with no ground available for safely experimenting with alternative frames. In sharp contrast, the Quincy case demonstrated dramatic shifts from local intractability to tractability, and, on a national level, back to intractability. Participants adopted a common place-based superordinate identity frame when conditions were ripe for change and when champions crossed the divide. Generally, then, the more that the parties' identity frames differentiated them from each other, the more intractable the conflicts remained. When parties developed common or overarching identity frames, some of the conflicts became tractable, at least temporarily.

This shift also led to new ways of characterizing those who had been seen as the enemy, and attempts to participate in joint problem solving across previously hostile groups. Not surprisingly, the QLG emerged with an egalitarian social control frame, which allowed many of those who may have preferred hierarchist or individualistic modes of social control to work together for the good of the community. In the Edwards case, stakeholders responded to the threat that the federal government would wrest control by creating a new semigovernmental body, the EAA. Although the EAA has triggered public outrage whenever it threatens to impose limits on specific activities, such as watering lawns, it is also characterized positively by significant champions. As San Antonio's mayor argued,

> It's made a big difference. First of all, it [the EAA] put everybody on an equal, or pretty close to equal, basis. We're all going to have to share the aquifer and that wasn't going to happen voluntarily. And so we needed to have that management structure in place to allocate water across the region and those that need more go find it, either from those that have extra within the region or go somewhere else. So I think it's essential to managing the aquifer over the long term. **[Edwards 84]**

Along with the EAA, economic incentives built into the developing water market structure have encouraged stakeholders to reframe themselves as partners who can find common interests, or as buyers and sellers. If it is possible to find common interests and to emphasize common identities with other parties, collaborative frames for conflict management become more feasible, and egalitarian frames for social control gain ascendancy. Whether as stakeholders or outside parties, we need to watch for such moments, when participants have the opportunity to revise disputes that had previously been judged intractable.

Part II

Water Cases

Chapter 7

Doan Brook: Latent Intractability

Sanda Kaufman and Mehnaaz Momen

This chapter uses the case of a threatened urban watershed, Doan Brook, to illustrate latent intractability that stems from the persistent absence of decisions to manage a natural resource, rather than from the deep-seated conflicting values or interests typically surrounding such decisions. This case lacks the typical behaviors of overt conflicts, such as hostile exchanges, lawsuits, or attempts to use political influence to bring about a preferred outcome. Instead, there is long-term failure to secure the sustainability of a scarce resource valued by its neighboring communities. The questions at the heart of this case include: Why the latent intractability? What consequences derive from it? And how do prevailing stakeholders' frames reflect the situation, or contribute to it?

Though there is a twenty-five-year history of efforts to manage Doan Brook, a recent event is used here to explore the nature of intractability and its relationship to prevailing frames. A regional public agency, the Northeast Ohio Regional Sewer District (NEORSD), decided to study collaboratively with bordering communities alternative means of watershed remediation and maintenance (1998–2001). The physical and historical characterization of the Doan Brook watershed is followed by a description of the participatory watershed study project and its stakeholders, and then an analysis of the connections between the frames of participants in this process and the latent intractability of watershed management.

The Watershed

Doan Brook, a Lake Erie tributary, courses through 11.7 miles of natural, dammed, channelized, and culverted stretches through quiet residential areas (85%); parklands of historical, natural, and recreational importance; and lakes (Jennings and Gardner 1998). It drains about 100 square miles of urbanized

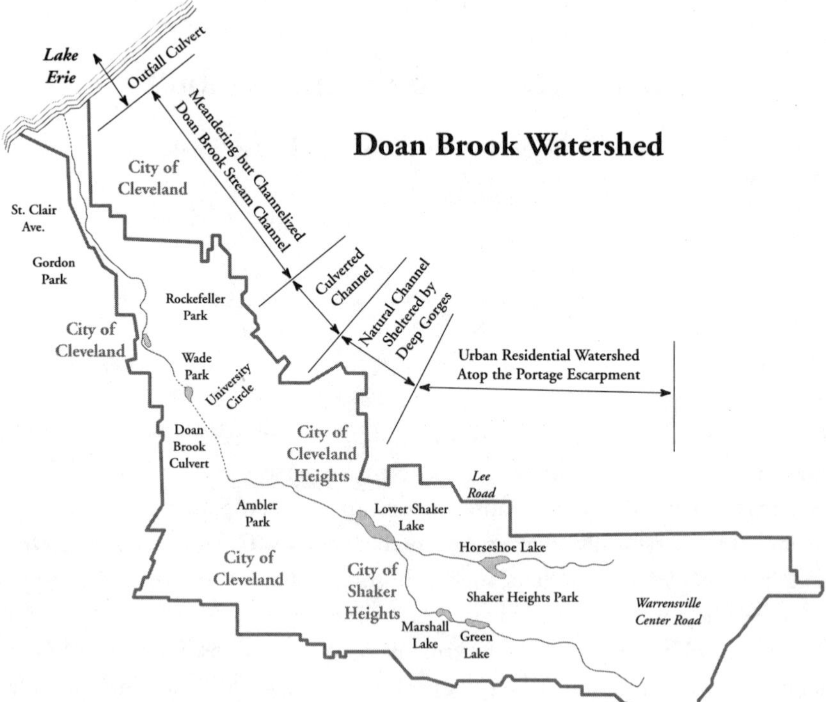

Figure 7.1. Shaker Lakes/Doan Brook Watershed, Cleveland, Ohio

land (Fig. 7.1) including Cleveland's eastern suburbs of Shaker Heights and Cleveland Heights, University Circle—the city's cultural hub—and several Cleveland neighborhoods (*Plain Dealer,* April 10, 1998).

Doan is a typical urban stream with poor water quality, rapid flow, flooding behavior, and sparse habitat, all consequences of its heavily built surroundings (pers. comm., Michael Walton, professor of biology, Cleveland State University, 2000). Factors common to urban areas—runoff loaded with lawn fertilizers and pesticides, stormwater and sewer overflows—contribute to its current predicament. Despite problems, Doan Brook is an asset for its neighbors. The lower part is the only bit of nature to which some of Cleveland's neighborhoods have easy, pedestrian access. The upper part, forming the (artificial) Shaker Lakes, is cherished by residents, who hike and bike along it and bring their children to watch wildlife.

The brook's gradual deterioration threatens to impair, and even curtail, current uses. In the lower stretches, water quality and safety concerns have led residents, especially younger or new ones, to ignore the brook's presence. In the upper portion, recreational use is limited and dropping as the lakes silt or become covered by green algae fed by the nutrient-loaded runoff. Despite this decline, Doan Brook continues to appear quite attractive and has retained the residents' affection, instead of stirring sufficient alarm and interest for anyone to take the actions necessary to safeguard and preserve it. Although some know and are concerned about its degraded state, most residents are largely unaware of any problems and would likely be very surprised if asked to pay mitigation* costs, very high according to some estimates. Since the brook's problems do not appear imminently threatening, those who would help make and fund decisions to ensure the brook's long-term health are unconvinced of the need for action. Reaching consensus among the many interested parties on remedial action is also a challenge. As a result, Doan Brook is quietly dying under the affectionate gaze of its neighbors.

Some watershed damage is irreversible. Other deterioration becomes increasingly costly to remedy in time, creating a pressing, if silent, need for remediation and management. Of those interested in the brook, some believe remedial actions should be ecosystem- or watershed-based. However, as is common for other natural resources, ecosystem boundaries do not match those of decision-making entities with jurisdiction over it, so there is no administrative framework for ongoing needs assessment, funding, implementation of plans, and monitoring.

Conflict around Doan Brook's management hovers under the surface. It is neither easily resolved, nor actively prosecuted, not least due to everyone's low expectations of imminent action. Despite a generally recognized need to prevent the costly, possibly irreversible, deterioration of Doan Brook, there have been few if any implementable† decisions to improve and manage the watershed. We explore some contributors to this peaceful, but environmentally damaging impasse, which we have termed latent intractability, and which is also found in contexts other than environmental conflicts. For example, despite broad consensus on the importance of quality education for all, many inner-city school systems remain neglected, mired in differences over standards,

* Mitigation—restoring the health of the watershed—may entail in this case a set of physical modifications, repairs, and new devices to protect the water quality and the habitat; redesign of ordinances controlling the ways in which new construction in the brook's vicinity contributes to the water pollutant loads; as well as changes in some of the ways in which municipalities carry out maintenance of open spaces surrounding the watershed.

† Public domain decisions are implementable (though not always implemented) when accompanied by agency mandate, resources, plan of action, and political support.

achievement assessment, or definitions of quality (Baum 2001) with persisting lack of tangible progress for the schools. The similarity resides in consensus on needs, coupled with prolonged failure to act that results in continued deterioration of a seemingly valued resource. In both examples parties may be subject to an "omission bias" (e.g., Baron and Ritov 1994). They tend to think of harmful consequences of acts as worse than equally harmful consequences of lack of action, which amounts to perpetuation of the status quo despite broad agreement on its inadequacy. The environment and the schools are the worse for it.

The next section sketches some key moments in the history of the Doan watershed, which through rather unusual civic-mindedness and private generosity became a public recreation resource near the turn of the twentieth century.

A Story of Civic Foresight

Doan Brook is named for Nathaniel Doan, believed to be the first non–Native American settler in the Cleveland area in the early 1800s, when the brook ran its natural course bordered mostly by forests and fields and by a few farms. A community of Shakers settled along the upper Doan in the late 1800s. They built a dam that formed the Shaker Lakes, and a water-powered mill whose few remnants are being considered for historic preservation.

Doan Brook began its transition into a public resource in 1882, when J. H. Wade developed 63.5 acres of his property into Wade Park, close to a major artery connecting Cleveland's two hubs. Wade's gift was followed in 1893 by W. J. Gordon's 122-acre estate at the mouth of Doan Brook, which became Gordon Park. In the same year, the State of Ohio passed a law allowing park commissioners to raise funds and purchase parklands (Eakin 1974). In 1894, the commissioners acquired from the Ambler family substantial parts of Doan's gorge area between the Heights suburbs and Cleveland, today Ambler Park. In 1896, the commissioners obtained from J. D. Rockefeller's Shaker Heights Land Company a large land tract, today Shaker Lakes Park (see Fig. 7.1). Rockefeller also gave lands to connect Ambler Park to Shaker Lakes Park, and 254 acres for Rockefeller Park, connecting Wade and Gordon Parks. Thus, within four years (by 1896), almost the entire watershed had become one continuous park. By then, neighborhoods, industry, and streetcars had replaced most of Cleveland's open space.

Giddings Run, an almost parallel stream, was diverted into Doan Brook and completely culverted, as was the portion of Doan passing through University Circle. Doan's lower stretch was channelized. In 1900, stone arch culverts over the brook connected the lower parklands with the drives overlooking them. Between 1915 and 1939, ethnic groups built along the brook "Cultural Gardens" commemorating World War I. As more features were added to the lower parkland, flooding became a threat to which the engineered response was brook channelization (Gooch 1998).

The Heights—Shaker and Cleveland—are Cleveland's oldest suburbs and closest to it, built in the early 1900s and completely enclosed by the newer eastern suburbs. Shaker Heights, path-breaking in its time, was built according to a plan that included provision of open recreation spaces along the Doan Brook, which endure to this day. In time, the Heights added walking and bike lanes with recreation amenities along the brook. Although Doan's corridor is by now the only nature-like element in an otherwise very densely built environment, its most scenic and natural components are the Shaker Lakes, the result of the Shakers' forceful intervention in nature's design. In this highly urbanized area, the lakes shelter migratory and local birds and small animals, offering wildlife- and bird-watching opportunities. In 1974, the U.S. Department of the Interior declared the 146 acres of parkland including the Shaker Lakes a historical site, with restrictions on re-zoning and on the building of highways or structures (*Plain Dealer,* Sept. 8, 1974).

As a consequence of the urban, largely paved Heights stretch of the brook, contaminated runoff has damaged Doan's water quality. The brook sustains a considerably less diverse land and aquatic habitat than could be expected based on its physical characteristics. Though appearance continues to be deceptively pleasing, discharges from combined sewer overflows impede Doan's recreational use and worsen water quality throughout the watershed. Extensive sedimentation threatens to gradually fill the Shaker Lakes.

For Cleveland residents, the lower watershed's spells of unpleasant odors, the crumbling sustaining walls, and the perceived lack of safety around the brook are more salient than any positive aspects, of which they rarely take advantage nowadays. Some, however, remember family outings and childhoods in the 1950s spent walking and even boating along the Doan.

Due to water speed and quantity after heavy rains, Doan poses great flood risks in University Circle, where the heavy traffic can be severely impeded. Case Western Reserve University, located in this area, had to outfit one of its sides with costly (and not particularly aesthetic) flood-resistant walls and elevated access. Flooding, especially in University Circle, and poor wet-weather water quality, mostly around the neighborhoods, are the most visible and aggravating watershed troubles, inconveniencing many. Since these salient nuisances occur mostly in Cleveland, it seems to many that the suburbs reap only benefits from the brook's presence, because the upper watershed problems are not directly apparent to the senses.

An opportunity to focus attention on the need for remedial action arose in 1998 when NEORSD initiated a project to bring the brook into compliance with Environmental Protection Agency (EPA)-mandated water quality standards for urban watersheds. The next section describes key moments during the past twenty-five years, when earlier opportunities for making watershed management decisions were missed, leading to the NEORSD project, the focus of this chapter.

An Eventful History of Inaction

Over the last twenty-five years there have been several attempts to maintain and improve Doan's natural environment. Problems have received periodic short-term attention especially after flooding incidents, when dams were repaired, flood debris was cleaned, and the wastewater treatment plants were improved (Table 7.1). In 1995, Horseshoe Lake (a Shaker lake) was dredged and its dam was reinforced. In 1997, the City of Cleveland built a costly dam on Doan Brook to reduce flooding in University Circle. The dam proved ineffectual because Giddings Run, the culverted Doan tributary, is largely responsible for floods but joins Doan below the dam. The 1999 final phase of a multiphase $1.8 million Corps of Engineers project involved draining the lower Shaker Lake, repairing the Shaker-built dam, and installing a state-mandated control valve in it to manage lake levels. The EPA-funded NEORSD project to assess collaboratively with the community watershed needs for compliance with water quality standards began in 1998.

Even before NEORSD's public participation initiative, Doan Brook had a rather rich history of public involvement, albeit in ways that do not converge to implementable decisions for its long-term sustainability (see Table 7.1). Differences over Doan Brook are rarely cause for overt community strife. Watershed problems seldom reach the local newspapers. Some residents and elected officials, with a keen awareness of their physical environment, take advantage of the frequent opportunities for education, debate, and consensus building. Focus groups with residents and nonprofit organizations reveal interest in the watershed's recreation potential, in having easily accessible nature in residential neighborhoods, and in the educational value of children's contact with nature. There is willingness to support, mostly in unspecified ways, someone else's action to ensure the Doan's long-term sustainability. Nevertheless, few implementable decisions are ever made to improve and maintain the Doan

Table 7.1. Time Line of Doan Brook Events

Date	*Event*	*Key Parties Involved*
1960–1970	Proposed Clark and Lee freeways over the brook defeated by citizen opposition	Local citizens, press
1966	Shaker Lakes Regional Nature Center founded	Local citizens
1970	Joint Committee on Doan Brook formed	Nature Center members
1972	Northeast Ohio Regional Sewer District (NEORSD) formed to focus efforts on sanitary sewage interceptors and on improvements to the wastewater treatment plans	
1975	Velocity breaker and trash rack built near railroad bridge at Martin Luther King Jr. Boulevard; University Circle culvert cleaned after the flood (between 3000 and 5000 tons of debris removed)	City of Cleveland
1978	Water Quality Management Plan developed	Northern Ohio Area Coordinating Agency
	Repair of the Doan Brook culvert under Martin Luther King Jr. Boulevard	Ohio Department of Natural Resources
1979	Inventory and evaluation for Shaker Lakes	Soil Conservation Services
1990	Repair of Horseshoe Lake	Ohio Department of Natural Resources
1994	Dam built in Cleveland Heights in the western section of the gorge to slow down storm water in University Circle	Shaker Heights, Cleveland Heights, initiated by Cleveland Water Pollution Control Commissioner (with public opposition)
1995	Water Quality Task Force created to identify current storm water and water quality issues, to educate citizens, and to make suggestions	Joint Committee on Doan Brook
1997	New retention basin built downstream from Martin Luther King Jr. Boulevard to reduce the peak flow into culvert from the upper watershed	City of Cleveland
	Drainage pipe installed in Lower Shaker Lake	Shaker Heights, Cleveland Heights
1998	Year of the Brook, special events and courses to educate the public	Nature Center at Shaker Lakes
	NEORSD project	NEORSD, engineering and public participation consultants, Public Study Committee

(*continued*)

Table 7.1. *Continued*

Date	*Event*	*Key Parties Involved*
1999	Sewer improvements, interceptor built	Regular Dry-Weather Sampling Program, Cleveland Heights, University Heights, NEORSD
	Downspout disconnect pilot project	City of Shaker Heights
2000	Dredging of Lower Shaker Lake	City of Shaker Heights
2001	Conclusion of the NEORSD project	NEORSD, engineering and public participation consultants, Public Study Committee

watershed, although some short-term decisions do get carried out, at times regardless of their long-range impact.

The Nature Center at Shaker Lakes (NCSL), a small nonprofit located in a facility surrounded by parkland near one of the Shaker Lakes, has championed Doan Brook issues since the early 1970s. Although it lacks broad formal authority, it has been very active and influential in mobilizing residents around various municipal policy decisions and initiatives to protect and enhance the watershed. For example, in the late 1960s, citizen opposition organized by a small number of Nature Center–affiliated residents defeated proposed plans for the Clark and Lee freeways that would have crossed the brook and destroyed its lakes section. The leader of this effort, today in her nineties, is still a member of NCSL, scrupulously attending its meetings.

NCSL brings Doan Brook to the attention of its public through several education programs introducing schoolchildren to their natural environment, as well as programs for adults, a Web site, and various regularly scheduled and special public events. For instance, in 1998, it initiated the Year of the Brook, a series of ice cream socials at various locations along the Doan, offering watershed tours. In a related initiative, NCSL elicited the preferences of residents, interest groups, and elected officials regarding the future of the brook. Five watershed scenarios were considered and discussed, ranging from a return to the presettlement state to heavy recreational use. Although they disagreed heatedly with the watershed facts underlying the scenarios, and with each other, participants expressed overwhelming preference for the "middle-of-the-road" scenario entailing some restoration and continuation of the current passive recreation along the brook.

In 1970, a NCSL initiative established the Joint Committee on Doan Brook to serve in an advisory capacity and coordinate activities related to the

Shaker Lakes and Doan Brook. Since then, the Joint Committee has been a key communication vehicle for involved citizens. Along with the Nature Center, it has tried to play a role in the ecological and historical preservation and maintenance of the natural resources of the Doan watershed. Members include a councilperson from each of the three cities in the watershed (see Fig. 7.1) (two of whom take turns chairing the monthly meetings), service staff, residents, and individuals with special interests such as historic preservation, the environment, and city beautification. Cleveland's presence at meetings is scant—the occasional resident or service staff person. When queried about this seeming indifference of Cleveland officials toward a significant city asset, residents and nonprofit organization representatives argue that the right approach toward their involvement has not been taken, or that the officials have yet to be persuaded of the benefits of their participation.

During Joint Committee meetings, elected officials and service staff update participants on the status of various initiatives and decisions affecting Doan Brook. The participants have the opportunity to ask questions about decisions and programs and raise concerns that range from the kinds of plants and trees to be planted at various locations to identifying a strategy for drawing a management plan for the whole watershed. For instance, there is Joint Committee consensus on a preference for native species whenever the Heights' service departments acquire funding for planting in public spaces. Everyone also seems to find environmental education valuable, and many participate in the NCSL-organized environmental town meetings at which faculty from the local universities discuss the fine points of watershed quality and habitat.

The Joint Committee meetings are convivial and seem the perfect forum for information exchange. However, the cities and even individual residents still manage to surprise by making decisions that affect the brook without apprising the committee. And, the fact that the Joint Committee members are on board for a specific decision does not ensure widespread community awareness or consensus. For example:

- In early August 2000 the Shaker Heights residents complained about "Green Lake," one of the Shaker Lakes whose surface tends to get completely covered with algae the neighboring residents considered unsightly. The City Council chose to purchase and release in Green Lake a number of (expensive) sterile fish that would eat most plant life in that lake, including the surface algae. This expeditious solution is rather brutal from an ecological point of view. Should it succeed (it has failed in the past, when the algae-destroying fish were eaten by the snapping turtles before they performed their task), it would disrupt the lake's ecosystem, possibly destroying important wildlife including other fish and snapping turtles. This is a prime candidate for consultation in the Joint Committee. However, the Shaker City Council took the decision only a few days after a Joint Committee meeting at which it was not brought up despite the presence of a Shaker councilperson.

- In Spring 1999, two willow trees appeared mysteriously on a portion of one of the Shaker Lakes that can only be reached by boat. This gave rise to a lively debate at the Joint Committee meeting. A resident argued that the willow trees reflected the will of neighboring residents who found the bald, raised portion of the lake unsightly. Others argued that, whether beautiful or not, the area provided important habitat for a species of birds who preferred such bald spots and who would no longer nest there if the trees were left in place, a claim disputed by some. Still others argued that the issue was neither aesthetics nor bird habitat, but rather the proper process for making decisions about public land: can any resident displeased with the aesthetics engage in private landscaping of public land? The matter was settled not in this venue, but rather by the stealthy disappearance of the willows, later found (with the help of an anonymous tip to the Service Department) discarded in a resident's yard. The Shaker Service Department replanted the willows at a different location near the lakes.
- In 1998, NEORSD initiated an interceptor project to mitigate effects of the obsolete sewer structures in Cleveland Heights and update their capacity to handle the current loads. Although approved by the municipality, the project quickly faced the wrath of residents who were eventually going to benefit from the project. Those living in close proximity to the construction area (South Park and Fairmount Boulevard) arranged meetings and distributed handbills to voice their dissatisfaction. They labeled the large sewer project the "excrement expressway" and opposed it on grounds of inconvenience from the construction noise, and concerns for the safety of neighboring housing structures. The opposition caused delays although it could not in the end prevent the construction of the interceptor, which was mandated for compliance with EPA water quality regulations.

These incidents capture several symptoms of latent intractability in the Doan impasse.

- Comity is not to be mistaken for commitment: Years of debates, environmental education of the participants, and discussion of shared concerns have not yielded even a warning, either from those who are Joint Committee members or from the other decision makers, of the upcoming move to "clean" Green Lake using introduced fish. Neither was the Joint Committee the forum where the willow problem was resolved. Rather, in a pinch everyone acted unilaterally instead of building, or submitting to, a consensus.

- The long-standing eagerness of Heights city officials to please or appease residents results in short-term fixes disregarding long-term consequences, as the Green Lake incident illustrates.
- Heights residents can get organized quickly in opposition to a decision whose implementation is imminent, as in the interceptor incident. This bodes ill for any attempts to improve the watershed that will impose costs on the residents. Therefore, if there is no current overt opposition to the idea of a watershed management plan, it may only be because the plan does not appear on the verge of implementation.
- Those who would demand action to remediate the watershed, and who stand a good chance to be heard, tend to notice short-range inconveniences such as the greening of a lake, a bald spot, or (temporary) noise, but seem rather indifferent to the more serious, long-range problems of poor water quality and lack of biodiversity in the brook.

The Joint Committee experience and the three examples point to recurring problematic aspects of participation and representation in public decision processes even at a relatively moderate scale such as watershed planning for Doan Brook. Few community members, and fewer in Cleveland than in the Heights, can devote the time necessary for informed, educated, consistent participation in public decisions. Those who do self-select, and they have rather predictable demographic and socioeconomic characteristics that enable their participation, but not effective representation of any constituency, since the community at large does not share their preferences. Consequently, their sanction of a proposed plan is mostly an individual expression not predictive of community reactions. Hence the latent intractability—the seemingly active, amiable, and participatory debate among the few, coupled with the indifference of the many, who only react to imminent decisions, of which the watershed plan is not one.

In recent years, NCSL has led efforts to facilitate watershed management planning for Doan that would ensure the brook's long-term health. It has identified data, management, and funding needs, and has researched various model structures such as partnerships and watershed authorities, used successfully to manage other watersheds. The difficulties in this endeavor range from the public's indifference and lack of awareness, to NCSL's persistent lack of resources, to the reluctance of the three city administrations to join in the effort. NCSL is a leader lacking effective following, which is surprising given Doan Brook's rather long participatory history and the seeming consensus on needs. Had the Joint Committee members been selected with commitment to represent the watershed stakeholders, it might have become more effective at fostering implementable management decisions. However, their tasks might also have become rather difficult. Conflict might have surfaced owing to deep-seated differences to be described in what follows, in the demographics and governance styles of the three municipalities involved.

In early 1998, when NEORSD obtained an EPA grant to study the watershed, assess needs, and engage in facility planning and building to help the brook attain EPA-mandated water quality levels (Ross and Chard 1999), it undertook three major tasks: a sewer system evaluation survey, facilities planning, and public involvement.

To comply with EPA grant conditions requiring public participation, NEORSD hired a consultant who assembled a Study Committee that became the target audience for NEORSD's study findings and solution proposals. The committee consisted of about fifty participants from the three communities surrounding the watershed, including residents, special interest representatives, elected officials, and service staff. Several Joint Committee members, including the NCSL director, elected officials, and municipal service staff of the three cities; some of the residents; and some of the special interest participants became members of the NEORSD Study Committee. The consultant organized and facilitated monthly two-hour public meetings according to a plan, presented to all from the outset, for the two-year duration of the NEORSD project, which ended in early 2001.

The outcome of this project consists of a set of NEORSD-proposed solutions for the water quality problems, with Study Committee input on a preferred solution. Despite drastic differences in views that surfaced during the two-year deliberations, there is no overt conflict, but neither is there consensus on the future of the watershed or on the best ways to improve it.

In what follows, we focus on the NEORSD project, beginning with a description of its stakeholders. A large portion of the information derives from the authors' attendance at Joint Committee and Study Committee meetings. The illustrative statements woven in the narrative were selected from fifty sixty-to-ninety-minute interviews conducted with NEORSD staff, consulting engineers, members of the Doan Brook Study Committee convened by NEORSD in compliance with EPA's public participation requirements, and with members of the volunteer Joint Committee on the Doan Brook.

The Constituencies

The Heights

Residents of Shaker Heights and Cleveland Heights value the characteristic greenery notoriously lacking in the newer eastern suburbs that have by now completely enclosed them. In the words of a resident:

> I live in Shaker and come along the parkland and it's a real positive amenity. We are members of the community, so we do things there.‡ **[1]**§

With relatively high per capita incomes and educational attainment compared to Cleveland, Heights residents tend to see themselves as enlightened and environmentally aware:

> I think residents of Cleveland Heights or at least this neighborhood may be a lot more environmentally biased than the other suburbs. I think it's a part of why people are attracted to this place because there are more liberally minded people here.** **[2]**

They hike around the brook, watch birds, come to the yearly Regatta event on the lakes organized by the City of Shaker Heights, and ride their bikes along paths old and new that stop short of connecting with the lower watershed bike paths. In fall 1999, many came to enjoy the sight of a stranded pelican on one of the lakes, and offered to help pay for it to be airlifted to Florida. However, not many know that the Shaker Lakes are formed by a brook called Doan, or that the same brook runs through Rockefeller Park in Cleveland. Nor are most residents aware that water quality in the brook falls below EPA-established standards for urban watersheds.

Judging by the gardening activity (Shaker Heights calls itself "the Garden City" and has an annual Landmark Home and Garden Tour) and by the look of the numerous carefully groomed, green lawns, it is also likely that few residents are connecting their own actions—heavily fertilizing lawns, watering them generously, and applying sufficient amounts of pesticide to keep weeds at bay—with Doan's poor water quality. The soil has high clay content, so most of the lawn water quickly runs off, carrying with it the fertilizers and

---

‡ Nonprofit Organization 6, Interview, paragraph 14

§ In subsequent chapters, this quote will be referenced as "Doan Brook 1," and subsequent quotes from this chapter as "Doan Brook 2," "Doan Brook 3," etc.

** Resident 3, Interview, paragraph 12

pesticides into the sewer system and into the brook. While other municipalities in the country have successfully passed ordinances curtailing fertilizer and pesticide use on private property, this strategy has yet to be tried in the Heights, although both cities have discontinued pesticide use on public lands. Elected officials and service staff believe that asking residents to change their gardening habits would meet with strong opposition:

> We already had a pilot project of disconnecting downspouts of 800 houses in Mercer and we had to fight hard to make that happen and I don't think it is a clear success. There were residents who were very angry about it and there were people who went door-to-door and we had to figure out which downspouts to disconnect (some shouldn't be disconnected because they could cause worse problems). . . . A lot of residents don't want change. I still have people irritated with me about the whole thing. It's easy for private citizens to say let's do this. People want change but they don't if they have to do it.[††] **[3]**

Cleveland

Cleveland, largest among the three cities along the watershed in terms of area, population, and economic activity (see Fig. 7.1), owns the land around Doan Brook, which it leases to Shaker Heights for the symbolic price of $1 per year. Historically, however, the two suburbs have spearheaded most initiatives around brook problems. Cleveland residents have the lowest level of participation in the Doan Brook committees, and its city officials appear to lack interest and involvement in environmental issues. The residents perceive Doan Brook mostly as a source of safety hazards and bad odors, possibly originating in the upper watershed. Flooding during heavy rainfalls and the rapid course of the water through its channelized stretch at all other times have caused children to drown, unable to climb back after falling into the rapid stream.

As focus groups with residents and neighborhood organizations in Cleveland told us, it wasn't always this way. Residents used to stroll along the brook with their family, just like the people in the Heights. Less than fifty years ago, Rockefeller and Gordon Parks were popular with children and adults, who fished, boated, or strolled through. Although in recent years there have been significant physical improvements, especially in Rockefeller Park, the lower watershed went through several decades of neglect while the neighborhoods

---

[††] Elected Official 2, Interview, paragraph 46

around it deteriorated physically, socially, and economically. The parks are cleaner and likely safer now, and there are new bike paths along them. Still, residents' perception of the two parks as unsafe for children at play persists despite improvements. The lingering negative image deters residents from seeking recreation along the brook, although it is the only open, green space in that part of Cleveland. Few venture to the Heights to enjoy the safer scenic stretch of Doan. In fact, few are even aware of the brook:

> The highest ownership is where you go right near the edge of the water. You see less knowing [awareness] down in Rockefeller Park because the elevation is so different, you get those giant walls that go right up to East Boulevard, where there is almost no sense of ownership.[‡‡] **[4]**

Although suburban residents complain about the lack of participation of their inner-city counterparts, they are not unsympathetic to their own account of it:

> Lower income people have better things to do with their time in terms of basic survival. . . . Environmental issues are usually much more represented by upper middle class college educated white folks.[§§] **[5]**

However, they feel differently about the lack of involvement of Cleveland's city officials. Some think Doan Brook's environmental problems are not sufficiently important to Cleveland's leaders:

> The city of Cleveland has the scales tipped in their favor. It's very rare that you ever have the mayor of Cleveland sitting down and treating the suburban mayors as equals[***] **[6]**

Elected officials have a reputation for getting involved only when it serves them politically:

> I don't imagine the city of Cleveland would have any interest in creating an [watershed] authority because it would mean sharing power.[†††] **[7]**

---

‡‡ Facilitator 1, Interview, paragraph 20

§§ Nonprofit Organization 3, Interview, paragraph 114

*** Elected Official 1, Interview, paragraph 24

††† Facilitator 1, Interview, paragraph 30

Or:

> Mike White [the Mayor of Cleveland at the time] will make the decisions. At least in the City of Cleveland what happens to it is what he personally approves in general.‡‡‡ **[8]**

In this view, participation is tantamount to sharing power, which Cleveland's mayor does not see as necessary. His decision to build the (ineffective) dam despite strong opposition from neighboring residents is consistent with this view.

Cleveland's residents appear wary of "extreme" environmentalists whose concerns shift the focus from the day-to-day problems of the inner city:

> The extreme environmentalist to me is the one who considers people as a problem, an invader. I don't see how when you come in with that bias you'll be able to be swayed in any direction even with fact.§§§ **[9]**

On the other hand, some prefer an opinion, even if differing from their own, to none:

> I prefer persons who are interested even if they have different opinions because if they have the right motivation that can be useful.★★★★ **[10]**
>
> Whether from Cleveland or the Heights, residents participating in the NEORSD Study Committee tend to have moderate to low expectations that their views will have an impact on NEORSD's choice of solution. In contrast, the environmentalists and citizen activists believe they will be able to influence decisions with their expertise and involvement:
>
> I think it [the level of public participation] changed because I got mad at a meeting. . . . When the minutes came back and my concerns had been recorded in black and white, people heard me and had similar concerns and it was addressed.†††† **[11]**

However, few participants, when asked how the study-generated information would affect their decisions, could be specific or point to information-sensi-

‡‡‡ Nonresident Stakeholder 6, Interview, paragraph 28

§§§ Service Professional 3, Interview, paragraph 59

★★★★ Service Professional 4, Interview, paragraph 18

†††† Resident 5, Interview, paragraph 29

tive aspects of their solution choice. Rather, many seemed to have preferences for solution types that predated study results and their analysis. For example, residents and environmentalists seemed partial to approaches relying chiefly on behavior changes and small-scale facility retrofits, whereas engineers and city service staff leaned toward comprehensive engineered solutions. Should it come to decisions, such philosophical differences that are impervious to information would likely lead to open conflict.

In their debates over preferences and solutions, participants in the Study Committee as well as members of the Joint Committee on Doan Brook have come up against a baffling array of government agencies entitled to make decisions that affect the brook, mostly without an obligation to fund any action. Some are described in the following text.

The Agencies

Doan Brook is subject to several governmental entities besides the three municipal governments of the Heights and Cleveland. NEORSD, the Northeast Ohio Area Coordinating Agency (NOACA), the Ohio Department of Natural Resources (ODNR), and the EPA make decisions that can, and do, affect the fate of the brook. NEORSD has been most actively involved in brook issues, especially in recent years, as a result of the EPA-mandated attainment of water quality standards in urban watersheds. NOACA has regulatory and advisory jurisdiction; ODNR approves the engineering design of dams such as the one on Doan Brook, for which it issues permits; the Army Corps of Engineers issues permits for wetlands and for dredging parts of the brook; Ohio EPA has regulatory jurisdiction, and USEPA dictates various standards, chief among which is, for Doan Brook, water quality maintenance.

Action is difficult under such circumstances. For example, Cleveland, the Heights, and NEORSD have to coordinate any storm water management efforts. Most such work requires EPA and Army Corps of Engineers permits. Processing the paperwork for the necessary permits to drain and dredge the brook in 1999 took eight years. Such dredging is needed periodically, but is not an item in the budget of any of the cities involved (*Plain Dealer,* Nov. 13, 1998).

Although standards and permits affect Doan Brook considerably, they do not come funded. The only government units having to allocate funds for non-sewer-related brook projects are the three municipalities. Some Study Committee members understand the consequences:

> I think you have to go a step beyond and say whose problem is this? Until there is an organization to deal with problems as they come up and they are in charge and can get the money, until then you can have a hundred ideas about what to do and how, and even where to get the money, and you won't do it because there is no one in charge.[‡‡‡‡]**[12]**

Therefore, they recognize the need for an organizational framework and some clear lines of responsibility to make concerted decisions that benefit the brook. However, when asked who they think is, or should be, in charge of making and implementing decisions, respondents share only one conviction: that they themselves are not. Quite a few believe the NEORSD will eventually make the key decisions that matter in the watershed's future:

> Obviously the NEORSD will call the shots on any capital project under their direct control, subject to some input from the committee.[§§§§]**[13]**

Some think the three city governments are key in making and implementing decisions regarding Doan Brook. Others believe the individual property owners will have the most say in what gets implemented. What matters with respect to the latent intractability is the apparent lack of information and the divergence of views regarding how such decisions are made and by whom. Also significant is the broadly shared view that someone else, other than the respondent, is in charge. Nevertheless, despite the seeming confusion and widespread perception that someone else can, should, or will act, the NEORSD study has created an expectation among Study Committee participants that an implementable decision will be reached regarding brook improvements.

Although the NEORSD process focused on water quality, the database it assembled for this purpose was useful in helping understand the causes and extent of the water quantity, flooding, and poor habitat quality problems. Despite differing conceptualizations of the decision process, Study Committee members believed decisions had to be based on up-to-date information about the watershed. They had mostly positive feelings regarding the scientific component of the study, though some had more confidence than others in the

---

‡‡‡‡ Resident 13, Interview, paragraph 21

§§§§ Facilitator 2, Interview, paragraph 24

role such information should play in decisions. One city official particularly keen on data stated hopefully,

> I think when the study is complete there will be enough definitive information that it will essentially direct the course of action or some potential course of action. All the wish-lists and unrealistic expectations will have to fall by the wayside.***** **[14]**

In what follows we focus on the NEORSD study process.

The NEORSD Project

To explore ways in which it could best meet EPA water quality mandates for Doan Brook, NEORSD hired engineering firm Montgomery Watson (MW) for study, modeling, and solution design. MW began with an extensive data collection effort including topography, water and habitat quality indicators, and flow measurements. At the monthly meetings, they briefed the Study Committee on findings, analysis, and computer-aided modeling. For example, they produced a set of contour maps for the various flooding levels corresponding to levels of precipitation that occur in this area with known frequency. On these maps they simulated and tested the effectiveness of various flood remedies such as removing support walls in the lower watershed, or clearing culverts of debris. They also traced the source and pattern of combined sewer overflows, the main cause of brook water contamination.

NEORSD also funded several microstudies of alternatives to the conventional engineering solutions of storage, purification, and tunnel facilities. These included bioengineered devices for reducing bacteria counts, as well as best practices that might reduce the need for the large structures that are typically components of NEORSD solutions. Maryland's Center for Watershed Management evaluated the brook and surrounding areas for possible changes in municipal and resident practices to reduce flooding and bacteria loads in the stream. The Center proposed to test practices such as disconnecting roof downspouts, modifying existing parking lots and driveways to reduce the amount of rainwater flowing directly to the brook, and provision of in situ filtering capability for the runoff in parking lots. The success of this class of remedies is contingent on behavioral changes, some drastic, on the part of the residents, and also on management practice changes on the part of the munic-

***** Service Professional 3, Interview, paragraph 43

ipal service departments. Both categories are very difficult, if not impossible, to evaluate and monitor. They are also sensitive to the level of maintenance that municipalities are able to provide, requiring long-term commitment. Although reportedly such practices have proven beneficial elsewhere, it is difficult to estimate their collective costs and effects on the water quality of Doan Brook because of the design and maintenance contingencies:

> Another thing we hear is that if we disconnect downspouts it will have a mitigating effect. Again, when questions were asked and actual percentages were given, the effects were very small. So when I am asked to order our citizens to do some fairly onerous things, I am finding out they won't have that much effect.[†††††] **[15]**

NEORSD's tool kit, in contrast, consists of fairly large devices for which performance measures are readily available. The engineering team can provide information on costs and watershed benefits, and prefers the relatively high level of predictability and control afforded by such devices during construction and operation. They are, however, bulky and less than aesthetically pleasing. They involve massive traffic and residential disruptions during construction, though they are almost maintenance free for long periods of time.

The Study Committee contributed a watershed vision and prioritized the watershed problems and criteria for evaluating proposed alternatives in four problem areas:

- Wastewater collection system management
- Flood control
- Storm water management
- Biotic systems management

The criteria included:

- Economic impact—capital cost, operation and maintenance cost
- Environmental impact—pollution reduction, impact on habitat and stream flowing
- Feasibility of implementation—constructibility, permanent land requirements, public acceptance, institutional constraints, and siting restrictions
- Operability—operating complexity, flexibility, reliability, compatibility with other facilities, and impact on downstream facilities

---

††††† Elected Official 1, Interview, paragraph 18

- Sustainable management of Lake Erie, public awareness, monitoring, organizational structure, and financing

The Study Committee also formulated some guiding principles for the study and solution phase. One key principle stipulated a range of solutions, from heavily built ones relying solely on engineering devices designed and built by NEORSD to ones relying on both physical and behavioral changes at the community level. The engineering firm proposed to examine for each area of concern a "do-nothing" alternative, one indirect intervention, and one direct intervention (read engineered solution). Committee members weighed the pros and cons of different philosophical approaches. In the project's last phase the Study Committee evaluated the alternatives proposed by the engineering firm for dealing with each of the four problem areas. The participants were asked to compare the (extremely technical and detailed) NEORSD-proposed designs and provide suggestions.

NEORSD has limited authority and resources. It has responsibility, mandate, and expertise for dealing only with water quality issues, leaving without remedy many of the other problems identified in the study. These problems may benefit from NEORSD's implemented plan only by synergy, rather than through direct planning and investment in solutions tailored for them. Therefore, a watershed management plan becomes more necessary and urgent to enable collection and allocation of resources for responding to the orphaned needs while the data collected for this project are still current.

The Study Committee meetings have fostered a collaborative spirit among participants. Meeting attendance was steady, although each meeting was attended by a different subset of twenty-five to thirty-five participants. Committee participation from Cleveland remained scant. Despite the presence of both elected officials and residents, there persists an overall lack of awareness about Doan Brook in the communities, especially in the neighborhoods of Cleveland.

Study Committee and Joint Committee members shared the perception that joint problem solving depends on a holistic approach to the watershed:

> [A] localized fix is like a Band-Aid. I think it's important for the cities to work together. We are all connected in this way so you can't fix locally, it's not going to work.[‡‡‡‡] **[16]**

Most interviewees voiced a preference for a watershed authority to overcome

‡‡‡‡ Resident 14, Interview, paragraph 27

the morass of partial, overlapping authorities currently affecting Doan Brook. As one resident remarked,

> It would be amazing if we could form a watershed group whatever it's going to be called, political group, with taxing.[§§§§§]**[17]**

The NEORSD public participation initiative is quite unique for this agency and for the Doan Brook area. The District's inclusion effort has been genuine, with costs in effort and resources. In recognition, participants in the Study Committee are mostly pleased with the whole process. Many interviewees tended to focus on the ongoing attempts to reach a solution, their participation in the public meeting, and the attempts to reach consensus. For instance,

> The process is good—a whole bunch of people talking about solutions instead of each being its own entity. Sometimes you can just force diverse groups to work on an issue but that doesn't happen unless they want to be there, and that appears to happen with Doan Brook.[★★★★★★]**[18]**

Interestingly, they also believe the process will not necessarily lead to a solution:

> The process hasn't resolved any issues with the brook. It's been a process of examining and getting a better understanding of the brook. I am participating in the process knowing full well that the bottom line is money.[††††††]**[19]**

Nevertheless, they set stock on the process itself:

> We are blessed with having an extremely sophisticated work group at the Joint Committee on Doan Brook watershed as a backbone for citizen outreach.[‡‡‡‡‡‡]**[20]**

This apparent harmony is problematic for several reasons. The participatory model itself (likely not on purpose) has lulled the Study Committee into a comfortable consensus mode that has discouraged challenges, especially since many have been overwhelmed by the complex technical details and feel out of their depth when questioning computer modeling output

§§§§§ Resident 13, Interview, paragraph 16

★★★★★★ County Official 2, Interview, paragraph 81

†††††† Nonprofit Organization 1, Interview, paragraph 20

‡‡‡‡‡‡ Facilitator 1, Interview, paragraph 19

or engineering designs. Residents and special interest committee members represent strictly themselves, with no duties to report to any constituency. The lack of community awareness about the brook's problems and the NEORSD project is therefore not accidental. The Study Committee's sanction of any solution is deceptive: it is due in no small measure to the fact that many feel either that no decision is imminent or that NEORSD will end up doing what it always does to resolve water quality problems. The history of the two suburbs' effectiveness in opposing implementation of projects makes it unlikely that any plans that will catch the communities by surprise or will impose costs or inconvenience will be implemented.

The interviews with Study Committee and Joint Committee on Doan Brook members yielded fifty different, detailed snapshots of their struggle to make implementable remedial decisions for the watershed. Since the interviewees came from three different cities and fall into nine categories of interests and roles (see Note on Sources and Table 7.2), their differences should not surprise: each respondent has a unique history, experience, and outlook on the environment in general and on Doan Brook problems in particular. However, while this is common to environmental conflicts, not all are either latent or intractable. We probe next how the respondents' frames relate to the observed long-term, peaceful impasse despite consensus on the need for action to remedy Doan Brook.

Table 7.2. Interviewees Grid

Stakeholder Groups	*The City of Cleveland*	*The City of Cleveland Heights*	*The City of Shaker Heights*	*Total*
Service professionals	1	1	3	5
Elected officials	0	1	1	2
County service employees				4
Regional agencies				6
Facilitators of the public participation process	0	2	0	2
Nonresident stakeholders				6
Nonprofit organizations	3	0	3	6
Nonaffiliated professionals	2	2	0	4
Residents	2	7	6	15
Total				50

Analysis

Can the respondents' frames—their sense-making regarding their own identity, other parties involved, and the decision-making process—account for the persistent impasse? Stakeholders frame each other largely in positive terms, but construe needs, solutions, and responsibilities quite differently. Based on their responses, we propose that the observed unusually collaborative atmosphere that fails to yield implementable decisions is rooted in the interaction between generally positive characterizations of self and others, based partly on mutual recognition of shared demographics and interests, coupled with differences in how stakeholders believe the conflict should be resolved, and by whom.

Identity Frames

The interviews revealed that respondents often held more than one of the institution, interest, role, and place-based identity frames (Fig. 7.2). Place-based identity, rooted in the location of either residence or work, seems widespread among all. NEORSD-affiliated parties tend to express institutional identity. Role identity frames were found especially among elected officials and service staff. Residents and environmentalists who got involved in order to protect some key interest, such as quality of life or a habitat, held interest-based frames. These identities often mapped into predictable preferences for proposed solutions.

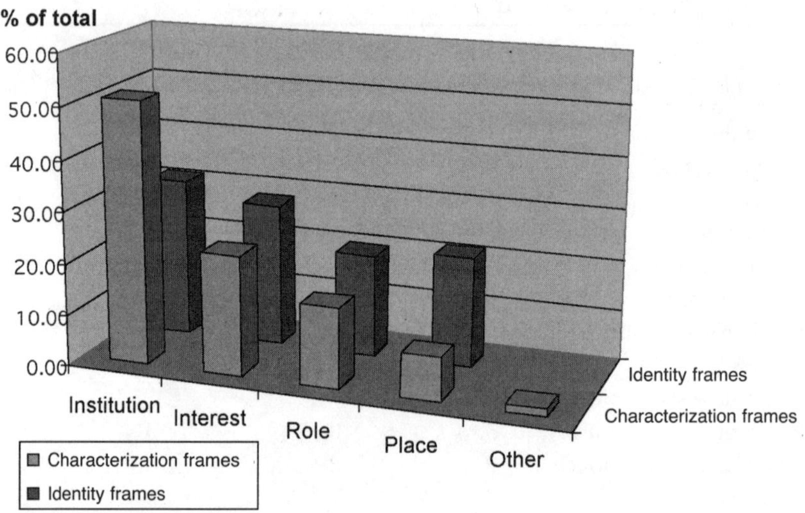

Figure 7.2. Characterization and Identity Frames by Role

Although we might expect only residents to hold place-based identity frames, others did too, possibly due to the nature of their roles. Municipal service staff members, for example, also relate strongly to place, even if they reside elsewhere than where they work, as many did. This is particularly significant here, since there are some considerable differences between Cleveland and its two suburbs. Suburban residents tend to refer to their involvement with the Doan Brook in terms of the many years they have been around it. They often express a sense of responsibility for the community resource tinged with proprietorship. **[1]** In contrast, when Cleveland residents voice their concerns about the brook, they tend to focus on the problems they face every day. Annoyance comes through more than pride of ownership, partly due to the lower homeownership rate and the higher transience. **[4]**

Most respondents representing agencies also identify very strongly with their institutions. This frame is present not only among the municipal, county, and regional officials, but also among nonprofit and nonresident stakeholders, although not everyone's involvement in the committee is due to professional affiliation. Some mentioned their strong identification with the mission, or the concerns, of their respective organizations.

Respondents with mainly environmental concerns tend to hold interest-based identity frames: They worry about losing Doan Brook as a (passive) recreation resource and consider themselves environmentalists or citizen activists on behalf of the watershed. Most of them believe in their own efficacy and ability to influence decisions with their expertise and involvement. **[11]** They were not numerous in the two committees, however, which may account for the lack of confrontation between them and the equally underrepresented Cleveland residents who tended to prefer remedies such as rebuilding the crumbling sustaining walls in the lower watershed, which environmentalists consider unwise. The consulting engineers explored removing lower watershed structures to restore the brook's natural floodplain, a strategy thought to alleviate the unsafe water speed and flooding risks, and the odor problems. There was a widespread sense that such a solution would be quite unpalatable to Cleveland residents because of their perception (expressed by some) that it would benefit others, such as University Circle's businesses, at their expense. **[5]**

Some environmentally oriented respondents also flirted with the possibility of opening the University Circle culvert to "out" the brook. At the time this alternative did not get much attention, appearing unrealistic due to costs, as well as traffic disruptions in one of the city hubs. However, a confluence of events made it suddenly viable. Construction of a new airport runway, a project dear to Cleveland's mayor, requires the culverting of another brook. To secure culverting permits, the City has to compensate by restoring another urban watershed. Opening the Doan culvert in University Circle became a prime candidate. Although this would be a large-scale undertaking, some environmentalists with interest-based identity opted for it, as a symbolic small step toward returning the brook to the earlier natural state of the watershed, which seems to have intrinsic value for them independent of other watershed consequences.

Committee members with different identity frames seldom confronted each other over their differences in the meetings. This contributed further to the latency of the conflict, by obscuring any differences. Should solution implementation become imminent, however, the place-, institution-, and role-based identities are sufficiently different and strongly held to bring out the conflict. Cleveland residents' long-held resentment regarding the perceived privileges of suburban residents may surface then. Service staff might openly disagree with the environmentalists' design and behavioral change schemes. Heights residents might oppose large-scale construction in their neighborhoods.

Characterization Frames

Characterization of others (see Table 7.3) evinces the same civility as the live-and-let-live identity frames. The characterization frames are mostly mild, possibly due to the reality of the convivial committee meetings in contrast to the unreality of the heavily technical solutions whose consequences are difficult to derive at a glance. Institutional characterizations were most frequent, followed by interest, role, and place (see Fig. 7.2).

Those claiming to represent environmental interests were targets of mildly negative characterization, especially from those who by institutional affiliation have to deal daily with concrete technical watershed problems (engineers and service staff). Some expressed weariness of the enthusiasm of those with strong environmental interests, but also some admiration for their intensity of purpose. **[9, 10]**

NEORSD has been correctly viewed by many as a key institution in the study process. Both it and the Nature Center benefit in general from a positive image. Not so the City of Cleveland, although this did not affect the characterization of its residents. Although the Heights residents and officials agree on the lack of participation by Cleveland city officials, opinions differ regarding the reasons. Some feel the issues around Doan Brook are not important to

Table 7.3. Characterization and Identity Frames Frequency by Role

	Characterization Frames		*Identity Frames*	
Categories	*Number*	*Percentage*	*Number*	*Percentage*
Institution	72	51.06	39	30.95
Interest	33	23.40	35	27.78
Role	22	15.60	25	19.84
Place	12	8.51	27	21.43
Other	2	1.42		
Total	141		126	

the Cleveland authorities. Others, especially in the Heights, see the Cleveland City Hall as tough, big, and with resources to do what it pleases, acting mainly for political advantage. The City's pattern of lack of involvement in meetings and decisions regarding the watershed has been accounted for by widely shared images of a heavy political machine that acts unilaterally and does not believe in consultative processes, with unwanted consequences for all its neighbors. **[6, 7, 8]**

In contrast, city residents are viewed with empathy **[5, 6]** and compassion for their economic and social problems that may well be exaggerated by lack of direct contact. Suburban knowledge of Cleveland residents' woes is likely mediated by evening television news and newspaper accounts, rather than derived from experience. Therefore, characterizations may tend to make allowances for an idealized image of poor Cleveland neighborhoods, perceived as less safe, more economically deprived, and more physically deteriorated than in reality. This is reciprocated by Clevelanders' characterization of elitist, self-focused suburbs, suggesting that some mutual reacquaintance is in order.

Many, regardless of their location, see the Heights residents and politicians as more active and interested in the watershed issues. They believe the two suburbs have more political clout than Cleveland and consequently will have the most voice and impact in any decision regarding the brook. **[2]** Some even count Cleveland out of the decision process, while others think the only way to resolve the brook issue is to get the attention of Cleveland's Mayor White, seen by many as Cleveland's sole decision maker. **[8]**

Do these frames play any role in the observed latent intractability of the Doan conflict? They may affect both the form and the substance of this conflict in several ways. For example, Cleveland residents' passive hostility toward the suburbanites, who reciprocate with misplaced paternalistic empathy, is not conducive to dialogue and consensus building. Although not openly expressed, there is a racial subtext to place-based mutual characterizations by residents, facilitated by the predominance of African Americans in the lower watershed. Although service staff showed more mutual familiarity and less hostility, they too tend to hold characterization frames about each other's political framework that may impede genuine collaborative processes, in which differences are acknowledged.

Conflict Management Frames

The majority of respondents adhered to a fact-finding frame. They claimed to value scientific information and research results to reach a decision. More than a third of respondents mentioned their trust in decisions based on data, **[12]** although most were unable to specify in what ways the NEORSD data inform their choices. Those who tended to prefer the "gentler" local solutions to the engineering ones also believed that the NEORSD-proposed alternatives will be rooted in the data and information NEORSD has collected, along with other experience and knowledge. Overall, many respondents adhered descriptively (regarding the current process) and normatively to a joint problem-solving frame, and talked about participation and alternatives. **[13]**

A number of people expect an agency in authority to decide, but remain vague about who this "authority" is, though when respondents use the term "authority" they usually mean either NEORSD or the city governments. Most believe the "authority" decides based on mandate; **[14]** some think that the "authority" will decide after consultation with the Study Committee, and although the final choice belongs to NEORSD's board, it will be influenced by everyone else in the committee; others believe the "authority" will base its decision on expertise.

Respondents expressed preference for a watershed authority (but lack of expectation that it will happen). **[17]** Many would prefer to see watershed problems handled by the passing of laws and regulations. It is unclear whether those in either category thought about the financial consequences of their preferred way of handling the conflict. A small number of respondents believe that all depends on what individual property owners decide, and they trust the market economy will resolve Doan Brook's problems.

Other Frames

The whole story frame—what it's all about—sheds some light on which aspects of this latent conflict are most salient to respondents: the issues at stake or the decision-making process. Those (few) whose whole story frame focuses on issues tend to pay more attention to the outcome of the conflict. They have definite expectations regarding the solutions, mostly focused on flood problems. Most respondents hold whole story frames focused on the ongoing attempts to reach a solution, on their participation in the public meeting, and on the efforts to reach a consensus. **[18, 20]** Although procedural uncertainty is high in general and in this project, citizens are not as a rule suspicious of efforts by government agencies to bring them to the negotiation table. For them, the public meetings offer access to information and open a rare avenue for participation. Irrespective of the level of influence the individual members expect to exert on the outcomes, involvement in community decisions seems to be highly satisfactory to everyone.

The outlook frames identify individuals' preferences for various solution scopes—total, partial, or specific. People holding total-solution frames value solutions for the whole watershed. **[16]** Partial-solution frames denote a preference or tolerance for different solutions for each part of the watershed, reached by consensus. Those holding such a frame prefer solutions agreeable to most, even if not comprehensive. People with specific-solution frames also believe in partial solutions, but seek to reach a decision by prioritizing problems rather than by consensus. For example, some respondents have mentioned flooding and safety issues as their priority. It is worth noting that individuals voicing these concerns belong to all stakeholder groups, although Cleveland residents are the only ones who suffer from the flooding. Everyone, whether directly affected or not, agrees that some watershed problems are more serious than others.

The conflict over Doan Brook is not resolved in the Study Committee not because the parties are not willing to reach an agreement or do not hold strong views and wishes, but because raising controversial issues does not appear to serve anyone's interest when implementation expectations are low. **[19]** The local media's lack of interest in a uniquely participatory process that could impact a large number of people in the Cleveland area is symptomatic of the perceived low likelihood of implementation.

NEORSD's project brought together stakeholders from the entire watershed, and EPA encourages watershed-based solutions. However, in this case, except for poor water quality, different sections of the brook have different problems that require different solutions and can be addressed almost independently of the other sections. That is, almost any improvement measure implemented in the Heights can only benefit the lower watershed, and no action in the lower watershed can inconvenience the suburban section. However, inaction is damaging to all. Interdependence, which usually makes debate and problem solving necessary, is obscured in this case by the possibility of unilateral action. Unfortunately for the brook and its neighbors, inaction yields a default outcome requiring no effort at joint decision making. Although it appears cost-free, this is arguably the costliest outcome to the communities in the long run, in terms of loss of resources and long-run costs of compliance with EPA regulation. In contrast, any remedial action involves resources and effort in the short run. It is quite a typical environmental quandary, lacking only a crisis or vocal advocates to become protracted. It seems latent intractability in environmental disputes is in some ways more insidiously damaging than open conflict, and more difficult to diagnose and tackle for lack of overt symptoms.

Conclusions

Understanding the dynamics of latent environmental conflicts can also help other classes of public decisions that face similar difficulties when trying to change the status quo, ranging from short-term flare-ups when personal convenience is threatened to long-term indifference toward ongoing deterioration.

Might the persistent dissonance between the apparent consensus in committees and the actual stalemate disappear if participation were broadly representative of the three communities' makeup? Although such participation is extremely difficult to achieve, it could surface some of the real barriers to action that currently held process frames are obscuring. It might help overcome them by identifying realistic responsibility lines and mutually acceptable structures that could implement collective decisions. It also has to be recognized, however, that despite the best efforts, even if genuine participation can be achieved, or perhaps because of it, some conflicts do remain intractable for long periods of time.

Note on Sources

Nine groups of stakeholders have been identified:

Service professionals: Service staff of Cleveland, Cleveland Heights, and Shaker Heights, involved in day-to-day environmental problems related to Doan Brook. They have access to information and to the economic and political resources of the cities.

Elected officials: Elected representatives on the city councils involved in policy issues regarding Doan Brook. They have considerable voice in the allocation of economic resources, and access to political resources of the cities.

Regional agencies: Agency and technical staff at the regional level, mandated with broad responsibilities that affect the planning and implementation of decisions concerning Doan Brook.

County service employees: Officials directly or indirectly involved in different service aspects (for example, sanitation) of the Doan Brook.

Nonresident stakeholders: Individuals sharing some of the residents' concerns and interests in the watershed, but not living near it.

Nonprofit organizations: Agencies around the watershed with a concern for Doan Brook and other environmental issues. Though they lack formal power, they are active as community representatives and are considered a major voice in their respective areas.

Nonaffiliated professionals: Outside experts indirectly involved with the Doan Brook situation based on their interests and concerns.

Residents: The citizenry of the three cities who will be directly affected by what happens in the Doan Brook, irrespective of their level of involvement in the decision process.

Facilitators of the public participation process: Individuals hired by the NEORSD to design and facilitate the meetings and workshops of the NEORSD Study Committee.

The focus groups were conducted with Cleveland residents and neighborhood associations in 2001. Led by one of the authors, the purpose was to promote interest in and resources for partnering with the Nature Center in restoring and maintaining Doan Brook.

Chapter 8

Portraits of Self and Others: State-Level Conflict over Water Regulation in Ohio

Carolyn Wiethoff, Roy J. Lewicki, and Craig Davis

> There is no meaningful environmental benefit. It [antidegradation] only results in delayed projects, duplicative work, [and] increased state bureaucracy, and fosters ill will between the development community and the [Ohio Environmental Protection] Agency.
>
> —Regulated Caucus Member **[1]***
>
> I find the idea of hurting economic growth [with antidegradation] laughable. With more protection, we get more growth. Environmental protection doesn't hurt growth, it enhances it.
>
> —Environmental Caucus Member **[2]**

In 1972, the U.S. Congress enacted the Clean Water Act to set specific limits on the amount of pollutants that a "point source" could discharge into the natural environment.† The act set a goal of "zero" discharge of pollutants, requiring individual states to define the water quality standards to which their dischargers must adhere. Based on this and subsequent legislation, state-level water quality standards (WQS) must:

1. include "use designations" for waters subject to the act, specifying how certain waters can be used in a manner that is at least as protective of water quality as existing uses;
2. specify water quality criteria sufficient to protect the designated uses; and
3. have an acceptable antidegradation policy.

* In subsequent chapters this quote will be referenced as "Ohio 1," and subsequent quotes from this chapter as "Ohio 2," "Ohio 3," etc.

† The act defines "point source" broadly to mean "any discernable, confined and discrete conveyance," such as a "pipe, ditch or channel" (Clean Water Act 33, U.S.C. 1311 and 1342).

Antidegradation policies ensure that the state agency allows water quality to decline only if this decline will result in important economic or social development. If water quality in any location is better than what is needed for the existing use designation, the policy allows for water quality to be degraded only if the person or company applying for a permit can prove that their project(s) would significantly enhance the economic and/or social environment in the surrounding area (Mullins and Vertrees 1995). An "acceptable" policy is one that sets high standards for this proof and requires each state to involve members of the general public in the process of deciding where, and by how much, water quality may be degraded.

This chapter describes a single episode in the ongoing debates over antidegradation standards. We begin with a brief overview of antidegradation policies and then introduce our setting: the Ohio Environmental Protection Agency's (OEPA) Antidegradation External Advisory Group (EAG). To provide snapshots of this dispute, we will then focus on three significant exchanges that took place during the group's tenure. We conclude with a description of the insights this conflict provides concerning the power of framing to create and sustain intractable disputes.

Overview of Antidegradation Policies

Generally, when water quality is better than that allowed by a state's WQS, the state's environmental agency may accommodate economic growth by granting permits that lower surface-water quality. States cannot grant permits that would lower water quality to the point where minimally safe environmental standards are no longer met. They are also required to protect the existing designated use of a waterway and extend extraordinary protection to "high-quality waters constituting an outstanding national resource" (Healy 1997, n. 44).

A state's antidegradation standards take effect only when the state environmental agency determines that a proposed project will degrade water quality. A common criticism of these programs is that the rules, though stringent enough on their face, are not actually applied by state agencies in every condition where water quality would be lowered beyond existing levels. Significant controversy exists as to when these policies should be applied and which permit requests will be subjected to antidegradation review standards.

Despite a large amount of attention and controversy fueled by these regulations, national studies reveal that 25 to 44 percent of the nation's surface water is not in compliance with state-mandated WQS, largely as a result of state agencies' failure to require antidegradation reviews for all projects that would lower water quality (Healy 1997). As a result, environmental advocacy groups have frequently filed lawsuits against both the U.S. and state EPAs. The suits seek to force these agencies to use the stringent guidelines and careful permitting practices required by their antidegradation policies in a wider variety of permit application reviews. As a result of this scrutiny, many state EPA branches have spent a significant amount of time and effort updating and maintaining their WQS and permit application procedures in response to court decisions (Chilson 1999).

The Ohio Environmental Protection Agency's External Advisory Group

The situation in Ohio is typical of those found throughout the country. The OEPA is required to submit updates to their antidegradation rules every three years. In 1992, the Agency's proposed changes were challenged in court by environmental groups who maintained that the Agency's plan for administering antidegradation permits had a number of legal and procedural flaws. Subsequently, the Ohio Supreme Court ruled in *Columbus and Franklin County Metropolitan Park District* v. *Shank* (1992), 65 Ohio St. 2d 86 *"Metro Parks"*) that OEPA was required to review every project that resulted in an increase in the amount of pollutants discharged. The language in the *Metro Parks* decision was a significant victory for environmentalists. It required the OEPA to conduct a full antidegradation review (including a detailed social and economic justification for the proposed project) for any project that would result in an increased amount of pollutants being put into the water, even if the project would not degrade the ambient water quality. Environmentalists' positions were strengthened when, in response to a second court challenge in 1997, the court ruled in *Rivers Unlimited, Inc.* v. *Schregardus* (1997), 86 Ohio Misc. 2d 78, 685 N.E. 2d 603 (*"Rivers Unlimited"*) that the OEPA's antidegradation policies remained inadequate, since the Agency was still using antidegradation review procedures only for projects threatening water quality deterioration that interfered with the designated use of the waterway. Again rejecting this interpretation of the code, the court held that "degradation" was defined as any increased amount of pollutant added to a waterway, and that all projects proposing such increases should be subjected to antidegradation review. This ruling strengthened the environmentalists' position in Ohio, but created what one OEPA representative called an "administrative nightmare." Because of the cost and time involved in a full antidegradation review, both the OEPA and those regulated by them wished to find a way to work under less stringent guidelines in the permitting process.

The *Metro Parks* and *Rivers Unlimited* cases generated a significant amount of press coverage in Ohio, pitting environmentalists and developers against one another in both local and statewide battles. Environmental groups began closely monitoring OEPA's permit application reports and filing injunctions against the Agency to force antidegradation reviews on any project that potentially would increase, by any amount, pollutants discharged to a stream. The notion of "one molecule of a pollutant" as the trigger for an antidegradation review became a realized dream for environmentalists and a nightmare for those seeking permits from the OEPA.

Naturally, court battles, injunctions, and public debates over individual permit specifications created a significant amount of tension over antidegradation rules in Ohio. In an attempt to mitigate this tension, address stakeholders' concerns more proactively, and resolve a large number of injunctions that blocked permitting, the OEPA decided to involve stakeholders in the 1999 revision of the antidegradation rules. Stakeholder involvement was a relatively new, yet potentially powerful, tool for the OEPA. In 1993, the Agency received a grant to explore a new mediation strategy that would facilitate public involvement in its rulemaking procedures. At that time, the Agency successfully used professional facilitators to move disputing parties toward the joint development of comprehensive rules on construction and demolition debris facilities. Building on this success, OEPA again hired outside facilitators to guide a stakeholder group through the process of developing rules to implement the Great Lakes Water Quality Initiative in Ohio's Lake Erie Basin. Through a series of meetings during 1996 and 1997, the group reached consensus on 80 percent of the issues they discussed; the rules were subsequently adopted with minimal opposition and no legal challenge (O'Leary, Yandle, and Moore 1999). Buoyed by this outcome, the OEPA's Division of Surface Water convened three additional groups in 1998 to discuss planned revision to rules covering water quality standards for the Ohio River drainage basin, total maximum daily load allocations,‡ and antidegradation. The OEPA formally identified its EAGs "as a means to educate and build consensus on controversial program issues" and

‡ "A TMDL [Total Maximum Daily Load] is a written, quantitative assessment of water quality problems in a water body and contributing sources of pollution. It specifies the amount a pollutant needs to be reduced to meet water quality standards (WQS), allocates pollutant load reductions, and provides the basis for taking actions needed to restore a water body" (OEPA 2000).

promised to "consider the recommendations of the EAGs when revising appropriate rules and programs" (OEPA 2000).

In March 1998 the OEPA sent written invitations to approximately 35 individuals throughout Ohio to participate on an EAG to discuss planned revisions to the state's antidegradation rules. Twenty-two individuals from a variety of organizations agreed to participate. At the initial planning meeting for the group held in April 1998, the OEPA formally identified each participant as a member of one of two distinct groups: the Environmental Caucus or the Regulated Caucus. Members of the Environmental Caucus included representatives from The Nature Conservancy, Rivers Unlimited, the Izaak Walton League, and a variety of environmental protection organizations. Members of the Regulated Caucus included representatives from the Ohio Home Builders Association, major municipalities in the state of Ohio, major utilities, chemical and other manufacturers, and law firms who typically advise and represent these groups in environmental litigation.

Each member of the Regulated Caucus was a designated representative of an established entity, expected to represent their group's interests in the EAG. Initially, OEPA envisioned separating this group into two distinct entities: one focused on point source issues, composed of industry representatives, and another focused on non-point-source issues, composed of homebuilders and representatives from municipalities.[§] However, participants at the initial meeting agreed that these groups generally shared a similar role; hence, they would band together into one caucus, even though some specific issues were not shared by all parties. Still, it was not uncommon to hear a Regulated Caucus member from the homebuilders association (who was mainly concerned with the permitting of non-point-source pollution) comment, "this part of the rule doesn't really impact our projects anyway" **[3]** when the discussion turned to point source allocation issues.

In addition to their somewhat strained coalition, Regulated Caucus members also had specified agency roles (based on their formal positions as legal representatives or "agents" of other entities) that occasionally constricted their participation. Six of the thirteen people assigned to the Regulated Caucus were attorneys; two of these individuals had been formally engaged to represent a client (or group of clients) on the EAG. Most of the members of the Regulated Caucus felt pressure to act as pure agents for their sponsoring organizations. As one attorney put it,

---

§ Non-point-source pollution is that which enters surface waters from no discernible point of origin, such as pesticides from lawns or salt from highway maintenance projects.

> [What is] frustrating for me [is when] my clients haven't taken an interest in advocating a position one way or another. So I sit there . . . I have my own personal opinions, but it is probably inappropriate for me to participate in that fashion. **[4]**

Naturally this was not the case for all representatives. Another attorney remarked in his interview,

> I have great autonomy with regard to my clients. I have their confidence and where it's necessary to accommodate or compromise that's generally okay with them. And when I draw the line, I'm generally supported. **[5]**

On the other hand, Environmental Caucus members typically belonged to more than one environmental group and were not expected to represent the interests of one particular association. Their charge was to argue generally for environmental protection. As one environmentalist put it,

> I'm not coming into this as a representative from a certain organization. Our premise is that we are here to clean the water of the state, maintaining good water quality and increasing that that is of poor quality. **[6]**

Occasionally, both the OEPA and the Regulated Caucus commented that the Environmental Caucus's role was to represent the broader public interest in the EAG process. Though environmentalists would occasionally acknowledge this as a reasonable expectation (e.g., "Well, our constituency, the public, has a right to be informed" **[7]**), they more often rejected the idea that they were agents of the public interest. As one Environmental Caucus member put it in his interview,

> Who is representing the individual landowners along these creeks that are all going to get more pollution? Do you see anybody there? They're not there. So we, the environmentalists, are supposed to be the third leg of this uneven stool [of the regulated caucus and OEPA]. We're not. We can't be. We can try. I tried desperately to represent the public interest. But we can't. **[8]**

Another caucus member noted in the April 1999 meeting,

> There's a difference in representative levels. Your clients know their jobs. We don't presume to speak for the public. **[9]**

The group began regular meetings in May 1998 and was scheduled to convene monthly.** A small consulting firm was employed to facilitate the group's activities. Meetings usually included eight to ten members of each of the two caucuses, who tended to sit on opposite sides of a U-shaped configuration of tables. Though cochairs had been elected by each caucus, there were usually no formal spokespersons for either group. The two facilitators and senior members of the OEPA sat at the open end of the horseshoe. Other OEPA members and observers (including one representative from a local newspaper who attended all of the meetings) sat in a ring of chairs outside the horseshoe.†† Working with OEPA, the consultants generated a monthly meeting agenda. The OEPA provided the group with "position papers" on proposed rule changes and modifications that were to be debated. Notes were taken on flip charts, and minutes of the meeting were produced. Each caucus met separately over a working lunch to discuss strategy and tactics, and key members regularly conferred with one another between meetings.

At the initial EAG meeting, OEPA identified ideal outcomes of the EAG process as (a) reaching consensus agreement on proposed changes to the existing antidegradation rule, and (b) achieving better understanding of the rule to allow more effective use of OEPA's resources (Novak 1998). The OEPA pledged to incorporate recommendations from the EAG into their proposed rule revisions on only those points where the two groups reached explicit consensus. On other issues, the Agency would note that the caucuses "agreed to disagree" and take their comments and concerns as advisory when drafting their proposal for revision. The Agency was committed to having all positions voiced during the EAG meetings.

The group spent its first two meetings identifying and prioritizing antidegradation issues to be discussed. OEPA took the EAG's recommendations for areas in which the rule could be revised and added their own concerns. The result was a detailed proposal for forty-three rule revisions. The group was charged with examining proposed revisions in three general areas: (a) the overall applicability of the law, and the types of projects to which it would and would not apply, (b) the process by which permits should be reviewed and

---

** Five meetings were canceled by OEPA owing to an office relocation and other administrative issues. Seventeen meetings were held from May 1998 to April 2000.

†† Owing to state regulations, all meetings were open to the public. However, meetings were not widely advertised, and access to the building in which the meetings were held was controlled by security.

evaluated, and (c) the manner in which water use designations would be determined and the extent of special protection that should be extended to particularly High Quality Waters (a specific EPA designation). The applicability question required the group to determine if all projects that increased discharge should be covered by antidegradation, even if they had little chance of resulting in the lowering of water quality. A number of specific types of projects were debated, including storm water drainage, temporary construction sites, and nonpoint pollution sources. The most significant *process* issue was the degree to which the public should be involved in the permitting process. Additionally, the question of how a project would be determined to have sufficient social and economic impact to justify the degradation of water was hotly debated. Finally, questions about the designation of High Quality Waters included the criteria for identifying a body of water as Superior High Quality or Outstanding High Quality, or, similarly, as being specially designated for extra protection under antidegradation law. EAG members also debated whether and how the waters downstream from a specially designated river should be protected.

Conflict Incidents in the External Advisory Group

Rather than presenting the full eighteen months of EAG deliberations in detail, this chapter focuses on three significant exchanges that occurred during our investigation of the group that shed light on the various frames developed by participants in this dispute. First, we will describe an EAG debate over a legislative bill regulating ditches in the state, an issue that was seen as the purview of the EAG. Second, we examine the process by which the group debated the use of surrogate parameters to test for specific pollutants as an example of their handling of technical issues. Finally, we focus on the debate over the antidegradation rule's applicability.

The Ohio Legislature Ditch Bill: The First External Advisory Group Crisis

Two days before the EAG's fourth meeting a local newspaper, the *Columbus Dispatch,* ran a story discussing OEPA's endorsement of an amendment to a bill in the Ohio legislature that would set water quality standards for ditches. Participants from the Environmental Caucus were outraged, believing that OEPA had circumvented the EAG process and taken their concerns directly to the legislature without citizen input. Though OEPA representatives explained that the Agency's actual endorsement of the amendment had been made before the EAG had been convened, the Environmental Caucus formally asked OEPA for assurance of the Agency's "good faith effort" toward the EAG process. Representatives from the Environmental Caucus interrupted the EAG's preliminary discussion of administrative matters at the October 8, 1998, meeting to raise their concerns and request a remedy.

The facilitators elected to acknowledge the concern but continue with the planned agenda, assuring the Environmental Caucus members that the issue would be addressed later in the day. The meeting then continued with a discussion of the technical issues and OEPA position papers planned for that day. Environmental Caucus members grudgingly participated in the open session, but once they convened in caucus for lunch, it was obvious that their concerns had not been allayed by a promise of future discussion. The Caucus agreed to ask that the entire EAG write a letter to the legislature expressing their displeasure with the process by which the ditch amendment had been introduced and endorsed. They agreed that the letter should not address the specifics of the legislation, but should reflect only the EAG's and OEPA's commitment to the EAG process. Environmental Caucus members were acutely aware of questions about the legitimacy of the EAG process. They agreed that without some formal expression of good faith from both OEPA and the Regulated Caucus, they no longer wished to participate in the EAG. As one member put it,

> We want antidegradation issues addressed at EAG meetings, not in professional lobbying groups or in the media. The process is being circumvented by this legislation, and I just don't like the thought of participating in a useless process. **[10]**

Ultimately, the group agreed that they would walk out of the afternoon meeting if the issue was not addressed to their satisfaction.

When the two caucuses reconvened in an open meeting after lunch, the Environmental Caucus formally asked the Regulated Caucus and the OEPA to join them in writing a letter to the ditch bill's sponsors. The letter would simply indicate that the regulation of water quality in ditches should be the purview of the EAG, and that moving the debate on this issue outside of the EAG forum thwarted the group's process. OEPA representatives agreed to take the group's concerns to the Agency director, and Environmental Caucus members volunteered to draft a letter to the sponsors of the bill. The group then turned its attention to the technical issues of the day: groundwater remediation, surrogate parameters for testing for pollutants, and the role of general permits in the antidegradation review process.

The proposed letter to the legislature was the first item of business at the next meeting on November 12. The Environmental Caucus presented a letter they had drafted and asked that all EAG members sign it to express their support. The OEPA's Division of Surface Water chief indicated that the OEPA director had already sent a letter to the senator supporting the bill and its amendment, but also encouraging the use of the EAG process rather than legislative action on this issue. The Environmental Caucus indicated that this was nice, but insufficient, and that the OEPA letter did not express strongly enough that significant changes to the antidegradation rule should not be made outside of the EAG process. As debate ensued, it became evident that the Regulated Caucus members were largely unwilling to sign the Environmental Caucus's letter. Expressing his frustration, one of the Environmental Caucus cochairs noted,

> The letter only says that the group exists, and we want a good safe message from the entire group asking them to honor our process. **[11]**

A member of the Regulated Caucus replied,

> There's no problem with that letter as you state it, but I can't sign it because I represent people and I have no authority. It is beyond the scope of representation here to get involved in a lobbying effort on behalf of the EAG. **[12]**

Another Regulated Caucus representative offered,

> How about if the letter is sent from the Environmental Caucus? We don't have to hold you up, and its okay with us if you send it. The letter should just come from the Environmental Caucus, and not the entire EAG. **[13]**

An Environmental Caucus representative shot back,

> But if you agree with the letter, why won't you sign it? **[14]**

To which the Regulated Caucus member replied,

> I can't. I have a [homeowners' group] membership that I represent, and without their stated consent I can't sign anything. **[15]**

Though somewhat placated by the Regulated Caucus's and OEPA's statements of support, members of the Environmental Caucus were generally unhappy about the situation. They did send their letter to the legislature, but issues of representation continued to be raised throughout the EAG process. It was not uncommon to hear members of the Regulated Caucus discuss their roles as agents for outside companies or groups, and even indicate that these agency roles hampered their interaction on the EAG. As one attorney put it,

> My clients tend to be conservative and low key and they don't want to get in people's faces and create controversy and so they don't get into these arguments at meetings like that. They don't appreciate me getting into them either. I have to be careful what I do. **[16]**

Ongoing Technical Disputes Regarding Surrogate Parameters

Though everyone associated with the Antidegradation EAG routinely commented on the length and complexity of the law, Caucus members disagreed about the value of complexity. Regulated Caucus members claimed,

> We want to avoid being caught in the web of antidegradation. . . . [O]ur purpose should be to narrow the scope of the rule so that people with projects that don't have an environmental impact aren't impeded by unnecessary rules. **[17, 18]**

They tended to focus on the negative outcomes associated with antidegradation rules, as illustrated by one attorney's comment,

> If we are unable to come up with a workable rule, economic expansion in Ohio will be limited. There are neighboring states with more workable systems where the people I represent would feel more welcomed. **[19]**

Similarly, another Regulated Caucus member noted,

> New antidegradation requirements are harmful to agencies that provide public services, and if regulations keep getting more complex they won't be able to provide those services. . . . I'm not sure the Environmental Caucus really gets that. **[20]**

On the other hand, Environmental Caucus members appeared to view the process as a means to gain additional advantages. They tended to focus on benefits that could be derived from an expanded antidegradation rule, as illustrated by comments such as,

> The bottom line is that we need a stream protection policy and this part of the Rule may be a back door to it. **[21]**
>
> We ultimately want to teach watershed groups that they need to think about water quality, and making them do an antidegradation alternatives analysis is one way to get at that. **[22]**

When a representative from the Regulated Caucus complained in an open meeting that "A rule of unprecedented length and complexity is getting longer and more complex," **[23]** an attorney with the Environmental Caucus replied,

> Complexity has a bad name. I call it good and necessary details. We're here to improve water quality in Ohio, and to do that, the devil is in the details. **[24]**

This difference in perspective permeated the EAG's discussion of the forty-three "master issues" they identified. The group's debate over the use of surrogate parameters for water quality testing provides insight into the typical way in which the EAG participants approached these technical and complex issues. The existing antidegradation rule required the OEPA to test water quality on a pollutant-by-pollutant basis. This was a costly and time-consuming process that both the OEPA and the Regulated Caucus wished to revise. The OEPA proposed a revision to the rule that would allow them to test for surrogates,[‡‡] rather than for each individual pollutant.

Once the OEPA's position paper on this issue was presented, Environmental Caucus members pelted the Agency with questions:

> If other characteristic waste streams could be identified, would OEPA propose other surrogates for consideration? **[25]**
>
> Are you willing to do a literature search on the correlation between treatment for ammonia and whether that impacts phosphorus removal? **[26]**
>
> Would this be used with large treatment facilities? **[27]**

When the debate shifted to the evaluation of unique parameters under the antidegradation rule, Environmental Caucus members were quick to note that

[‡‡] Surrogates are single parameters used to represent several pollutants in the entire waste stream. For example, under the OEPA proposal, the Agency would test only for ammonia–nitrogen and use this test result to gauge the treatment performance and environmental impact of smaller waste treatment plants.

testing for bacteria should not be compromised because it is the only parameter that protects recreational uses of water. Generally, the Environmental Caucus's questions revealed their suspicion that the OEPA would use relaxed testing guidelines to slacken water quality standards indirectly. As one representative put it in a closed Environmental Caucus meeting, "This issue paper requires us to rely on the EPA as trustworthy, which we may not be able to do." **[28]** Throughout the morning briefing session, the Environmental Caucus asked the Agency to clarify the limits it would place on the use of surrogate parameters and proposed careful wording for the law that would specify the boundary conditions for such testing.

While in their closed session during this meeting, Environmental Caucus members continually commented on the need to protect themselves and the environment from the "polluters" on the regulated side. In this particular meeting, the main room had been divided in half with a moving partition to accommodate the closed lunchtime meetings of both caucuses; the coffeepot was on the Regulated Caucus's side of the room. When one member of the Environmental Caucus desired a cup of coffee, she commented that she was heading "into the lions' den." **[29]** When another Caucus member volunteered to get the coffee for her, she accepted with professed gratitude, saying, "I don't know if I'm up for going in there right now." **[30]** When reflecting on the general meeting progress, another Environmental Caucus member commented that it was difficult to know if OEPA was answering their questions thoroughly, because "they [OEPA] typically can't answer honestly with industry in the room." **[31]** In the final open debate, Environmental Caucus members expressed their concern that this would be a "slippery slope" situation where ammonia would be used inappropriately as a surrogate for more dangerous parameters.

The Regulated Caucus, on the other hand, was much more concerned about specifics of the proposed regulation than actions or motives of the Agency and the Environmental Caucus. Their questions on the initial proposal were a quest for specific information, such as, "How much time will the Agency save in the permitting process by testing for surrogates?" **[32]** "How will the Agency determine whether a waste facility is domestic or industrial?" **[33]** Participants in the Regulated Caucus's closed lunchtime meeting did not mention any issues of the Environmental Caucus's motive, but instead focused attention on how surrogate modeling would be accomplished and how domestic and industrial waste facilities would be defined under the proposed rule.

While the motivation of the Environmental Caucus was not at issue during this closed meeting of the Regulated Caucus, the former's technical expertise was often called into question. Regulated Caucus members made comments suggesting that environmentalists were generally unaware of the intricacies of applying for and receiving a permit from OEPA. Environmentalists were characterized as strident, illogical, and uninformed during many of the Regulated Caucus's closed meetings.

Applicability Debates: "The Elephant in the Corner"

One of the most contentious issues facing the EAG was the general applicability of the antidegradation law. The Regulated Caucus maintained that the OEPA should require antidegradation reviews only in instances where a project was likely to result in a significant change in ambient water quality. The Environmental Caucus, relying on the language in the *Metro Parks* decision, argued that antidegradation review should be triggered every time a permittee wished to increase the discharge of pollutants to a body of water by even a single molecule. The Environmental Caucus's arguments on this point were direct and often strident. As one environmentalist put it,

> Our argument begins and ends with *Metro Parks.* The rule is triggered with an increase in the discharge of pollutants to the stream. . . . I presume that anything that violates *Metro Parks* would violate federal law as interpreted by the [Ohio] Supreme Court. **[34]**

Generally, the Regulated Caucus saw their opponent's position on this issue in a very negative light. One Regulated Caucus member described the Environmental Caucus's position this way:

> [T]he Environmental [Caucus's position is] . . . taken to the extreme: there should be zero pollution. I mean, you should really not add [anything] . . . there should be some controls or regulation or whatever to really minimize any risk to human health or wildlife . . . it's this kind of zero-risk perspective. It also tends to be a "when in doubt use the most stringent requirement" [perspective]. **[35]**

Another Regulated Caucus colleague agreed.

> I think that in general the environmentalists' side is unwilling to bend. They seem adamant in their position. . . . The Environmental Caucus needs to have realistic expectations and not "ask for the moon." **[36]**

On the other hand, the Environmental Caucus clung to their position that the introduction of even a single molecule of waste into the water was, de facto, pollution. Arguing that "there's no reason to pollute if you don't have to," **[37]** they routinely referred to the Regulated Caucus members as "polluters" during these disputes. Comments such as "There's an obligation of polluters to learn the law" **[38]** and "Your activities that pollute need to be within the rule" **[39]** were commonly heard during open EAG meetings. Environmental Caucus members maintained that the regulated entities had an obligation to provide significant social and economic justification to increase the amount of materials put into a waterway: "We need to see if the benefits of this action benefit society, not just the polluter." **[40]**

Increasingly, members of the Regulated Caucus took exception to being labeled as polluters. One of the Caucus members remarked,

> Frankly, I'm getting a little sick of this perception that the regulated entity always wants to do the wrong thing. **[41]**

Another agreed:

> [F]rom my personal standpoint I don't enjoy meetings where you're treated like a polluter. **[42]**

These members continued to argue that the Environmental Caucus's position on the definition and scope of degradation was untenable and unworkable. The group held two special meetings devoted solely to the applicability issue, and was unable to reach consensus on the myriad details surrounding this question. The Environmental Caucus continued to argue that the *Metro Parks* decision was the binding principle for Ohio's antidegradation law, and that any project resulting in a single molecule's increase in discharge must be subject to antidegradation review. Environmental groups continued to file lawsuits and injunctions against the OEPA to force them to conduct such reviews throughout the EAG process. The Regulated Caucus continued to argue that the *Metro Parks* decision was flawed, and would result in an unworkable antidegradation regulation. As one of their representatives put it,

> The point of this process should be to protect water quality, and water quality should be defined with regard to the concentration of pollutant in the water. If the concentration decreases as the result of a project, it is hard to see a rationale for antidegradation review, even a streamlined one. **[43]**

Then, midway through the EAG process, a new OEPA director, Chris Jones, was appointed. Jones had been the government's attorney of record in the *Rivers Unlimited* case, and in this capacity was very familiar with both the court's ruling in *Metro Parks* and the arguments surrounding it. Shortly after Jones's appointment, the Regulated Caucus sent him a letter asking that he make a final decision on the applicability question so that the EAG could move forward on other issues. The Environmental Caucus quickly countered with a legal brief of their own outlining the OEPA's required compliance with the *Metro Parks* decision. Their position was clearly stated: "anything that violates *Metro Parks* would violate federal law as interpreted by the [Ohio] Supreme Court." **[44]** The Regulated Caucus reply: "I think we have an unreasoning *Metro Parks* phobia in the room." **[45]**

In response, Jones formally met with the EAG in May 1999. At this meeting, representatives from both the Environmental and Regulated Caucuses made formal presentations of their position. In his opening statement, Jones noted that,

> I've read the letters that you've each prepared on the issue and I understand that you have a fundamental disagreement on applicability, but . . . if that's the issue that's holding you up, then I'll make that decision so you can move forward . . . [but] what I'm most interested in learning today is about those issues on which there might be potential consensus so that you can all move forward. **[47]**

During his questioning of the Environmental and Regulated Caucus presenters, Jones noted that the two groups seemed to be receptive to discussing the possibility of a "scaled review" process, where smaller projects would be exempted from various parts of the antidegradation review process. During this meeting, Jones asked the Regulated Caucus representative,

> What if we did a scaled social and economic justification and it had one less public hearing? If we can do a scaled review that is acceptable to both parties, then applicability is looking a lot less significant. . . . Are you opposed to scaled review? **[48]**

The Regulated Caucus member answered,

> No. Well, there's no visceral response from the environmental community either. **[49]**

Jones announced that he would not make a decision on the applicability issue but would instead send the group back to seek out areas of consensus. He said:

> Look, I assume the law will be appealed. I'm still shocked that GLI [the Great Lakes Initiative] hasn't been appealed. But that's what we want to get to, something that's an agreement like the GLI folks reached. We want to move the process along and focus on where there is agreement. **[50]**

Based on this mandate, a member of the Regulated Caucus volunteered to create a matrix that would allow the group to discuss specifically what kinds of projects should be subject to what types of antidegradation review procedures. In designing and discussing the matrix, the EAG was able to reach consensus on a majority of types of projects, allowing the OEPA to conduct scaled antidegradation review (including minimal public participation and streamlined alternatives analyses) on a number of renewal and expanded discharge permits. They ultimately "agreed to disagree" on a number of significant items, including whether streamlined review processes should be applied to projects discharging to already low quality waters and whether projects that resulted in a net environmental benefit should be subject to antidegradation review at all.

It is important to note that the actual role of the OEPA vis-à-vis the EAG was never clearly defined. In one sense, the Agency served a mediating function. Agency representatives, particularly the Division of Surface Water chief, actively worked with the facilitators to guide the group toward a consensus agreement. OEPA members often suggested compromise positions. As the Division chief phrased it during the February 1999 meeting:

> We've gone through all this pain, and we want the full EAG to have the opportunity to hammer out compromises before we have to come in and reach a decision. **[51]**

Members of the Environmental Caucus seemed to be particularly motivated by this view of the Agency as a mediator. As one representative put it,

> I think the best outcome for this EAG process would be to develop rules that the environmental and regulated communities and Ohio EPA would mutually agree upon. I'd like to have as much consensus as possible. **[52]**

Members of the Environmental Caucus often expressed frustration when the group was unable to achieve consensus, as evidenced by this comment from a meeting early in 1999,

> The process is all about moving toward shared attempts to solve problems, working together for reasonable solutions. We should share the same goals, though I am not certain we do. **[53]**

The Environmental Caucus members also saw the EAG as a way to learn more about the technical aspects of the antidegradation law. As one representative put it,

> I really think we should be focused on developing a clear definition of "antidegradation." We need clear definitions of the process which is currently too cumbersome. **[53]**

Another echoed this concern,

> I hope there is time to get the mechanics and specifics of the rule plainly articulated to all our [Environmental Caucus] members. **[54]**

On the other hand, the Agency clearly had the final decision-making authority of an arbitrator. They had the legal mandate to draft, ultimately, the final rule revisions, but pledged to take both sides' arguments under advisement when preparing the new rule. In a personal interview, one OEPA representative said,

> We wanted to allow the parties to bring up issues that they had with the rule, discuss those issues, see if we could reach consensus on the set of changes to the rules, and if not, at least we identified areas that we could agree to disagree but both parties felt like they had an opportunity to bring their issues or concerns and discuss them regarding the antidegradation rule. **[55]**

Members of the Regulated Caucus generally viewed OEPA representatives in their arbitration role. As one representative said,

> [T]he Agency nominates the wording of what they would like to happen. If environmental advocates and regulated communities agree, they move forward with their recommendations. If stakeholders don't agree, they move forward with their recommendations. The Agency is in the driver's seat; if we can't agree, the default is the Agency's position. **[56]**

Another Regulated Caucus member indicated that this view of the Agency was behind his strategy in EAG meetings when he said,

> Consensus is nice, but that's not why I'm here. I'm here to make my best possible arguments to the Agency that advance our position on how the rule should look. That's my job. **[57]**

Another Regulated Caucus Member concurred:

> On many aspects there are deep divisions—it will be hard to come close on some issues, and on others it is just impossible. All we can do is try to give the Agency the best read on our positions that we can. **[58]**

The Outcome

In April 2000 the EAG met formally for the final time. At this meeting, the group again heard from Director Jones, who summarized the results. He noted that the OEPA had decided that, consistent with the *Metro Parks* decision, antidegradation review was to be triggered by the activity of adding pollutants or changing pollutants in a receiving stream. He also identified a number of areas of consensus that were identified, such as changes to the general permit process, a streamlined plan for public involvement in the process, and guidelines for the protection of Superior High Quality Waters. He acknowledged that the group had been unable to achieve consensus on the protection of Low Quality Waters, in situations where there was no change in water quality and/or permit limit levels were being increased, and on what actually constituted a net environmental benefit. Our interpretation of the way in which these outcomes aligned with the positions of the Environmental and Regulated Caucuses is presented in Table 8.1.

Reflecting on the process, members of the Regulated Caucus were generally displeased. They noted that the point of the process should be to protect water quality, and that water quality should be defined as the concentration of pollutant in the water. If the concentration actually decreased as a result of a project, they maintained, then there was no rationale for an antidegradation review. Similarly, an Environmental Caucus member noted that,

> [T]he question of protection of low quality waters is a philosophical position that we will never waver from. We're not entirely pleased with the outcome here. **[59]**

In his final comments, Jones acknowledged the group's displeasure with the outcome:

Table 8.1. Outcomes of the EAG Process

Issue	*Decision/Outcome*	*Caucus's Position Most Supported by the Outcome*
Overall applicability of antidegradation law★	Degradation is defined as "one additional molecule of pollutant" introduced to the water	Executive decision by OEPA director consistent with *Metro Parks* and *Rivers Unlimited* decisions and supportive of Environmental Caucus's position.
Provision for scaled review of some projects (vs. complete antidegradation review for all covered projects)	Scaled review allowable for specified types of projects	Specifics of the scaled review procedure negotiated by the EAG. Overall idea of scaled review supportive of Regulated Caucus's position.
Inclusion of antidegradation review in the general permitting process	Scaled review allowable in most instances	Specifics negotiated by the EAG. Neither caucus's position fully supported.
Procedures for protecting Low Quality Waters	EAG could not reach consensus	Director will announce OEPA position on the issue.
Coverage of projects whose current permit levels allowed for an increase in pollutants discharged	EAG could not reach consensus	Director will announce OEPA position on the issue.
Definition of "net environmental benefit" and process for determining whether significant social and economic justification for projects exists	EAG could not reach consensus	Director will announce OEPA position on the issue.
Protection of High Quality Waters	Significant antidegradation review required for all projects on surface waters with special high quality designations	EAG reached negotiated decision; final ruling most favored Environmental Caucus's initial position.
Use of surrogate parameters in testing for pollutants	Agreement that some surrogate testing is appropriate	EAG reached negotiated decision. Neither caucus's position fully supported.

★The Regulated Caucus position was that the following kinds of projects should be exempted from review, whereas the Environmental Caucus believed that they should be subject to review: groundwater cleanup/remediation activities, General Plan permits, projects with nonchemical pollution sources, and new sources connecting to an existing sewer treatment works.

> It is clear that not everyone is satisfied with the outcome, but we do appreciate the work you've done to bring us to the point. I'm sure we'll be revisiting the issue. **[60]**

One of the Regulated Caucus members was more succinct:

> It's a foregone conclusion that all this will wind up in court. **[61]**

The OEPA planned to have a draft rule available for public review and comment in summer 2002. The Agency will make changes to the rule if necessary in response to public comment, and then will file the proposed rule with the Joint Committee on Agency Rule Review in early 2003. Another public comment period and public hearing will occur in the fall of 2002, and the final rule revisions will then be submitted to the Ohio legislature for approval.

Analysis

The debate over water quality standards in Ohio is a recurring one. The parties involved in this EAG had interacted with one another before in both legal and rule-making forums, and most acknowledged that they would come together again in similar situations in the future. These individuals (and in many cases their clients) continue to pit themselves against one another in court cases, regulatory battles, and public debates despite their partially successful efforts to achieve consensus in the EAG.

We hypothesized that there was a synergy between the parties' views of themselves, characterization of the other disputants, and frame of the conflict situation itself that contributes to the continuation of their dispute. Therefore, we analyzed the parties' identity, characterization, conflict resolution, and gain/loss frames to determine how they both shaped participants' behaviors during this dispute episode and contributed to the dispute's ingrained intractability.

Identity Frames

Generally, our data reveal that EAG participants brought dual identities to the EAG table: they were individuals with private opinions and interests, and professional advocates defending the interests of their constituents. The former identity was significantly more prevalent in the Environmental Caucus, whereas the latter was more often cited by Regulated Caucus members.

When Regulated Caucus members talked of themselves as advocates, they identified themselves with clients' interests. **[4, 5, 12, 15]** In the role of agent, they framed EAG discussions as instrumental to achieving the terminal goal of economic development in Ohio. These individuals were "pure" agents, in that they identified primarily with the roles of their client organizations. Indeed, the sense of agency was so strong amongst Regulated Caucus members that some expressed frustrations with having to keep their own opinions quiet during these discussions. The reader will recall the comment from one attorney:

> I have my own personal opinions, but it is probably inappropriate for me to participate in that fashion. **[4]**

On the other hand, Environmental Caucus members were more like "free" agents in these discussions. These individuals tended to reject both social and institutional identities, choosing instead to align their identity with personal interests and beliefs about environmental protection. This was reflected in self-identification comments such as "We are here to clean the water of the state." **[6]**

The linkage of personal identity with interests intensified this dispute, largely because Environmental Caucus members' primary identities were inherently linked to their arguments. Consequently, they often responded to attacks on those arguments quite personally, which added emotional intensity to the debates. On the other hand, Regulated Caucus members' agency roles sometimes seemed to allow them more personal distance from the dispute, lessening their emotional involvement in debates. Indeed, as noted in the applicability debates, individual members of the Regulated Caucus were quite upset at being personally labeled "polluters." **[41, 42]** During their personal interviews, many of these individuals noted that they, and their clients, were not in the business of polluting. Thus the Environmental Caucus wanted the discussion to be about people's personal identities, while the Regulated Caucus believed that there was not a place for personal identities at the table.

On the Regulated Caucus side, members' agency roles contributed to intractability by making it difficult for the EAG to reach negotiated settlements. These individuals made it clear that their approval authority was in many cases limited by their membership. In addition to limited decision-making authority, Regulated Caucus members may have felt that their agency relationships required them to adopt strong argumentative stances in these negotiations. As we noted, these discussions took place in an open forum, and these formal agents may have had their ability to compromise thwarted because large concessions may have appeared to be weak or inappropriate representations of their clients' interests.

Additionally, each caucus tended to view its own identity as the "appropriate" one for the EAG. Environmental Caucus members often cited the importance of passionate defense of environmental resources to the EAG process, whereas Regulated Caucus members were more likely to talk about the need for the EAG to formulate simple, legally defensible regulations. Then, when each side began to characterize the other, they used their own standard of "appropriateness" and found the other lacking, as noted in the next section.

Characterization Frames

We found that most members of the Environmental Caucus characterized Regulated Caucus members as attorney/advocates, often using the label of "lawyer" in a derogatory way when they talked about the Regulated Caucus's overly rational, argumentative, and detail-focused behaviors. Interestingly, however, although Environmental Caucus members overtly acknowledged that Regulated Caucus participants had formal responsibility to serve as agents for other entities, environmentalists often tacitly identified Regulated Caucus members as personalizations of the entities that they represented. Environmental Caucus members often referred to Regulated Caucus members themselves as polluters during open and closed meetings, apparently ignoring any distinction between the agent and the party the person represented. It may be that, because environmentalists viewed the Regulated Caucus members as emotionally uninvolved in the EAG debate, they reasoned that Regulated Caucus members had little passion for environmental issues on a personal level. It thus became relatively simple for the environmentalists to brand Regulated Caucus members as polluters because they assumed that these agents shared the values, and hence the culpability, of their principals.

It is also possible that environmentalists were frustrated by the absence of the "real" regulated community. The Regulated Caucus comprised not business owners or elected officials responsible for development, but their representatives or agents. Consequently, Environmental Caucus members had no true outlet to express their displeasure with current development practices or to seek understanding from a perceived nemesis. Additionally, because regulated entities were largely represented by legal counsel, the discussion was usually located at the level of legal detail with little attention paid to the underlying philosophical differences between the parties. In this forum, Environmental Caucus members may have been unable to express their more general positions on environmental matters.

As we have noted, environmentalists seemed to approach the EAG as a forum for education and consensus where collaboration was a real possibility. Regulated Caucus members, on the other hand, tended to view the EAG as a mechanism to present arguments to the OEPA rather than to resolve differences with environmentalists. It is likely that the very composition of this group was problematic for Environmental Caucus members because it did not provide a forum in which they could act out their desired identities as personally charged defenders of the environment.

Members of the Regulated Caucus characterized Environmental Caucus members as less technically sophisticated about the legalities of environmental regulation. Many Regulated Caucus participants pointed to the large number of technical questions raised by the Environmental Caucus as evidence of the latter's inability to understand water quality regulations. Regulated Caucus participants also voiced frustration about the inability of the EAG to reach concrete, legally defensible settlements and cited the Environmental Caucus's "overly passionate and irrational" arguments as one reason for this failure.

The two caucus's characterizations of the OEPA also differed dramatically. The OEPA's role in this dispute was difficult to characterize in a singular way; indeed, three roles were visible. During the monthly meetings the Agency acted as a technical adviser, facilitator, and mediator. An OEPA division chief chaired each meeting, and staff members made numerous presentations and were always available to answer questions. Working with the professional facilitators hired by the OEPA, the division chief encouraged the group to reach agreement on issues wherever possible; in this sense, they were a mediating third party. However, ultimately the OEPA was an arbitrator: they reviewed arguments presented by both sides to develop the final rule. Our data indicate that the Environmental Caucus's characterization of the OEPA was more consistent with the mediator and technical adviser roles, while the Regulated Caucus's characterization reflected the arbitrator. The Regulated Caucus's acknowledgment of and appeal to the OEPA as adjudicator prompted them to make their appeals supporting resource utilization stronger and more directly persuasive than the Environmental Caucus's appeals for resource protection. On the other hand, the Environmental Caucus made significantly more requests for information, asked more direct questions, and focused more on achieving consensus than did the Regulated Caucus.

The caucuses' differences in their characterization of the OEPA were likely prompted by differences in their own identity frames. It may be the case that environmentalists focused on the mediator role because seeking compromise was more consistent with their identity frame. On the other hand, presenting strong arguments was more consistent with the advocate's identity expressed by most Regulated Caucus members, and so they were more likely to view the OEPA as an audience for their advocacy.

Conflict Management Frames

Just as they viewed the OEPA differently, the two sides also had significantly different frames of the EAG's purpose. For the Environmental Caucus, the EAG process was primarily seen as a fact-finding and/or consensus recommendation forum. Members said that their role was to "raise issues" and "increase awareness" so that the OEPA would make an "informed decision" when drafting the new antidegradation rule. Consistent with this frame, one of the Environmental Caucus's primary tactics during EAG meetings was to voice questions to other participants, and members often phrased their arguments in the form of questioning. As noted above, this contributed to the Regulated Caucus's characterization of the environmentalists as naïve and unable to comprehend the technical issues in the antidegradation debate. Still, this view of the conflict was strongly consistent with environmentalists' identity frames of "pure" personal advocates for environmental protection.

On the other hand, Regulated Caucus members more often framed the conflict as one ultimately decided by an authority (the OEPA). They viewed themselves as agents/advocates, and were more likely to generate arguments and persuasive statements directed toward the OEPA. Our analysis of exchanges in EAG meetings revealed that they asked far fewer questions than did the Environmental Caucus, and also that they addressed the OEPA in a positive, argumentative stance more often than did their environmental counterparts. Again, this is consistent with the identity frame of legal agent/representative expressed by most members of the Regulated Caucus.

Gain/Loss Frames

As noted in Chapter 1, a wealth of evidence supports the notion that people evaluate outcomes differently if those outcomes are presented as potential for gain or for loss (Kahneman and Tversky 1979). Perceived losses are more salient than commensurate gains, such that reducing a loss is seen as "worth" more than forgoing a gain (Kahneman, Knetsch, and Thaler 1990, 1991; Knetsch 1998). For example, people are likely to act more aggressively to avoid losing $10 than they will to gain $10. In negotiation situations where people believe that they are in danger of losing $10, they find it difficult to concede ground toward agreement, whereas if they view a negotiation as a possible means to gain $10, they are more likely to make concessions and reach an integrative agreement (Bazerman, Magliozzi, and Neale 1985; Neale and Bazerman 1985). In fact, when parties approach a conflict focusing on what they might lose (a loss frame), they are more likely to escalate conflict rather than compromise (Bazerman 1984). On the other hand, if they focus on what they might gain from an agreement (a gain frame), they are more likely to seek compromises (Neale and Bazerman 1985).

The presence of gain/loss frames in environmental disputes is well investigated. In traditional environmental discourse, developers embrace a gain frame, whereas environmentalists view conflicts from a loss perspective. Developers typically argue for the building of new projects or the commercial use of resources by emphasizing economic benefits such as an increase in jobs or convenience for local citizens. On the other hand, environmentalists typically tout the losses that will result from the destruction of natural resources. These argument postures have a general tendency to encourage corresponding risk-seeing and risk-averse postures between the two groups: people tend to be risk-seeking when faced with potential gains, and risk-averse when faced with potential losses (Kessler, Ford, and Bailey 1996). It is likely the case that, because developers typically have significantly greater resources at their disposal than environmentalists do, they approach each conflict from a position of relative superiority. In this mind-set, developers view negotiated outcomes through the lens of a gain frame because, from their already-established powerful position, they are relatively certain that they will not lose ground and instead seek only to better their position. On the other hand, environmentalists possess significantly fewer resources and are typically in the weaker position at the negotiating table. Each conflict is consequently viewed through the lens of a loss frame because any compromise potentially weakens their already vulnerable position.

However, in the EAG, it appeared that this traditional assignment of gain and loss frames was reversed. Environmentalists focused on the potential benefits of an expanded antidegradation law, arguing that this could have positive outcomes such as educating watershed groups and providing stream protection. **[21, 22]** On the other hand, members of the Regulated Caucus focused on the potential losses in revenue, jobs, and development that could result from a more stringent rule. **[18, 19, 20]** One possible reason for this reversal is that the Environmental Caucus was perceived by all parties to wield power in these negotiations because of their victories in the *Metro Parks* and *Rivers Unlimited* court decisions. Indeed, the entire EAG process was initiated partly because of OEPA's desire to avoid future legal battles. From this position of power, members of the Environmental Caucus took an unusual gain/benefits–focused frame reflecting a degree of optimism about the regulatory process. Their willingness to view the OEPA as a mediator, and their stated desire to reach negotiated compromise through the EAG process, are evidence of the relatively conciliatory posture more common to disputants who view themselves in a position of relative power. Similarly, the Regulated Caucus's view of the OEPA as an arbitrator, and their tendency to make more strident arguments with less tendency to compromise, is consistent with disputants using a loss frame who are unwilling to suffer further losses as a result of the conflict episode.

Intractability

The two caucuses' differing identity and conflict management frames contributed to the intractable nature of this dispute as the parties viewed themselves as, in the words of one Environmental Caucus member, "ships passing in the night." EAG members often voiced frustration that they were "not heard" or "not communicating" with one another. **[53]** We posit that disputants' frustration was at least partially caused by differences in the sides' frames of the process itself, which were inextricably linked to their identity frames and subsequent competing characterizations of the OEPA. While environmentalists were seeking consensus, the Regulated Caucus was busy making strong argumentative statements to the OEPA that were designed to persuade the Agency in its final rule making.

First, the two caucuses' frames of the conflict were connected to their competing conflict management frames. The Environmental Caucus had a basic interest in keeping the debate alive so that their interests were voiced in as many places as often as possible. By casting the EAG as a fact-finding process and a forum for consensus, they could more easily view their participation as a terminal goal, valuable simply because they were able to obtain information and voice opinions. On the other hand, the Regulated Caucus's conflict management frame supported reaching an end to the EAG process quickly while simultaneously losing as little potential for development as possible. While the Environmental Caucus viewed the EAG as an end in itself—a forum to advance their individual interests—the Regulated Caucus saw the process as a means to an end: a revised rule that would benefit their clients.

Similarly, the relationship between gain/loss frames and the parties' relative positions of power in this negotiation contributed to its intractability. Research on the effect of gain/loss frames in negotiation suggests that participants with a negative/loss frame are less likely to accept settlement solutions and more likely to escalate conflict (Bazerman 1984, Neale and Bazerman 1985). Historically, this has been the position of environmentalists, as evidenced by such things as the prevalence of "militant" environmental activists such as the Earth Liberation Front (ELF) and environmentalists' heavy reliance on court action and injunction. However, in the EAG, members of the Regulated Caucus adopted the defensive postures associated with the loss frame. This suggests that it is the parties' relative power vis-à-vis one another that prompts them to adopt a gain or loss frame of a conflict, rather than the actual content of their positions. Still, regardless of where it resides, any party's loss frame contributes to dispute intractability. In this context, recall the comment from a Regulated Caucus member: "It's a foregone conclusion that all this will wind up in court." **[61]**

Conclusion

Ultimately, although the OEPA should be applauded for its serious effort to engage in constructive dispute resolution mechanisms, the characterization frames that participants had of the OEPA in dispute may hinder the success of the Agency's endeavors. In this case, the Agency was required to play a number of roles during the dispute resolution process, and each party's choice to prioritize one of those roles over others contributed to shared frustration with the process and, ultimately, the intractability of this dispute. Certainly each of these roles is necessary for the Agency. First, staff members must be present to provide technical information to the disputants to allow them to focus attention on specific new proposals and revisions. Second, when the Agency behaves as a mediator, they encourage the parties to express interest-based arguments that could be used to find common ground and reach a mutually acceptable solution. On the other hand, the OEPA ultimately has the legal mandate to propose rule revisions. In this position as arbitrator, their presence prompts the parties to present strong positions and try to make the best case for them.

Our study of the Antidegradation EAG demonstrates how intractability can be traced to the disputants' frames. Though all parties approached the dispute rationally, each prioritized the component(s) of the Agency's roles that were consistent with their own identity frames. The Environmental Caucus viewed the OEPA as a mediator and attempted to provide interest-based arguments consistent with their interest-based identity frame, whereas the Regulated Caucus framed the OEPA as an arbitrator and, again consistent with their own institutional and agency identity frames, behaved as strong advocates for their clients' positions. Consequently, the parties' differing identity, characterization, and conflict frames combined to thwart the consensus-building process: one side sought consensus through a mediator, while the other made strong arguments directed to an arbitrator. Generally, these data provide insight into the conflicting roles and impacts of mediators and arbitrators. More specifically, our analysis suggests that the OEPA and its sister agencies need to pay careful attention to how their roles are being framed in these dispute resolution processes, and specifically how disputants' own identity, conflict management, and gain/loss frames shape their views of both these agencies and the negotiated processes they facilitate.

Note on Sources

The information in this chapter was derived from interviews with members of the EAG and documents prepared by these individuals for submission to the OEPA and/or review by group members. The first author also transcribed verbal statements made by EAG members in both open meetings and private caucus sessions.

Chapter 9

Comparing Water Cases

Roy J. Lewicki, Sanda Kaufman, Carolyn Wiethoff, and Craig B. Davis

The Ohio Environmental Protection Agency's (OEPA's) Antidegradation External Advisory Group (EAG) and the Doan Brook watershed management process presented in the previous chapters seem to have a great deal in common. Both took place in the state of Ohio, both were concerned with protecting water quality, and both occurred during the same period of time. But on closer inspection, differences between the cases exist that are directly related to variations in participants' frames. The purposes of this chapter are threefold: first, to explore the components unique to watershed management that are illustrated by these two conflicts; second, to comment directly on the ways in which participants' characterization, identity, and conflict management frames contributed to the disputes' intractability; and third, to highlight some of the other similarities and differences between the cases that are instructive. Finally, we provide a summary of the theoretical and practical implications of these analyses.

The Complexity of Watershed Management Issues

Water is a necessary ingredient for a healthy, functioning ecosystem (Benson 1996), but the science of measuring and managing water quality is fraught with uncertainty (Wagner 2000). Some of this difficulty is inherent in the nature of water. Substances added to a river upstream are disseminated downstream—sometimes quickly and sometimes slowly. They accumulate in the stream bottom and in downstream vegetation, often making their effects difficult to see or evaluate (Peters and Meybeck 2000). Pollutants may enter a stream from a specific point (a "point source") such as a drainpipe. Other pollutants enter from nonpoint sources, such as runoff from agricultural fields. Pollution caused by nonpoint sources is difficult to identify and assess. Moreover, because pollutants can enter a watershed at multiple places, determining the "net" damage to water quality that results from any single activity is particularly problematic.

Watersheds are complex and dynamic systems that can both change quickly and erode quietly over time (Cannon 2000). As demonstrated in the Doan Brook case, deterioration may continue for long periods of time without creating a "crisis point." In the absence of dramatic degradation incidents, such as major oil spills or chemical dumping, water quality is likely to erode in slow and largely unnoticeable increments that are difficult both to measure and to predict. A buildup of pollutants may not be evident until damage to plants and animals living in the stream is obvious to the naked eye. Badly polluted streams may seem, to the average observer, to be normal and healthy. Unfortunately, once visible damage occurs, pollution is usually so severe that a complete restoration of the stream habitat is impossible.

Such incremental deterioration problems have typically been described by behavioral scientists as entrapment or sunk-cost psychology, in which a problematic situation deteriorates, requiring a decision as to what to do next (Staw 1976, Teger 1980). The decision involves risk because the future is unclear, and returns on investment are ambiguous. In classic sunk-cost dynamics, the decision is made to "throw good money after bad" to rescue a bad decision. In contrast, in these water quality standards cases, it is the *absence* of decision that contributes to further deterioration, because it is difficult to determine when, or at what point, a river's status changes from "clean" to "polluted."

Because of the uncertainties inherent in water quality assessment, debates over the quality of water can run the gamut. They can either remain largely latent until a crisis point is reached, as in the Doan Brook scenario, or they can be speculative "finger-pointing" debates about hypothetical crisis points and impacts, as was the case with the EAG. In both cases, conflict between groups is assured, but it often takes on very different forms and manifestations.

Water-based conflicts are exacerbated by the fact that different areas of a watershed can have remarkably different features and water quality. Ecosystems vary widely within the same watershed, each uniquely created by the area surrounding the waterway, activity in or near the water, and characteristics of the water. Consequently, activities that have little or no effect in one part of the watershed can be highly detrimental to aquatic life elsewhere. More pragmatically, people upstream and downstream are likely to view the watershed and its quality control issues very differently. Again, the Doan Brook case is illustrative: residents in downstream Cleveland not only experienced different effects of polluted water, they also valued the brook for different reasons than did residents of upstream Shaker Heights and Cleveland Heights. Much like the parable of the blind men and the elephant, stakeholders at various points along a watershed are likely to view it in dramatically different ways, prompting disagreement on its nature and properties. These differing perspectives have the potential to create and exacerbate conflict.

Recognizing these dynamics, current conventional wisdom—and practices of federal agencies, environmental groups, and water resource users—suggests that watersheds should be managed holistically rather than by focusing on particular quantity or quality issues in specific places (Benson 1996). Both the Doan Brook and EAG cases are examples of this principle, though in slightly different ways. The EAG case study represents a statewide, results-driven attempt to set general policies protecting water quality, rather than focusing on any particular watershed. In general, Doan Brook is more properly viewed as an example of "watershed democracy" (Benson 1996), where all parties affected by or interested in a particular watershed work together to determine antidegradation solutions that will be most appropriate for the entire system.

Both cases are also illustrative of current trends in water quality management. In today's political climate, environmental decision making typically involves significant public participation (Spyke 1999). Federal and state environmental agencies are increasingly committed to getting public input from affected and interested stakeholders. These agencies recognize that consensus-based management decisions enhance cooperation from these parties—a particularly important commodity in cases where natural resources reside in whole or in part on private property (Benson 1996). Indeed, previous research suggests that the overall success of watershed management initiatives may correlate directly with the extent to which the public is involved in the decision-making process (Wagner 2000). Recognizing this, regulatory agencies in the state of Ohio, like their counterparts around the country, are increasingly turning to citizen advisory groups and ad hoc groups of stakeholders as partners in developing and implementing water quality management regulations.

Comparing Doan Brook and the External Advisory Group on Key Frames

In this section, we will compare the two cases. We will begin with several clear-cut similarities and differences. We will then compare the two cases on the three dominant frames—characterization, identity, and conflict management. Finally, we evaluate the two cases on the spectrum of intractability discussed in Chapter 2.

We can start with some preliminary and self-evident distinctions between the Doan Brook and EAG cases. First, as we have previously noted, the disputes are prima facie similar because they both deal with water quality issues in the state of Ohio. Moreover, both disputes were formally facilitated at regularly scheduled meetings, with set agendas. Additionally, both were convened by a regulatory agency or commission for the expressed purpose of obtaining citizen involvement in the water quality management process.

The largest difference between the disputes is that, while Doan dealt with a single watershed and therefore focused on brook-specific evidence and instances, the EAG was charged with developing water quality mandates for almost all state waterways, and consequently tended to focus on generic and theoretical positions in the absence of reference to a specific waterway. Previous research has demonstrated that people are more willing to take action and make sacrifices to restore a particular place than to promote abstract ideas of water quality (Adler 1995). Consequently, the lack of opportunity for place-based identity in the EAG was possibly problematic, for it may have prompted members to adopt more polarized, abstract positions, rather than seeking an implementable compromise for the good of a specific individual watershed.

The climates and tones of the two disputes were also quite distinct. While parties in the Doan dispute were largely friendly with and supportive of one another, those on the EAG were often overtly hostile toward each other. This may have been the result of the large percentage of lawyers involved in the EAG. Because lawyers are professional adversaries, they tend to view the world in competitive terms and fight to "win" to preserve the positive regard of their client(s). Similarly, the parties in the EAG had a history of interaction that may have contributed to the adversarial tone of their meetings. Whereas Doan Brook participants were generally coming together for the first time, members of the EAG viewed their participation as only one episode in an ongoing drama of conflict.

Another important difference between the two cases is how the parties at the table were selected. The OEPA invited known stakeholders to participate in the EAG, whereas participants in the Doan Brook conflict largely self-selected into slots designated by the Agency for various kinds of stakeholders. This may create an interesting trade-off in the way that representatives are selected for participation in these initiatives. The danger of using stakeholder groups invited by an agency is that people in those agency roles may be more loyal to their constituency and less likely to compromise in joint problem-solving efforts (Law 1999). In contrast, the danger of parties self-selecting into designated slots is that the parties really don't effectively speak for any given constituency. As a result, if consensus is achieved, it may not mean much at the time of implementation. Care should be taken that the chosen representatives can and do effectively speak for their constituency, but at the same time that they are not wedded to an inflexible "party line" and are capable of modifying their position in the interest of group consensus.

Conflict Management Frames

In some respects, parties in the Doan and EAG disputes had remarkably similar conflict management frames. First, participants in both cases tended to view their conflicts as fact-finding initiatives. A majority of interviewees in the Doan case indicated that they saw the gathering of information as a primary reason for their involvement in the dispute; 42 percent of identity-related comments from EAG members similarly supported this position. From our analysis of these cases, it is obvious that one important reason people chose to become involved in watershed management groups was to obtain information about both current water quality and proposed management strategy alternatives. To that end, most people viewed and valued their involvement as an opportunity to learn.

Similarly, participants in both disputes often talked about participation in the decision-making process as a mechanism to air their thoughts and positions. As one of the Doan Brook interviewees put it, "The process is good—a whole bunch of people talking about solutions instead of each [area of the brook] being its own entity." **[Doan Brook 18]** A lawyer on the EAG put it even more strongly, "I'm here to make my best possible arguments to the Agency that advance our position on how the rule should look. That's my job." **[Ohio 57]** Interestingly, it seems that the OEPA, a regulatory agency involved in both disputes, shares this participatory conflict management frame. An OEPA representative interviewed in the EAG scenario noted that a key purpose of the EAG was to ensure that "both parties felt like they had an opportunity to bring their issues or concerns and discuss them." **[Ohio 55]**

But, while providing a "voice at the table" is certainly an important component of locally based watershed management programs, one key difference between the Doan Brook and EAG case studies is in the relative importance that participants placed on having that voice. One potential weakness in consensus-based watershed management programs is that they can be more procedural than substantive, focused on giving individuals a role and voice in the decision-making process rather than (or even at the expense of) significantly improving water quality (Benson 1996). It seems that participants in the Doan

Brook watershed management process framed the conflict procedurally, while the EAG participants framed the conflict substantively, perhaps because of the actual differences in the decision-making authority given to stakeholders in each group. For the EAG, those who would have to abide by antidegradation regulations (i.e., the Regulated Caucus) were charged with reaching an actual negotiated resolution with environmentalists to produce a law that both sides could "live with." The OEPA assured the participants that where compromise was reached, the agreed-upon language would be incorporated into the revised law. Thus there were many opportunities for potential substantive gains for both caucuses. On the other hand, Doan Brook representatives had no such mandate, nor were they granted even provisional decision-making authority. Consequently, those who participated in the process were likely motivated by the opportunity to gain voice.

A significant difference also existed in the way that each group viewed the potential for technical solutions to their respective conflicts. Although both groups ostensibly focused on the importance of consensus-based decisions and joint problem solving, the nature of their consensus was different. For Doan Brook stakeholders, consensus took the form of placing near-blind trust in the technical models presented by the EPA and/or the Sewer District, because they viewed these agencies as a trustworthy source of technical expertise. Here, consensus potentially could be obtained simply by mutually embracing the most appropriate or acceptable technical solution provided by a knowledgeable authority. Recall the quotation from one Doan Brook participant: "Obviously the NEORSD will call the shots on any capital project under their direct control, subject to some input from the committee." **[Doan Brook 14]** On the other hand, members of the EAG believed in their own expertise and spent more time challenging the OEPA and questioning their technical standards. The peppered questions and heated exchanges in the debate over surrogate parameters **[Ohio 17–33]** provide a vivid example of this perspective. For the EAG, consensus had to be obtained partially through the joint development of the group's own technical solutions, rather than through shared reliance on solutions generated by someone else.

This difference may be the result of the relative levels of experience held by members of each group of stakeholders, which served to strengthen the mandate and representation of each group. Participation in debate over water quality issues has a particularly high "information cost" because it takes significant time and effort to understand fully the complexity of a watershed, the impact of various pollutants, and the full effects of technical proposals (Wagner 2000). Most participants in the EAG had more experience with water quality management issues than did those in the Doan Brook scenario. Many EAG Regulated Caucus members were attorneys who specialized in water management, and most of the Environmental Caucus members at the table also had expertise in this area. (In fact, one member of the Environmental Caucus was a former employee of the OEPA's Division of Surface Water.) On the other hand, many of the Doan Brook stakeholders were private citizens without an extensive technical background in this area. It is logical that they would choose to rely on the expertise of those with more experience, whereas EAG members had the relative luxury of relying on their own and their colleagues' expertise. It is likely that EAG members viewed the conflict as less procedural and more substantive largely because they had a more sophisticated grasp of the technical issues being discussed.

Characterization Frames

The EAG and Doan Brook cases have a similar cast of characters. Various levels of the Environmental Protection Agency are involved directly or indirectly through funding of the decision processes and through regulatory requirements that made these processes necessary. Environmental interests are also the major "protagonists" in both cases. Both cases had regulatory agency conveners—OEPA for the EAG, and the Northeast Ohio Regional Sewer District (NEORSD) for Doan—and both had access to agency-provided professional facilitation of meetings. The group size and composition, however, was quite different. The EAG had twenty-three members, each belonging to one of two interest-based caucuses. The Doan Brook Study Committee was larger and more fragmented, with about fifty members representing nine different key stakeholder interests, not including the convener. In addition, EAG members had much more group cohesion, more individual and mutual clarity about whom they represented, and a much stronger mandate (at least on the Regulated Caucus side) than was the case for Doan Brook. It is interesting therefore to observe the differences in characterization frames operative in the two cases, and to explore some reasons for, and consequences of, these differences.

In terms of clarity of stakeholder role and representation, as well as balance of expertise levels, EAG and Doan Brook cases represent two extremes. From an observer's point of view, it seems the results are unsatisfactory at both ends. The EAG process failed to produce an across-the-board agreement at the table, while the Doan Brook process yielded a kind of passive consensus that may not mean much when the time comes for NEORSD to implement water quality enhancement measures.

EAG participants had formal roles, and labels that reinforced them, as well as a shared history of other encounters. On the one hand this can add clarity at the negotiation table regarding who knows whom, who knows what, who represents whom, and who can commit to what actions. On the other hand, such role clarity, combined with a history of past interaction among these specific individuals, produced very sharply defined and rather negative characterization frames that impeded the process. The already culturally entrenched "tree hugger versus polluter" (social do-gooder versus social villain) framing dynamic was amply played out in this conflict, strengthened by the parties' self-identification, by the OEPA's labeling of the two key groups, and even by the way in which each meeting's agenda created time and opportunity for the gathering of separate caucuses. So it is not altogether surprising that the parties held reciprocal negative frames (refer to examples), likely formed before this EAG process, then enhanced by it, and in turn affecting it. These frames may have acted as filters that privileged information supporting them and discounted inconsistent information (Bazerman 1998), lessening the chances of any change in relationships and trust occurring in the face of new evidence. So the crisp representation and the role clarity may have fueled the negative frames, thereby preventing a more collaborative tone and more information sharing for the crafting of an integrative solution.

In the Doan Brook case, the parties had long held their respective roles as agency or service staff members, engineers, residents, environmentalists, or elected officials. However, although some subgroups existed, not all participants in the two-year study process knew each other from previous interactions. Any previous interactions between the parties were among role representatives, rather than among specific individuals. For example, municipal service staff had interacted with environmentalists and residents before, but not necessarily with the individuals involved in the study process. Therefore, although parties held some characterization frames predating the study process, the study was also an opportunity for participants to get acquainted with each other without preexisting personal baggage. Interestingly, the parties held a number of mildly negative characterization frames about the institutions and groups from which others came (e.g., Cleveland versus suburbs, service staff versus environmentalists, and engineers versus lay public), but these were not actively played out in the study group interactions.

Partly because of these "benign" characterization frames, the atmosphere in the Doan process was quite friendly and respectful throughout the two-year monthly meetings. Those interviewed for this project did not even privately express sharp negative characterizations of others (e.g., staff about environmentalists, or residents about agencies). Is there a downside to this positive atmosphere? It depends on the point of view. From the participants' perspective, the process was satisfying and successful, especially given that their dominant conflict management frame was to defer to expertise in watershed management problems. From an observer's point of view, the lack of genuine "agents" representing specific stakeholders with clear agendas, coupled with the pattern of past events, suggests that the consensus may be misleading in predicting public reactions to implementation efforts as NEORSD begins to build the solution it has proposed. Consensus within the study group is not expected to translate readily into wider community consensus about what should be done to improve the water quality in the brook. In fact, the conflict could be intensified once participants and nonparticipating stakeholders face the consequences of actual construction in the brook, rather than the currently abstract proposal many have embraced.

In the EAG case there was a polarization of roles and a balance of expertise, while in the Doan group there was a broad representation of interests and a strongly unbalanced distribution of expertise, both of which were reflected in the characterization frames. With some exceptions, EAG group members saw the caucuses at relative parity with respect to their own understanding of technical issues related to water quality standards, environmental models, and regulatory issues and processes. In contrast, the Doan Brook study group had clearly designated experts—NEORSD staff, consulting engineers, other consulting specialists, and municipal service staff—and a number of residents, environmental activists, and others with almost no understanding of environmental, modeling, and engineering knowledge. This pattern of knowledge distribution had a predictable impact on how parties characterized each other's trustworthiness. Members of the EAG group challenged each other on substantive issues more than did members of the Doan study group, who tended to characterize the technically adept parties as knowledgeable and trustworthy.

Finally, the EAG and Doan groups differed in ascribing intentionality to others. In EAG, the environmentalists ascribed to the Regulated Caucus responsibility ("intent to pollute") that was clearly irksome to the latter. In the Doan case, there was a pervasive lack of ascribed intentionality for the poor water quality. Residential use of fertilizers and pesticides, failure to deal with pet waste in the streets, and the expansion of paved surfaces (parking lots and new buildings) were major contributors to the Brook's degraded state. But there was no overt characterization of any groups as responsible, although some of the solutions discussed and even preferred by many participants involved behavioral changes on the part of the anonymous culprits.

Identity Frames

Parties in both disputes were relatively quick to adopt strong agency identities, particularly when they were formally aligned with or represented an organization. In the Doan Brook case, representatives from municipal, county, and regional entities, as well as those from nonprofit organizations and other nonresident stakeholders, each primarily identified themselves as agents or representatives. Members of the EAG not only aligned themselves formally with either the Environmental or Regulated Caucus, but also identified themselves primarily in terms of the companies, organizations, and constituencies that they were employed to represent. In both disputes, then, people at the table naturally took on agency roles. It was sometimes stated, and often implied, that participants' words and actions were those of their constituents, rather than a result of their personal interests in the dispute. Indeed, one of the key difficulties in the EAG process—the debate over a letter to the legislature regarding the "ditch bill"—occurred because Regulated Caucus members did not believe that they could step outside of their agency roles and sign the letter, despite their personal support.

Also, in both cases, participants identifying as "environmentalists" were quicker to frame themselves in a societal role (a citizen concerned about the environment) rather than taking on an agency-based identity (representing a particular organization or constituency). Though environmentalists were outnumbered by other stakeholders in both case studies, they often spoke of their desires and abilities to champion the causes of environmental protection and consensus-based decision making through their participation. In both cases, environmentalists saw inherent value in having the opportunity to voice their interests in a public forum. Recall the comment from Doan Brook: "When the minutes came back and my concerns had been recorded in black and white, people heard me and had similar concerns and it was addressed." **[Doan Brook 11]** Similarly, a member of the EAG's Environmental Caucus voiced his belief that participation in the EAG would enable him to personally bring important environmental issues to the forefront: "Our premise is that we are here to clean the water of the state, maintaining good water quality and increasing that that is of poor quality." **[Ohio 6]** In both disputes, the framing of one's identity in a societal role was more often found with environmentalists and citizen activists than with any other group of stakeholders.

The most obvious difference in identity framing between the two conflicts was largely a result of the nature of each dispute. Because the EAG dealt broadly with all waters in Ohio, there was little sense of "place-based" identity in this conflict. But this was an important component of how parties in the

Doan dispute identified themselves and each other, as illustrated by one resident: "I live in Shaker and come along the parkland and it's a real positive amenity. We are members of the community, so we do things there." **[Doan Brook 1]**

Previous research suggests that the Doan approach, coupling place-based identity with local autonomy over a watershed, should yield successful environmentally protective decisions, provided that participants in the decision-making process appropriately represent all affected stakeholders (Cannon 2000). In fact, one of the expressed purposes of the U.S. EPA's community-based environmental protection programs is to build a "sense of stewardship" around places that encourages local residents to comply with locally made decisions and to monitor other residents' actions (Siedenfeld 2000, Wagner 2000). Though the long-term effects of both the EAG and the Doan Brook processes have yet to unfold, we can speculate that one of the keys to the ultimate improvement of Doan Brook's water quality may reside in regulatory agencies' abilities to engage all affected stakeholders more actively in the substance of the discussion, and to facilitate consensus on a solution.

It is important to note that there was relatively little identity-based conflict in the Doan dispute, whereas in the EAG there were clear "battle lines" drawn for environmentalists and regulated entities and the two sides were overtly antagonistic toward one another. It may be that when an outside party actually names parties' identities, as when the OEPA designated the "Environmental" and "Regulated" caucuses on the EAG, it enhances participants' tendencies to frame their own identities in ways that polarize disputants and heighten perceptions of conflict between the parties. Similarly, most members of the EAG had engaged one another as disputants before this conflict episode, many as direct combatants as trial lawyers in court. These previous encounters may have sharpened tendencies to think of others on the EAG in terms of "us" and "them." Social identity theory, and other popular views of identity such as personal construct theory, all conclude that the presence of others who differ in salient values or characteristics heightens individuals' sense of identity vis-à-vis those values or characteristics (Eagly and Chaiken 1999). Therefore, in the EAG scenario, the mere presence of attorneys representing chemical companies heightened Environmental Caucus members' sense of their own identity as "protectors" of the environment. On the other hand, parties in the Doan Brook conflict had not had similar past experiences with one another; consequently, their identity frames may not have been as salient because previously learned defensive reactions would not have been triggered in this conflict.

Finally, it should be noted that there is potential for conflict in the place-based identities brought forth by the Doan dispute. One problem with water quality disputes is that watersheds are viewed differently by people who are upstream and downstream of one another, often because water quality is different in each place. Residents in downtown Cleveland already view the brook quite differently than do those in Cleveland Heights and Shaker Heights. Consequently, place-based identities could potentially exacerbate conflict in the future, particularly if different interests, and perhaps already-competing interest groups, come to be identified with different places along the brook.

Dispute Intractability

Are the two cases equally intractable? Are any differences reflected in the operating frames? Conflicts are intractable when they are long-standing, elude resolution, and vary in intensity over time (see Chapter 2). EAG and Doan Brook have some of these characteristics to different extents, which accounts in part for the different kinds and levels of intractability they exhibit.

Both EAG and Doan revolve around water quality issues and share the attendant dilemmas discussed earlier, including the difficulty of contending with nonpoint pollution sources, assessing and containing damage in various sections of the same watershed, and dealing with the invisibility of damage. That is, they both manifest a broader underlying conflict of some twenty-three years, sparked by federal and state regulatory events mandating water quality standards whose attainment is costly and difficult to implement, both technically and politically. The parties involved, or, more aptly, the roles they enact—regulator, municipal service staff, regulated industry, etc.—have had past encounters in this protracted and iterative conflict and will likely meet again. Even if some dispute episodes are resolved, the underlying conflict is not likely to see resolution, partly because no single episode can address all of the key issues in the conflict. In this light, both cases can be said to elude resolution because of their episodic nature. Where they differ strikingly is in the intensity of the particular conflict episodes we explored.

Of the eight key issues in the EAG case, the group resolved only five; three failed to garner consensus and were therefore left for the OEPA to decide. OEPA's position on the three unresolved issues could be challenged in the courts if any of the parties are dissatisfied with the outcome. Such dissatisfaction is bound to occur because the OEPA decision will satisfy either one side or neither side (had there been a position acceptable to both caucuses, they probably would have managed to obtain consensus). The seed of continued strife lies in the fact that the efforts to resolve the conflict satisfactorily addressed only certain parts of the problem. The comment from one Regulated Caucus member during the last meeting of the EAG is telling: "It is a foregone conclusion that all of this will wind up in court." **[Ohio 61]**

In the Doan Brook case, the study group had apparently sanctioned the engineered solutions proposed by NEORSD. But, here too, resolution has been incomplete, increasing the likelihood of the conflict resurfacing. In Doan, the incompleteness rests in the poor quality of stakeholder representation, greatly diminishing the meaning and value of the consensus. Those largely unaware of the NEORSD process and its outcomes, including most residents of neighborhoods in the three affected municipalities, will soon face NEORSD attempts to implement large-scale construction projects. Judging from past experience, residents in the two suburbs will be especially quick to oppose inconvenient and costly physical change, especially when they do not clearly understand the need for it.

The parties in the two disputes clearly differ in their absolute "level" of conflict. As we have noted, Doan Brook has been described as a "latent conflict," in that the parties were largely engaged only for purposes of voice, but not in a way that pushed for major substantive improvements in the brook's water quality. In contrast, the EAG may be described as a setting where the conflict level was moderate to high, in that both sides were constantly pushing for specific substantive outcomes in the wording of the new regulations. These conflicts thus differed significantly in their "ripeness" and in the level at which the parties engaged them. One can argue that for Doan Brook to be resolved, the conflict will require "stimulation"—that is, key stakeholders will have to become more proactively engaged in both searching for and pushing for substantive resolution to degradation in the brook. In contrast, for the antidegradation task force to achieve consensus on a new set of water quality standards, the conflict will require some degree of "tempering" to help the parties listen more effectively and work more creatively toward protecting water quality in ways that minimize economic impacts. Both conflict stimulation and conflict tempering can be managed by reframing dynamics. In the first case, the identity, characterization, and issue frames may need to be enhanced to "arouse" the neighborhood stakeholders toward a more aggressive push for management of Doan Brook; in the second case, the identity, characterization, and issue frames may need to be refined, or managed through mediation, to create new language to which all parties will agree.

Conclusions and Recommendations

The key contributors to intractability in the conflict process are the parties, the issues, and the social systems in which the conflict is embedded (Chapter 2). We review below these key components and the ways they played out in the two Ohio watershed management cases.

Parties and Issues

EAG and Doan Brook, one an over-ripe and the other an under-ripe dispute, show two faces of intractability that derived from the marked difference in the level of technical sophistication of their respective parties. EAG participants had a high level of understanding of the issues at stake, despite their complexity. Each understood the issues well, understood their opponents well, and understood the intricacies of the process in which they were engaged, as well as the alternative process options (OEPA ruling, court challenges) when they failed to agree on new rules. As a result, the parties were engaged to the point of quasi polarization, largely because of their ability to translate issues and alternatives into consequences for themselves and their constituencies. In contrast, issues were far too complex for many of the participants in the Doan Brook study group, who were often overwhelmed by the amount and technicality of the information they believed they had to master to arrive at an acceptable solution. Consequently, parties tended to focus instead on the process, which they could more readily understand, at the expense of the outcome. As a result, they were much less engaged by the issues and allowed the technical experts to control what happened.

Social Systems

The two cases were very different in scale. The EAG process addressed antidegradation standards for the entire state of Ohio, while Doan Brook dealt with a small urban watershed and local constituencies. It seems the scale difference was reflected in some of the frames. In the context of the statewide case, the resulting parties' relationship was agency-based and "professional–adversarial." The Regulated Caucus consisted of agents from major developers, and all the parties had encountered each other in a variety of other environmental forums. In the Doan case, the relationships between parties were more personal and friendly. In both cases, these differences created clear consequences in terms of the identity and characterization frames previously described.

Conflict Processes

Finally, the two cases were also quite different in conflict processes. In the EAG, conflict had clearly grown to the polarization stage (see Table 2.1). Each had strong preferences for its own group, had clear negative stereotypes of the other group, and minimized their communication except when formally at the table. There was some evidence of segregation, but not very strongly. In contrast, at Doan Brook, the conflict stayed primarily at the discussion stage. In fact, it was the general absence of intense conflict around a specific incident or crisis—defined in Table 2.1 as a "contained and focused commitment to resolving issues"—that may have under-engaged the parties and minimized their ability to achieve any significant resolution.

Frames

In addition, differences in identity frames were likely the result of the nature of the two disputes. The EAG's statewide scope meant that participants sought broad standards to sustain water quality across a variety of situations and contexts. In this broad context, it made sense that participants would view themselves and others in terms of their agency roles and general beliefs or principles. On the other hand, Doan's local scope encouraged participants to focus on a specific context and engendered a sense of place-based identity that was absent in the EAG dispute.

Outcomes

Finally, we need to inquire about the impact of the two cases on the environmental outcomes. For the EAG, the impact will be new antidegradation rules that should enhance the quality of water throughout the state of Ohio. For Doan Brook, the ultimate outcome will be measures to improve water quality in the Doan Brook. Where does the environment fare better? Is it in the wake of protracted EAG negotiations? or following the convivial but latently intractable Doan study?

In the EAG case, failure to reach consensus leads the OEPA to make recommendations for new rules, a "worst case scenario" that ostensibly would protect the environment to some extent. It is noteworthy that the parties were able to reach consensus on the majority of issues: the process clearly had merit if we evaluate it in light of the substantive outcomes on which the caucuses were able to agree. However, in the significant areas where the EAG failed to reach consensus, each party can, and likely will, challenge the OEPA decisions in court. In this regard, the environment is protected only so long as the court rules in its favor, which is by no means certain.

In the Doan case, the parties do not appear to clearly perceive the consequences of failure to agree on watershed management measures. They seem to misconstrue the absence of final decisions as tantamount to absence of consequences. The consequence of inaction is further deterioration of the watershed: "Cleveland fiddles and Doan burns." It appears that, because the rules for engagement and subsequent follow-up activities were relatively poorly defined in the Doan Brook case, there is more room for inaction and consequently a higher likelihood of water quality degradation in the long run (see the discussion of role-ambiguous social systems in Chapter 2).

Ironically, parties in the Doan Brook dispute were more conscious of the merits of participating in the decision-making process than were members of the EAG. In the EAG, participants were driven both by strongly held principles and by role responsibilities that had been ingrained through years of interaction. Consequently, their interaction did relatively little in terms of changing participants' minds: instead, it sharpened their characterization and identity frames. Though it had valuable outcomes, the process itself was viewed as only another episode in their ongoing dispute. On the other hand, Doan Brook participants viewed the process more developmentally, valuing it not only as a forum to voice their ideas and concerns, but also as a means of obtaining technical information. Consequently, their tendency to view the conflict through the lens of a process frame was enhanced, whereas identity and characterization frames were relatively less important.

Theoretically, these disputes shed light on both the importance of framing and the nature of dispute intractability. Differences in identity, characterization, and conflict management/process frames exacerbated conflict among the parties in the EAG. But in the Doan Brook case, conflict was minimal between individuals who, despite differing identity claims, shared a common view of the conflict as a search for a technical solution to the watershed's problems. Together, these disputes provide strong evidence for the power of framing to both intensify and moderate conflicts. Similarly, these disputes provide evidence that intractable conflicts can take two forms: latent and manifest. Though many water quality issues take the form of latent conflicts because of difficulties associated with accurately assessing the presence and effect of pollutants in a watershed, it is still appropriate to view these disputes as intractable.

Practically, our analysis of these disputes suggests that conflict episodes may be more readily resolved if participants share a common frame of the dispute resolution process. Convening agencies and third parties would be well-advised to carefully articulate the goals of the process and the role that each participant is expected to play when putting together watershed management advisory groups. Similarly, parties to the dispute should have a clear understanding of expected and desired outcomes of their interaction, and shared criteria for evaluating proposals and decisions. Though water quality disputes can properly be called intractable, it is possible to achieve consensus in particular episodes of this conflict if the process of debate and compromise is carefully managed.

Part III

Toxics Cases

Chapter 10

The Story of Drake Chemical: A Burning Issue

Ralph Hanke, Adam Rosenberg, and Barbara Gray

Dealing with hazardous waste is a challenge for the United States. As of January 2001, there were 40,000 toxic sites in this country, including 1700 on the Superfund National Priorities List. These sites include abandoned waste storage or treatment plants, chemical facilities, as well as weapons manufacturing and mining facilities, and they pose the greatest threat to public health and the environment. The Comprehensive Environmental Response, Compensation, and Liability Act (CERCLA), otherwise known as Superfund, became law December 11, 1980, and is the largest single project of the Environmental Protection Agency (EPA). CERCLA's focus is to provide remedies for toxic waste sites and to ensure the public health and well-being of the citizens of the United States.

In the beautiful and wooded Appalachian Mountains of central Pennsylvania lies the Bald Eagle Valley. Flowing through this valley are the Bald Eagle Creek and the Susquehanna River, both of which are part of the Chesapeake Bay watershed. Where the Susquehanna River and the Bald Eagle Creek meet lies the town of Lock Haven. Lock Haven is home to an inordinate number of bladder cancer cases. Researchers eventually linked these cases to the site of Drake Chemical Inc. (Drake) in the southeast section of the town. What was unearthed at this Superfund site—and what happened at the site—is not nearly as pretty as the surrounding countryside.

This chapter examines what happened at the Drake site between 1984 and 1999 and provides an overview of the conflict at the Drake site. We do not pretend to know what should or should not have happened in this dispute nor do we profess to know whether incineration was the appropriate means of remediation. Our concern is with the frames the disputants used and how those frames contributed to the extensive, and sometimes very acrimonious, conflict about incineration; and so we invite you to join us on a journey examining a very fascinating, and at times perplexing, conflict.

History of the Site

Killsdonk Chemical first built a chemical production facility on the Drake site in the late 1940s. Drake Chemical Inc. bought the property and manufacturing facilities in 1962. Drake manufactured chemical intermediates—wholesale chemicals that serve as raw materials for other chemicals—for producers of dyes, pharmaceuticals, cosmetics, textiles, and pesticides. The company produced chemicals in small-batch kettles, and whenever they improperly mixed a production run, overproduced a compound, or lost an order they dumped the chemical mix into the lagoon ponds behind the facility. Chemical sludge filled these unlined lagoons, and leachate from the lagoons moved steadily toward the Bald Eagle Creek.

Drake operated in this fashion until the early 1980s. At that time, the Pennsylvania Department of Environmental Regulation (DER), now the Pennsylvania Department of Environmental Protection (DEP), enacted stringent environmental regulations prohibiting Drake from disposing of chemicals on their property and mandating them to clean up and seal the lagoons. In January of 1982, Drake filed for bankruptcy, due mainly to the high cost of complying with the tougher environmental regulations.

Drake Chemical left the site highly contaminated, particularly with a compound called Betanepthalamine (BNA). BNA is a semivolatile organic material that absorbs through the skin and is implicated in bladder cancer. Because of the presence of BNA, Drake was one of the first properties identified as an abandoned hazardous waste site under the Superfund Act. By 1984, Drake reached the top-ten list of Superfund sites and became eligible to receive priority funding for remediation.

The Government Steps In

In 1984, the EPA wrote the first of three Records of Decisions (RODs) for the Drake site. A ROD is a public document that delineates the remediation process approved by the EPA for cleaning up a Superfund site. The first ROD was primarily concerned with slowing the flow of leachate through the ground. Remediation activities under this ROD included partially excavating contaminated soils, capping the remaining contaminated soils to inhibit the flow of leachate from the site, and temporarily disposing of excavated sediments in a storage facility constructed on-site (EPA 1984).

The first ROD was effectively a stopgap measure and did not arrest the flow of leachate. It also did not address the source of many of the problems: the buildings, materials, and sludge on the site itself. Therefore, the EPA proposed a second ROD, and remediation under this proposed ROD included draining and removing the lined wastewater treatment lagoons, removing all buildings and debris, incinerating all chemicals and sludge in an off-site Resource Conservation and Recovery Act (RCRA)-permitted incinerator, placing extraction wells around the site, and then, finally, capping and abandoning the entire site and keeping it off-limits to the public. Capping and abandoning the site meant putting a layer of clay over the contaminated soils to prevent rainwater from leaching into the soils, thereby isolating the contaminants from the groundwater aquifer.

Consistent with EPA policy, the remedial project manager (RPM) for the site held a public meeting in September 1985 and presented this proposed ROD to the local Lock Haven community. Only Lock Haven City Council representatives were present at the meeting, and they opposed the EPA's decision to cap and abandon the site because they were uncomfortable about capping a property located in a floodplain. Furthermore, they opposed abandoning the site because they wanted to see the property return to productive use on the Lock Haven tax base. City Council's resistance initiated the first major conflict over the Drake site.

During the next six months the EPA, DEP, and City Council examined alternatives to the proposed ROD, including a proposal to remove all contaminated soils with disposal at a toxic waste landfill site. As City Council considered this proposal, the DEP agreed to it. At the same time, however, the U.S. House of Representatives passed the Superfund Amendments and Reauthorization Act (SARA), an amendment to CERCLA, in October 1986. SARA stressed permanent remedies and innovative treatment technologies in cleaning up hazardous waste sites. An EPA employee said, "[T]he landfill option was now the least preferable and actual treatment, getting rid of the problem, the most preferable." SARA also prohibited litigation to block cleanup once a ROD chose and formalized a method of cleanup for a Superfund site. This point of law would ultimately play a large role in the ensuing conflict.

Four elements were now present in the conflict. First, and foremost, the EPA wanted to treat the site to eliminate the leachate because all the parties became increasingly concerned that the chemicals from the Drake site would soon enter the Chesapeake Bay watershed system. Second, SARA's proposed changes were looming. Third, Pennsylvania did not have an appropriate landfill facility to handle the contaminated soil. Fourth, Lock Haven City Council wanted the Drake site back on the tax rolls. The confluence of these four factors prompted the EPA to eliminate the "cap and abandon" portion of the proposed ROD. This modification met with everyone's approval, so the EPA signed the second ROD in May of 1986 (EPA 1986). As part of the cleanup, the EPA carried out a series of Remedial Investigation/Feasibility Studies (RI/FS) on the contaminated soil and groundwater. The studies indicated that the contamination covered the entire area and extended to the water table. In 1988, the EPA completed the RI/FS, and the EPA project manager announced another public meeting to propose the third ROD.

This ROD proposed excavating the contaminated soils, sludge, and leachate lagoon sediments at the site and decontaminating that material using a transportable, on-site incinerator (EPA 1988). The EPA held the public meeting for the third ROD in September 1988. Very few people attended this meeting as well. According to an EPA employee, all but one of the participants at the meeting liked the idea of incineration. This employee expressed surprise that no one at the meeting questioned how safe incineration might be. A Lock Haven City Council member present at the meeting stated that he found nothing wrong with the incineration process because "I understood the mechanics of the process and did not see anything to be concerned about." Thus the proposed ROD was accepted and supported at the public meeting. The EPA signed the third ROD on September 29, 1988, and began the third phase of the cleanup.

When the EPA signed the third ROD, they had no set procedure for developing bid specifications on an incinerator: "There wasn't an outline to follow." In addition, the EPA found it difficult to assign someone to Lock Haven for the extended period required for building and managing an incinerator. Therefore, the EPA turned to the Army Corps of Engineers to help develop the specifications for the project and, eventually, to handle the day-to-day engineering and contract management of the incineration process. The Army Corps of Engineers was very precise about the bid specification process; consequently the EPA did not release the call for proposals until the spring of 1993.

While the bid specifications were developing, the EPA held another public meeting in August 1992. At that meeting, they presented the first of three risk assessments they would ultimately write for the Drake site. An EPA employee emphasizes that the EPA took the initiative to write this risk assessment to help the community find out about the risks associated with incineration. Although not as detailed as the two later risk assessments, this first assessment concluded that incineration did not pose an appreciable hazard to the community.

The seven-year delay in building the incinerator fostered a number of complaints. For example, one state environmental official expressed dismay over the EPA's management of the project during that time. One official put it this way: "It, uh, took 'em a very long time and a whole lotta money." It took roughly another year after the EPA let the contract to set up the incinerator. However, incineration did not commence as planned in 1994. According to a DEP employee, "The dirt was ready to go into the incinerator and then there was a stop."

The AIR That We Breathe

That stop was the result of an environmental citizens' group called AIR (Arrest the Incinerator Remediation) whose members opposed the incineration. AIR came on the scene in the summer of 1994, just as construction of the incinerator was about to begin. AIR's involvement represents the beginning of the major, protracted conflict on the Drake site. As far as the City Council, DEP, and the EPA were concerned, AIR literally came out of nowhere. As one agency official put it:

> I would be really interested if they could cough up some good solid reasons why they chose to make this such a career, for years, from so far away as from out of the county. Why they didn't do something before. **[1]***

AIR believed that the incinerator posed three major problems. First, the incinerator would emit dioxin—a particularly dangerous substance. Second, atmospheric thermal inversions in the Bald Eagle Valley would trap dioxin emissions within the valley, thereby increasing health risks. Third, the proposed kiln-style incinerator was outdated, dangerous, and likely to emit unknown gases into the environment. According to an AIR member, "When the chemicals are coming out of the stack, nobody knows what is coming out."

These concerns surprised the EPA. To the EPA, AIR members seemed inflexible and unnecessarily worried given that the first risk assessment showed incineration was safe. According to an EPA employee, "AIR was unwilling to listen to what we had to say." AIR countered that they had listened to the EPA but did not like what they heard.

> I think EPA gets away pretty easily by having technologies and risk assessments that are so complicated that the guy on the street can't read them and that's part of the way they win. They win with technical jargon. **[2]**

---

* In subsequent chapters, this quote will be referenced as "Drake 1," and subsequent quotes from this chapter as "Drake 2," "Drake 3," etc.

Furthermore, AIR believed that the risk assessment was fundamentally flawed.

> [EPA] said, well even if a little bit of dioxin does come out the stack, it is okay because it is not as much as the background level of dioxin because it is everywhere. That is crazy. That is like saying, well if water is dripping into a cup and the cup is half full and we put one more drop in there, they are saying that that one more drop is okay, but no, that one more drop makes the cup fuller. **[3]**

Other members of the community also got involved in the dispute. For example, one member of the Environmental Affairs Committee of Lock Haven City Council (EAC) expressed concern that the incinerator would be unable to achieve the high level of burning efficiency expected by EPA scientists. This person also disliked the possibility that the burn would release harmful heavy metals such as mercury, chromium-6, and beryllium. Other members of the community who eventually joined AIR shared these kinds of concerns. One such person reflected on how little they knew about incineration at the time.

> I can remember at the time, I read it in the paper, and I thought yeah, there you go. You got all that poison out there, if you burn it, and then we won't have that poison any more. . . . But I knew very little about incinerating back then. Some of the folks who started the AIR group convinced me that there was a lot more there, a lot more to this, than met the eye. **[4]**

On the other hand, another EAC member did not feel threatened by the burn. This person believed that soil incineration posed a very small risk to healthy individuals especially when comparing the risk of incineration to the risk of leaving the site without remediation. A member of City Council at the time expressed similar views, arguing that as far as they were concerned the EPA and DEP scientists had satisfactorily addressed the issue of the heavy metals and therefore there was little health risk involved with the burn.

Fearing for the safety of the people in the community, AIR proposed a prototype closed-loop system (i.e., one that produced no emissions whatsoever) to replace the incinerator. The closed-loop system boiled the polluted dirt, gathered the contaminant by-products in containers, and shipped those containers off-site. The EPA states that they were aware of the closed-loop technology that AIR preferred and opposed the system because they believed that it would not work adequately in a large-scale operation like Drake. That disagreement meant the conflict soon became very public and acrimonious. The EPA held several public meetings at the end of 1994 and throughout

1995 designed to engage AIR and others in a public input process. AIR, however, did not see these meetings as conducive to public input.

> Some of the meetings that they had for us they would announce the day before. A lot of people (in Lock Haven) are working people. They would have it in the middle of the day which people couldn't [attend] on short notice like that. Or they missed the one single article, little ad in the paper. Nobody really knew much about it. They really didn't advertise well. **[5]**

A Distinct Increase in AIR Pressure

Therefore, AIR went on the offensive. For one, they did not believe the EPA when the EPA said the closed-loop system would not work. Indeed, AIR saw a more sinister motive behind the EPA's decision to stay with the proposed rotary kiln incinerator. AIR believed the EPA did not wish to adopt their (AIR's) "perfectly acceptable" system because the Army Corps of Engineers was "in the back pocket" of the incineration contracting company. Further, members of AIR believed that the EPA's science was "bought," either through pork-barreling or private industry influence.

> They brought in the dike levy first. They broke the spirit of the people with the dike levy project. People fought their hearts out against the same Army Corps of Engineers that is now running this project and then after they break people's spirit with that they come in on the heels of the dike levy project the same Army Corps of Engineers and says, now we've got an incinerator for ya. Anybody want to fight? And people went "Hell no. We don't want to fight. We can't fight. There is no sense fighting." And that's exactly what they wanted. Because they didn't want anybody interfering with this larger pork barrel, that was a bigger pork barrel than the first pork barrel that came through. **[6]**

To further strengthen their position, AIR recruited members throughout the region and mobilized student support at Lock Haven University. In addition, they instituted a letter writing campaign to state, local, and federal representatives asking them to approach the EPA and demand they shut down the incinerator—which many representatives did. AIR also sought an audience with Vice President Gore. To convince City Council to ask EPA to reopen the ROD and consider alternatives to incineration, AIR regularly attended Lock

Haven City Council meetings. At one point in 1995, AIR was able to persuade City Council to send a letter requesting the EPA reconsider the ROD. However, City Council reconsidered that stance and quickly withdrew the letter. Other than this small deviation, Lock Haven City Council remained firmly in favor of incineration. Further, most members of the council were very unsympathetic to AIR and saw AIR's actions as overly aggressive. As one member and local elected official put it:

> The vocal minority, the people who are nasty, just nasty. I mean, you have to sit at a council meeting to see . . . the hatred. You just sit there and you try to make real judgments; it's real problems. Someone sat there and gave me a lecture on my role in government, someone who I don't think can pick up and carry my jock strap. **[7]**

Nevertheless, AIR had more success at the county level as one of their members ran for a county seat on an anti-incineration platform and won.

> [I]n the face of my election, . . . claiming that if I got elected I would do anything in my power to stop the Drake Incinerator . . . [there are still] a lot of . . . arguments that people will use against the AIR group . . . (such as) "where were you eight years ago or nine years ago" and my answer to them is "I was in college." So, you know . . . your life priorities change as you get older and as you learn more about the situation. **[8]**

This victory provided AIR with important financial support and power as many of the local county councils soon voted in favor of sending money to AIR to support their attempt to stop incineration. In fact, the Clinton County Commissioner's Office would eventually join forces with AIR to launch a lawsuit aimed at stopping the incinerator.

In addition, AIR recruited the support of the local farm bureau and the local farming community. AIR argued that by contaminating the valley with dioxins, the incinerator would subsequently poison the farmers' crops and livestock and thereby put the farmers out of business. Indeed, AIR approached two major grocery chains that wrote letters clearly stating they would not buy produce grown in the Lock Haven area unless it was tested for dioxins and shown to be safe. One of the proponents of the incineration saw these efforts to recruit support from the farming community in a dim light.

> The bottom line was that those kinds of things I believe were criminal. To say that this is going to cause cancer . . . you're going

> to die of cancer, or this milk is going to be ruined, or [Major Grocery Chain] is not going to buy product . . . all those kind of things are just blatantly not true. . . . To make believe that the soils are going to be contaminated and the fields are going to be contaminated and the milk two valleys over is going to be undrinkable—these are criminal kinds of things. **[9]**

AIR members also took a pledge of nonviolence. To ensure they could keep that pledge and still forcefully fight incineration, AIR hired a trainer so they could learn methods of nonviolent civil disobedience. That disobedience included chaining themselves to the fence at the Drake property in an attempt to halt the incinerator. In spite of these efforts on AIR's part, not all proponents of the incineration believed that AIR members took that pledge of nonviolence seriously.

Reactions to the Pressure

AIR hoped chaining themselves to the fence might gain national exposure and force the EPA to abandon incineration. Although the regional television stations and the regional daily newspapers covered the event, AIR was unable to garner the national attention they sought. Worse, many DEP and EPA officials considered these activities as nothing more than a nuisance and further reasons to disregard AIR and their concerns.

> Most of the time I just wouldn't talk. I just wouldn't talk at all. I wouldn't meet with them. They went overboard. **[10]**

Further, a member of EAC argued there were better ways for AIR supporters to accomplish their goals than chaining themselves to the Drake site or practicing civil disobedience. In addition, this person recalls how he eventually found AIR's tactics so atrocious that he could no longer get himself to hear what AIR had to say.

> [My son] is a registered Independent. One day, when this dispute was really firing up, he was greeted on the street by a group of younger AIR members . . . and was genuinely harassed—I mean to the point that they seemed to indicate that, ah, there might be some pushing around. My son served four years in the U.S. Navy and knows how to take care of himself, and he finally looked at them and said, "Look, I'm tired; I'm just out of work; all I want to do is go home. I don't think you really want to press this any fur-

> ther" and sort of walked through them to his car and came home. That they would do this—it took me a long time to get over the anger it aroused in me, and I would, if you press me to the wall, have to admit that yes, it gave a certain edge to my participation in the debate; and they foreshortened my ability to see merit in any of their arguments. **[11]**

In spite of AIR's genuine dedication to what they saw as a very real danger, proponents of the incineration saw many of AIR's tactics in a very negative light. For example, a former member of AIR paints AIR's actions with very dark brush strokes.

> I tell ya, there's nothing more frustrating when you ask [the AIR leaders] a question and it's not answered. There's nothing more frustrating when you ask a legitimate question, and you get the run around. Now, I think that they do this, to frustrate ya just to move on and not worry about what they're looking at. **[12]**

Another former member adds

> And then I'd ask a million and one questions of the AIR leaders. But asking the million and one questions also means taking some of the answers and believing that [they are] true, and that's not something that I felt AIR was willing to do. Everything was a lie, it didn't matter what was said [by the EPA and city council], everything was a lie. Well, okay if you want to feel that way, but that's pretty narrow-minded. **[13]**

AIR's response to these kinds of frames was that faulty or flawed data—provided by the EPA and other institutions—duped people into believing incineration was safe and leaving AIR. Furthermore, the AIR leaders contended that one of the individuals who left AIR was "a mole planted by City Council" and therefore this person's interview and condemnation of AIR should not be taken seriously.

Further, one government employee suggested that AIR could engage in behaviors that were harmful against "innocent" people and such behaviors prompted some supporters of incineration to label many of AIR's behaviors as "scare tactics." For example, on the Monday following the 1997 Super Bowl, AIR accused Drake cleanup workers of drinking on the site during a series of trial burns. To substantiate their claim, AIR members showed the EPA supervisors a dumpster within the Drake complex that contained both empty beer cans and pizza boxes. To AIR, this discovery was very significant and indicated at least two things. AIR believed that it demonstrated that people on the site could potentially be mishandling the incineration equipment and thereby exacerbating the potential damage to the community. Furthermore, AIR saw the beer cans as evidence that the EPA was unable to adequately supervise the activities at the incinerator.

In response to AIR's claim that drinking was occurring on-site, the EPA removed five employees from the site and tested them for alcohol. Their tests were negative and the EPA claimed that there was no evidence of actual drinking on the site. Further, some proponents of the incinerator speculated that AIR planted the cans and the pizza boxes since "they knew exactly which dumpster to go to." AIR denies this accusation stating, "We had an informant who told us which two dumpsters always contained pizza and beer boxes." Although no one has yet substantiated or disproved whether AIR planted the materials, the situation led an agency official to characterize AIR as follows

> And I do believe the leadership of this particular activist group has lied to their own members because I'm sure they don't check either. They believe in the people who are leading them. And they sound very rational unless you manage to push them over the edge. You present this as a truth and your own people believe it. They don't run over and check. So, you know, it's fostering fear unnecessarily. **[14]**

In spite of these strong words, AIR held firm to their position that drinking on-site was a serious problem they had exposed through their vigilance.

> Based on a tip from a garbage hauler, we were told that beer and pizza were the foods of choice on-site and that we would find both at anytime. Thus, video camera in hand and in the secured area of the site, we started searching dumpsters and videotaped empty six packs mixed in with calibration documents in bags. We didn't accuse them, we caught them! **[15]**

In another attempt to alert people to the danger of incineration and the proponents' willingness to lie about the safety of incineration, an AIR member, frustrated with the DEP's lack of responsiveness to the video they took of the incinerator "discharging emissions," as AIR put it, wrote in a newsletter that a member of the monitoring staff was a perjurer. Such tactics met with stiff oppositions by the proponents of the incineration. As one DEP official stated,

> That was just wrong . . . and so, you know, when they do stuff like that. If they called me names because I represent the government, I wouldn't like it but I'd tolerate it. When they called her a perjurer, that really made me mad. So, any consideration that I would have given him in the future is gone. He's done. I don't think he cares, or he knows but . . . **[16]**

AIR, on the other hand, maintained they needed to adopt a confrontational stance to protect the safety of the community and deal with the tactics of those in favor of the incinerator.

> You get to a point where you become very battle hardened and you realize that you are not going to get the truth from somebody unless you pull it out of them under oath. Sitting around the table with them is a waste of our time, and our time is a premium. . . . You know, I mean the amount of our lives that we've put into this fight has been a tremendous investment of time. Emotion, time, money, health. I mean you name it, we've run ourselves ragged trying to stop this project and we've tried everything. We've tried conflict resolution, we've tried dialogue, we've tried everything right into court. And, here we are. **[17]**

The Environmental Protection Agency's Response

The EPA responded to AIR's concerns three ways. First, they carried out a new risk assessment to replace the second one. Next, they undertook what became known as the "moss-bag study." Third, they built a specialized meteorological station next to the Drake site. The new risk assessment purported to address the dioxin possibility as well as the concerns expressed by AIR about the thermal inversions in the Bald Eagle Valley.

The EPA considered the moss-bag study a very innovative approach for measuring the presence of dioxins. Animals do not absorb dioxins directly. Rather, plants absorb dioxins from the air and water and then animals ingest the dioxins by eating those plants. Therefore, to avoid slaughtering farm animals—and to avoid potentially embarrassing a local farmer—claimed the EPA, "we placed moss bags throughout the region to measure for the presence of dioxins." To AIR, the moss-bag study was nothing more than "filler," a way to assuage the public and to make up for broken promises. Furthermore, AIR felt the moss-bag study represented a turning point. The EPA worked very closely with the Farm Bureau, the local farmers, and the major grocery chains. In the end, these organizations were convinced that incineration was safe. AIR, on the other hand, felt "cut out" of these meetings and, therefore, that their trust was broken. The Farm Bureau's change of heart was particularly painful for AIR since a member of the Farm Bureau had originally been very outspoken in their criticism of incineration. A member of AIR made no bones how they felt about the "traitor" who eventually revised her appraisal of the incinerator's safety.

> I trust her absolutely as much as I trust the padding under that carpet to make me not slip over there, which is not very much on that little rug. Okay? **[18]**

The EPA designed the meteorological station to measure atmospheric conditions and show if an inversion was occurring. The idea was to provide a local "check point" for shutting down the incinerator. The readings made at the weather station were also "broadcast" to the community through a downtown storefront. As far as AIR was concerned, "We don't think it worked, and besides, it did not measure the chemicals of concern." Nevertheless, this service was very soothing to one City Council official:

> Those were two of my biggest concerns in the beginning because, the push was from AIR that it affects children and old people first, and that was a big concern of mine. But you know once you see the readings, and you see the test results, and see that there are no real big fluctuations, and that you're dealing in the billionths and trillionths, it doesn't make as much of an impact as when somebody is talking about [how] it's going to get into the breast milk and babies are going to be slow, and have problems. That kind of stuff, unless it's really substantiated, doesn't hold water. **[19]**

It is important to note that the EPA was very proud of these efforts and they felt they had addressed the concerns expressed by the public in a fair and scientific way. One EPA employee said that the moss-bag study and the Farm Bureau's satisfaction with its results showed that the EPA provided "conflict resolution where a resolution is possible." This same person, however, also thought that AIR did not establish open communication:

> [AIR's mind] was made up. They felt that incineration is the wrong thing to do no matter how safe you can show it to be. Their stance was one more dioxin molecule is a bad thing and there is no gray

area . . . and . . . there was nothing I could say or do to make them feel I was protecting them. **[20]**

A long-term member of AIR substantiates that concern. This person and his spouse practice a lifestyle that incorporates many aspects of living off the land. He believed the incinerator directly endangered their lifestyle:

> Even a minuscule amount, whatever amount comes out of that stack at Drake is more than we had before. Or whatever comes out of the water that is coming down out of the stack is more than we had before. So wherever it goes, whether it goes on the grass that the cows eat and the deer eat, or into the fish, it is a fat stored toxin. So, if you are eating something that is contaminated, it is building up, every bit is stored. They have more than what is on the ground. We are hunters here. If we are eating deer meat, we are eating whatever they have absorbed at a higher level. **[21]**

A Courtin' We Will Go

In an attempt to alleviate such fears, the EPA presented the results of the new risk assessment at a public meeting in December 1995. In January 1996, AIR rejected the risk assessment and in conjunction with the Clinton County Commissioner's Office, filed a suit against the incinerator in the Williamsport, Pennsylvania, federal court. The session in Judge Muir's court proved momentous for both sides. On the second day of the trial in March 1996, the EPA decided that the new risk assessment was, as an EPA employee put it, "not good enough and that it needed to be done over." The EPA stated in court that they wanted to refine portions of the risk assessment and come back to the court when it was finished. Judge Muir immediately adjourned the hearing and created a court order that delayed the incineration indefinitely.

AIR was ecstatic. As far as they were concerned, they finally had indisputable proof that the government regularly lied about the Drake cleanup process. This ecstasy is understandable given AIR's expressed concern that incineration could "annihilate" the population in the valley.

> I think there is a very, very real chance of people having preexisting conditions that are susceptible to that type of contamination. I think there is a real risk of premature death and illness for those who are susceptible to that kind of contamination. And maybe for

> the Drake workers themselves. There may be a possibility that a lot of them will have bladder cancer. I hope not. **[22]**

AIR's joy proved to be short-lived however. After asking for a series of extensions, both AIR and the EPA returned to Judge Muir's court in August 1996. Ironically, Muir did not consider the refined risk assessment but ruled that no one can challenge the remedy at a Superfund site—incineration in this case—once the remedy has been started. The time to challenge a remedy, argued Muir, is before it is started or after it is completed. AIR appealed Muir's decision to the Third Circuit Court in Philadelphia, where it was upheld in June 1997 by a vote of 12–0. AIR subsequently filed a petition with the Supreme Court in September 1997. The Supreme Court rejected that petition in January 1998, and, subsequently, the Clinton County Commissioner's Office distanced itself from AIR.

As far as the EPA was concerned, "[T]he conflict was resolved because it went to the Supreme Court and the court said incineration cannot be stopped." The DEP was also satisfied, regardless of the legal ruling, that incineration was indeed the way to go.

> The whole risk assessment issue and their review of the risk assessment; to a person like myself who is scientifically based but not in all of these fields, able to understand it, but not qualified in any of them. Gave me a reassurance . . . of what EPA and my people have been told. **[23]**

While all this legal jockeying was going on, the EPA continued to refine the risk assessment—now known as the third risk assessment—by using data from a number of trial burns during late 1996 and early 1997. The EPA presented the findings from these trial burns to the Lock Haven community at a regular series of public meetings. Again, the EPA was proud of how they were involving the community in the process.

> I think you need to know that we have presented the facts of this incineration project, the actual data we've collected. We have been very forthcoming and open with the entire community. **[24]**

Similarly, it is important to note that AIR did not believe the veracity of the EPA's data and publicly stated that the EPA was blatantly lying about their data and findings at these meetings.

In its final analysis, the third risk assessment compared the expected cancer rate after incineration with the normally occurring rate (i.e., the base rate) of cancer within the local population. The EPA's risk assessment estimated that if 10 million people ingested every bit of emission from the incinerator over two years, then only one additional person would be expected to develop some form of cancer. Many people complained about the way the EPA presented their findings to the community. In particular, they were frustrated about what they perceived as the inability of EPA scientists to use language appropriate for an audience of nonscientists. Because EPA scientists used complex statistical procedures and unfamiliar terminology, it was difficult for community members to understand the results of the assessment studies. Therefore, they felt that the EPA scientists trivialized what they, the citizens, considered significant health risks. As one city councilman put it, the EPA scientists "never took off their scientist's hat and put on their grandfather's hat."

After the risk assessment was completed, a review panel of fourteen academic scientists from around the country deliberated over the assessment's findings. The panel then met in Williamsport in January 1998 for two days of public meetings. At those meetings, the panel concluded that the assumptions behind the risk assessment and its methodologies were very conservative, and that the assessment was scientific, safe, and free of bias. Following the review, the regional administrator for the EPA met with AIR and all of the local governmental bodies at Lock Haven University. The EPA used the results of the third risk assessment to publicly argue that incineration was safe. AIR was no more satisfied with this assessment and its peer review than it was with the original assessments. AIR complained that the EPA allowed only one recommended scientist from AIR to serve on the review committee. As far as AIR was concerned,

> Every other person on that peer review was an industry person or a researcher, who had received money from the EPA for research. So they stacked their own peer review and expected us not to see it. Or else didn't give a shit. I don't know which. And when they submitted their findings, they had this big peer review sham . . . during the day in Williamsport so that Lock Haven people couldn't get to it."† **[25]**

AIR tried to offset the results of this review by holding their own "Real Review" in Lock Haven at the end of January. AIR hired some of their own scientists and researchers and invited some prominent environmentalists to

† The distance between downtown Williamsport and downtown Lock Haven is roughly 25 miles and takes approximately 35 minutes to travel by car.

attend this review. This review panel concluded that the EPA placed "policy before good science" and that the incineration should not proceed.

Nevertheless, the thermal destruction facility began operation in March 1998. However, within three days the DEP filed two Notices of Violation on the incinerator; and, under state nuisance statutes, AIR filed a suit in state court against the contractor conducting the incineration. Because the incinerator was implemented as part of a federal contract, the suit was transferred to federal court, where Judge Muir granted two days to hear AIR's request for a restraining order. Judge Muir listened to the testimony on both sides and concluded there was no proven case of imminent threat to health, and declined the request to stop incineration. Further, Muir rendered a judgment stating that the matters involved in this case, as in the previous case, could not proceed because of CERCLA and, furthermore, they did not fall under state nuisance ordinances; thus he dismissed the case.

AIR appealed once again to the Third Circuit Court of Appeals, where the deposition was heard in Philadelphia during February 1999. During the deposition, one of the three panel judges supposedly argued that the appeal of AIR was a moot issue because incineration would be completed before the appeals court would be able to reach a decision. At that point, AIR's legal representative allegedly said that AIR was trying to establish the principle that any form of incineration is harmful. That statement suggests that for AIR, the incineration debate had moved beyond a safety issue for the Lock Haven community and was now a national concern about citizens' rights associated with government-sponsored cleanups. In spite of this concerted attempt to stop the incineration, an EPA official argued that by December 1998, "[T]here was really no conflict that we could see, other than AIR proceeding with the appellate case." Similarly, a DEP official at the time held that

> There is only one answer to this. That is to finish it as quick as possible. The pain will not go away until after that. It diminishes once you get past the court case but your best defense is to treat early first. Because they can say whatever lie they want. And the second things is to keep the pedal to the metal. And, you get it [the incineration] done as fast as you can, because that's the only thing that's gonna make it go away. **[26]**

In spite of courageous efforts, AIR was unable to garner enough public support to stop incineration. Members of AIR claimed it was because the government had broken the spirit of the town:

> Let's face it . . . people like to win. People don't like to lose, and I think that after they saw the dike levy go in, they saw . . . [fighting the government to be] a losing battle . . . [and that] we [the government] don't care whether you want this incinerator or not, we're going to build it and we're going to burn it and you're going to breathe it. That's exactly the attitude from the beginning. There was never any, never once, any serious discussion about another method. Even though the EPA had every opportunity in Clinton County to try other methods . . . What I've seen here reminded me of the storm troopers of Nazi Germany. **[27]**

They reiterated this many times:

> Yeah, and we hate them because they have no integrity, because they lied and because they are fighting us with our own resources. **[28]**

The Court of Appeals did not grant AIR its second appeal and the EPA completed the incineration on April 22, 1999—Earth Day.

Frames and Situational Factors: The Sources of Intractability

The following analysis focuses primarily on the conflict between 1994 and 1999. A number of situational dynamics and the sociolinguistic frames held by the stakeholders can explain the intractability of the Drake conflict during those years. A model of the interrelationships of these factors appears in Figure 10.1. Three factors—misconceptions, differences in risk perception frames, and social identity frames—contributed to the stakeholders' negative assessment of the credibility of information provided by other stakeholders. These negative assessments led to a cycle of damaging communication, distinguished by negative characterization frames, selective listening, and suspicion and mistrust. This cycle along with social identity frames prompted the disputants' choice of conflict management frames. These conflict management frames, together with the cycle of damaging communication, led to the intractability of the dispute.

Misconceptions

Misconceptions played a predominant role in the conflict during the turbulent years. Misconceptions differ from ignorance and indifference. In this case, each disputing party appeared to honestly believe it had the best interests of

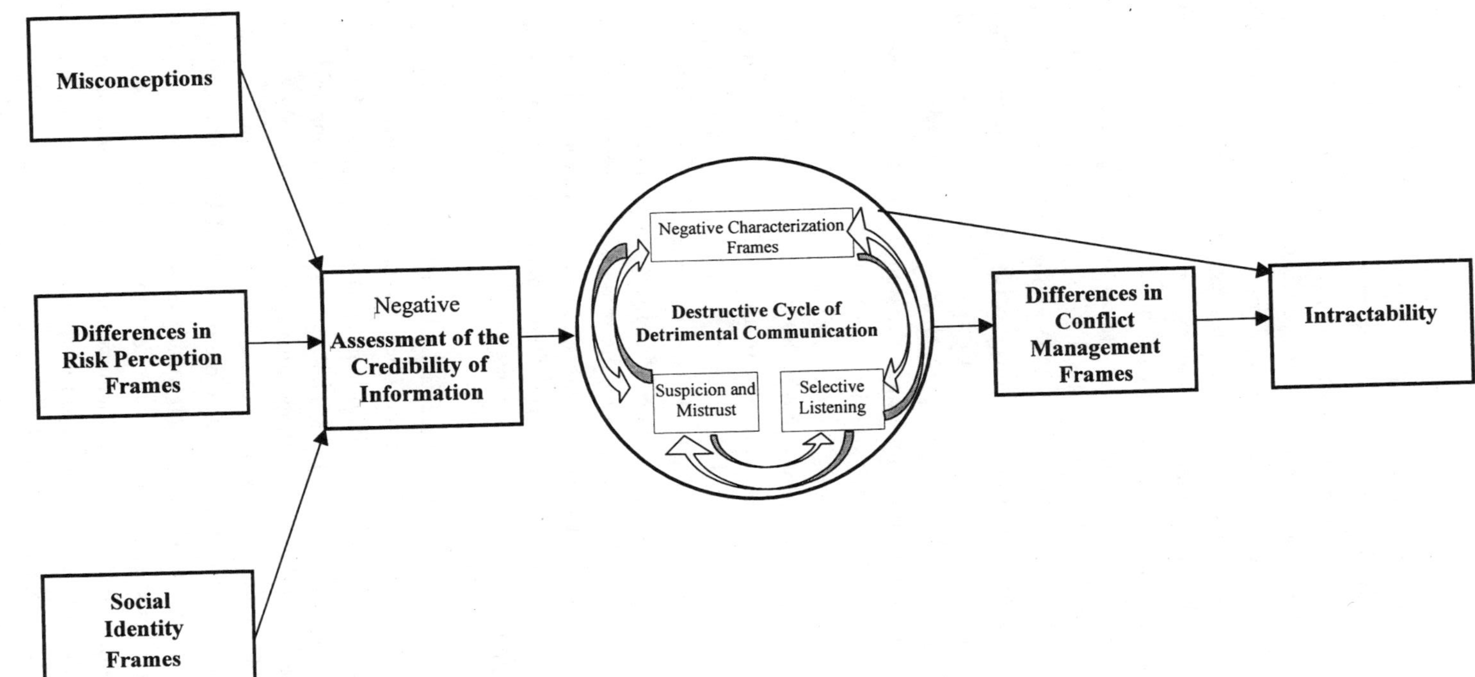

Figure 10.1. Model of Interrelationships among 3 Key Factors in the Drake Dispute

the residents of the Bald Eagle Valley at heart when it made decisions, wrote recommendations, or took actions related to the Drake site. Rather, misconception describes the condition whereby the parties often misunderstood the effects of their own actions. From this perspective, misconceptions were abundant during this dispute, and they were not limited to one side or the other.

For example, the EPA did not come across as concerned with how accessible they were when they communicated their risk assessments. **[5]** Furthermore, the technical nature and length of the second and third assessments made them virtually incomprehensible to the public at large. A common reference to "those big binders over on the shelf" suggests the degree of intimidation associated with the assessments. One opponent even accused the EPA of obfuscating the risk assessment on purpose. **[2]** In spite of these criticisms, one does well to keep in mind that the EPA acted in what they believed was good faith. They saw their scientific approach adequately expressing their deep level of concern for the environment and the well-being of the people in the Bald Eagle Valley. Unfortunately, the EPA misunderstood how the other disputants perceived their actions.

Lock Haven City Council was also guilty of misconceptions. For example, the City Council did not seem amenable to an inclusive process when it came to making decisions about the Drake site. A member of the council expressed how the decision to clean up the Drake site was not and should not be a democratic one, although this person agreed that many people believed otherwise. This person asserted that citizens have the responsibility to elect officials to office who, in turn, decide what should be done. This attitude did not leave any room for AIR and their concerns. Therefore, it was not surprising that AIR soon opposed the Lock Haven City Council with as much vehemence as they opposed the EPA.

AIR also suffered under misconceptions. For example, many people in the group were lifelong members of the Lock Haven community. Further, the AIR leadership team lived in the Bald Eagle area since the mid-1980s, and all of them had working ties to Lock Haven. Nevertheless, none of the AIR members attended the public meetings during the 1980s and early '90s. It was only when the incinerator was about to be built that AIR formed and started vociferously opposing incineration. The members of AIR did not see anything untoward in that move. As one of their members put it, "my priorities changed as I got older." AIR's lack of early involvement, together with their sudden and ardent opposition to the proposed incineration, prompted some agency officials to speculate that AIR's opposition to the incineration was at best capricious and at worst opportunistic. **[1]**

AIR's rationalizations about their lack of early involvement, the EPA's stridently technical approach to risk assessment, and Lock Haven City Council's noninclusive approach to decision making are all examples of the many misconceptions present in this dispute. These misconceptions led the parties to think they were not contributing to the problem. Worse, though, they encouraged the parties' opponents to doubt the veracity of the information the parties provided. That doubt eventually turned into outright skepticism: "I could have a piece of paper and stand there and hold it up and say I have a white piece of paper in my hand and they would say no, it's not white."

Differences in Risk Perception Frames

A variety of factors can influence risk perceptions. For example, cultural theory predicts that individuals perceive a variety of risks in a manner that supports their way of life (Wildavsky and Dake 1990). Others argue that disputes about risk reflect disputes about the legitimacy of existing political and economic arrangements (Hilgartner 1985). Studies of community risk perceptions identified three types of lay publics: sponsors, guardians, and preservationists (Elliott 1988). Sponsors focus most strongly on expected outcomes, preservationists focus most strongly on potentially catastrophic events, while guardians focus moderately on both. These differences come about not because sponsors are more rational than preservationists, or even that they think more like scientists and engineers. Rather, they come about because sponsors trust the current system for managing risks, and believe in their spokespersons. Guardians and preservationists, on the other hand, view the hazards as exceptional and requiring special attention. Guardians and preservationists tend to focus on health and safety concerns as well as aesthetic and cultural consequences (Elliott 1988).

Risk perception frames expressed in this dispute reflect the influences outlined above. Those risk perception frames also influenced the assessment of the credibility of information. **[19]** Supporters of the incineration who saw the risk associated with the incineration process as low, described AIR's information as "X-files science," science that could not be and should not be taken seriously. **[9]** Conversely, most members of AIR felt that the risk involved with incineration was far too high. **[22]** As a result, they became highly skeptical of information provided by the EPA and DEP. **[3]** Further, members of AIR thought that the EPA's science was "bought," either through pork-barreling or private industry influence. **[6]**

What was never in doubt for any party in the dispute was that science should be the final arbitrator in determining risk. A citizen says, "[N]ot that [EPA's] answers weren't correct by giving the scientific formulas and the four-inch binders, but the way it was presented to the public wasn't done in a way that made people trust their answers." An opponent to incineration echoes a similar sentiment about the preeminence of science. "They're a worthless agency if the truth isn't part of [it]. . . . First of all science is truth. That's what I was always taught." Nevertheless, different perceptions of what science said about the risk involved led to differences in assessments of the credibility of the information provided by other stakeholders. While AIR held the risk assessments were "fundamentally flawed" and a "stack of lies," a DEP official held that "this was the best risk assessment [the EPA] had ever seen [and] it gave me great confidence in the decision."

Social Identity

The parties' social identities contributed to the intractability of this conflict by leading disputants to doubt the veracity of certain information and by influencing their choice of conflict management frames. Although all parties expressed concern for the well-being of the public, a distinction can be made between those people who saw themselves as protectors of the public and those who saw themselves as scientists working for the public. For instance, those individuals who tended to have identities as protectors of the public and informed advocates for the well-being of the ecosystem rejected the credibility of the information provided by the EPA and other institutions. **[2, 3, 4, 8, 25]** Conversely, those people who viewed themselves as scientifically oriented professionals working for the public tended to be both in favor of incineration and supportive of the information provided by the EPA and other institutions while remaining skeptical about the concerns raised by AIR. **[9, 19, 20, 23]**

One important identity for AIR was that they are a nonviolent group. To reflect this commitment, AIR members took a pledge of nonviolence. To ensure they could keep that pledge and still forcefully fight incineration, AIR hired a trainer so they could learn methods of nonviolent civil disobedience. The nonviolent social identity is very important to AIR, and any suggestion that they might be otherwise irritated AIR members to no end: "We went out of our way throughout the Drake fight to be nonviolent, taking a pledge to always be peaceful," and their reaction to threats to their nonviolent social identity was to invoke adjudication conflict management frames: "We don't care whose quote it is, it's false and you are liable if you print it." Similarly, the EPA, DEP, and the Lock Haven City Council all saw themselves as honest, decent individuals—caretakers, if you will—who held the best interests of the community at heart. This "caretaker" identity is as important to these groups as AIR's nonviolent identity was to them. Suggestions that they might be otherwise **[28]** led members of these groups to adopt authority decides based on expertise conflict management frames, as reflected by a DEP official. **[26]**

Perhaps the most compelling example of the role social identity played in this conflict comes from an individual who expressed a strong personal identity (beyond that of most people in central Pennsylvania who also hunt and fish) as a person who lives off the land and eats wild game. This person believed the EPA's risk assessment would support an incineration that would force them to give up living off the land and thereby lose an important part of their identity. **[21]** These examples demonstrate that social identity frames contributed to the intractability of the conflict in two ways. The first is by influencing how disputants judged the credibility of the information provided by others in the dispute. The other is in terms of the threats to personal identity and how they led directly to differences in conflict management frames. These differences in conflict management frames, in turn, directly contributed to the intractability of the conflict. As far as the disputants were concerned, their opposition simply did not have any sense of who they were or how incineration influenced those identities.

Cycle of Destructive Communication Behaviors

Once the parties dismissed the credibility of their counterparts in the dispute, they initiated a cycle of destructive communication behaviors. Three elements make up that cycle of destructive communication: negative characterization frames, selective listening, and suspicion and mistrust. The disputants expressed suspicion and mistrust in a variety of ways. Some members of AIR felt that the EPA did not intend to clean up the site at all. "There is a tremendous amount of money and we believe that there is a deal between Superfund employees and the contractors. They have no intention of cleaning up the Drake site. It is all about perception and looking nice." They also believed that former members were not to be trusted. **[18]** Similarly, an agency official reflects the lack of trust many proponents of the incineration felt about intentions of the members of AIR. **[11, 14]**

The literature on conflict clearly establishes the impact of mistrust on selective listening. If groups mistrust each other they tend to see each other as the enemy, develop negative stereotypes of the other group, develop hostility, and thereby find it easier to maintain negative stereotypes. Further, if circumstances force mistrusting groups to interact, each group is likely to listen more closely to their own representatives and not listen to the representatives of the other group, except to find fault with his presentation. In other words, group members tend to listen only for that which supports their own position and stereotypes (Schein 1970, Sherif 1958). Others have shown that negative beliefs validate negative feelings, and negative feelings legitimize negative beliefs. Further, once a group sees another group as undesirable, it tends to gather information to support that view. That action leads to selective evaluation of behaviors, the discovery of confirming evidence, and attributional distortion (Pruitt and Rubin 1986).

Both government officials and opponents of incineration provided evidence that selective listening was at work in the Drake case. One elected official, who kept a distance from the dispute, held that one of the main problems with the people close to the dispute was that they were unwilling to hear the whole story: "I mean, they should give themselves the chance to have an open mind until somebody can prove that it's all wrong or all right. Otherwise, there's no sense in even trying to solve it." A citizen who was once sympathetic to the AIR cause was even more succinct. **[13]** Another example shows how one incinerator advocate came to have a very profound struggle with AIR and found it almost impossible to listen to what they had to say. **[11]**

In addition to producing selective listening, mistrust often leads to the use of negative characterization frames by people on both sides of the dispute (Schein 1970). These negative characterization frames also influenced both selective listening and trust. One agency official characterized AIR leadership as liars who mislead their members and that characterization led to fear and mistrust. **[14, 16]** A local elected official expressed similar sentiments. **[7]** Another local agency described their relationship with AIR as one of total lack of communication. **[10]** Negative characterizations by AIR members were no less incendiary. **[25, 27, 28]** These exchanges of negative characterizations influence the level of trust and selective listening that, in turn, influenced the level of negative characterization. In addition to selective listening, an individual suggested that the dispute produced autistic hostility (Newcomb 1947), in which parties stop interacting and communicating. **[10]**

Conflict Management Frames

The cycle of destructive communication described in the preceding text, along with the social identity frames of the disputants, served as a catalyst for the formation of incompatible conflict management frames. Those frames included authority decides based on expertise, authority decides after consultation, fact-finding, struggle, sabotage and violence, adjudication, and appeal to political action. For the most part, opponents to the incineration used adjudication, appeal to political action, and struggle, sabotage, and violence conflict management frames, whereas those in favor of the incineration used authority decides based on expertise, authority decides after consultation, and fact-finding frames, although the opponents adopted some fact-finding frames as well.

As indicated, the opponents to the incineration believed they needed to adopt a confrontational stance. **[17]** The supporters of the incinerator also took a somewhat confrontational position. Nevertheless, one might argue they coated their position with a layer of "justified" authority. **[26]** Ironically, when pressed, both sides of the conflict expressed what could be termed as their preferred, as opposed to enacted, conflict management frames. The preferred conflict management frames are the frames that the disputants used when asked how they think the conflict could be best resolved. Their enacted conflict management frames are the frames the disputants used when explaining what they were doing to resolve the conflict. One former member of AIR used a fact-finding frame, arguing that people should talk about issues and receive answers to their questions. **[12]** Other members of AIR as well as the government agencies echoed that sentiment. **[4, 24]**

In addition, both sides of the conflict employed joint problem-solving frames when asked about their preferred approach to resolving the conflict. An AIR member expressed the need for discussion of the issues:

> [T]he way you work it out is to talk real-speak with people. You sit down at a table and you talk real-speak. And if that fails then you should have an access to the courts. I don't think that everybody should rush to court and I, when I gave that quick answer, it's not only because I am feeling so angry about this particular site right now. But I do think that people should have the option to sit down and discuss things. The problem is if you don't and the government goes ahead and does these things recklessly you don't have any other option except court.

An agency official expressed a similar view:

> Both sides need to be heard and need to listen to each other. I believe in interest based negotiation, if you know what that is? Okay. That's very, very important. And you know I got no clue what the [AIR members] are really afraid of. . . . [B]ut they did

> serve some good purposes. I mean we would have never done the moss bag studies. We wouldn't have done some of the risk assessments if nobody had argued. We would never have gotten to the second or third part of the risk assessment or the peer review. . . . We probably wouldn't have put that second scrubber on. . . . So, their concerns caused improvements in the process . . . so I wouldn't tell you he had no good impact. His problem was, he wanted all or nothing, so he got nothin'.

Those preferred frames suggest that the disputants could have found a common ground for conflict management. Unfortunately, those preferences were not the strategies that the disputants enacted. Instead, they adopted more confrontational conflict management frames and ended up in an intractable conflict where neither side understood each other and both sides eventually ceased to express any concern for the other side's perspectives.

The Final Analysis

A number of situational factors and sociolinguistic frames serve to influence the intractability of this conflict. The first factor is the misconceptions held by the disputants. These misconceptions led the parties to think they were not contributing to the problem when, in fact, they were. The misconceptions of the parties resulted in poor sharing of information, lack of participation, and reliance on others to solve the problem. Inadvertently, AIR, the City Council, and the EPA directly harmed the communication process. The EPA's misconceptions led them to overestimate the effectiveness of their community outreach process. City Council's misconceptions made it difficult for them to include AIR's concerns. AIR's misconceptions made it difficult for them to see that people had taken the problem at Drake very seriously long before AIR got involved. Had these misconceptions not occurred, it is conceivable that the dispute would not have been as acrimonious; certainly, one would expect fewer negative assessments of the credibility of information provided by the disputants.

The differences in risk perception frames expressed by the disputing parties, on the other hand, seem to be in keeping with this kind of conflict (Elliott 1988). As such, these frames would likely contribute to some negative assessments about the information that each party presented. Nevertheless, had the differences in risk frames been the only negative element in this dispute, one would expect the negative assessments of the credibility of information might not have escalated to full-blown skepticism. Similarly, the social identity frames of the disputants also led to negative assessments of the credibility of information provided. If the disputants had threatened each other's identities less, it might have been possible for the groups to better hear each other's information (Schein 1970) and to avoid incompatible conflict management frames.

Misconceptions, risk perceptions, and social identities all influenced the stakeholders' assessments of the credibility of the information provided by the other parties. Unfortunately, the effects were mostly negative, and the parties doubted the veracity of the information that they provided each other. Therefore, when the EPA argued that dioxins could not be formed in the incineration process, AIR simply did not believe them. Similarly, when AIR complained about particulate emissions from the incinerator, the DEP and EPA essentially dismissed those claims out of hand. The high level of skepticism about the credibility of information provided by other parties directly contributed to what we identify as the destructive cycle of detrimental communication.

Three elements make up the detrimental cycle: selective listening, negative characterization frames, and suspicion and mistrust. "Suspicion and mistrust" refers to the deep-seated doubt the disputants held about each other. That doubt included a genuine belief that members of the opposition were potentially dangerous, were lying, and held malice in their heart. Selective listening is the act of filtering the conversations of other people for ideas that suit one's own perspective. At times, disputants did not hear the entire story that an opponent was trying to tell. At other times, disputants attended only to those parts of a conversation that substantiated their position, or ignored those parts of a conversation that demonstrated an error on their part. In-group members use negative characterizations to vilify out-group members and maintain in-group cohesiveness and solidarity. In this dispute, the negative characterizations were particularly foul, and they included references to Nazism, assertions of willful dishonesty, and insinuations of violence. The three elements interacted with and fed back on each other to create a morass of (mis)perceptions among the disputants. Once mired in that morass, the parties were unable to communicate in a constructive fashion.

This morass had two effects on the conflict. On the one hand, it led to differences in conflict management frames. On the other hand, the destructive cycle of detrimental communication also directly influenced the intractability of the conflict. Further, the (lack of) understanding they developed in the cycle of detrimental communication determined which conflict management frames the disputants adopted. Unfortunately, the adopted frames were at different ends of the conflict management spectrum.

These differences in conflict management frames inevitably contributed to the intractability of the dispute. On the one hand, opponents of the incineration process argued that legal arguments, political action, and civil disobedience were required because the incinerator represented a direct attack on their rights as American citizens and so adopted and championed adjudication conflict management frames. On the other hand, the proponents of the incinerator believed they had the authority and expertise required to know incineration represented a scientifically sound approach to cleaning up a dangerous chemical soup. Therefore, they adopted authority decides after consultation conflict management frames, but eventually championed authority decides based on expertise conflict management frames. The disparate nature of the frame held by the disputants when coupled with the (mis)communication of the cycle led both parties to dig in their heels and refuse to deal with their opponent's deeply and, we believe, honestly held convictions about incineration. In the final analysis, the proponents of the incineration, perhaps secure in the power vested in them by CERCLA, blithely denied there was a conflict as they completed the burn at Drake. Meanwhile, the members of AIR, perhaps enraged by the lack of power vested in them by CERCLA, came to despise the government agencies and promoted the fight over incineration at the Drake site as their first battle in what we suspect will be a protracted war about environmental safety in the United States.

Note on Sources

The information in this chapter was derived from a number of sources, primarily from interviews with state, federal, and local government officials, civic leaders, activists, environmentalists, and community residents. The time line of the events and certain claims were corroborated and clarified using the *Lock Haven Express* from August 1994 through November 1999, the Drake Chemical Administrative Record (provided by the EPA) from 1984 to 2000, and federal Supreme Court and state court documents relating to the court cases.

Chapter 11

When the Parents Be Cancer-Free: Community Voice, Toxics, and Environmental Justice in Chattanooga, Tennessee

Michael Elliott

Chattanooga has forged a rich and varied history. Over the past forty years, the city, and in particular the downtown, underwent a series of economic and political transitions. A dynamic industrial economy declined significantly during the 1960s and '70s. In the face of growing pessimism, substantial civic and political efforts helped the city forge a new vision. Chattanooga reenergized both its economy and its sense of community. For many residents, these forty years marked a time when the city *reframed* its identity and perspective, to become something reborn and bolder.

But not all residents participated equally in this rebirth. In the folds and corners of the city stood neighborhoods that remained tied to the old industrial base. For residents of these communities, forty years brought economic decline and a long struggle to alter the toxic legacy of an industrial past. Alton Park and Piney Woods stood out as the most severely impacted of these neighborhoods.

Chattanooga, then, is a city where most residents dramatically reframed their identity as a community, their relationship to decision making and conflict management, and their conceptions of others in the community. Here, too, Alton Park and Piney Woods fought to transform themselves in ways that paralleled the larger community, despite being caught in recurring patterns and frames that resisted change. It is the story of these two neighborhoods, within the broader context of Chattanooga's transformation, that we explore in this chapter.

Chattanooga Reinvented

History

Lookout Mountain, Missionary Ridge, and the Tennessee River bind historic Chattanooga into a compact and beautiful setting. Strategically located, the city grew up as a gateway between the East Coast and the Midwest, facilitating the movement of resources and goods around the Appalachian Mountains. Because of its strategic location to transportation and natural resources, Chattanooga grew into a significant industrial city, becoming known as the Dynamo of Dixie in the early 1900s.

By the 1960s, however, Chattanooga was growing sickly. Compared to other southern cities, Chattanooga had the highest percentage workforce in manufacturing, but industry and commerce were in sharp decline. Between 1950 and 1970, many foundries closed, stores shut down, and the city lost 10 percent of its population to the suburbs. Chattanooga was left choking in the legacy of its old industry: a derelict waterfront, decaying structures, toxic sites and streams, and highly visible air pollution.

A Legacy of Pollution

Chattanooga is located on the Tennessee River, as it pierces the Cumberland Plateau. The particular geology of the plateau accentuates the city's topography. Very long and steeply sloped ridges, stretching for miles, tower up to 1500 feet above narrow valleys. In the days preceding environmental regulation, the extensive network of streams and rivers provided for convenient disposal of industrial waste. At the same time, the mountains served to trap industrial air emissions. As a result, both air and water were highly polluted.

Well before national environmental awareness grew in the late 1960s, Chattanooga residents were well aware of pollution in their city. Smog was so thick that on some days, drivers needed headlights to see at noon. During this period Chattanooga residents came down with tuberculosis at three times the national average (Graham 1999). Airborne substances were commonly blamed for damaging the paint on automobiles and houses and for killing local vegetation. Water pollution in local creeks and rivers could not be masked; fish kills sometimes occurred in area lakes and rivers and people became ill from odors rising from the waters.

Air Pollution in Chattanooga

In 1969, federal air pollution officials at the U.S. Department of Health, Education and Welfare (HEW) awarded Chattanooga a distinction that it did not want. Because of problems with particulates, smog (ozone), and nitrogen dioxide, the 1969 HEW report called Chattanooga the "worst polluted city" in the United States. In response, Hamilton County, under state authorization, established the Hamilton County Air Pollution Control Bureau.

The Bureau organized itself to develop regulations based as much as possible on a consensus of industry. The Bureau shared draft regulations with local industry, particularly with the Chattanooga Manufacturers' Association, and encouraged feedback. Significant effort was made to resolve issues. The Bureau preferred to facilitate compliance through the use of seminars, workshops, and information-sharing rather than through direct enforcement.

Despite significant accomplishments, Chattanooga was classified as a nonattainment area under the Clean Air Act in 1974. The Bureau began to consider more controversial regulations, including a ban on new incinerators and heavy fines for noncomplying industries. These changes were blocked by local business leaders who were concerned about slow industrial growth and unemployment. By 1976, the state air agency and the U.S. Environmental Protection Agency (EPA) considered taking control of Chattanooga's air program. The Bureau responded by creating a Community Advisory Committee to allow a wider range of interests to participate in air pollution decisions, and gradually expanded regulations.

With manufacturers investing millions of dollars in pollution control equipment and some of the most polluting industries closing operations, air quality improved dramatically. By 1981, Chattanooga's ambient air quality met Clean Air Act standards. By 1989, Chattanooga complied with newer standards set in 1977, one of only a few metropolitan areas in the nation meeting all federal air quality standards.

Chattanooga's Water Problems

As early as 1964, the Stream Pollution Control Board (SPCB) of the Tennessee Department of Public Health identified significant pollution problems in the streams and rivers in Chattanooga. Thirty-five area industries were discharging treated or untreated waste into the Tennessee River or its tributaries. Only after passage of the Federal Water Pollution Control Act of 1972 did conditions improve. With regulatory changes, the development of a comprehensive sewer and wastewater management system, and more effective control over storm water management on industrial sites, the quality of local waters greatly improved in most stream and river segments. However, some creeks, including Chattanooga Creek, remained severely impaired.

Economic Decline

As the overall environmental quality of the region improved significantly, the city faced a continuing crisis. Improvements in air and water quality were coupled with the shutdown of many industrial facilities. Some facilities closed because they could not meet clean air standards, but many more closed because their obsolete factories were no longer competitive in internationalizing markets. The city was losing its economic base.

The city also was coping with an archaic form of governance that limited its capacity to innovate. Chattanooga was run by an elected commission, in which at-large elections were held for five commissioners, each of whom ran a specific set of departments. Thus the city had no independent executive or legislative branch; all budgetary and interdepartmental decisions were made by the commission. City government provided little leadership as the city drifted. As Jack Murrah, executive director of the Chattanooga-based Lyndhurst Foundation, notes, in the early 1980s, "there was a sense of doom in the air, and the future seemed foreclosed" (Motavalli 1998).

The City Participatory

In the early 1980s, three events served to demarcate Chattanooga's transformation. First, the Lyndhurst Foundation, a local philanthropy, redirected its energies and resources to support the environmental, cultural, and physical renewal of Chattanooga. The Foundation helped establish an urban design center in downtown Chattanooga to popularize ideas of sustainability, diversity, and mixed-use development. Second, local governments appointed the Moccasin Bend Task Force to plan an undeveloped peninsula located across the Tennessee River from downtown. The task force embraced an open and inclusive process, conducting over sixty-five public meetings throughout the community. Subsequently, the task force expanded its focus to include all 22 miles of the Tennessee River corridor within Chattanooga, and involved citizens in hundreds of public meetings. Third, a handful of civic leaders visited Indianapolis to learn about the Greater Indianapolis Progress Committee. For twenty-five years, the Committee had used broad-based participatory and consensus-building techniques to promote social and economic redevelopment. The team committed itself to create a similar process in Chattanooga.

The emerging sense of community participation gained additional impetus in 1984. Chattanooga Venture was formed with support from the Lyndhurst Foundation, the Chamber of Commerce, and the city's planning commission. Venture was created to engage the full community in the task of promoting environmental, social, and economic revitalization of the city. Venture organized itself as a convener, bringing diverse groups together in a problem-solving setting.

Venture first promoted a community visioning process called Vision 2000. Fifty community members were trained in facilitation, visioning, and nominal group techniques. These members facilitated a six-month series of public meetings in which more than 1700 citizens participated. The resultant Tennessee Riverpark Master Plan built on Chattanooga's natural beauty, history, and industrial infrastructure by creating an extensive system of public space with new industrial, commercial, and residential development. The twenty-year plan was largely implemented within a decade, and visibly transformed the downtown. A city planner notes:

> In the Chattanooga community, there is such an industrial identity in how people think about jobs, and yet there is a tremendous appreciation for the natural beauty and the environment. For so long, the pendulum supported an industrial mindset. But I have been witness to the swing back, to balance and appreciation for environmental features as assets, as issues of value for a community. Before, it was jobs and payrolls and taxes. Now, we give value to beauty and tree coverage and clean water. **[1]***

Citizen involvement remains a central tenet of public decision making in the city. In 1992, Venture initiated ReVision 2000. This time, 150 people were trained as facilitators, and more than 2600 residents participated in nine community meetings. More recent significant public participation processes include Futurescape (1996), a regional growth management planning process involving over 2500 city and county residents in a "visual preference survey"; IMAGINE Eastgate (1998), with over 300 people participating in a "design charette" for the neighborhood surrounding a failing mall; and "Recreate 2008" (1998), with hundreds of people involved in a visioning and planning process for revitalizing the city's parks system.

The City Sustainable

In the 1990s, civic leaders in Chattanooga conceived of a new economy for the city, one based on sustainability. The city's slogan called for "economy, ecology, equity." Chattanooga is now focusing on the Southside Project, a 380-acre brownfield redevelopment just south of downtown. David Crockett, city

---

* In subsequent chapters, this quote will be referenced as "Chattanooga 1," and subsequent quotes from this chapter as "Chattanooga 2," "Chattanooga 3," etc.

council chairperson (and descendant of one of Tennessee's most famous frontiersmen), notes:

> Within the 500-acre area of downtown, we were faced with a very ambitious brownfield exercise. There's an art to doing it so that you don't get bogged down, and full public participation—which we had—is crucial. There have to be both wingtips and hunting boots under the table. (Motavalli 1998) **[2]**

The city is promoting housing, an eco-industrial park, and a conference and education center. In addition, the City Council and the Chamber of Commerce are cooperating on a public/private partnership called the Environmental City Project, which seeks to promote clean industry and environmental awareness within the region. Another project, the Environmental Initiative, seeks to develop a national center for environmental information and business.

The city, once known as The Most Polluted City in the United States, is now widely known as The Sustainable City. In 1996, the United Nations Habitat II Conference in Istanbul recognized Chattanooga as one of the world's twelve "Best Practice Cities." Chattanooga also received a 1996 award from the President's Council on Sustainable Development. Vice President Al Gore noted that Chattanooga "has undergone the kind of transformation that needs to happen in our country as a whole" (Motavalli 1998). Chattanooga has also been described as one of six "smart cities" (Koerner et al. 1998) and as one of the country's ten "Most Enlightened Towns"(Madison 1997). In 2001, National Public Radio highlighted Chattanooga in its *What Makes a City Great?* series (Stamberg 2001). Chattanooga remains a city in transition. As David Crockett notes, "We don't say we're a model. We say we're a living laboratory" (Graham 1999).

Alton Park and Piney Woods

Chattanooga's remarkable success, however, has not been uniform. Focusing primarily on issues of ecology and economy, the city has made less progress on its third stated sustainability goal: equity. Inasmuch as environmental issues are often tied to race and economic disparity (Bryant 1995, Bryant and Mohai 1992, Bullard 1990), poor neighborhoods across Chattanooga continue to struggle with the city's legacy of pollution.

African Americans make up 20 percent of Chattanooga's population. Racial tensions here are less significant than in many southern cities, but race nonetheless exacerbates difficult divides. In 1971, rioting over school busing left one African American dead and many more injured. In 1980, several businesses were firebombed after an all-white jury acquitted two Ku Klux Klansmen accused of shooting and wounding four black women. Chattanooga responded in the late 1980s by establishing the Chattanooga Human Rights/Human Relations Commission to hear complaints about discrimination and to help resolve community problems, and in 1990 the city revised its charter to better separate legislative and executive powers and to elect legislators by district, thereby improving neighborhood and minority representation.

Community Characteristics

Alton Park and Piney Woods are contiguous neighborhoods situated in South Chattanooga. The neighborhoods are located 3 miles south of downtown, in a deep valley between Lookout Mountain and Missionary Ridge. They are bounded by the foothills of Lookout Mountain and Chattanooga Creek to the west and east, the state border with Georgia to the south, and Interstate 24 and the Tennessee River to the north. As such, the neighborhood and street grid are physically isolated from other neighborhoods in Chattanooga. This isolation is underscored by a city planner:

> One problem with Alton Park is that it's not really between anywhere and anywhere else. . . . That's one reason that forty, fifty, sixty years ago a lot of bad stuff ended up in Alton Park. It was easy to say, "Well, let's just put it down there where no one will notice it." It's near the Georgia border, there's not a lot of political cohesion there, and it's marshland that's cut off from the main part of the city by the creek. **[3]**

For the past eighty years, Alton Park and Piney Woods have been home to many of the city's most polluting industries. Contiguous with the central city, the area was far enough removed to provide easy access to cheap, developable land. Equally importantly, the land was flat and well served by the waters of Chattanooga Creek. A neighborhood activist recalls:

> When I was young, I walked to school. I passed those factories every day. I got sprayed on a bunch. It was something I just did because I had a goal, to get to school and back home. . . . It was the industries that caused the problems, and we figured we couldn't do anything about the industries. The [city] would talk

> that they would do something about it, but they wouldn't. That leads to a feeling of being an unwanted stepchild. You say you're gonna do something and you never do. **[4]**

Another resident notes:

> Oh this was a "fine" community. Everything was real; it was a community that we had pride in. My mother had her flowers in the garden and she belonged to a flower club, and she would trade flowers off with some of the white women. . . . Well, it's not like that now. Each community deteriorates with age, and this is an aging community. **[5]**

As industry grew, so did the residential community surrounding it. From the 1930s through the 1960s, the community changed from predominantly white to predominantly black. A neighborhood association civic leader recalls the in-migration of African Americans:

> Whites lived out here, but they got to where the plants had so much pollution that they moved out. All the white people sold out and moved. . . . Many blacks lived on the Westside. We had churches and a lot of residences over there. Then urban renewal come through and the city bought out lots of these people. That's why we bought out here. Because . . . we didn't have anyplace else to go. **[6]**

As the neighborhood grew increasingly African American, industry continued to grow. A resident describes the transformation this brought about:

> To me, the best aspect of the community is its beauty, even in the winter. It sits on the side of a mountain that has great scenery. . . . When I was born and raised here, if you got in trouble around the corner your mama knew about it before you got home. The people who lived . . . on the street I grew up on—they're still there. But industries moved into the neighborhood. They were invited thinking that it would bring prosperity, but they caused a lot of problems that were not foreseen. In the past, good things happened because the people worked together. It was a neighborhood where you had doctors, lawyers, baker men, retail, pharmacies, everything that a community needed was there when I was growing up. The only thing that you have now is manufacturing, chemicals. You got one or two little stores, and it's just not a community anymore. It's

> just a place where people go and live until they can get out and go someplace else. **[7]**

The two neighborhoods now house 5300 individuals, 98 percent of whom are African American. Incomes are substantially below the city average. Industrial and residential areas are in close proximity. Large industries are often surrounded by single-family homes. Three public housing projects, six schools, and three recreation centers are located in the area. Alton Park Health Center and Alton Park Middle School border the heavily polluted Chattanooga Creek. As a neighborhood activist notes, with the neighborhood located beneath Lookout Mountain where many of the city's elite lived, the residents felt a pervasive sense of separation:

> I was always told to beware of those who stand high on the mountains and look down. A lot of people who stay up on these hilltops have been shrewd in the past and have constituted a lot of games that we didn't know the rules to. I can't say they were hateful, they weren't hateful, they were just businessmen, you know, just looked after their own interests, and we just weren't one of them. Yep, we just weren't one of them. **[8]**

Organizing the Community to Engage in Struggle

Environmental problems within the community continued to emerge while the rest of the city began to grow cleaner. This juxtaposition between citywide improvements and continued neighborhood degradation in Alton Park and Piney Woods initiated a struggle involving industry, government, residents, and community groups. Moreover, while local industry had historically employed neighborhood residents, this employment decreased as industrial restructuring created demands for more specialized labor, and increased mobility allowed workers to commute greater distances. As one neighborhood activist described:

> The industries might at one time have been a major force of employment for the community but they are not anymore, because those [who work] here no longer live in the community. The community is left reaping the after-effects of what has been planted years before. All of the exposure and chemical spills that happened twenty years ago are just now beginning to surface in

> the health of the community in the way of respiratory problems, asthma and heart conditions, and cancer. **[9]**

In the early 1970s neighborhood residents became more concerned about air and water pollution and began to hold community meetings. One resident describes the change:

> I worked as PTA president, as classroom homeroom mom, volunteer, whatever. My kids used to be in school right across from Velsicol [a chemical manufacturing firm]. All four of them went there, but the school was closed because there was such a problem with the chemicals from the plant that the students couldn't play outside because of the fumes. My oldest daughter passed out at school one day and we had to go and get her. I am sure that was just one particular incident out of many. . . . That was a long time ago and we didn't have . . . any dialogue at all with the company. We saw each other as enemies because they did not show that they were interested in the community, and we did not have an opportunity to sit-in or talk with them or discuss anything with them. It was the industry against the community. And our lack of knowledge prevented us from getting involved or knowing what to do or how to do it. **[10]**

A second longtime resident adds:

> When I was in Memphis at the Bob Hope Hospital for leukemia, one of the things that blew my mind was that most of the people was from Chattanooga. Chattanooga is very polluted, and it disturbed me very bad. I had a lawyer friend, who just moved to Arizona because her asthma has become so bad. She had to leave here because she said it was about to kill her. My grandson—he's just so sick with asthma, I don't know why. But I think it has something to do with whatever they pumped underground in the Chattanooga area. Whatever is in the air. Sometimes you can wake up early in the morning, and I can look at my car and just see so much stuff, like chemicals that fell out of the sky overnight. Like, I'm telling you, I think that a lot of pollution still be let out around here, but at night time, when people are sleeping, because you can see the results in the morning time when you get up. **[11]**

This concern was highlighted by a series of events in the 1970s. In 1970 the Chattanooga–Hamilton County Air Pollution Control Bureau found extensive and severe damage to plant life in Alton Park and on the adjoining Lookout Mountain. Tests indicated that the damage was caused by the herbicides dicambia and tricambia. Both were manufactured by Velsicol Chemical Corp. Alton Park residents filed a class-action suit against the company. The suit, which grew to include 150 families and six companies, sought actual and punitive damages for harm to their property and an injunction against release of air emissions. The suit was settled in 1979 for $235,000. Payments to individuals ranged from $300 to $2,500. As a condition of the settlement, residents could not sue Velsicol for similar damages in the future. A local elected official notes:

> At that time there was hardly any government regulations to address air pollution, the groundwater, the creek, so a group of Vietnam veterans who lived out here organized the Black Veterans Affairs Organization and started to address all the chemical companies. . . . People died of cancer that did not even relate to the types of cancers found elsewhere in the county. That became an alarm. We started saying to the county health department "you come out here and you tell us what is wrong with us out here." But the department was part of the local system so we had to get people from the federal government involved. As veterans we felt that we had a right, that we had paid our price. We said "Okay, if we are getting sick from Agent Orange in Vietnam, there is a company that is doing Agent Orange here in this community." The City of Chattanooga did not want to admit that we had a problem. The city fathers fined polluting companies that make millions of dollars just $100 or $500. That's not a fine, that's a slap in our face. We wanted something like $20,000 a day, that gets their attention. So we started checking politicians' records to see who was giving them financially, we found out that a lot of those companies was financing a lot of politicians that were running for office, and therefore we felt like that was influencing their way of thinking. **[12]**

A number of groups formed during the late 1970s to mid-1980s to try to improve the community, including the Alton Park/Piney Woods Community Coalition, Turning Point, Progressive Improvement League of South Chattanooga, STOP (Stop Toxic Pollution), and a student group from the University of Tennessee at Chattanooga (UTC). The student group was to have a striking impact on the community. A neighborhood activist explains:

> One of the things about pollution and chemical companies, it is never a racial line. It draws a community together, both white and

> black. It is one of the most unique things I have ever seen. UTC was an upper-middle class school that had no ties in the community. During the early '70s, the new chancellor wanted the university to play a role. Students, white students, started coming into the black community and saying, "Are you aware that these companies are doing this to you?" The students came out and they were all white, at a time when we didn't let white people come out here, okay, because we was in that mode, we would just as soon shoot them. And all of a sudden these kids, white girls coming out here with their white hair and rags on their head, we just said, "What kind of students are these, with long hair and jeans and sitting on the floor," but they knew what they were talking about. So they began to go into the neighborhoods and talk to the mothers, because they were girls. They were the ones that was telling us how to go to a creek and do our own investigation. . . . And from there the students and STOP came in with Greenpeace and all these other organizations who had knowledge as to what these chemical companies were doing in other parts of the country. So now we know it is not just us alone. **[13]**

In the 1980s and early 1990s, an increasingly militant perspective emerged within the community. Environmental issues linked with housing and public safety, with job opportunities and education, to provide a wide array of grievances against perceived injustices. Public housing proved a focal point of this discontent, with a community organizer leading public housing residents in protest against the city:

> Miss Dixon played major. Miss Dixon went to jail. But she went on demonstrating, she stopped traffic, she made things happen. She defied the law. She organized the residents to say we are just not going to take it any more. They wouldn't pay rent. They brought babies and children to city hall, packed it with children, babies hollering and crying and the parents not about to stop them from crying while the city hall was trying to do its business. They took rats and things down and let them go in city hall. They caught the biggest rats they could find from Alton Park and they marched to city hall and they let them go—created a big mess down there. Finally the mayor conceded. Said come and talk to us because she refused to stop the demonstration. Jesse Jackson came in to meet with the group and help in the march. They was not backing, they

> were going to take rats down there everyday, they would do that and they got on national television. So again a community to be effective does so by demonstrations, voting, and being full of information. **[14]**

Conflict over Health

Health concerns continued to arise among Alton Park and Piney Woods residents. In 1983 the residents demanded that a health study be conducted to determine whether the pollutants in the air and water were contributing to poor health in the community. A local public health department study did not find any significant difference between the health of neighborhood residents and that of other residents in the city. The state's public health study concluded that residents suffered from excess respiratory problems, but that death rates or major diseases did not significantly differ from other parts of the city. The study also determined that toxic pollutants and particulates were all below legally allowed levels. These studies were met by residents with widespread skepticism. A community organizer described the reaction:

> The state health department . . . found problems, but there was no pinpointing one company out there as the polluter. . . . So, when the health survey was done, it was like, most of the problems people were having was coming from inside of their houses, from household chemicals to the type of heating they were using. They never pinpointed that the chemicals being used at Velsicol and other plants could be cancer-causing materials. I mean, people were just dying from cancer, and women were having miscarriages from inhaling all of that stuff over the years. We did our own survey . . . without the health department, without EPA being involved, to actually sit and talk about who's dying in the neighborhood, and how many miscarriages. We found that a lot of women have had miscarriages, and a lot of children . . . had respiratory problems. Now mind you, the health survey did say that there was a lot of respiratory problems out there in the community, far more than what was in the control group, but they wasn't going to say that it was caused by pollution. **[15]**

Because of ongoing community concern, several additional studies were conducted during the 1990s. The most recent health study, completed in 1997 by the Agency for Toxic Substances and Disease Registry (ATSDR), again found no significant difference in disease rates between Alton Park and Piney Woods and other local communities. As viewed by an industry manager:

> If you go back to the 1970s and some of those early studies, you will see that the air bureau seemed to lead the way in those things, and rightly so. The air pollution control bureau is the closest thing Chattanooga has to experts in the area. But a lot of times people do not want to believe them. We hear about all these cancers, people dying of cancer because of pollutants. Well, the studies don't say that. The study says it is a pretty normal rate here. And I have studies of my plant and my people that work right here by the chemicals and everything is normal. They say everybody is dying of cancer, and I say everybody I know is dying of cancer too. People die of cancer. I think people think we must be lying to them, because there has to be a reason why they are dying of cancer. **[16]**

Conflict over Toxic Contamination: Brownfields and Superfund

In mid-1980, another community battle emerged when Velsicol Chemical Corporation made plans to construct an impermeable clay cap over an 18-acre chemical waste dump on its property. The dump, known as Residue Hill, had been used as a waste site for over twenty years before it was closed in 1973. The cap was necessary because groundwater in the area was becoming polluted by leachate from the dump. The cap was designed to prevent further migration of water and soil pollution. A toxic waste forum was held in November 1980, with Velsicol as the primary target of the meeting. Among the residents' concerns were the safety of Residue Hill's cap, odors emitted by Velsicol, and the hazardous chemicals that had recently been found in a pool of water on the Piney Woods school playground.

Within a year of the capping, more sources of pollution were brought to the residents' attention. The Chattanooga Task Force of the Tennessee Toxics Program found many dumps, some containing chemical waste, along the banks of Chattanooga Creek. Throughout the 1980s, waste sites continued to be discovered in the Alton Park/Piney Woods area until there was a list of forty-two suspected hazardous waste sites in the Chattanooga Creek watershed, eleven of which were designated as state Superfund sites, with six of those located directly on the creek's banks.

Despite considerable efforts to promote remediation, no sites were cleaned up until the mid-1990s. Community residents felt ignored by government and industry alike. One resident described the community's strategy as follows:

> Okay, I'm very spiritual. One of my questions once to a minister was, "Why do [you] have to preach the same sermon over and over every Sunday?" And he said, "You can preach to some folks, and they hear the message one time and understand it. There might be someone else sitting in the congregation, and you gotta preach the same message to them twenty times before they actually hear it. They hear it, but they didn't hear it." . . . You should keep saying the same things over and over until someone listens. Don't go to the next step—keep on telling them until someone begins to listen. I believe that's what made the [city and industry] listen—'cause we kept on saying the same thing over and over again. **[17]**

The Struggle between Velsicol and the Neighborhood

Within this context, concern about waste generation and industrial pollution continued to rise in the community. In the late 1980s and under new ownership, Velsicol began to invest heavily in the environmental performance of their facility. As the environmental engineer notes:

> The managers of Velsicol, the owners of Velsicol are very ethical people. I am not talking tree huggers, but I am talking ethical people who believe in reducing pollution. Our CEO came to us back in '86, right after the managers bought the company. We started doing Form R hazardous air pollutants reports for the Toxic Release Inventory [an inventory of hazardous emissions and transfers]. We had never done this before. People said, "Oh, you guys know what you put out," but we didn't. We never looked at it, we never added it up, we only worried . . . about pollutants in terms of what the regulators told us to do. We started looking at these numbers, these huge numbers. Our CEO said, "I want those reduced by 90 percent. I am going to give you a period of time, the money and resources to do it, but I want it reduced 90 percent." **[18]**

Most of the air emissions were volatile organic compounds, primarily solvents used in the chemical manufacturing process. The plant engineers designed a system for reducing off-gassing and for collecting and thermally destroying the gases that were emitted. At a cost of over $3 million, the system would collect fugitive emissions, feed them into a computer-controlled incinerator, and reduce air emissions into the neighborhood by 90 percent. None of this was required by regulation.

The afterburner needed an air pollution permit to operate. Despite significant benefits to the neighborhood, the hearing hall was packed with hundreds of community residents opposed to the proposal. Residents did not trust the company, and believed that any action taken by Velsicol would be detrimental to the neighborhood. The Air Quality Control Bureau issued the permit over the strident objections of the community. As an industrialist who participated at the meeting noted,

> Mostly, these meetings are for venting, and to me a venting meeting is a waste of time. I guess it makes the people who are screaming and hollering feel good, but nothing gets accomplished. It's just a regulator sitting there. What do you say when you have such irrational people. Voices get lost in the commotion, like the lady that comes up to me and says, "I have a two-year-old child. Can you tell me is this chemical going to hurt him?" That is a legitimate concern. Not some guy who says, "I think we should go back to the stone ages, and I would just like to blow your plant up." People who just blow-up. **[19]**

Velsicol's corporate managers, operating out of Chicago, came to realize how detached the company had become from the community. The company and the community were at an impasse. The managers began to appreciate that despite improvements in environmental quality, the company's history of poor relations would keep it locked in conflict with its neighbors.

> We had a public hearing to get a permit to manage hazardous waste. This hazardous waste had been managed in this plant for fifty years, nothing changed. But . . . we had to have a public hearing. The public really had no power to change anything on that permit, because technically there was nothing wrong with the permit. But so many people came and vented about a lot of things. At that point, the company thought that it was getting a bad rap, that we had a lot of initiatives to reduce pollution and nobody in the community cared about this. We were really not asking the community residents what they thought and people inside Velsicol started looking for a better way to do business with our neighbors. **[20]**

This realization led to the first systematic effort by an industrial company to meet directly with residents of Alton Park and Piney Woods. Velsicol invited its most ardent critics to sit down with managers from the company through an ongoing community advisory panel. The panel consisted of seven neighborhood civic leaders, three representatives from environmentalist organizations, a community organizer, a chemistry professor, the Local Emergency Preparedness Committee executive director, and a program director from Chattanooga Venture. The panel met with the plant manager and its operations and environmental managers. During its first year in 1992, communication among the advisory panel members proved difficult. Distrust was high, the dialogue wary. Panel members focused on the long history of community impacts. A Velsicol engineer notes:

> The history of the area is full of neglect. A lot of industry has shut down over the years. Most of them were the '50s and '60s industry that weren't too keen on environmental issues. People get stuck thinking in the historical perspective. . . . To overcome this takes a lot of good faith effort to turn things around. You have people who say, "Well I remember this release or this fire" and you go back and you find out they are talking twenty years ago, twenty-five, thirty, forty years ago, but people still think about those things because they are in their minds. But we have a lot of people in the neighborhood that are willing to take us at face value and help us get to a point of action. You can talk so much, but after awhile you got to act. We are not PR people, we are engineers, and we are not used to seeing, asking for people's inputs. We are learning and the community is learning. The community is the same way, they are not used to being able to give input. They have been able to vent at public hearings but that is not actually inputting or dialoguing or getting things done. **[21]**

The panel has changed significantly during the ten years of its existence. An environmentalist on the panel notes:

> The community advisory panel had a whole lot going for it. When it first started out, Velsicol did not have a clue. They knew they needed to clean up the environment and they knew what some of the complaints were, but they did not know how to connect to the people. I saw a big change in attitude by both the residents and the company. Every once in awhile you would get a new community

> person in there that had not been part of the discussions and they had an axe to grind, and it would start over again, but you began to see panel members and then community members standing up to defend Velsicol. **[22]**

A neighborhood activist adds:

> I blame the sources [of pollution] for not taking responsibility thirty years ago. . . . But before the laws were there and before the community response was there, they didn't have to [protect the environment]. So [some industries] are making the process of manufacturing cleaner and more efficient. They install better systems, like storage tanks that used to be under ground are now built above ground so that you can see what is going on and more readily fix problems. And when a problem exists I don't think they try to hide it as much as they used to. They know that the community is concerned, and they want to work with us to try to improve not only the health of the community but to improve the community too. . . . If we could work together harmoniously and have an open dialogue we would be nearer to solving the problems. But we still haven't arrived at that point yet. We have a few companies that work with us. Velsicol is the leading one in this particular area, in working with us. Maybe what Velsicol is doing could calm some fears about involving community leaders or residents in the decision-making process. Because a lot of people, you know, don't do better because they don't know any better and that is true of the community also. You have to know before you can do. Knowledge is a powerful force if used in the right way. **[23]**

Another community participant on the advisory panel describes the process in these words:

> Back then officials and owners of plants were more ignorant about what was going on. They were trying to ignore the problem instead of facing the problem. People right now, not everybody, have a tendency to listen more and try to do something about it. The city councilmen, the commissioners, people like Velsicol Chemical Company—now listen. They had to listen. People began to complain to the air pollution control board over and over again, and they started coming out and investigating. Stuff got in the newspaper and on television. . . . The more people began to real-

> ize what was going on, the more of a threat it became to these industries, and so they had to listen. They began to change their way of thinking, and instead of sealing off their thoughts, just walking away from it, they began to sit down and see what's going on. Some of the issues got dealt with, and some of them didn't. But guess what? At least they were aware how the people thought. Listening is the first positive step to dealing with it. People beginning to listen makes a big difference. **[24]**

This dialogue has not changed the basic interests of either the company or the community. It has, rather, altered the manner in which the company managers and community representatives work together to resolve difficulties. As Velsicol's environmental manager notes:

> A lot of us think, well, I am a rational person, I can figure out what my neighbors want. But that's not true. I found out from all the years on the advisory panel. . . . What I am concerned about has nothing to do with what my neighbor is concerned about. You have to ask people. Ten years ago, we . . . thought in terms of "We are abiding by all the regulations. Leave us alone." We didn't talk unless forced to by law suits or regulation. . . . We are starting to see more to it. Just because we're under regulations doesn't mean we're good as far as the community is concerned. So we started looking and realized that there probably is something we can do about the odor, about the traffic. So now, when we've got a problem, let's talk about it and see if we have a rational explanation for it or if we can fix it. **[25]**

He goes on to say:

> If you deal with residents like we do on the advisory panel, the first issue we have to address is like they do in the Middle East. You have to first acknowledge we all have the right to exist. You know it is easy to go in and say, "We just don't want you here, we want you out of here. We want zero emissions." That type of conflict is hard to resolve, because we rely on this job to feed our families. If we work past this issue, we can look at health effects of pollutants, how the company can better control pollutants, and whether cleaner substitutes can be made. That's what we are trying. . . . If you asked me what my long-term goal is, I would like people to say, "I love to live across from your plant." Will that ever happen? I don't

> know. Industries have to generate some community assets. You have to have some reason why people would want to live near a plant other than working here because we are too mobile of a society. People can now work on one side of town and live on the other side. We have a social responsibility to start looking at other ways to help the community, to become an asset to the neighborhood. **[26]**

Current Perspectives

The evolving collaboration with Velsicol represents only one segment of the overall community conflict. Alton Park and Piney Woods neighborhood organizations continue to struggle not only with Velsicol, but with numerous other industrial companies for changes in environmental practice and social responsibility, with city government for resources needed to clean up the community and to rejuvenate its infrastructure, and with state and federal environmental agencies over the cleanup of the remaining contamination. The legacy associated with coking operations, organic chemicals, pharmaceuticals, metallurgical and foundry operations, tanning and leather products, wood preserving, textiles, and brick making remains. Many specific issues generate intense conflict that ebbs and flows from one dispute to the next. This includes an ongoing dispute over the cleanup of a 7-mile segment of Chattanooga Creek, a segment so polluted that it is designated as a federal Superfund site. Yet the conflict has changed. As a neighborhood activist notes:

> In the '70s, a little small group got together and was trying to talk to the Air Pollution Board. It looked like they were getting nowhere. But they just persisted. When those folks died off, then a fresh group that knew a little bit more stepped in . . . and they persisted. And then it came to our time. . . . It took all of that and all those years. We cannot say that it was one group—it was all the groups, all the concerns over the years that brought about the change. It took so long because the people needed to rise up. We were surrounded by all this pollution. Going in little groups. But that just didn't make any waves. When we come together in large numbers—that makes a difference. **[27]**

Embedded into this sense of progress is a linkage not only with the protection of human health through environmental protection, but also the potential for integrating nature into the community. As an elected official from the neighborhood put it:

> So all these things would not have happened if the community would not have taken its stand on environmental issues. It would have been business as usual, but now . . . you got industry recognizing that this is an environmental community that is very interested in the environment, saving birds, trees, the creek and fish and all this. Before, African Americans have never been conscious of saving creeks, it has never been an issue, but then once the blinders were taken off our eyes, we said, "Look, we don't have to go out into the suburbs to see nature, we got it right at home." So now we are bringing urban greenways to the community. It changes the focus of where communities can go, it changes race relationships, because everybody has a common ground in nature. **[28]**

Many community residents are cautiously optimistic about the changes that are now spilling into their neighborhood. Despite the fact that the Chattanooga Creek cleanup generated conflict similar to what was found in the Velsicol case, the community organized itself to resolve differences. As a neighborhood environmental activist notes:

> EPA came up with the idea about the community advisory group. The community was so divided during that time and we just couldn't make decisions. One group is going one way and another going another. STOP was knowledgeable about the environment, but we needed . . . to get full community input about what we should do. It was a good process, a timely process. At least in the '90s, we sat down at the table and discussed what was going to happen in the community. And from generating and discussion, things changed around. The government turned around, and we began to see what could be done. **[29]**

Yet, other community activists and residents remain deeply distrustful of this move toward dialogue, and toward the industry and government agencies that are willing to engage in dialogue. A community organizer summarizes her feelings:

> Basically I think the government's just feeding them something to keep them quiet and hoping that it will just soon die down. I think they're doing just a little for the community right now, and they

> say, "You see this big, nice thing we're gonna put in here, you look at this nice stuff that we're gonna do, and forget about these other things." It's all a facade for them to forget about the real issue. No, it's not fairly done. It's trickery, it's politics. . . . The old soldiers that are here now will keep the focus on what the community needs. But when they die down and the younger people take over, I don't think they will keep the focus. The government's . . . setting up small organizations outside of the community, instead of working with organizations that are already organized. They do this in order to strip out the community leaders and burn out the people, because [it's hard to] continue meeting on Monday, when they're meeting on Tuesday for these other projects. They're burning them out. It's just strategy that they're using against them to make them lose the focus, and they're not doing them fairly. **[30]**

After three decades of conflict over environmental degradation in the neighborhood, conditions in the neighborhood have improved but remain a significant problem, and the struggle continues. Progress is difficult, as a citywide civic leader describes:

> There is a sense of community, but also several different communities and factions. . . . So there seems to be a broad agenda with general support, but when you try to make any progress in dealing with a particular issue, the little agendas distract from the bigger picture. . . . We definitely have done some great things with the riverfront area in Chattanooga, but I don't think we have achieved that kind of success in Alton Park/Piney Woods. There is a lag. . . . I still have a great hope for the community, but we are not there yet. There is still much to be done. **[31]**

Residents of the neighborhood believe the air is cleaner but remain mistrustful of plant operations and industrial by-products. The Alton Park and Piney Woods communities are still highly industrialized. A neighborhood resident and schoolteacher describes this combination of hope and determination:

> Racial integration, cooperation and working together has made the most difference to Chattanooga. If cooperation and communication were to happen, we wouldn't have all these other problems. But some industries . . . are denying that they have a part in this. As long as they can hold out and not admit any responsibility, then they are off the hook. And so they are evading the problem by pre-

> tending it doesn't exist. And so it is going to be up to the community and the elected official and the government and all the industries together to bring them into their responsibility through laws and different rules in order that they can be held accountable. **[32]**

Many of the residents remain angered by the protracted fight to stop the degradation of their community, and feel that their health is still threatened. A community activist notes:

> Interest in pollution issues has dropped. They told us the coal tar was a quick thing that, because of Superfund, would be done immediately, but to continue to clean up would be a long-term project. We fought so hard. And now we're tired. We did get something done, but it was just so hard; it was a struggle. We're not giving up, but I don't even get a chance to attend the meetings like I should. I'm tired. **[33]**

Few sense that the conflict itself will disappear. The resources needed to complete the work are too great, thereby ensuring that neighborhood and city interests will remain divergent. A city planner explains:

> Alton Park and Piney Woods will gradually improve as a place to live but it is going to be a very, very slow process. There is just beginning to be the will in the city organizations to put the resources into that community. . . . Alton Park/Piney Woods could rest relatively high on the city's priority lists, because a fair number of people have begun to see that area as the test case, the challenge. Let's see if we can make this work. But the neighborhoods closer to downtown are the ones that are getting the most emphasis now. It seems easier to leverage the success of downtown just by proximity. You work something in this block, so you go to the next block and the next block and work it out. Alton Park starts about 34th Street, so that's quite a few blocks to go. **[34]**

As a result of such prioritizing, neighborhood activists believe that this is a struggle that they must pass on to their children.

> The very people who are here will not be here when the work is finished. It will be a whole group of new people. The question is: are they prepared to fight? We have to keep fighting. The industries are still around. You got to always watch, no matter what the deal is, you got to continue to watch because they are about making a

> dollar. That is what we had in 1970. People were dying. We don't want those companies to ever think that we are not watching them. But we're all getting old. Deborah is getting old. Mr. Jackson is getting old. I am getting old. Who is going to take our place? . . . What is going to happen when everybody thinks everything is all right? It can't be because the residue is always going to be here; that can never change. You cannot go down there and dig it up. It will be here for 100 years. **[35]**

And, in the eyes of one resident, the struggle will not be over until the health issues are addressed:

> When we find that the community is not getting sick like they were, and little children that's been born into the community, they are not contracting asthma or emphysema or cancer, and the parents be cancer-free, then we'll know that this has really had an impact on the community. **[36]**

Frames and Intractability in Alton Park and Piney Woods

Chattanooga offers both a challenge and a possible model for the management of intractable conflict. On the one hand, this conflict over toxic pollution that has been ongoing for more than thirty years continues to pose difficult and challenging issues. On the other hand, the dynamics of this conflict have changed considerably. As a community, Alton Park and Piney Woods residents appear to be more conscious of the frames that they use to interpret the conflict, and of the malleability of these frames to community interpretation. They have developed a lateral network of ties characterized by trust and reciprocity between community members (e.g., mobilizing coalitions between various neighborhood organizations), as well as vertical ties characterized by a degree of trust and reciprocity with power holders and decision makers (e.g., bridging relationships between the community and external organizations such as Velsicol and EPA). These mobilizing and bridging networks enhance the social capital available to the neighborhood, thereby increasing the community's capacity to resolve conflict and to gain voice and power (Gray 1999). Residents, public officials, and industrialists have also developed specific conflict management skills, both as individuals and as an interrelated community.

In the following sections, we will examine how frames contributed to these changes. First, we will analyze the identity and characterization frames that disputants adopted in the period from the 1960s through the 1980s. Second, we will explore the evolution of conflict mode frames in both the city and the neighborhoods, and how changes in the former helped catalyze changes in the latter. The final section investigates the impact of changes in conflict mode frames on identity and characterization frames.

Identity and Characterization Frames through the 1980s

How do community residents view their own identity and characterize other stakeholders in this conflict? First, we encounter a tension within the larger community. On the one hand, Chattanooga has an "industrial identity," which tends to bind the civic identity to jobs, payroll, and taxes. **[1]** This identity grows from a long history and tradition, in which Chattanoogans developed a dynamic economy from an industrial base. This identity is symbolized by the "wingtips" under the table. **[2]** On the other hand, the industrial development tended to obfuscate Chattanooga's other primary identity as linked to "natural beauty and the environment." **[1]** Chattanooga is located in a physically beautiful site, a place where a river, valleys, and mountains form a dynamic landscape. As long as the air and water were heavily polluted, Chattanoogans exhibited stronger linkages with industry. These linkages, however, led to a designation of Chattanooga as the "most polluted city in the United States." Moreover, the decline of heavy industry corresponded with regulatory shifts that improved environmental quality. A rebalancing of these identities became possible. **[1]** An environmental identity was symbolized by "hunting boots" under the table. **[2]**

In Alton Park and Piney Woods, early indications of identity seem much more tightly linked to community and to victimization. Images from the past suggest a tightly linked community, in which children were nurtured by the community as a whole, women raised gardens, and racial tolerance was practiced. **[5, 7]** Yet, these identities are at crosscurrents to images of victimization. Blacks are forced out of the Westside and end up buying homes from whites who are fleeing the pollution of Alton Park and Piney Woods. **[6]** Industry moves in and displaces community enterprises. **[7]** Children are "sprayed" with pollution on the way to school each day, and consider themselves to be an "unwanted stepchild" to industry and city government. **[4, 10]** Younger residents leave the community as soon as economically feasible, thereby adding a sense of abandonment to that of separation. **[9]** Those who stay behind experience high incidences of "leukemia" and "asthma." **[11]** This victimization identity is both interest- and place-based—rooted in interests focused on reducing pollution and protecting residents' health, and place-based because the hazards are specific to the Alton Park/Piney Woods communities.

For many, this sense of separation (both physical and social) from the rest of Chattanooga gave way to an identity of activist or protestor. Vietnam vets "felt they had a right" and had "paid the price" to demand action. **[12]** Miss Dixon "played major" by protesting and going to jail. Yet, even in this sense of protest, community residents present little sense of a racially excluding identity. They saw themselves as black, but not as anti-white. Even the one reference made to not letting "white people come out here" was linked to a specific time period, when blacks were "in the mode." **[13]** The same activist asserts that pollution is "never a racial line. It draws community together, both white and black." **[13]**

The identities of industrialists exhibit a similar degree of flexibility. On the one hand, industrialists hold rationality and action as core to their identities. They note that "we are not PR people, we are engineers" and believe that "you can talk so much, but after a while you got to act." **[21]** They also strongly reject "venting" as a legitimate mode of discourse, in part because while it helps people who are "screaming and hollering feel good . . . nothing gets accomplished," **[19, 20]** and in part because such venting is frequently an attack on the integrity and intentions of industry, and therefore an attack on their identity. As one engineer put it, "like they do in the Middle East. You have to first acknowledge we all have the right to exist." **[26]** On the other hand, once this basic right for industry to exist is acknowledged, at least some industrialists recognize that rational decision making requires dialogue as to what everyone values, since these values are not self-evident. **[20, 25]** For these individuals, being workers in industry also meant they were members of the community in which the industry was located, with responsibilities to that community. **[26]**

Characterizations

In the early years, characterizations often promoted separation between groups. Community residents characterized other stakeholders as aloof and distant. Industry would talk about doing "something" but would never do it. **[4]** Children were told to "beware of those who stand high on the mountains and look down" because the well-to-do lived on Lookout Mountain above the neighborhood. **[8]** The well-to-do were "shrewd" and constituted "games" that excluded poor African Americans. **[8]** Industrialists would release a lot of chemicals "while people were sleeping" that would fall "out of the sky overnight." **[11]** City officials were indifferent to the problems of the residents. **[12]** Similarly, industry and political leaders also reinforced the separatist identity of the neighborhood residents as well as their invisibility. Residents were people who "screamed and hollered" and who wanted society to "go back to the stone ages." **[19]** Industry would ignore its neighbors, unless forced to interact by a lawsuit or public agency. **[25]**

Interestingly, even in these earlier years, many residents suggest a desire for tolerance, not only of blacks by whites, but also of whites by blacks. For many, anger seemed muted by a vague sense of possibilities, and of the humanness of all people. Explicit images of environmental racism are not used. Rather, the images are more globally construed as issues of environmental justice, and the perpetrators of the toxic legacy are described as "ignorant" and "irresponsible," but not "hateful." This leaves open the door to improved working relationships between the community, industry, and public officials, since the various stakeholders do not presume that the bad conditions experienced by the community are the result of deliberately bad intentions on the part of other stakeholders.

The Evolution of Conflict Mode Frames

Conflict mode frames shift dramatically, first within the city and later within the neighborhoods. Until the 1970s, the city and the neighborhoods shared a single conflict mode frame: authority decides based on expertise. In addition, Alton Park/Piney Woods residents also framed the conflict in avoidance and passivity. The data suggest that other frames—notably fact-finding, joint problem solving, appeals to political action, and struggle—that would be activated later in the conflict were not active in this early phase. In the city, authority frames gave way to a bold invitation to a new relationship of consensus building by civic leaders who stood outside of public office, yet wielded considerable influence (joint problem solving). In the neighborhood, these frames gave way to a protracted struggle, involving lawsuits, protest, and persistent political action (struggle, adjudication, and appeal to political authority), and finally yielded to a partial negotiation process (fact-finding and joint problem solving).

In the city, the transformation is easier to delineate. Chattanooga's decline spurred new thinking. The city drew in ideas, processes, and expertise from other cities that had previously navigated the economic dislocation associated with industrial restructuring. The city had residents who had remained civically engaged and were willing to invest financially both in the process of consensus building and in the implementation of the plans that emerged. Equally importantly, Chattanoogans exhibited little overt conflict over either the process or the resulting recommendations. In the early 1980s, consensus was being built among people with shared interests and concerns, in the presence of leadership who trusted the process enough to let it succeed. Eventually, success built on success as participatory consensus building processes were employed in a number of community visioning settings.

In Alton Park and Piney Woods, few of these larger conditions existed. The neighborhood was more skeptical of expertise although open to the conditions of other communities. **[13, 15]** Civic engagement was more uneven, and financial resources considerably lower. Conflict, both amongst the neighbors and between the neighbors and outsiders, was considerably more intense.

Frames that delineate how best to manage conflict are therefore more divergent. In the 1970s, community activists saw little alternative to political and legal action, and to protest and civil disobedience. **[12, 13, 14, 15]** These actions, however, never involved a large cross section of the community. Rather, individuals took on responsibility to address problems as they saw it, and generated many small community organizations centered around charismatic leadership. The relationship between the community groups was at times cooperative and at times competitive. **[27, 29, 31]** Vietnam vets protested against "Agent Orange here in this community." **[12]** Students and STOP and Greenpeace linked up to organize against the industry. **[13]** A community housing advocate "went to jail" for shutting down city hall with babies and for releasing rats. **[14]** Community residents conducted their own health survey when the state health department's survey did not answer their questions. **[15]**

Yet, this dominant frame gives way to a decidedly more mixed frame involving not only struggle and protest, but fact-finding and joint problem solving. Movement appears to occur in both directions. Industry clearly is altered by previous protest and community concerns. In some sense, the neighborhood has forced industry to respond by mobilizing and gaining voice through protest (power frame) and by "saying the same things over and over until someone listens." **[17]** With a change in management comes a change in industry frames toward the communities' concerns. Managers who see themselves as "ethical people who believe in reducing pollution" look for a "better way to do business" with their neighbors. **[18, 20]**

These changes grow from two sources, each linked to the larger changes that were altering Chattanooga. The neighborhood consistently demanded a higher standard of performance from both the industry and public officials. These movements were linked to rising expectations within the neighborhood, based in part on observations of improvements made in Chattanooga as a whole. Second, the citywide community culture also promoted higher expectations of what constituted appropriate industrial and governmental action within the two neighborhoods. Chattanooga and the nation's growing awareness of negative consequences of environmental pollution, and the development of a regulatory infrastructure to deal with it (e.g., Superfund), also changed the expectations. As such, both industry and public agencies were encouraged to improve environmental performance and relationships with community residents.

As in Chattanooga's experiments with consensus building, Alton Park and Piney Woods' more tentative experiments with dialogue and negotiation yielded initial successes that fed expectations for yet even greater levels of dialogue and accommodation on industry's part to community concerns. "Racial integration, cooperation and working together" are seen by some as the preferred way of resolving differences. **[32]** Whether this will prove as successful in the two neighborhoods as it did in the city remains unsettled.

The Impact of Conflict Mode Frame-Shifts on Identity and Characterization Frames

Identity and characterization frames shift substantially amongst those activists most directly involved in dialogue processes. Today, residents talk about themselves in terms of being knowledgeable, a threat to the industry, and persistent. **[23, 24, 27, 32]** African Americans are seen as "conscious of saving creeks" and concerned with nature. **[28]** Residents talk with a stronger sense of power. Yet, several community leaders exhibit a tiredness, a sense of aging. Not only are they growing older, but so is the community. **[5, 33, 35]** They yearn for younger leaders to pick up the mantle of responsibility.

Characterization frames have changed even more dramatically. Residents make frequent reference to how officials and owners of plants were ignorant "back then" and were not responsible "before the laws were there." **[23, 24]** Many residents refer to former antagonists in more accepting terms. Companies "do serve a need" and "listen more and try to do something about it." **[23, 24]** Likewise, industry exhibits a considerably more empathetic perspective and a clearer sense of responsibility both to open dialogue and to change corporate behavior. **[24, 25, 26]**

These frames are not universally shared, and some residents remain deeply suspicious of the intent behind dialogue processes as well as their impact. "Basically I think the government's just feeding them something to keep them quiet" and the government is "burning them out" by drawing them into too many dialogues. **[30]** Yet this perspective is in the minority. Most respondents not only support the changes, but link improvements in corporate and governmental behavior directly to the processes of dialogue. Thus, in the minds of many of the residents, shifts in conflict modes toward dialogue directly led to more collaborative identity and characterization frames, as well as concrete improvements in environmental quality. Progress indeed had been made toward a time when "the parents be cancer-free." **[36]**

Note on Sources

The information in this chapter was derived from newspaper articles and from interviews with community residents, activists, business leaders, environmentalists, civic leaders, and public officials. Newspaper articles were collected from the *Chattanooga Times* and the *News-Free Press.* The time span covers forty years from the 1960s forward.

Chapter 12

Framing Effects in Toxic Disputes: Cross-Case Analysis

Michael Elliott and Ralph Hanke

Across the country, thousands of communities now struggle with efforts to protect ecosystems, public health, and community well-being from the impact of contaminated sites. These communities share much in common with Chattanooga, Tennessee, and Lock Haven, Pennsylvania, where issues of toxic chemicals led to deeply felt and difficult to resolve conflicts. In this chapter, we will examine the events and conditions found in Chattanooga and Lock Haven, and explore why these disputes have been difficult to resolve, how the framing of these disputes contributed to intractability, and how reframing may have contributed to de-escalation over time.

Why Toxic Management Disputes Are Often Difficult to Resolve

Chattanooga and Lock Haven are both industrial communities. While Chattanooga's industrial sector is considerably larger and older than Lock Haven's, both developed these sectors in the first half of the twentieth century. As was typical of this period, industrial facilities were located in valleys adjacent to stream and river systems. Rivers provided transportation, water for processing, and dumps for liquid waste. Also typical for this era, industries disposed of wastes through land burial and lagoons, and by emitting pollutants into the air. Over time, many sites came to be contaminated.

The cleanup of contaminated industrial sites poses many difficult choices. Further, disputes over the cleanup process are often intense for several reasons. First, a plethora of federal and state legislation governs remediation of contaminated sites, with different laws setting differing requirements and responsibilities for local, state, and federal government; the various owners and operators of the facility; and the surrounding community. Second, effective cleanup is often very expensive, running into the tens of millions of dollars for a moderately complicated site. Costs increase significantly as sites are cleaned to higher standards. Third, each waste management technology poses its own risks. And fourth, the debate intensifies when the concentrations of chemicals in the ground are extremely small, when contamination comes from multiple sites with multiple owners, or when the site is inactive (a "brownfield" site) or abandoned (a "Superfund" site) (Hird 1994, Mazmanian and Morell 1992).

In this context, disputes often linger for many years, simply because cleanup requires many resources from a variety of stakeholder groups. In Lock Haven, Drake's manufacture of small batches of chemical intermediates left a broad array of chemical wastes that Drake could not afford to clean up when it filed for bankruptcy in 1982. In Chattanooga, the Alton Park and Piney Woods neighborhoods contained forty toxic landfills and numerous contaminated industrial facilities. Many of these sites were contributing to soil and water contamination, which residents feared was harming their health. In both communities, federal and state agencies, particularly the U.S. Environmental Protection Agency (EPA), were active participants, bringing national and state stakeholders into local disputes.

The Impact of Frames on the Conflict Dynamics

In these contexts, how do frames contribute to the intractability of these disputes? To answer this question, we will examine the interrelationship of four frames—risk perception, identity, characterization, and conflict management—and their impact on intractability. As shown in Figure 12.1, these frames alter the capacity to resolve environmental disputes by changing disputants' preferences for outcomes and problem definitions, by altering patterns of communication and interaction, and by directly altering the disputants' willingness to resolve the dispute.

Risk Perception Frames

As discussed in Chapter 1, stakeholders in a dispute may perceive the likely outcomes and potential risks associated with future actions differently. Because of these differences in perception, individuals and stakeholders may disagree fundamentally on which problems to address, and the appropriate response to the problem. In Chattanooga, this was made manifest when residents of the neighborhoods began to link the toxics in their environment with the sicknesses they experienced in their lives. Residents in the 1960s and '70s focused

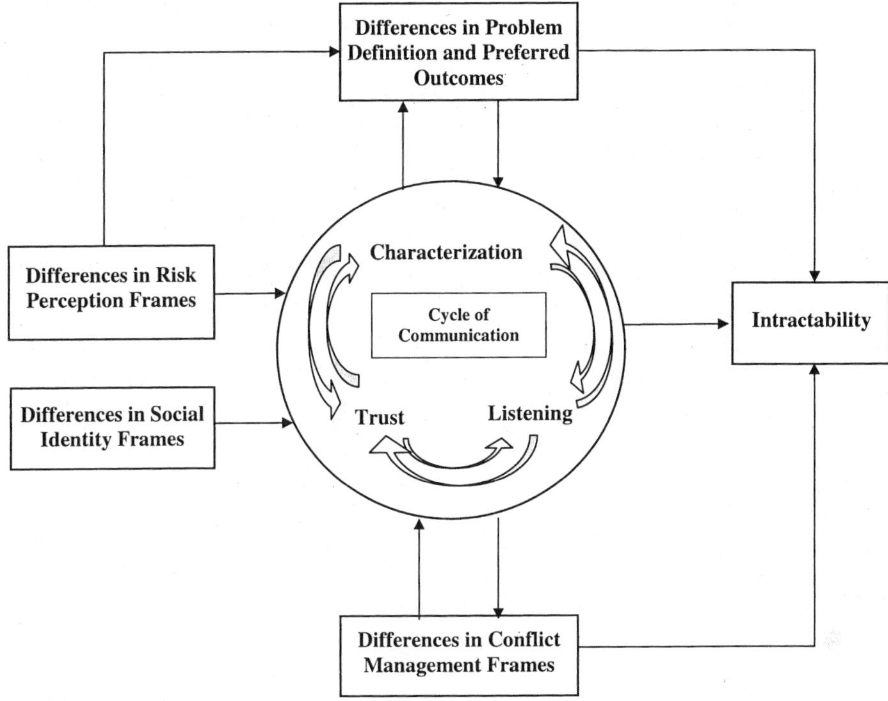

Figure 12.1. Model of Interrelationships among Four Key Factors in the Drake and Chattanooga Cases.

almost exclusively on the acute effects of exposure (lung, eye, and nose irritation; bad odors), while residents in the 1980s and '90s also worried about chronic effects (asthma, cancer). As one resident explained,

> My grandson—he's just so sick with asthma, I don't know what the problem is; I don't know why. But I think it has something to do with whatever they pumped underground in the Chattanooga area. Whatever is in the air. **[Chattanooga 11]**

Beginning in the 1980s, residents demanded that the county health department conduct studies of public health. Residents believed that the studies would pinpoint specific chemicals that were causing respiratory illness and cancer in the community. When the studies did not determine that the neighborhood residents faced an elevated incidence of disease, residents explicitly rejected the public health studies as biased or insufficiently precise. Studies conducted by the Agency for Toxic Substances and Disease Registry (ATSDR), a division of the U.S. Centers for Disease Control, were deemed better only in that they uncovered evidence of lung impairment. Meanwhile, residents conducted their own study by "sitting and talking about who's dying in the neighborhood." Residents were particularly concerned with children and the elderly, who seemed to be sick more often, and made explicit links between the diseases they found (asthma, cancer) and the chemicals in the environment.

Residents in Lock Haven remained largely unconcerned about the risks associated with Drake until the 1980s. Two events catalyzed a greater sense of disquiet. First, a cluster of bladder cancers was identified in the community. Betanepthalamine (BNA), a semivolatile organic compound found on the Drake site, had been implicated in bladder cancer. Because EPA staff considered BNA highly risky, they listed the Drake site as one of their ten highest priority Superfund sites in 1984. Second, EPA decided to treat the Drake soil by means of on-site incineration. This decision led to the formation of a community group called Arrest the Incinerator Remediation (AIR). AIR organizers were expressly concerned with incineration-based air pollution risks. These residents believed that incineration would release dioxins and other unknown chemicals into the air and were convinced that thermal inversions would keep these chemicals from dissipating, thus poisoning the residents of the valley. As one member notes: "I think there is a very, very real chance . . . of premature death and illness for those who are susceptible to that kind of contamination."

As in Chattanooga, AIR consistently expressed skepticism about the risk assessments presented by the EPA. Their skepticism ranged from doubt and suspicion to incredulity. AIR contended that both the methods and the results of the risk assessments were flawed. In particular, they argued that the risk assessments did not account for the presence of dioxins in the incinerator output, the local thermal inversions, or the effects of the incineration on the old and the young.

In both communities, various stakeholder groups held widely differing perceptions about the health risks associated with toxics and their management. Introduction of new information by government officials or by community residents did not alleviate these differences in perception, nor did stakeholders in either community change their risk frames significantly during the conflict. AIR, for example, saw incineration as a "technology that is on the way out in this country" and argued that "we do not want to be the last of the guinea pigs." Their opposition to the incinerator as overly risky never faltered throughout their campaign against incineration. Conversely, the EPA held that incineration did not pose a substantial risk to the community, that their risk assessments were "very conservative," and that the incinerator was "state of the art and the best technology available." These fundamental differences in how risks were perceived remained unaltered over the course of the conflict.

Similarly, in Chattanooga, where significant progress has been made to reduce exposure to toxics, perceptions of the risks involved remained highly divergent. A community resident exclaims that "people were just dying from cancer, and women were having miscarriages, from inhaling all of that stuff over the years." At the same time, an industrialist notes that,

> The studies don't say that. The study says it is a pretty normal rate here. And I have studies of my plant and my people that work right here by the chemicals and everything is normal. They [community residents] say everybody is dying of cancer, and I say everybody I know is dying of cancer too. People die of cancer. I think people think we must be lying to them, because there has to be a reason why they are dying of cancer. **[Chattanooga 16]**

These two individuals had worked together to reduce exposure to chemicals, but remained divergent in the ways they framed the risks that result from that exposure.

Other instances also demonstrate the differences in the risk frames. Many of the comparisons and concerns raised by members of AIR suggest that they saw the Drake incineration process as comparable to the processes and outputs of a permanently sited waste incinerator. Similarly, in Chattanooga an industrial air pollution control device was interpreted by the community residents as being a hazardous waste incinerator. While the EPA and the industries involved made distinctions between these various technologies, neither AIR nor the residents of Alton Park accepted the distinctions as useful, believing instead that proponents of the cleanup actions were creating distinctions to obfuscate the facts.

In these examples, risk perceptions contributed directly to distrust of those stakeholders who held differing risk frames. The stakeholders found it difficult to trust those who came to such different conclusions when faced with the same evidence. Public officials in both communities concluded that residents were overly concerned about risks with very low probabilities. Activists in both communities felt that the government agencies employed flawed techniques of analysis since the results were inconsistent with their own assessment of the risks.

Equally important, differences in risk frames led to changes in characterization frames. In both communities, stakeholders explained differences in risk frames by negatively characterizing the motivations and abilities of the other stakeholders. Community activists believed that government officials deliberately obfuscated the facts. They characterized the risk assessment and ATSDR's findings as government chicanery, while promises of risk reduction were seen as "feeding the residents something to keep them quiet." On the other hand, government officials and industry characterized activists as "loud mouths," as people who want society "to go back to the stone age," and as "irrational" people.

One of AIR's most defining characteristics is their call for "zero emissions." They fought for closed-loop systems, which they believed to be technically feasible, because even "one extra molecule of dioxin" was too much. This flew in the face of the EPA's approach to remediation. EPA held that varying levels of emissions create varying risks and that certain levels of risk are acceptable. AIR refused to accept that approach as a viable way to consider the outcome of incineration. To them, the risk estimates merely served as justifications for their interpretation that the EPA was "annihilating" the Lock Haven community. The disparate approaches to emissions practiced by the opposing parties represented a hurdle in communication that neither side would ever overcome.

In Chattanooga, many residents also demanded that industry completely eliminate their emissions. Despite differences in risk frames and preferred outcomes, however, stakeholders in Chattanooga could often focus on potential gains that both sides recognized would reduce risk. While risk frames held by residents differed significantly from agency officials and industrialists, residents were able to work with both groups. For example, an industrialist noted that conflict associated with community demands for zero emissions are

> hard to resolve, because we rely on this job to feed our families. If we work past this issue, we can look at health effects of pollutants, how the company can better control pollutants, and whether cleaner substitutes can be made. **[Chattanooga 26]**

Many residents share this desire for a pragmatic progress as well, but with a strong sense of needing to constantly watch these industries, to carry on the struggle, from one generation to the next:

> The very people who are here will not be here when the work is finished. It will be a whole new group of people. The question is: are they prepared to fight? We have to keep fighting. The industries are still around. **[Chattanooga 35]**

Identity Frames

The two cases also illustrate the impact of identity frames on conflict dynamics. The cases share characteristics that are often found in toxics disputes, but also present an unusual twist on some of these common themes.

Both communities are in the process of redefining themselves. In Chattanooga the shift is more dramatic, if only because the city is larger and the changes more pervasive. The switch from the *Dynamo of Dixie* to the *Sustainable City* is more than just a change of mottos.

Alton Park and Piney Woods grew up within a vibrant industrial complex. In these African American neighborhoods, residents worked in the local industrial facilities. Over the past quarter century, however, industry restructured, many facilities closed, and the workforce of others became better educated and was drawn from a more widely dispersed area of Chattanooga. Today, the majority of workers in many Alton Park and Piney Woods industrial facilities reside outside the neighborhood. Residents rarely identify themselves as economically linked to industrial employment or incorporate industry into their sense of identity. Rather, industry has become "the other," outside and apart:

> The industries might at one time have been a major force of employment for the community but they are not anymore, because those [who work] here no longer live in the community. The community is left reaping the after-effects of what has been planted years before. **[Chattanooga 9]**

Industrialists also sense this division, drawing a line between themselves and those outside their fences. At the same time, in Chattanooga there remains a sense of a larger community, to which both residents and industrialists belong. Each side includes itself in this larger community, linked by a common place and overlapping interests, and acknowledges, albeit weakly, some form of shared identity.

Lock Haven, on the other hand, is a small central Pennsylvania town. The population is primarily Caucasian and working class. Like Alton Park, the average per capita income is quite low, making this one of the poorer areas in the United States. Many AIR members believe this socioeconomic feature motivated the EPA to use incineration in the first place. In Lock Haven, the physical manifestations of industrial restructuring have been smaller, but the impact may well be more pervasive within the community. The closing of two chemical companies, coupled with the departure of Piper Aircraft Company, changed the area from a reasonably secure and thriving enclave to one mired in economic decline. These circumstances left many residents feeling vulnerable.

In the context of these industrial shifts, three identity frames appear to predominate. Residents primarily identified themselves as either defenders of justice or victims. Industrialists and public officials most often saw themselves as rational experts.

The Defender of Justice

In both Lock Haven and Chattanooga, community activists believed that they were defending the community against environmental injustices. Given their perception that the risks associated with the toxics were significant, activists moved to protect their community against the threats imposed by outsiders. This was particularly apparent in Lock Haven, where the intensity with which activists experienced this social identity increased significantly over time. At the beginning of the dispute, AIR saw itself as a grassroots organization focused on ensuring the safety of the Lock Haven community. As time went on, they came to see themselves as protectors of more fundamental public goods, including "our very fundamental rights as Americans." In the end, AIR saw itself as freedom fighters resisting the oppression of government.

In Chattanooga, the Alton Park and Piney Woods residents noted conditions of environmental injustice, and also saw themselves as central to the creation of a more just future. Activists referred to themselves as "spiritual" and likened their political action to a minister who has to preach the same sermon repeatedly every Sunday. They also likened themselves to Vietnam veterans who learned about Agent Orange and fought for government action to right the injustice resulting from their exposure to it. Further, they made distinctions between industries that were "going through the process" of cooperation and remediation, and those who were "denying that they have a part in this." Finally, they talked about their role in keeping the struggle going, for 100 years if need be.

At the same time, activists were more integrated into the wider community, and included not only neighborhood residents, but also community leaders, public officials, and, at times, industrialists who worked with the community. In contrast to Lock Haven, the activists in Chattanooga noted that resolving these injustices was not their work alone. They called on the larger community to listen and act:

> It is going to be up to the community and the elected official and the government and all the industries together to bring [the indus-

> try that seeks to avoid cleanup] into their responsibility through laws and different rules in order that they can be held accountable. **[Chattanooga 32]**

In a particularly telling story, one very politically oriented resident described how white college girls came into the neighborhoods "at a time when we didn't let white people come out here" to help the community with environmental problems, how the community wondered "what kind of students are these, what kind of kids are these, with long hair and jeans and sitting on the floor," but how over time the students and the community came to work together. **[Chattanooga 13]** In this neighborhood within Chattanooga, then, environmental justice was not seen as identical to environmental racism: "One of the things about pollution and chemical companies, it is never a racial line. It draws a community together, both white and black." **[Chattanooga 13]**

The Victim

Community residents also identified themselves with memories of their injured history, with being a victim. These memories could be old and enduring. The fight over incineration at the Drake site was the second major battle in Lock Haven in one decade. The first battle had been about a dike levy designed to protect the city from future flooding of the Susquehanna River. This battle had raged for a number of years and divided the town into two distinct factions. Many of the players in the Drake dispute had also been involved in the dike levy dispute. This history of serious community disagreement colored their framing of the Drake conflict.

The Alton Park and Piney Woods neighborhoods had experienced decades of environmental insults. Adults remembered going to schools and needing to hold their breath as they passed in front of industries. They recalled children being "sprayed" with chemicals and gardens being destroyed by air pollution, and felt powerless to stop the problems.

> It was the industries that caused the problems, and we figured we couldn't do anything about the industries. They would talk that they would do something about it, but they wouldn't. That leads to a feeling of being an unwanted stepchild. **[Chattanooga 4]**

Industry did more than pollute the neighborhood. They transformed the community from one with "doctors, lawyers, baker men, retail, pharmacies, everything that a community needed" to one where

> the only thing that you have now is manufacturing, chemicals. You got one or two little stores, and it's just not a community anymore. It's just a place where people go and live until they can get out and go someplace else. **[Chattanooga 7]**

Industry was not the only source of victimization however. The neighborhoods are located at the base of Lookout Mountain, where many of the city's elite lived.

> I was always told to beware of those who stand high on the mountains and look down. A lot of people who stay up on these hilltops have been shrewd in the past and have constituted a lot of games that we didn't know the rules to. **[Chattanooga 8]**

In this light, the city relocated African Americans from the Westside through urban renewal just at the time when white families living in Alton Park sought to move away from the pollution. As a result, Alton Park and Piney Woods transitioned from white neighborhoods to black ones.

> I can't say they were hateful, they were just businessmen, just looked after their own interests, and we just weren't one of them. **[Chattanooga 8]**

The Rational Experts

In Lock Haven, the social identities of the EPA, the state Department of Environmental Protection (DEP), and the city council also intensified. Earlier in the dispute, they saw themselves as reasonable, scientifically oriented professionals. This identity was institutionally based, particularly for EPA and DEP. As environmental professionals, these officials legitimized their decision-making authority by appeals to scientific rationality. The more AIR challenged the legitimacy of these claims, the more important these identities became to the public officials. They spent ever more time emphasizing their objectivity and ability to come to grips with the scientific aspects of the incineration process. As one proponent pointed out:

> I am a chemist and I know that it is impossible for anything harmful to be coming out of that stack at those temperatures. . . . It's just not possible. **[Drake 9]**

Some public officials and industrialists working in Alton Park and Piney Woods, on the other hand, gradually expanded their conception of their identity. Civic leaders increasingly described the problems facing Alton Park as "our problem" or "Chattanooga's problem." They referred to residents from the neighborhood as "neighbors." They continued to talk about themselves as "rational," but came to understand that being rational did not preclude dialogue with their neighbors: "We are engineers, and we are not used to seeing, asking for people's inputs. We are learning." Ethics became increasingly part of their identity: "The managers, the owners are very ethical people. I am not talking tree huggers, but I am talking ethical people who believe in reducing pollution." Industry no longer felt isolated from the community around its fence line: "We have a social responsibility to start looking at other ways to help the community, to become an asset to the neighborhood." **[Chattanooga 18, 21, 26]**

Thus, in Chattanooga, we find a distinct pattern whereby previously separated groups have broadened their social identity to a more inclusive one. At the same time, their core identities remained intact, and it is easy to imagine a reversion to old identities in the face of perceived betrayal or failure. Conversely, in Lock Haven the disputants' identity frames became more differentiated and ingrained as time went on.

Conflict Management Frames

As we noted in Chapter 1, it is possible to view conflict management frames residing on a spectrum ranging from more interactive to less interactive (Keltner 1994). A significant difference between Lock Haven and Chattanooga is the repertoire of conflict management frames adopted by the disputants. While the disputants in Lock Haven at times sought to adopt more interactive frames, disputants soon found themselves in an escalating process involving increasingly less interactive conflict management frames. Chattanooga, on the other hand, began with the elite seeking to resolve conflict through authority and expertise, and neighborhood residents framing conflict management as requiring struggle and adjudication. Over time, both groups transitioned from these divergent frames to ones in which each adopted more "joint problem solving" frames.

At Drake, city council members were first to respond to EPA's remediation proposal. The City Council eventually set up an environmental assessment committee to handle the Drake site and any concerns that might arise from it. As such, the EPA, Pennsylvania DEP, and Lock Haven City Council formed a powerful triumvirate that was essentially in favor of incineration. Government officials contended that these three levels of government took into account all the considerations and concerns of the community. The members of AIR, however, clearly felt alienated from these government agencies. AIR did not see any of these three groups representing their concerns and perspective. With the emergence of AIR as a stakeholder in the conflict, both the EPA and AIR emphasized fact-finding conflict management frames. AIR and the EPA both thought that science should be the final arbiter at the Drake site. However, they could not agree on what science was saying about the risk of incineration.

Although both sides maintained the fact-finding frames throughout the dispute, their other conflict management frames began to diverge rapidly. AIR sought help from national groups such as Greenpeace, GreenLaw, and the Sierra Club for community organizing and adjudication. These appeals to political action and adjudication frames emerged as AIR sought to galvanize the community around their cause. The citizens elected one of AIR's founders to a county commissioner post, based on his anti-incineration platform. That individual then persuaded the other county commissioners to support AIR in its first court battle with the EPA. As time went on, however, AIR's political clout diminished. The county commissioners eventually withdrew their support for AIR's legal stance after the Third Circuit Court of Appeals ruled that under the Comprehensive Environmental Response, Compensation, and Liability Act (CERCLA), AIR could not sue the EPA. The members of AIR felt disenfranchised and angry, fighting three governments that, from AIR's perspective, were trampling on their rights as American citizens. As incineration became increasingly likely, AIR reframed the conflict as one requiring struggle. Meanwhile, the EPA maintained their authority decides with consultation frame, shifting to an adjudication frame only in response to AIR's lawsuits and only for as long as was necessary to counteract AIR's challenge to EPA's authority.

In Chattanooga, the conflict management frames were more multifaceted, varying over time. In the 1960s and '70s, government and elected officials primarily held authority decides conflict management frames, while Alton Park and Piney Woods residents resisted through political action and direct struggle. A group of Vietnam veterans organized the Black Veterans Affairs Organization to address problems with industry and elected officials. Other residents worked with the students from the University of Tennessee, Chattanooga, and with Greenpeace to organize a neighborhood-based environmental group called Stop Toxic Pollution (STOP). Residents organized demonstrations, stopped traffic, brought rats to city hall, and defied the law. Residents talk of this time as a period of confrontation.

During the 1980s, Chattanooga began experimenting with community visioning processes and other forms of civic participation and engagement. It was the decade of Chattanooga Venture, of Vision 2000, of downtown revitalization, and of appreciation for Chattanooga's natural beauty. These changes largely bypassed Alton Park and Piney Woods neighborhoods that were physically, socially, and racially separated from most of the city. Yet, during this period, the conflict management frames within the neighborhoods also gradually shifted. Industry became somewhat more attuned to a sense of social responsibility and to the need for engagement with the community. Public officials became more confident in the use of consensus building. Community activists brought experiences from one neighborhood to the next, increasing the pressure for collaborative problem-solving processes. Simply ignoring the problems was no longer an acceptable approach to managing the conflict.

During the 1990s, more collaborative conflict frames came to dominate the thinking of public officials, residents, industrialists, and activists. To the activists, industry and public officials listened because

> the more people began to realize what was going on, the more of a threat it became to industries, so they had to listen. They began to change their way of thinking, and instead of sealing off their thoughts, just walking away from it, they began to sit down and see what's going on. **[Chattanooga 24]**

Residents increasingly felt that "racial integration, cooperation and working together have made the most difference to Chattanooga. If cooperation and communication were to happen, we wouldn't have all these other problems." **[Chattanooga 32]** Industrialists felt that they were "getting a bad rap" despite initiatives to reduce pollution and they needed "a better way to do business with [their] neighbors." The conflict management frames therefore evolved simultaneously among all the major stakeholder groups. As each group moved toward "joint problem solving," the willingness of one stakeholder group to engage in dialogue with other groups proved mutually reinforcing, as dialogue led to changes valued by the various disputants.

Assessment of the Communication Cycle

What are the impacts of the frames discussed above? How did risk perception, identity, and conflict management frames play out on the patterns of communication found in Chattanooga and Lock Haven? In particular, how do they account for the differences in the communications found in the two communities? As was already discussed and shown in Figure 12.1, each of these frames directly affects the communication cycle. We will now explore impacts on three major elements of this cycle: openness to listening, levels of trust, and characterization of others in the dispute.

Openness to Listening

In the final analysis, neither side of the Drake dispute was very open to listening to what the other side had to say. One person suggested that to AIR "everything was a lie, it didn't matter what was said, everything was a lie." The EPA was also unwilling to listen because they perceived that "AIR was in the grips of an individual who made a living from fighting incinerators . . . and . . . we've heard all that stuff before and it's nothing new."

In Chattanooga, on the other hand, disputants saw value in listening.

> People . . . have a tendency to listen more and try to do something about it. The city councilmen, the commissioners, people like Velsicol Chemical Company—now listen. . . . Listening is the first positive step to dealing with it. People beginning to listen makes a big difference. **[Chattanooga 24]**

Similarly, industry moved from a deep concern about the "irrationality" of community residents to one where,

> when we've got a problem, let's talk about it and see if we have a rational explanation for it or if we can fix it. If they say we want [industry] to shut down and leave, well we are not going to do that, but we'll sit down and listen. **[Chattanooga 25]**

Trust and Mistrust

Very significant differences in levels of trust exist between Lock Haven and Chattanooga. Some members of AIR felt that the EPA did not intend to clean up the site at all.

> [W]e believe that there is a deal between Superfund employees and the contractors. They have no intention of cleaning up the Drake site. It is all about perception and looking nice. **[Drake 18]**

Many of the disagreements occurred between individuals. AIR did not trust many of the individuals on the Lock Haven City Council, the DEP, or the EPA. AIR accused many of these individuals as being blatantly dishonest and working in concert to maximize their share of the pork barrel. Conversely, members of the DEP, EPA, and Lock Haven City Council viewed AIR members as individuals who distorted facts, used scare tactics, or did not understand the situation.

By comparison, a community activist in Chattanooga noted:

> When a problem exists I don't think [industries] try to hide [pollution problems] as much as they used to. They know that the community is concerned, and they want to work with us to try to improve not only the health of the community but to improve the community too. **[Chattanooga 23]**

This is not to say that they trust their good intentions.

> You got to always watch, no matter what the deal is, you got to continue to watch because they are about making a dollar. . . . We don't want those companies to ever think that we are not watching them. **[Chattanooga 35]**

Yet, despite this concern, there is a sense that at least some industries, if carefully watched, will perform responsibly. Similarly, industrialists also came to believe they could work effectively with members of the community, move beyond struggles over whether the industry should survive, and focus on more tractable issues of pollution prevention, health protection, and community improvement.

Impact of Selective Listening and Mistrust on Characterization

Both communities have a strong sense of boundaries between those who are internal to the community and those who are external. Like many small towns, Lock Haven expects much of newcomers before they are considered part of the local fabric. The disputants played upon the distinction between insiders and outsiders. Members of the EPA characterized themselves as well liked in the community, often talking about how people addressed them by their first names when they walked through the downtown. Similarly, a high-ranking DEP official emphasized the importance of the many friendships agency officials developed at Lock Haven City Hall while they were working on another project.

In juxtaposition to this sense of belonging, proponents of the incineration characterized AIR members as outsiders who really had no business being involved with the incinerator. They regularly pointed out that the founding members of AIR came from two counties away and therefore could not have the best interests of the community at heart. Similarly AIR characterized the insiders at Lock Haven as more concerned with lining their own pockets and those of their friends than caring for the well-being and health of the people of Lock Haven.

Characterization frames in Lock Haven intensified even more than did identity frames. At the beginning of the dispute, AIR characterized proponents of the dispute as "reckless," "using poor technology," and "so-called experts." By the end of the dispute AIR referred to the ATSDR as a "public relations arm of the EPA," and branded the EPA as "liars," "sneaky," and "hypocritical." The proponents of the incinerator were as unsympathetic in their descriptions of AIR. Members of AIR were "blatantly inflammatory," "narrow-minded," and prone to using "X-files science."

Characterizations made by disputants in Chattanooga, by contrast, were both less hostile and held more tentatively. Further, negative characterizations decreased toward the end of the '90s. While a few activists talked about the changes as a facade and trickery, most acknowledged that industry and public officials brought something of value to the community.

Similarly, into the early 1990s, industrialists felt that residents were irrational, concerned primarily with venting and getting media attention, and antagonistic. Managers, with experience primarily in public hearings, considered public meetings as somewhat perilous, to be avoided when possible. These managers now hold public meetings and meet with activists at the community organization's offices. Industrialists still talk about those who want to take us back to "the stone ages," but in general, they reserve such characterizations for a few select individuals, not activists or residents in general.

Intractability

How can we best make sense of these frames, and their impact on the tractability of the two conflicts described? In some ways, we may be tempted to think that the Drake site conflict was more tractable than conflicts found in Chattanooga. The core dispute between AIR and the EPA lasted approximately five years, and EPA was able to complete its incineration of contaminants at the Drake site under the protection of the courts. However, this dispute can be better seen as a single incident in a larger national dispute over air quality, incineration, and dioxins. That conflict has been raging since the 1960s and does not look to be close to resolution. Moreover, at the Drake site, the conflict was "resolved" bluntly, with one side proving powerful enough to enforce its will on the other.

Conflicts over toxics in Alton Park and Piney Woods, on the other hand, have been explicit for forty years. Residents sense that it will be ongoing for another "100 years" because "the residue is always going to be there. . . . You cannot go down and dig it up." Yet, in many ways Chattanooga exhibits signs of tractability, a conversion of the conflict from an overt dispute into a civic problem. The potential clearly exists for the issues to revert to old patterns of conflict, but the potential also exists for more collaborative patterns to emerge.

In comparing the two cases, the similarity between the actions taken by public officials and industrialists in each community is striking. In both communities, federal and local agencies or industry moved to clean up contaminated sites, and community groups opposed their efforts to do so. In both communities, residents were concerned about the health effects of the contaminated sites and of the proposed remedial actions. In both communities, periods of intense struggle between the parties developed. Yet, the conflict dynamics in the two communities eventually diverged, with Lock Haven caught in an escalatory cycle and Chattanooga entering a de-escalatory cycle.

From the beginning, AIR was aghast at what they viewed as a flawed and dangerous technology that they believed would only serve to poison the local population. They could not understand that anyone could be in favor of incineration unless they were "in the back pocket of big business." By contrast, the EPA could never understand why AIR was so concerned about the incineration process. The EPA trusted its risk assessments and believed incineration was very unlikely to harm anyone. These disparate views of the risk involved with incineration served to undermine communications, foster distrust, and increase negative characterizations of opponents in the Drake case. As a result, the dispute maintained a steady path away from collaboration.

In addition, the participants engaged in an intensification (escalation) of social identity and negative characterizations that left them unwilling to adopt conflict management strategies that could lead to resolution and collaboration around the remediation. Those conflict management choices, in turn, reinforced the escalation of the conflict. The intensification of the "us vs. them" approach resulted in public shifts in allegiance by some members of AIR. Former members would argue that AIR was too inflexible and unwilling to consider alternatives. AIR saw these changes in allegiance as betrayals. In the end, AIR distinctly moved from a focus on pollution (interests) to the protection of basic freedoms (rights). This shift from interests to rights led AIR to escalate the conflict beyond Drake to other sites and communities as well as to the Supreme Court.

Chattanooga, however, entered a de-escalatory cycle. Most importantly, communitywide dynamics caused conflict management frames to shift. These dynamics led toward collaboration and the design of consensus-building processes that successfully resolved difficulties in the downtown and close-in neighborhoods. This experience altered conflict management frames not only amongst the participants in these processes, but more globally throughout Chattanooga. Activists developed skills in collaboration. New norms of legitimacy around "environmental quality" and conflict modes developed, among both elites and residents. Changes in conflict modes in turn promoted new understandings of community identity, changes in communication patterns, and reductions in negative characterization.

These changes are self-reinforcing, as new patterns of communication promoted more effective problem solving, and new identities focused attention on problems of concern to the community. A neighborhood-based environmental activist described efforts by EPA to clean up a Superfund site in Alton Park, a process that started as being very conflictual, as follows:

> It was a good process, a timely process. At least in the '90s, we sat down at the table and discussed what was going to happen in the community. And from generating and discussion, things changed around. The government turned around, and we began to see what could be done. **[Chattanooga 29]**

Conclusion

Chattanooga and Lock Haven each faced difficult problems associated with toxic contamination. These two cases, however, demonstrate that while such conflicts are often intractable, changes in risk perception, identity, conflict management and characterization frames are sometimes possible. Moreover, changes in frames can have a significant effect on the conduct of the conflict, even when core issues remain difficult to manage.

In particular, the cases suggest that independent frames are interactive. Changes in conflict management frames or identity frames create changes in communication that affect listening, trust, and characterization frames. The cases suggest that changing conflict management frames may be easier than changing other frames, and that changes in conflict management frames may be powerful precursors to de-escalatory cycles in communication. Further, the cases suggest that when identity frames are softened, broadened, and made more inclusive, they encourage a positive cycle of communication. On a more cautious note, the cases also suggest that while risk frames have powerful effects on communication cycles and preferences for outcomes, they appear to be resistant to change. However, the cases do not explore the impact of more robust fact-finding and joint problem solving conflict management frames on risk frames, since neither community engaged in such processes.

Part IV

Growth Management Cases

Chapter 13

Colorado Growth-Related Environmental Conflicts

Robert Gardner, Carol Conzelman, Karen Mockler, Kim Sanchez, and Guy Burgess★

The state of Colorado is riding a wave of economic growth and expansion that, for the foreseeable future, shows little sign of abating. With growing economic opportunities in the booming technology and information sectors, Colorado's cities and towns are experiencing both a rapid influx of newcomers and a redistribution of existing residents. Over the past ten years, Colorado has added 800,000 new residents, 80 percent of whom have been absorbed into the Front Range Urban Corridor—a 200-mile stretch of nearly contiguous cities located on the western edge of the Great Plains. Nestled at the base of the Rocky Mountains, these communities lie in an area traditionally cherished for its wide open spaces, untamed wilderness areas, and extraordinary scenic splendor.

As a result of these developments, many Front Range communities are facing a proliferation of conflicts and disputes involving land use politics, environmental protection initiatives, economic growth strategies, and residential development plans. Not surprisingly, different communities, each with a unique sense of history, place, and politics, encounter different sets of conflicts and disputes regarding the most effective way to handle commercial and residential growth.

The region's newcomers and old-timers represent a broad spectrum of political, economic, and environmental orientations. People are drawn to the region by its booming economy, seemingly endless selection of outdoor recre-

★ This chapter was truly a group effort. Individual sections were written by Carol Conzelman (El Paso County), Karen Mockler (Larimer County), and Kim Sanchez (Boulder County). The overall paper was organized and edited by Rob Gardner (who also did some of the writing). Guy Burgess directed the project and helped edit the manuscript.

ational opportunities (such as skiing, biking, hiking, fishing, hunting, and four-wheeling), dry, sunny climate, environmental consciousness, and entertainment and cultural life. Corporations and businesses are also interested in the West with its relatively large supply of undeveloped or "vacant" land. They especially like the fact that the area's scenic beauty and amenities attract a relatively large and highly educated workforce. In fact, the area is quickly becoming one of the premiere hot spots for the growing computer and technology sector (the corridor from Boulder to the Denver Tech Center constitutes what some analysts consider to be the next Silicon Valley). The newcomers, together with "native born" Colorado residents, give the region a diversity of perspectives concerning land use and environmental policy. This diversity, in turn, engenders increasing friction between the multiple contingencies that represent the region's population.

In this chapter, we explore differences in the ways in which the various parties frame the tensions between growth and environmental protection in three communities along the Front Range Urban Corridor: Larimer County (Fort Collins), El Paso County (Colorado Springs), and Boulder County (Boulder). Development in this semiarid region is possible primarily in fairly narrow corridors nourished by irrigation and municipal water from the mountains to the west. Since large-scale urban growth is not really practical in such a mountainous area, development is primarily occurring just east of towns located at the base of the mountains (note the crosshatched areas in Figure 13.1).

Our project employed a somewhat different methodology than that used by the other cases reported in this volume. Rather than conducting detailed analysis of a single case, we conducted a somewhat less formal, comparative analysis of three separate cases. We focused on the differing ways in which Colorado citizens frame underlying, long-term, intractable conflicts surrounding growth issues. As such we have not attempted to document the detailed proceedings of each case but rather to understand the full range of ways in which people think about the underlying issues. To do this, we deliberately chose disputes involving people at both ends of the political spectrum. Rural El Paso County (east of Colorado Springs) is perhaps the most conservative area in a generally conservative community. It is a place where large numbers of citizens still question the legitimacy of central planning. At the other extreme lies Boulder, a community that has been pursuing centrally planned growth control measures as long as any other community in the country. Our third case, Fort Collins, represents an intermediate community that is being pulled in both directions.

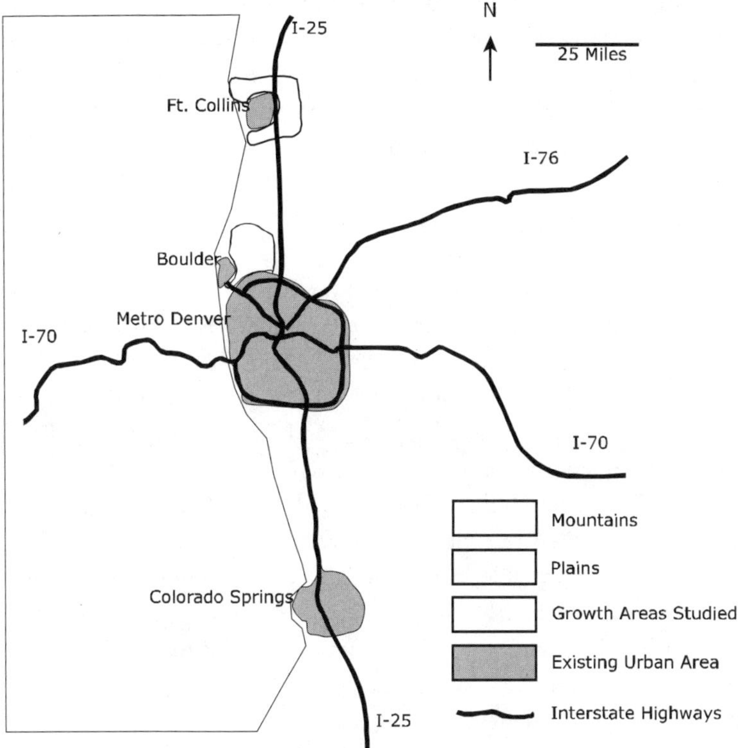

Figure 13.1. Colorado Growth Project Communities

In each case, our interviews focused upon those growth-related disputes that were of greatest public interest at the time of the study. In Colorado Springs, the conflict revolved around a controversial proposal to extend the zoning system into the previously unzoned eastern part of the county. Here the debate focuses upon whether planners and county officials should have the authority to decide which land uses are best for the community. By contrast, planning was accepted in Fort Collins and Boulder where the debate centered on how their respective regions should be planned (rather than debating whether planning was or was not appropriate). In Fort Collins, the focus was a complex debate surrounding a growth management initiative called City Plan and in Boulder public discussions considered the interplay between residential growth control, job growth, and housing prices.

As you can see, the arenas in which the disputes were being played out differed from community to community. In Colorado Springs, years of tension were finally coming to a head in a climactic public meeting of the county commissioners. While there have been numerous, volatile growth-related events in the history of Boulder and Fort Collins none were pending during the period of the study. As a result, the responses that we received focused less on a specific dispute and more on the general issue of growth management.

Larimer County

Founded as a military fort on the Cache La Poudre River in 1864, Fort Collins marks the north end of a population explosion that stretches south along Colorado's Front Range to Colorado Springs and beyond. The city has consistently ranked as one of the fastest growing metropolitan areas in the nation over the past fifteen years. Population figures for Larimer County and Fort Collins illustrate the phenomenon (see Table 13.1).

By 1997, Fort Collins's population had reached 106,000. In fact, "population growth in the area is so relentless that government officials have all but conceded that growth is inevitable; they implicitly accept planning department projections of a 57 percent increase in population by the year 2020" (Furniss 1998). Given that residents and city officials have conceded to the inevitability of growth, the largely rural communities surrounding Fort Collins have engaged in a grand debate with the city's native and incoming residents to determine the fate of the city and its surrounding municipalities.

The conflict over growth in Larimer County centers around three key issues: property rights, environmental preservation, and community vitality. Activists on all sides of the issue are squaring off to preserve what each party

Table 13.1. Population Figures for Larimer County and the City of Fort Collins, 1950–2000

Year	*Larimer County*	*Fort Collins*
1950	43,554	14,937
1960	53,343	25,024
1970	89,900	43,337
1980	149,184	65,092
1990	186,136	87,758
2000	251,494	118,652 (35.2% change from 1990)

County data: http://www.census.gov/population/cencounts/co190090.txt

City data: http://library.ci.fort-collins.co.us/local_history/topics/contexts/table1.htm

views as their "natural" right. For example, property-rights advocates consisting of farmers, ranchers, and developers hold firmly to the belief that they have a right to sell and develop their private landholdings as they please. In the eyes of one such advocate, county and city officials were dubbed as "liberal bureaucrats." For this and other property-rights advocates, government regulation and intervention strategies such as zoning, land-use restrictions, and growth boundaries are viewed as unnecessary impositions on landowners' rights to sell and develop land that is "rightly theirs." Represented by a growing body of activists, these individuals advocate a free-market approach to growth, and reject government planning and regulation as economically unsound. One such activist sees a limited role for government in this dispute:

> Government doesn't need to tell people that they can only build a berm 3 feet high, or plant a tree 2 inches in diameter. Government should only do what people can't do for themselves. And, if neighbors end up with a nuisance problem, under the law, they go to court. When you start making a list of the approved landscaping plants for development, dictating the height of fence, [or] making laws [stating] who can live in a home, that goes outside the bounds of health, welfare and safety, in our opinion. [People] have decided it's the government's job to solve neighborly squabbles. That's something society has evolved. It didn't happen 50 or 100 years ago. But we've suddenly become a society that expects someone else to solve our problems. **[Larimer 1]**

Alternatively, vocal opponents to market-driven approaches argue that leaving planning and growth decisions to the forces of supply and demand takes the power to shape and direct the future of the community out of the hands of the citizenry and puts it into the hands of a few profit-minded individuals or companies. One resident of Larimer County argues that:

> Individuals have become more greedy. They want to profit regardless of the community's rights or goals. They believe they have a personal right to do whatever they want, and I'm really pissed off that they feel they have an inherent right to make a profit from their property, and [they feel that] anything that would interfere with the increase in the value of their property is legally wrong. They consider investment in land to be guaranteed to profit, whereas investment in the stock market is not. **[Larimer 2]**

Mirroring this view, another resident states:

> All that conflict is a result of rapid growth that made the greedy greedier, and the general public more uneasy about what's happening. It's largely a result of having to make a lot of changes quickly in order to keep up with the rate of growth, instead of a gradual evolution everyone would get used to. I think the feeding frenzy from 3000 realtors in a town of 100,000 people has stoked the coals of the property-rights movement's opposition to the revision of our master plan and our county code, and it's largely based on greed, profit-making and an unwillingness to create desired conditions that most members of the community can agree upon. **[Larimer 3]**

Although many see profit and greed as driving the motivations of key stakeholders in the growth management process, as illustrated by the previous two perspectives, others find that the market, short of promoting greediness and vice, actually reflects the needs, wants, tastes, and desires of the people buying and developing property in the county. One resident feels that the market will take care of planning concerns because it truly reflects what the residents want rather than reflecting the needs and interests of the planners. She argues:

> In large part, market forces will take care of it if the market forces are there. We are facing a lot of demand and pressure; a lot of people do want to come here, so there are a lot of people to buy houses if they're the houses that people want. Developers can change the way they do business and be successful. But if the people don't want what the planners think they want, then this could all be an academic pipe dream. **[Larimer 4]**

Deviating from the positions of those residents who are wary of developer-driven or profit-driven growth strategies, land-use advocates perceive members of the planning boards as outsiders who do not understand the rural, ranching culture and the history of the land. This mismatch of worldviews has created a bifurcation between those working to maintain a sense of community and seeking a high quality of life and those who feel a sense of entitlement because they have owned, farmed, and ranched the land for generations. Because of the bifurcation of rural and urban residents populating Larimer County, many argue that differences in worldview and vision for the future often conflict between residents. One Fort Collins planning department official points out that "the hardest concept for people to accept was that we need to be thinking of ourselves as an urban community, rather than a suburban or rural community." **[Larimer 5]**

Added to the tangle of competing factions are small but vocal groups of environmental advocates who perceive any development as a threat to the native plant and animal life and the prairie ecosystems. Among the issues central to environmental activists are national protections for rare, native species such as the Preble's meadow jumping mouse and development boundaries around the Poudre River. However, their policy suggestions come into direct conflict with the growing and increasingly vocal community of land-use advocates. This contingent of landowners and developers consistently puts up a strong fight against these environmental policy proposals because they infringe upon the property owner's self-proclaimed "right to make an honest living." This intergroup conflict, some feel, is largely unproductive and prevents true political collaboration. One land-use advocate points out that the demands of many of the environmental advocates make compromise and cooperation difficult:

> People should understand when ideology should give way to working together. The Sierra Club has got a lot of angry people—that's not compatible with good politics. We're learning nationwide that people don't like that. They're condescending toward people who don't [share their views]. **[Larimer 6]**

Another resident questions whether the end results of environmental activism produce beneficial results for all citizens and taxpayers. Bitterly, he states:

> [Environmentalists] publicly beat on their chests that the world is going to hell in a handbasket, but in the end, their wildlife stuff and effective downzoning is the cat's meow. They're getting everything, and government's going to end up paying for it, because we have one impact fee after another. I think the Sierra Club ought to be proud of themselves. I think they've accomplished more than they even know they've accomplished. **[Larimer 7]**

The assumed right to do what one wishes with one's property or land conflicts directly with an environmentalist ethic that privileges the public good over private "rights." One resident summarizes this tension cogently:

> Between environmentalists and property-rights people, it's not a question of factual disagreements but of different values: private

> gain versus public good. Some groups actually value economic growth, and [are hoping to attract] more people, and I don't [agree]. Those people need to read "Tragedy of the Commons." The commons are never protected. **[Larimer 8]**

To address these issues and problems associated with population and economic growth, citizens and administrators began to take steps in the last decade to ensure the upkeep of both the natural and the human environments. For example, substantial open-space purchases were financed with a .25 percent sales tax (passed in 1992); partnerships with Great Outdoors Colorado—a lottery-funded land trust agency—allowed for the purchasing and preservation of open space, parks, and trail land; and contributions from conservation trust funds and Larimer County, and a second, countywide open lands sales tax (passed in 1995), made available the funds to balance residential and commercial growth with environmental preservation. As a result, the City of Fort Collins now owns more than 4000 acres of natural land, including more than 1000 acres along the Poudre River. These parcels of land have been set aside as "undevelopable"—used only for wildlife habitat preservation and low-impact recreational use (such as hiking, biking, and climbing)—and they therefore buffer areas of the county from runaway growth.

However, despite countywide initiatives to purchase protected land and open space, many land-use advocates argue that these purchases inhibit the economic growth and vitality of the region by making certain parcels of land off-limits to commercial development. Because of their power and influence in community decision making, developers and other land-rights advocates are able to get their message heard in public arenas. As a vocal and well-funded interest group that opposes land-use restrictions, they claim that they truly reflect the majority of citizen sentiment.

Despite their vocal opposition to preserving prime land for recreational or environmental open space, many feel that the developers' power and money have considerable influence on the public discussion surrounding land use and zoning. One observant resident points out that certain individuals have a greater influence in swaying public opinion around the open space issue:

> There's not the appearance that people that favor open space outnumber [land-use advocates], though they do. Land-use people can say they represent the majority—it's obnoxious, but they can say it and people believe it, and it's catching on. **[Larimer 9]**

For environmentally minded residents, open space purchases and natural land preservation symbolize more than a simple environmental ethic or an oppositional stance to commercial or residential development. Instead, open space preserves the connection to the natural environment that makes a certain place or region of residence habitable and welcoming. For one resident, the natural environment provides a sense of solace in an increasingly stressful and hurried world, and the failure to protect these lands results in a loss of this protective function:

> Psychologically, the loss of open space and natural areas where we get our inspiration and our tranquillity have an adverse effect on how we deal with stress and all other daily activities. **[Larimer 10]**

Mirroring this view, another resident adds:

> Humans should still be able to experience their environment—exclusionary preservation isn't the solution. People need to be integrated with their environment. **[Larimer 11]**

For many Larimer County residents, the integration of the natural and residential environments provides a key feature or amenity that makes Fort Collins and its surrounding towns and villages a unique and high-quality place to live. Although some residents argue that the preservation of the natural environment threatens the economic vitality of the region by limiting the amount of commercial growth, others hold that the natural environment and open spaces are economic resources in and of themselves. Consequently, as some residents argue, the denigration of natural spaces through residential and commercial development actually becomes an economic liability to a region. Illustrating this point, one resident mentions:

> One of the reasons people move to Colorado is because of all the great open space. Very few move here to live in zero lot housing, where walls are nearly touching each other. **[Larimer 12]**

Although developers, land-rights advocates, and other citizens supporting the development of protected lands point to key concerns over the long-term economic viability of the region, opponents feel that the quality of life and community dynamics facilitated through preservationist land-use policies have just as much long-term economic impact.

Regardless of one's particular stance toward open space, the region continues to grow. With its increased population, Fort Collins has become part of a national trend in which automobile use is growing at a faster pace than population. These extra vehicle miles threaten Fort Collins's ability to deal with traffic congestion and air-quality problems. A congestion-management plan indicated that automobile use would have to be curtailed, and this goal became the catalyst for the City Plan. Drafted in March 1997, the City Plan looks at how to balance different forces represented by growth. It sets out to (1) redefine urbanism and urban spaces, (2) generate a different pattern of development for dealing with transportation issues, and (3) engender a better sense of integration between neighborhoods and new commercial developments. The stated goal of City Plan was to develop growth in ways that accommodate competing visions and interests.

For example, new standards for commercial development, such as maximum block-size restrictions, were intended to make newer parts of town look more like the street frontages of Old Town, or downtown Fort Collins. These standards arise out of certain residents' beliefs that economic growth in the commercial and retail sector necessarily damages the vitality of the community by introducing national chains to a local economy once supported by local, independent businesses. One resident argues that this growth stems from the fact that commercial interests see Fort Collins as a virtual gold mine due to its moderate size and location just to the north of Denver:

> Fort Collins has been a distinct community. We're just on the verge of losing that, and becoming a suburb of Denver. Becoming an urban metropolis of our own, way past community involvement. That 100,000 population has encouraged three new supermarkets to open. Kmart and Wal-Mart are both doubling. And it's all based on that 100,000 figure. So it's triggered a lot of extra development. It just seems like a chain reaction—more stores lead to more people lead to more stores. **[Larimer 13]**

The influx of chain stores and strip malls, many argue, leads to a loss of true or genuine community identity. Certain residents feel that these new stores can be found in virtually any other community across the United States, and fear that Main Street, Fort Collins, will become Main Street, Anywhere, USA. Additionally, some residents feel that a loss of local ownership of businesses could result in a reduced commitment to the interests and vitality of the local community. In the words of one resident:

> I don't like that major streets are becoming strip shopping centers for chain stores; chain stores don't have vested interests in the community. They're not owned by local entrepreneurs. **[Larimer 14]**

At the residential level, planners in Larimer County rezoned the entire community to resist the sprawling proliferation of the gated communities and enclave developments found in other Front Range communities. This action was a direct response to developers who have chopped open spaces into physically and geographically isolated subdivisions and to citizens who have challenged these developments. Decrying the aesthetic aspects of these quickly growing housing developments, one resident states:

> I don't like the new suburban developments being constructed on the fringe of the city. I don't like the way the houses look, the way they sprawl into agriculture land. I don't like the fact there are acres and acres of new suburban homes. **[Larimer 15]**

Also targeted by the plan were developments that fragmented the countryside with ranchettes (houses built on enough land to support horses or small farm animals). One resident contrasts the sprawl of multiroom houses and consumption of large parcels of land in Larimer County to the lifestyle of Caribbeans she encountered while in the Peace Corps:

> People [in the Caribbean] were simply living on a lot less and just as happy. They did not need telephones, TVs, cars, and in a lot of cases, electricity and running water. And they definitely did not have 500-square-feet-per-person houses. That's where sprawl and consumption come together, in these giant prairie houses that we're building. **[Larimer 16]**

She argues that such sprawling growth across the countryside not only leads to greater consumption of manufactured and natural resources but also divides neighbors from each other and the rest of the community. According to the City Plan, however, all subdivisions have to be connected to the larger community to prevent civic isolation. In addition, based upon detailed studies of the land-use needs projected for the next twenty years, the plan established urban growth boundaries and adopted tough development and land-use regulations, especially in newly developed "greenfield" areas.

Despite plans to prevent sprawling growth within the city and county, many feel that efforts need to be integrated and coordinated among the neighboring communities. Although, for example, if one municipality creates urban-growth boundaries and purchases open space to curb development, a neighboring community may have conflicting plans. This situation could potentially lead to spillover growth from one community into the next—if not from direct development itself, then from traffic, pollution, and noise. To rectify this situation, one resident calls for regionwide coordination and cooperation:

> [We need] regional cooperation in dealing with these issues. In Fort Collins, we can do the best we can to manage growth, and if Windsor [a neighboring town] doesn't do anything, they'll still build right up to our boundaries and drive on our streets and pollute our air and our efforts will go to naught. The good thing is maybe we still have the time to do something with them. But there's still a lot of competition, distrust, big fish/little fish mentality. **[Larimer 17]**

Short of halting all development, the City Plan's Partnership Land-use System (PLUS) would try to save most existing open space by clustering new development. Due to public outcry, however, the enforcement arm of the plan, what's called "the code," is still being revised. Among public concerns is the hotly contested 20/80 policy, which recommends that all new rural development be clustered on no more than 20 percent of a site, leaving the remaining 80 percent open and undeveloped. This is opposed by the land-use community because it essentially requires them to contribute to the community 4 acres of open space for every acre developed. By most accounts, one of the most progressive of three county commissioners, is pushing for transfer development units (TDUs), another alternative to sprawl, which would concentrate development on lands closer to the center of town. While providing a flexible, market-based approach to the allocation of development rights, this plan is still opposed because it forces private landowners to forsake the development potential of much of their property.

However, despite plans to curb runaway growth and sprawl, many argue that planners still have to keep in mind the forces of market demand. Although new urbanist projects are attractive to community-conscious planners and developers, those seeking to live in the area may have different wants and desires. One developer argues that the market must ultimately drive the housing decisions in a particular area:

> The criticism from the development community is that while, in theory, a new urbanist project can be viable financially, the local market isn't there and we're mandating and describing a product that people around here don't want. They want a suburban, low-market product. **[Larimer 18]**

In other words, unless people are seeking to relocate or build in ways that are consistent with these planners' design specifications, there may be a loss of market value or demand for these new housing units in the area. Although attractive to planners, these new urbanist projects may conflict with developers' plans and visions for the area. One resident boils the conflict down to what he calls a "chicken and egg" question:

> Planners can point down to Boulder and Longmont, with plenty of examples of new urbanist projects that are wildly successful, but nobody's been doing them up here. Developers challenge their numbers; they challenge development numbers for not looking at what people are doing in other parts of the country. **[Larimer 19]**

For the majority of residents and county officials, the question continues to be what, if anything, to do about growth. Those who equate sprawl with a declining quality of life are pitted against a landowner community that sees its options evaporating. They believe the code has been thrust upon them by a bunch of city folks who don't know anything about living in the country. Rural residents feel they've been blindsided by new changes to the code, and are very vocal about it.

The manner in which residents, officials, planners, and developers approach growth and sprawl in Larimer County boils down to what each group identifies as its central causes. Because Colorado and the rest of the Front Range are experiencing both rapid and profound growth unparalleled in the region's history, a definitive answer or set of solutions proves difficult. Many individuals locate the problems associated with growth in the rapid influx of Californians and easterners to the area and a redistribution of existing residents within Colorado. Where some argue these trends are disturbing, others, like this Fort Collins resident, argue that growth is a necessary result of progress:

> I believe you have to continue to grow in order to survive. A lot of what we've come to enjoy are the results of progress, and unfortunately, with progress comes population growth, not just births but immigration, not just from other states, but other parts of Colorado. **[Larimer 20]**

Another resident challenges the idea that outsiders are the cause of the growth problem.

> Some people in Fort Collins who don't like the changes growth has wrought complain that it's the newcomers who are causing it.

> This is a myth. A lot of it is birth rates and people have kind of overlooked that. It's [a question of] dealing with our own people and making room for our children to live in the community. **[Larimer 21]**

Even defining growth as a problem becomes a contentious issue. Many longtime residents of Colorado recall that throughout the 1980s, the state was not faring well economically. The growth of industry and commercial and residential development was viewed as a boon to the state's economy. However, now that the majority of residents in the region have moved to the region within the past decade, many see the residential growth as problematic. According to one resident, "people moving here were seen as a real feather in the cap." He continues:

> But as Colorado and Fort Collins started to flourish economically, a real dichotomy [formed] between the folks already there and whoever followed them. People who've even moved here in the recent past have a tendency toward drawing up the drawbridge. In other words, [new residents are saying] "now that we're here, we need to stop this growth thing." **[Larimer 22]**

Everyone says they're concerned about preserving the area's natural beauty and amenities such as open space and clean air and water. But as soon as economics enters the picture, lines are drawn. With vigilant citizen action on both ends of the political spectrum, the central majority has stayed largely silent, although the Fort Collins newspaper and numerous public officials have admonished residents to stay involved. Master plans, they say, have little clout without continuing citizen action.

El Paso County

El Paso County, an area larger than Rhode Island and located in the southern part of the Front Range, is presently experiencing both rapid growth and relentless sprawl. From a physical, western boundary near the summit of Pike's Peak, the county sprawls eastward across vast prairies that extend from the foothills of the Rockies to the Kansas border. Although self-described as a community with almost endless economic and development opportunities, El Paso County is experiencing the effects of sprawling development stemming from a traditionally relaxed, free-market approach to growth. As the region experiences growing traffic snarls, disappearing prairie lands and open spaces, and a spiraling cost of living, the citizens of Colorado Springs and the surrounding areas are increasingly sensitive to quality-of-life issues that are compromised by relentless and uncontrolled growth. The debate continues between property-rights advocates who favor a laissez-faire approach to growth and those concerned citizens and policy makers who are turning to growth-management alternatives.

El Paso is the fastest-growing county in the state in terms of population. Its population has expanded by more than 83,000 since 1990, making it the third-largest county in Colorado with approximately 510,000 people. Colorado Springs, the major city within the county, is the fastest growing metropolitan area in the state with a 3.0 percent annual increase in population (Table 13.2).

The city of Colorado Springs, which is about a ninety-minute drive south of Denver along Interstate 25, has a metropolitan area of 183 square miles. Covering a land mass as large as San Francisco, Boston, and Washington, D.C., combined, 40 percent of its area is still undeveloped (or "vacant," as the city's Internet Web site announces). The area boasts a wide variety of geological, wildlife, and recreational attractions, such as Garden of the Gods (an awe-inspiring red rock formation), Royal Gorge (where the Arkansas River has created a deep chasm from its descent out of the mountains), natural carbonated springs, fishing streams, and hiking and biking trails. East of the mountains, the city's developed areas lie on a huge expanse of prairie and farmland (as of 1995, 63% of the land was zoned agricultural). At 6035 feet, the climate is pleasant year-round, but still progresses through the four seasons. The crime rate is exceptionally low, over a quarter of the population are college graduates, and there is only a 4.7 percent rate of unemployment.

Table 13.2. Population Figures for El Paso County and City of Colorado Springs, 1940–2000

Year	*El Paso County*	*Colorado Springs*
1940	54,025	~37,000
1950	74,523	~45,000
1960	143,742	~70,000
1970	235,972	~136,000
1980	309,424	~215,000
1990	397,014	~283,112
2000	516,929	~360,890 (27.5% change from 1990)

County data: http://www.census.gov/population/cencounts/co190090.txt

City data: http://www.publicpurpose.com/dm-uscty.htm

El Paso County is not known for its cultural diversity, however, and it has a reputation for being extremely conservative in both religion and politics. Contained within its boundaries are the United States Air Force Academy, Fort Carson Military Reservation, and the U.S. Olympic Training Center. Since 1992, the county has become the home to more than seventy national and international Christian ministries and "para-church" organizations. Republican citizens solidly outnumber Democrats, and this margin is only increasing. In the 1998 elections, for example, the Republican contestant in each category received the most votes, often by a wide margin. Every county official (including the five county commissioners) is a Republican, as is the city's mayor, and every state representative from El Paso County.

Publicity for the city accentuates its favorable stance toward growth. In materials and documents describing the region's growth and development, the city's Web site (http://www.colorado-springs.com) repeatedly uses the word "vacant" to describe the expansive tracks of open space and prairie lands to the east of the city. "Growth has pushed development up into the foothills and out onto the plains in the east. . . . Colorado Springs prides itself on its small-town feel while steadily growing." The city ducks any contradictory interpretations of these statements by claiming that, "The influx of newcomers (nearly one-third of the population has lived here for four years or less) adds to its character."†

A traditional stance that opposes growth control and favors market-driven approaches to economic development has created a prodevelopment populace. Containing few planned communities, the area is home to numerous low-density housing subdivisions and strip mall developments that are beginning to spread out into the vast eastern portion of the county. Although residents and surrounding communities are feeling the effects of El Paso County's sprawling development, efforts to regulate development through zoning laws or land-use restrictions are viewed by the majority of the citizenry as a threat to their freedom to do as they please with their land and property. This sentiment has environmentalists, policy makers, planners, and others concerned about sprawl up in arms about the scant environmental concern shown by many of the residents.

Growth is accepted by residents of El Paso County as an inevitable fact of living in a desirable location, and the only major concern they have is that there needs to be proper planning for the future. In other words, if there is a

---

† Since the original quotes were collected, the information on the Web site has changed and no longer contains the document from which the quotes were taken.

problem, it is only the *manner* in which the county is growing, not the fact that it *is* growing. Differing opinions concerning the way future development is handled lie at the center of the growth dispute in El Paso County. For a vocal majority of the residents, there is enough land and space to accommodate both new and existing residents, which therefore translates into a hostile attitude toward zoning and other growth-control measures, especially among those residents of rural eastern El Paso County. "Most of us who live in the country are quiet, law-abiding, hard-working citizens. We don't understand the need for more laws and regulations," **[El Paso 1]** states one concerned resident living in the eastern portion of the county.

In El Paso County, many residents are dismayed by the rapid and ill-conceived nature of sprawl, but few would say they are philosophically against the episode of growth that Colorado is experiencing. They realize that theirs is an appealing place to live, and they shy from denying others the right to enjoy the area. It seems that many people who favor growth, or accept it as a natural result of historical forces, neither problematize its ill effects, nor consider its negative externalities.

Many residents compare the growth of this region to other "problem areas" in the country, and state that they need not worry because the problems are worse elsewhere. One resident compares the growth in Colorado Springs to his native California. Shrugging off the idea that growth is something to be concerned about in Colorado, he asserts, "this is nothing compared to the San Fernando Valley near Los Angeles where I'm from." **[El Paso 2]**

Though this resident considers that growth may pose a problem for residents in the long term, he does not feel it is something about which residents should become overly alarmed—growth is simply much worse elsewhere. Another retired planner adds that he is not necessarily against residential and commercial development, but that "it just needs to be slow and steady" to provide adequate jobs for its residents and to ensure the responsible upkeep of the surrounding environment.

Those who work as professional planners are often able to conceptualize the adverse effects of growth differently than the general population. Responsible and prescient planning is clearly a theme of central importance to planners and county officials when considering the impacts of growth. However, given that Colorado Springs has a tremendous amount of land east of the city limits available for expansion, few residents, officials, or developers are concerned about using up the large stock of property in the county. These points suggest that the average person in El Paso County thinks about growth according to a short-term time frame, and with an individualistic orientation instead of with broader community or environmental interests in mind.

These competing beliefs create an enormous amount of tension between residents who decry any attempts to regulate land use and those whose professional experience and training tell them that unchecked growth and sprawl are not in the best long-term interests of citizens or the community. The entire process led many citizens to believe that their elected officials were not truly representing the majority viewpoint. Two residents speaking into a microphone at a public meeting about an extremely controversial zoning proposal illustrate this tension:

> I'm not going to try to talk any more sense into you, because it's obvious three of you don't know what sense is. Three of you [county commissioners] obviously don't have any concern for anybody but yourselves and your political careers. We're going to take you to court every time you turn around and we will kick your ass. **[El Paso 3]**

Another resident adds:

> Europe is at war now because they're not countries that are run by the people. You three [county commissioners] are the instrument that is driving this country to what Europe is doing now. Every time you enchain these people you are driving them further and further towards civil war. This is what causes a country's civil unrest. How dare you do that to us, by what right do you drive us into a big fight? You've got citizens here who are pissed off at you, do you not listen? **[El Paso 4]**

The three commissioners who were in favor of zoning, however, were convinced that they needed to plow ahead and implement zoning whether the majority of the people liked it or not. They felt that they were responding adequately to the letters and phone calls they had received from residents who wanted zoning, that the plan was sufficient, that zoning was inevitable given current growth pressures, and that people were simply going to have to adjust to the changes. Many, like this resident, however, were skeptical and would rather leave the community decisions up to the people rather than elected officials:

> Citizens should be able to vote on this matter. If the board votes for zoning today, I believe that this action will alienate the citizens of eastern El Paso County to a degree that will be the cause of

> great dissension within El Paso County for many years to come. And probably into the next generation. I cannot believe that this will benefit El Paso County, and it will ultimately cause more harm than good. We all believe in the Constitution of the United States but we interpret it differently. In spite of our differences, would we not have done much more good by working together in the spirit of cooperation and fellowship rather than bitter adversary? Let's set aside the zoning plan and work on a plan that each side can live with. **[El Paso 5]**

Although a vocal majority of residents speaking their mind at this meeting saw the attempts to zone or place restrictions on land use as a threat to democracy, another resident attending the meeting provided an alternative take:

> Had the majority had their say when women were given the right to vote, none of us women would be here, and [two female commissioners] would not be commissioners, and blacks would not be allowed to vote had the majority of people had a say. Thank goodness the commissioners have the ability to do the right thing. **[El Paso 6]**

The atmosphere of the gathering was almost desperate, given the fact that most of the 300-plus people in attendance abhorred the very idea of zoning and were on the verge of panic that their treasured way of life was about to change at the hands of county officials who seemed insensitive to their needs and opinions.

Despite the fact that many perceive growth in the area as an inevitable outcome of progress and economic growth in the county, there are vocal advocates of growth control who feel that public officials have a responsibility to all members of the community, not simply to special interests who aim to profit individually or commercially from a laissez-faire approach to land-use management. Despite the largely market-driven approach that has historically characterized growth policy in the area, many are urging policy makers to rethink their traditional course of action. Arguing that elected governmental officials should more faithfully represent their wants and desires, one resident adds:

> Citizens of Colorado have said loudly and clearly that growth is a major concern and priority, so government must respond and pass the Responsible Growth Act. You can educate individuals and make them feel guilty about the issue, but the bottom line is to

> convince elected officials that they have a duty to the people to contribute to the betterment of their community. **[El Paso 7]**

This former planner decries the traditional top-down approaches characterizing many legislative actions and community enhancement programs and states that residents must be involved in the planning and growth discussions. Others see such a balanced approach as more fully meeting and respecting the needs and desires of the residents in the county, reflected in this El Paso County resident's statement:

> [T]he consensus on a statewide basis was that some form of standard public notification and input process was preferable to unrestricted growth. And I'm of that mind myself, and I applaud the commissioners for helping us to get equal rights under the law. **[El Paso 8]**

Although most residents would prefer a negotiated or balanced approach to growth management, few are willing to concede on freedoms and liberties they feel are basic to their roles as citizens and property owners. After the extremely heated public hearing on this controversial zoning plan, many left the meeting fuming and frustrated over the lack of cooperation between competing parties. One angered participant observes:

> And now there's a mass influx of people out there, and as you've heard tonight, where's the respect and understanding and consideration for each other? If there was that kind of respect and consideration between people out there we wouldn't need zoning. But now we need something, I believe it to be an arbitrator or a referee. We need zoning out there. **[El Paso 9]**

According to others though, the possibility of compromise on zoning is hopeless. Resorting to ad hominem and personal attacks, many, like this commissioner, feel that a consensual outcome is difficult if not impossible:

> It is not possible to reach an agreement on this issue because it has disintegrated to the level of personal agendas and deep-seated emotions of philosophy. It is possible to find a solution in most cases, but not the way this has gone. **[El Paso 10]**

Although policy makers and elected public officials have given the public the opportunity to voice their concerns at various public forums, many residents are frustrated because they feel that their perspectives are not adequately considered. This sentiment has led a number of citizens to view their elected officials as "a government of bureaucrats, hungry for power and for money." **[El Paso 11]** One resident reminded the commissioners' meeting that "those in power who practice tyranny and despotism are known as tyrants and despots. When this fight ends I'm sure that will be your legacy." **[El Paso 12]**

Additionally, because those in opposition to zoning felt slighted by the city officials, the dispute had escalated to a game of political wrangling that many saw as leading nowhere. One frustrated resident states:

> The inflammatory rhetoric surrounding zoning is increasing on both sides: it's unproductive, it's hurtful, and it distorts the issue. If the zoning plan was a good one, people would support it, but the problem is that people do not feel heard or understood. **[El Paso 13]**

Despite the differences of opinion on the matter, the city is grappling with the controversial idea of managing its population accretion and concurrent sprawl. An unstated rule of the county's growth policy is that developers decide what gets built where. This approach is supported by a market-based philosophy that appeals to conservative purists who believe that too many government rules interfere with private-property rights. Two residents mirror these concerns that developers have more power to influence public growth policy than the average citizen. Upset at the forcefulness of certain public figures, one rural resident states:

> Nobody seems to be for [zoning] except for the staff of a few developers and people who want to use other people's property without paying for it. Yet three good members of the Republican party sit here and try to force it down our throats. **[El Paso 14]**

Advocating a similar distaste for governmental intervention, another resident adds:

> Now it's clear to me that you can't legislate nirvana. We don't build the new city; private development does. We need more developers and private sector to embrace the new vision. **[El Paso 15]**

Realizing that unrestricted growth may not be in the best long-term interests of the region, the City Council has decided to take a more proactive step to "get a handle on growth" by creating a development guide for all of Colorado Springs. A citizens' committee is currently considering six land uses (commercial, residential, industrial, institutional, office, and open space) and how they can be configured into a layout for the future. These examples of official thinking show that growth may be of mounting concern in the area, but their primary considerations are controlling the cost of living and maintaining the quality of life. This sentiment, however, conflicts with some of the deeply held values of the local residents, especially those living in the rural, eastern portion of the county and city. One rural resident describes the core values shared by many eastern El Paso County residents:

> If someone asked me to describe a typical resident of eastern El Paso County, I would have to say there is none. We are as different as snowflakes and as individualistic as America itself. We share a common love of freedom, and a fierce respect for our flag and constitution. Basic to the liberties we hold so dear is our land, specifically that piece of property we have toiled a lifetime to call our own. We realize that with freedoms and rights come responsibilities. The vast majority of us living out east are highly responsible citizens. We vote, pay our taxes, bother no one and maintain our property well. **[El Paso 16]**

The rural/urban split between interested parties characterizes one of the central tensions of the growth dispute in this region. For many rural residents, their land and property is something for which they have worked long and hard. One rural resident explains this sentiment:

> These people are the last of the true pioneer spirit and the type of people who came out here and founded this area, who lived and endured the 100-mile-an-hour winds and no running water. I bought four 40-acre parcels, I lived on them for two years without a well. I sold my prized possessions to get a well. I built a ranch on raw land, and I feel like I have a real nice place now. **[El Paso 17]**

As a result of their long struggle to secure lands that are now considered their own, they interpret any attempt to control or regulate land use as a threat to their natural and God-given freedoms. This El Paso County resident points back to traditional American values of freedom and natural rights to justify his contempt for big government:

> Our founding fathers were given a vision from God , who gave us this land in the first place, to set up this nation with a government run by the people. As part of that vision, they were given an understanding that it was the nature of bureaucrats to want more power and more money and to create more bureaucracy to get it. To me,

> the issue here is whether our future here will be that of people who will govern themselves under the unique form of government we have today, or whether we will gradually allow governments to steal virtually all of our rights until we have reverted to the type of government our forefathers came here to escape. **[El Paso 18]**

In summary, the growth dispute in El Paso County is characterized by a competing set of groups and interests. On one hand, the geography of the region will allow for a tremendous amount of growth to the east of Colorado Springs given the large stock of land available for development. On the other hand, planners and city officials know that the attractive natural environment and the high quality of life will not be sustained unless they approach growth through zoning and land-use regulations. The dispute centers around the majority of residents who prefer a market-driven, laissez-faire approach to growth, and those residents, county commissioners, and environmentalists who seek to uphold the integrity and sustainability of the region.

Boulder County

Boulder County is located on the eastern edge of the foothills of the Rocky Mountains, about 20 miles northwest of the city of Denver, and spans a diverse range of high plains and small mountain communities. Containing 273,112 residents, Boulder County is one of the most attractive regions in the state due to its proximity to Denver, the cultural center of the Rocky Mountain West, and the expansive mountain playground that offers access to a range of hiking, biking, and winter sports facilities.

As a vibrant, progressive community of 92,000 residents, the city of Boulder constitutes a prime cultural and recreational destination for those living in and around the Denver Metro region. Touting miles of biking trails, strategically placed pedestrian crosswalks, an award-winning rapid transit system, and a populace sensitive to the changing shape of its community, Boulder is received as a city that takes a proactive stance toward growth. Since Boulder was one of the first communities to have a well-established growth management program, it follows that it was also one of the first places to discover what could go wrong. Consequently, this discovery launched the citizens of Boulder County headlong into a wrangle of competing views and perspectives related to growth.

The City and County of Boulder are considered by many to be pioneers in growth management policy. During the boom in residential and commercial growth following World War II, the City refused to provide water and sewer service to any property outside of its municipal limits to prevent growth beyond already established boundaries. In 1959, the City established its first urban service boundary, called the Blue Line, which runs along the base of the scenic Flatirons and surrounding foothills that characterize Boulder's scenic mountain backdrop. Designed "to protect the foothills from development which was considered imminent and extremely detrimental to the natural beauty of Boulder," and to help maintain its fragile ecosystems, this zoning line limits growth along the Front Range by restricting the extension of water service above a certain elevation (de Raismes et al. n.d.). Today, the Blue Line is obvious from anywhere in the city: above the line there is an abrupt end of development and beginning of open space. Beginning in 1967, the City of Boulder also implemented a .4 percent permanent sales and use tax to support an open space program for the community (the tax is currently .73 percent). To date, the program has bought and zoned nearly 30,000 acres of open space (de Raismes 1999).

In 1970, Boulder created its first comprehensive plan, a policy initiative that "set the tone for further City and County cooperation and introduced the concept of staged urban growth in the Boulder Valley" (de Raismes et al. n.d.). The plan was a sketchy, yet integral planning map designed to accommodate future growth prospects while managing the existing and preparing for future open spaces in the city limits. Since the 1970s, the City and County of Boulder acquired a growing stock of open-space land and have protected the region from runaway growth characterizing other major urban centers. However, the growth outside of Boulder County in the surrounding counties and communities has placed Boulder in a precarious position of balancing new growth and development while maintaining a community unique in character and diverse in natural amenities.

The most visible indicator of growth in Boulder County is the rapid and profound residential development, as witnessed by the expansive construction of new homes, condominiums, housing developments, and subdivisions sprouting up within the county and, especially, along US-36, the 25-mile freeway leading to Denver. Within the county, population has increased rapidly in a relatively brief period of time. For example, four other towns in the county have grown dramatically over the past two decades: Superior has grown from a population of 208 in 1980 to 5400 in 1998; Louisville has increased by 13,232 people (70%) since 1980, Lafayette by 11,462 (56%), and

Table 13.3. Population Figures for Boulder County and the City of Boulder, 1940–2000

Year	*Boulder County*	*City of Boulder*
1940	37,438	12,958
1950	48,296	~20,000
1960	74,254	—
1970	131,889	66,870
1980	189,625	76, 685
1990	225,339	83,312
2000	291,288	94,673 (13.6% change from 1990)

County data: http://www.census.gov/population/cencounts/co190090.txt

City data: http://www.co.boulder.co.us/lu/demographics/city_pop2000pdf; http://.ci.boulder.co.us/comm/history/

Longmont reached a population of 58,173 in 1998—a difference of 15,173 (35%) from its 1980 population (Table 13.3).‡

The level of growth reflected in these cities reflects a consistent pattern across the county. Within the City of Boulder, growth figures (Table 13.3) are slightly smaller due to the fact that the city has reached a point of relative build-out and currently has restrictions on building height within the city limits. These factors, along with the intentional buffering of open space, has limited growth within the City of Boulder proper, but has displaced some of its potential growth elsewhere in the county.

Employment growth is one of the primary factors identified as driving residential growth in the cities of Boulder County. Within Boulder County, employment has grown from a total employment of 89,760 in 1980 to a total employment of 166,768 in 1998. In particular, the region has been identified as having one of the fastest-growing technology sectors in the United States. The area is home to numerous Internet start-ups and communication technology leaders, drawing to the Front Range a cadre of well-educated workers and technicians. Information and computer technology giants such as IBM, Storage Tek, Sun Microsystems, and the expansive Interlocken office park have located their operations in the county, creating more jobs and drawing an increasing number of people into the Boulder County area. While the city of Boulder was once the employment center for Boulder County, its share of

‡ U.S. Bureau of the Census, City Planning Departments 1999.

county employment has been decreasing in recent years due to increased employment elsewhere in the region.

Employment growth in Boulder County continues to expand annually, with more growth predicted for the future. The Denver Regional Council of Governments (DRCOG) projects that by 2020, 304,370 new jobs and 148,370 new housing units will be created, which equates to 2.05 jobs per new residence (DRCOG 2000). And, while the City of Boulder is expecting to bring in 24,000 more jobs, it only plans to build 3700 more housing units, according to the City of Boulder Planning Department.[§]

One planning official for the City of Boulder explains that "growth" in Boulder County has largely been a symptom of employment growth in the area. He states that increased employment growth in a limited housing situation has consequently created a "jobs–housing imbalance," where the daytime population is fundamentally different from the nighttime population. This imbalance developed because Boulder has continued to encourage commercial growth, business growth, and economic development so it could develop a stronger tax base, while, at the same time, controlling the number of houses being built within the city limits.

Boulder's basic growth-management framework (consisting of comprehensive plans, blue-lining, open space acquisition, and residential growth management) worked well to curb some of the adverse effects of development until the 1980s, after which the economy experienced rapid employment growth. From 1980 to 1990, Boulder's population grew by 6600 while the number of jobs in the city grew by 26,000. As a result, an increasing number of nonresidents made a daily commute into Boulder. By 1993, rapid job growth in Boulder began to cause a "political crisis" of sorts, and concern about jobs became a leading issue. People were worried about the projections of job growth, relative to projections of residential growth, and wanted to do something about it.

The citizens of Boulder tend to be characterized by a solid and almost ubiquitous environmental and communitarian ethic. These deeply held values intensify the conflicts between those advocating economic and residential growth-control strategies and those advocating the interests of developers and businesses. On one hand, Boulder city residents value a high quality of life preserved through community vitality initiatives and "smart growth" policies. On the other hand, however, economic growth and residential development are necessary to maintain this quality of life and to open Boulder's amenities to a

[§] University of Colorado Urban Sprawl Conference, 1999.

broader and more economically diverse population. In many ways, growth is a contentious issue in Boulder County because it splits the value commitments of many of its residents. An understanding of what growth means to the people of Boulder and Boulder County can be gleaned from the many "solutions" that are being proposed for dealing with the growth problem.

Interestingly, the City of Boulder, frequently cited as one of the best examples in the country of how growth can be effectively controlled, is not necessarily revered in Colorado Springs. One city official for Colorado Springs put it most pointedly:

> Boulder's growth management did not work well. It forced bedroom communities to spring up all around the town, and then the City of Boulder itself did not get taxes from them. Furthermore, there is not enough variety of housing prices in Boulder [i.e., they are too high], so Boulder is a poor example of how growth should be managed. **[Boulder 1]**

Concerned that the City Council wasn't moving fast enough to deal with this job and housing issue, citizens who wanted to slow down the rate of job growth came forward to address the issue themselves. In most areas, the thought of turning away jobs or reducing commercial growth would never enter a policy maker's mind. However, the imbalance between rapid job growth and limited residential growth has created a tremendous demand for housing within the city and has thus drastically inflated the cost of already existing housing. One city planning official discusses the ironies of housing and growth management in the area:

> The housing strategy talked about rebalancing jobs and housing by looking at potential for housing growth. Job growth in the community, the growth of the University of Colorado, and this whole issue of growth management are still on a collision course, and how we unravel those things is still going to be an issue. Boulder has arguably contained sprawl. We have maintained this compact human-scale city, we've maintained a relatively high quality of life, encouraged a high quality of economic development, and we've protected the environment. But on the other hand, housing prices have increased beyond the reach of many who would like to live, work, or go to school here in the community. Our job growth has arguably generated sprawl elsewhere, and the policies we've used to get there have felt overly burdensome to some of those in the community. **[Boulder 2]**

At the center of the conflict between concerned citizens and businesses lie the dual issues of spillover growth and affordable housing. Many Boulder County residents living both inside and outside of the city limits observe that the City of Boulder's restrictive growth policies and open space policies—which limit the rate and amount of growth in the city—have caused growth to spill over into surrounding areas. The primary goals of purchasing protected open-space land were to preserve the natural prairie environment, to provide low-impact recreational spaces for Boulder County residents, and to buffer the community from relentless growth both within the city limits and from neighboring towns and counties. One elected county official explains the logic of purchasing open space, both for the city and for the county as a whole:

> Boulder and Louisville [a neighboring town] are landlocked and so have decided not to grow anymore. But then cities like Lafayette and Longmont are growing by leaps and bounds so we have agreements with those cities, but they have large planning areas. So we do what we can in the interim to buy up as much open space as possible so that when we renew the intergovernmental agreements there will be less space to have to grow into. **[Boulder 3]**

Using this logic, the protection of a quickly disappearing stock of open, undeveloped prairie land is a strategy used to more carefully plan for the future. This planner sees intergovernmental agreements (IGAs) as "vital" to managing growth in a smart manner because such agreements are the "only way you're going to get cities and counties to sit down together." These agreements also "allow the city and county to work together better" by providing more planning and coordination as to where growth will and will not take place. **[Boulder 5]** By acting in the present to plan for future growth and future growth agreements, Boulder County has been able to buffer certain communities and neighborhoods from runaway growth and spillover development.

One county commissioner supports the movement toward IGAs because these agreements tend to break down the conflicting agendas and visions for the region. He states: "We've influenced several jurisdictions which may have had differences in the past to sit down and focus on the positive side of what we can do and what we can mutually agree upon." He continues:

> The idea of an IGA is to get the cities and counties thinking more in a regional kind of way and thinking about the impact on their neighbors. The potential is for a more shared vision . . . intergovernmental agreements are one way of sort of finding what that

> shared vision is for the future. . . . IGAs become a way of putting that vision for the future into a language that creates binding agreements between entities and into maps which really become the basis for determining where growth will happen and where it won't, and where preservation will occur. **[Boulder 6]**

Despite their cooperative benefits, the question of who will pay for these planning agreements and open-space purchases remains. Traditionally, a majority of residents have voted for tax increases within the city and county to aid in the purchase of additional open-space lands, and therefore view open space as a valuable policy option in the management of growth. One resident, however, points to some of the negatives of open-space policies:

> Open space is a positive thing because it's preserving land from development. But there are also negatives to it. One phenomenon that often occurs is that open space is purchased to preserve the natural setting of the area, but then the land is sold to the government and the public, who has purchased the land with tax dollars, and the public demands access to it. And unless you are very, very careful, everything you want to preserve and half the values you want to preserve are no longer there. **[Boulder 7]**

In many ways, managing growth through open space purchases presents an interesting paradox. On one hand, growth and development in the area allow for more money to be poured into the public coffers through sales and property tax revenues. According to one planner, this extra revenue "allows us to buy more open space" and takes the burden of funding these projects off of the local taxpayer. A county official adds that

> economic prosperity usually means healthier taxes and a more prosperous public sector than you'd find in parts of the country where growth isn't happening. . . . [In these growth areas,] you'll probably find a citizenry that is motivated by growth to preserve the quality of life, [something] that they wouldn't be motivated to do if there weren't growth. **[Boulder 8]**

For there to be enough money to fund open space and other community preservation projects, the region, therefore, needs to allow for commercial and residential growth.

On the other hand however, this growth and development limits the amount of land that can be designated as protected or open space—especially in areas that are reaching a maximum level of build-out. One elected official from Boulder County explains this paradox clearly:

> They [developers] always say that you have to grow or you'll die. I don't believe that, because cancer is growth too and it will kill you. . . . We wouldn't need to buy more open space if there wasn't so much growth occurring. **[Boulder 9]**

Another common drawback to open space is that by limiting growth within one region, the growth is displaced to other, neighboring communities. Although the intended goal is to limit growth and development of the region, growth in surrounding areas creates a housing crunch on the local market, thus making affordable housing difficult if not impossible to find in the city. This unintended consequence of Boulder's growth management policies is explained by one planning official as potentially exclusionary:

> When [an urban growth boundary] becomes an exclusionary tool, that's when we run into some problems talking about the appropriate mix between jobs and housing in communities and dealing better with our transportation system because of that. If there is no affordable housing within a set, contained area, then urban growth boundaries can irresponsibly be used as a "red line" to exclude the poor. However, how much is related to the boundary itself and how much is related to the land-use mix within the boundary is an arguable discussion. Growth management inside cities has the potential to, in a sense, create another form of a "gated" community. **[Boulder 10]**

Most of the housing boom in Boulder County has occurred outside of the city limits in cities and towns such as Superior, Lafayette, Longmont, and Louisville. As their residential areas grew, these communities of Boulder County decided that they wanted commercial growth as well. So the whole development of southeast Boulder County was, to a significant degree, facilitated by a sprawl effect where development spilled out from the city of Boulder into neighboring communities. This irony is well articulated by one resident:

> The irony of the open-space system, combined with the pretty strict growth regulations, is that it preserved the city of Boulder geographically, but in doing that, what happened is the driving up of property values to the point of Boulder being an elite community. **[Boulder 11]**

Outside of housing concerns, residents identify community vitality as a central concern within the overall growth issue. For many, the growth in the area is fundamentally changing the contour of the community itself. One concerned resident argues that the largest impact or change engendered by growth is on the social or community aspects of the city due to the influx of national chains and "big box" retail stores. She states:

> Basically [growth is] changing the social side of the city. Yes, [city officials] preserved the city spatially, but socially, they didn't preserve anything. So Boulder's growing into an elite community. This elitism is present everywhere you look. You look down on Pearl Street. All the commercial areas downtown are changing. It seems like every week there is a new going-out-of-business sign up on the windows on East Pearl Street. So whether you look at it residentially or whether you look at the commercial changes, it's changing and millionaires and corporate businesses are moving in. **[Boulder 12]**

Citizen concern spawned a series of political events, which culminated in a "Slow Growth" campaign for the November 1995 ballot. Their proposal would have limited nonresidential building size to 13,000 square feet and would have been implemented over a period of five years. When the business community caught wind of the Slow Growth initiative, sparks began to fly. They argued that other cities that implemented restrictions on economic growth like Santa Barbara, Pasadena, and Walnut Creek, California, experienced immediate decline in the health of the local economy. When the Slow Growth campaign was proposed by the citizens of Boulder, businesses warned that they would leave town if the initiative was passed. The business community voted "no" on this campaign, and consequently, Slow Growth failed at the election. One Boulder Chamber of Commerce representative gives a possible reason why this initiative was a failure at the polls:

> I think it's the tool that doesn't work in the system. I like growth management. I think growth management is incredibly important. I think every community in Colorado should be exercising growth management. Boulder and Boulder Valley have a fantastic comprehensive plan and again that's one of the umbrella pieces in this all, but when you get down to the implementation side of things, I think that's where we have really gone awry. We make it so unpleasant and so uncomfortable for people that they don't do it

> here. There's obviously a whole contingency in the community that says "excellent." What happens in the governmental side of thinking is that when Boulder starts to lose its sales tax revenue and says that we need to be at X level in order to be able to supply police, fire, our various parks, all that kind of business but yet the sales tax revenues also show that our piece of the pie is shrinking and only taking in Y amount. Instead of thinking about how you make the process friendlier, you make life so hard for people that they don't want to participate. It fosters a competitive environment: Re-zoning. That's why Amgen [a biotechnology firm] went to Longmont. That's why a series of people have gone to Longmont because the Boulder system is so unfriendly and so unpredictable. And you have to go through this major site-review process, which is this totally nutty thing. Talk about cumbersome, expensive, unpredictable. **[Boulder 13]**

The differences between commercial and residential growth control are subtle but quite significant. Residential growth control limits new construction and reduces the number of people who can move into a community (while also increasing housing prices). Since voters are all existing residents who already have a place to live in Boulder, they tend to be supportive, and people who would like to move in can't vote. Commercial growth control has a very different cost–benefit structure. The community's entrepreneurial businesses are terrified of rules that may prevent them from expanding should they become successful. As a result, many convincingly threatened to leave should commercial growth control be enacted. Since many voting residents wanted to keep their Boulder jobs this was a threat that got enough attention to tip the political balance.

Despite the negative effects of spillover growth, and despite the problems generated by a restrictive business environment, Boulder County planners continue to view the City of Boulder's growth-control policies as saving Boulder's unique setting and quality of life from the negative effects of the growth that it would otherwise have experienced. Economically and environmentally, the City of Boulder has curbed the negative effects of growth and sprawl, but has sent many employed within the city limits to find more affordable housing in other areas of Boulder County, influencing sprawl conditions in neighboring cities.

Chapter 14

Analysis of Colorado Growth Conflict Frames

Robert Gardner and Guy Burgess

This chapter compares and contrasts the three cases (Boulder, Larimer, and El Paso Counties) presented in Chapter 13. We explore three primary frames: identity frames (how individuals and parties think about themselves), characterization frames (how parties think about and characterize the identities and positions of opposing parties), and conflict management frames (the processes through which individuals prefer to address the conflict). This cross-case comparison will draw upon quotes and perspectives described in Chapter 13 and will draw from the discussion of framing and intractability from Chapters 1 and 2. We also examine how these frames used by participants in growth-related environmental problems affect the intractability of the conflict and communities' ability to deal with these problems.

The Project

This analysis and the three case studies presented in the previous chapter are based upon in-depth interviews with thirty-six community leaders and draw from insights provided by another five experts invited to a graduate seminar on the topic. We also conducted an extensive document search that included a substantial number of valuable Web-based materials. Drawing on our interview and archival data, as well as perspectives and public comments from three quite different Colorado communities, we compiled a sample of quotes representing the various ways that people think about growth. However, we made no effort to calculate the number or proportion of people who adhere to each view. We also did not seek to identify the number of moderates who see both sides of a framing issue and can't quite make up their minds. Our goal was simply to collect examples of the various ways in which people think about the growth issue. Therefore, we offer only a limited window into framing behavior in our three communities rather than an exhaustive or representative study. A more comprehensive assessment would undoubtedly yield a much more complex and diverse picture.

In the sections that follow, we illustrate and analyze the various frames using brief quotation segments. (Full quotes are presented in the preceding chapter. A few new quotes not appearing in the preceding chapter have been cited in this chapter for supplemental illustration.) In presenting these quotations, we have removed proper names and have included minimal identifying material. This reflects the confidentiality of our interviews and our desire to focus upon the general issues of framing without becoming a party to the conflicts we studied.

Readers will also note that the three cases presented here are somewhat different from the cases considered elsewhere in this volume. Rather than focusing upon a tightly defined issue, we looked at a cluster of three dissimilar disputes surrounding growth-related environmental conflicts. While this approach allowed us to observe a broader range of frames it also reduced the depth with which we could examine each community.

Identity Frames

Identity frames reflect the various ways in which individuals affiliate with meaningful bases of identification, including demographics, location (or sense of place), social role, institutional or group affiliation, and interests. As rhetorical theorist Kenneth Burke reminds us, identification with a particular set of values, affiliations, and perspectives imply their opposites—those values, affiliations, and perspectives with which we disagree (Burke 1950). Therefore, just as certain sites of identification can provide a source of identity, opposing sites of identification can also be indications of what individuals reject. Analyzing these frames sheds light upon the various ways individuals see themselves in the context of the conflict.

Because individual arguments, concerns, and values are often inextricably tied to their core identity, challenges to a person's views on growth-related issues are often perceived as a threat on a very personal level. As we noted in Chapter 1, threats to core aspects of one's identity contribute to the overall intractability of the conflict (Rothman 1997). While we found that identity frames in our cases were rooted in demographics, place, societal or institutional role, group affiliation, and interests, it was the interest-based identities that seemed most important in fueling the conflict in our growth cases. This is where we've focused most of our attention, with place, societal role, and demographics discussed as they overlap with our primary focus.

Interest-based identity frames form among groups of people with shared political causes that are usually based upon shared values. These frames determine which groups people most closely identify with (or against) and include the particular values, interests, and positions associated with the distinct interest or interest group. These identity markers tend to revolve around prominent social issues, political philosophies, or organized advocacy groups. Since people who live in the same place tend to have overlapping interests, it is common in growth-related conflicts for place-based frames to reinforce identity frames based on interests. The opposite can also be true. People with different images about how a place should be managed can develop quite competitive intergroup relationships organized around these competing views of place. With respect to growth-related issues, it is common to find contending interest groups fighting over the future of places like Boulder, Fort Collins, or eastern El Paso County. In our work, we identified five common interest-based identity frames: freedom, commons, progress, community, and environment. We compare and contrast how these played out in each of the three communities.

Freedom

The first cluster of identity-based interest frames addresses the common assumption that growth management is a public policy problem. Individuals who frame the growth issue as one of individual freedom and property rights believe that everyone should be free to pursue their own self-interests in whatever manner they choose (within legal limits). They believe that growth management should be a private sector rather than a public sector issue. They are also convinced that the routine exercise of individual responsibility takes care of most problems and that individuals can work out the remaining problems among themselves. People who tend to frame issues in this way identify closely with an ideology that is skeptical of government involvement in growth management processes. Thus groups whose interest-based identities are oriented around the freedom frame also pursue an individualist orientation with respect to views of social control. With respect to societal roles, they see themselves as being in direct opposition to government regulators and bureaucrats.

In our study we found most adherents to these frames living in eastern El Paso County, with several Fort Collins residents also expressing similar frames. The following quotations illustrate how this frame was expressed:

> Our founding fathers were given a vision from God. . . . the issue here is whether . . . we will gradually allow governments to steal virtually all of our rights. **[El Paso 18]**

> The mood in this audience tonight is about as close as you'll ever get to the mood of our nation when it was founded over 220 years ago. These people understand what freedom is all about. They understand that the government that governs least governs best. They live day to day by the libertarian motto: "live and let live." They haven't been tainted yet by micro-managing government or numbed by all the rules and regulations that we live by in the city. But now tonight you're about to change that without batting an eye. You're going to destroy the last bastion of freedom left along the Front Range. **[New Quote]**

> We don't understand the need for more laws and regulations. **[El Paso 1]**

> Basic to the liberties we hold so dear is our land, specifically that piece of property we have toiled a lifetime to call our own. **[El Paso 16]**

> [We're the] last of the true pioneer spirit. . . . [We] came out here and founded this area. **[El Paso 17]**

The republican spirit embodied in the quotes above illustrates how these individuals' conceptions of self as "American" and "law abiding, land-owning citizens" influence their leanings toward social control frames that champion a limited governmental role in land-use policy. Because their interest-based identities are rooted in their respect for traditional, libertarian values, these identity frames leave little, if any, role for what they see as "excessive" governmental intervention in the conflict. As interest-based frames, these residents object to governmental "bureaucracy" and meddling. Therefore, they see themselves as ambassadors of the Constitution and traditional American values.

Commons

Another group of people come to the issue with an almost visceral reaction to the way in which growth is transforming the landscape and their communities. They frame their interest-based identity on what they are against: sprawl, growth, and, to a significant degree, change. They want to keep their neighborhoods and communities "the way they were," and reject the acquisitiveness and materialism that seem to accompany prosperity and growth. This commons orientation frames what these individuals see as problematic with or symptomatic of growth and development. This orientation also constitutes an interest-based frame that is supportive of community preservation and environmental protection. With respect to social control frames this orientation overlaps considerably with the egalitarian-local frame endorsing local, community-based governance for their neighborhood or region.

This framing obviously has a strong, place-based component, since the commons (which people are seeking to protect) is, by definition, a concept that focuses upon place and regional identity. A core component of individual identity is, therefore, affiliation with a particular region's culture, lifestyle, and geographic characteristics. Changes in physical and environmental surroundings associated with population growth can either negatively or positively impact people's conception of their quality of life. Consequently, for people espousing a common frame, growth is seen as threatening to the welfare or preservation of the place they cherish and therefore to their place-based identities. The following passages illustrate this orientation:

> Fort Collins has been a distinct community. We're just on the verge of losing that, and becoming a suburb of Denver. **[Larimer 13]**
>
> I don't like that major streets are becoming strip shopping centers for chain stores; chain stores don't have vested interests in the community. **[Larimer 14]**
>
> People [in the Caribbean] were simply living on a lot less and [were] just as happy. . . . That's where sprawl and consumption come together. **[Larimer 16]**

Many respondents felt that sprawl was making their communities look nearly indistinguishable from one another and thereby eliminating the uniqueness of the places to which they were attached. Their orientation as "anti-consumerist" or against large, corporate, "big box," chain stores signifies an interest-based identity frame that interprets the influx of national chains as a threat to the smaller, locally run establishments that are seen as a significant contributor to community identity.

When sprawling growth encroaches on historically unique and geographically separate communities, the creeping development toward and within the boundaries of these communities is interpreted, by many, as a threat to the very boundaries that make the region unique and separate from the areas surrounding it. Consequently, it is perceived as a threat to one's very identity when these boundaries become blurred.

Progress

Of course there are other residents whose reaction to growth is quite the opposite. They see growth and prosperity as, on the whole, beneficial to their local communities. Although they do realize that there are some problems (e.g., increased congestion) that occur while local infrastructure struggles to catch up with the growing population, these problems are perceived as minor when compared with the larger benefits of growth. Smog, congestion, and sprawl are simply part of the cost of progress, and an essential part of the quest for human betterment. And, the problems experienced in our study communities were often seen as much less severe than those encountered in the nation's large metropolitan areas.

These sentiments constitute both place- and interest-based identity frames. Many realize and are appreciative of the fact that they live in a place that people living elsewhere in the country regard as a vacation destination. People recognize that this attractiveness fosters growth, and growth must be managed in a way that preserves what is attractive about the place, while still securing growth's benefits.

> [Y]ou have to continue to grow in order to survive. . . . with progress comes population growth. **[Larimer 20]**
>
> [P]eople move to Colorado because of all the great open space. . . few move here to live in zero lot housing. **[Larimer 12]**
>
> [P]eople complain that it's newcomers who are causing [growth]. This is a myth . . . it's [a question of] dealing with our own people and making room for our children to live in the community. **[Larimer 21]**
>
> This [growth] is nothing compared to the San Fernando Valley. **[El Paso 2]**

As place-based identity frames, these quotes illustrate how individuals compare their region to other regions (and thus residents of these regions) before considering the particular challenges facing Colorado. As self-identified Coloradans, or members of their specific local community, they feel a significant stake in the outcomes of growth policies because these decisions will invariably affect the nature of communities with which they identify.

These frames consider the effects of growth on both regional and personal identity. As a region, the very same amenities that draw people to Colorado contribute to the growth and development that undermine those amenities. Consequently, residents' special attachment to place becomes threatened as both the built and the natural environment change.

While some newcomers see the problem of growth and development as far worse in other regions of the country, many longtime residents still maintain a picture of "the way things were" in their individual and collective frames, and see the new growth as a threat to their imagined community. Longtime residents and newcomers from more-congested areas enter the growth discussion with competing frames, which are largely irreconcilable and therefore contribute to intractability.

Community

While some individuals focus on the physical effects that growth has on the natural environment, other stakeholders focus on the social effects. For these individuals, growth is transforming the underlying sense of community and changing the character of the neighborhoods in which people live. They realize that these changes require a different way of thinking about their community and, by extension, themselves. This produces a different kind of place-based and interest-based frame—one that prioritizes the effects of growth on social relationships:

> [Growth is] changing the social side of the city. . . . [City officials] preserved the city spatially, but socially, they didn't preserve anything. . . . Boulder's growing into an elite community. **[Boulder 12]**
>
> [W]e need to be thinking of ourselves as an urban community, rather than a suburban or rural community. **[Larimer 5]**

Identity frames can be quite complex. Some Boulderites, for example, seem to define their community as consisting only of city residents. People who work or study in the city but live elsewhere are somehow not considered part of this identity group. For example, one person credited Boulder's residential growth control program with having contained sprawl and protecting its identity even though its dramatic employment increases had forced a significant proportion of its workforce to live in the sprawling and expanding bedroom communities located outside the growth control area:

> Boulder has arguably contained sprawl. We have maintained this compact human-scale city, a relatively high quality of life, [and the] environment. But on the other hand, housing prices have increased beyond the reach of many who would like to live, work, or go to school here. **[Boulder 2]**

There are critics, of course, who believe that Boulder's image as a carefully planned and progressive city simply neglects the effects of the spillover growth caused by Boulder's success. These individuals identify themselves as being part of a larger growth region characterized by sprawling development. And they tend to be more interested in increasing the quality of life associated with these developments.

This ability of place-based identities to develop at different levels makes it far more difficult to craft workable compromises on difficult growth-related issues than it would be if everyone adopted the same interpretation of the boundaries. Narrower, subcommunity frames make it easier for people to avoid, in their own minds, responsibility for larger problems that they have helped cause. And this contributes to the intractability of the growth problem more generally. While Boulder offers the clearest example of this dynamic, the same process clearly affects other communities along the Front Range as well.

Environment

While many look at the social or sociological impacts of growth, others frame it in terms of its impact on the natural environment. They see themselves as defenders of a constantly shrinking natural environment, which they believe is on the brink of catastrophic collapse. Their identity is one rooted in their environmental interests and, as a result, they tend to see human society itself as the enemy and, for some, a cancerous growth on the planet. While based upon environmental interests, these frames also tend to be place- or location-based since they focus upon Colorado as a place of extraordinary natural beauty, wide-open wilderness, and diverse ecosystems. This frame focuses upon protecting the environment for its own sake and goes beyond the simple desire for outdoor recreational opportunities. For many, it is almost a spiritual view of the environment.

> Psychologically, the loss of open space and natural areas where we get our inspiration and our tranquillity have an adverse effect on how we deal with stress and all other daily activities. **[Larimer 10]**
>
> Why the West? Because growth seeks places that aren't used up . . . yet. I've always thought the term "growth" was oxymoronic. I've known people who died of growths. In Colorado, growth has meant the destruction of 30,000 acres of wildlife habitat a year, caustic air, and an overcrowded back country. Colorado and the West aren't growing. They are shrinking. **[New Quote]**

> Some groups actually value economic growth, and [are hoping to attract] more people, and I don't [agree]. Those people need to read "Tragedy of the Commons."* (Hardin 1968) **[Larimer 8]**
>
> [Public funding of open space has negatives.] . . . the public demands access . . . unless you are very, very careful, everything you want to preserve . . . is no longer there. **[Boulder 7]**

For these individuals who identify with the surrounding natural environment, both spiritually and symbolically, growth poses a challenge not only to Colorado's characteristic beauty, but also to the very values and identities of its residents. By rooting their orientations to the growth issue through environmental interests, these respondents see themselves as, first and foremost, protectors of the environment. By focusing exclusively upon environmental protection, adherents to this frame give little consideration to the benefits of growth and development. This framing can make it difficult for them to consider the possible advantages of a growing tax base with its ability to increase funding for open-space purchases while also paying for environmental cleanup efforts. Residents with environment-based and growth-based interest frames are often diametrically opposed to one another. This combination of frames contributes to intractability by making it harder for people to see win–win opportunities presented by collaboration between environmental and development interests since both sides tend to assume an uncompromising, positional stance.

Characterization Frames

A relatively impartial bystander who listens to the growth management debate is likely to be struck by the extent to which people seem to be talking past each other. Frequently, it seems as if the parties are not seriously considering the possibility that opponents may have valid points. Instead, there is a tendency for people to focus upon unflattering characterizations of opposing parties and positions.

This negative labeling of opponents and the positions that they advocate constitutes negative characterization framing. These frames commonly result in stereotypes in which the views and interests of opposing parties are viewed as so indefensible that they are worthy only of ridicule. As framing strategies,

* In "The Tragedy of the Commons," Garrett Hardin depicts what can happen to a community commons when everyone increases the number of animals that graze there.

these cognitive schemes contribute to the escalation and overall intractability of the conflict by fueling greater hostility and mistrust between parties. Additionally, the negative characterization of opposing parties pulls disputants away from potentially fruitful communication and collaborative conflict resolution strategies by demonizing the "enemy."

Similar to identity frames, characterization frames work to solidify the positions and identities of those making the characterizations (Smyth 1994, Tajfel and Turner 1979) while simultaneously limiting the need to consider the merits of opposing positions. In the same way that identity frames work to protect or define the identity of a particular stakeholder, characterization frames provide an out-group against which these views can be reinforced. This characterization framing can increase intractability as opposing parties view each other's arguments as less and less credible.

In this section, we explore the presence of five key characterization frames used by parties in the growth conflicts we studied: profit and greed, last settlers, bureaucracy and power, environmental meddling, and elitism. As with identity frames, we will focus primarily on interest-based frames while supplementing this discussion with instances of place-based, institutional-based, and societal role characterizations.

Profit and Greed

In the Colorado growth dispute, it is common for pro-growth and -development interests to be characterized negatively by anti-growth parties as profiteers who are ripping off the community for selfish gain. When parties frame their opponents as "thieves" or "criminals" it is easy for them to conclude that opposing views deserve, and thus receive, no serious consideration. This type of interest-based, characterization framing depicts the pro-growth contingent as possessing a fervent thirst for money and profit at the expense of community interests.

> Individuals have become more greedy. They want to profit regardless of the community's rights or goals. **[Larimer 2]**
>
> . . . rapid growth that made the greedy greedier. **[Larimer 3]**
>
> I don't see any positive aspects to growth. There are a few individuals who have benefited from that growth . . . e.g., the high school graduate who became a contractor and is now "loaded." Only because of good timing have some people benefited, where they would not have been successful otherwise. However, few people realize the advantages of growth. The income brought in by

> these few wealthy individuals is not a benefit. **[New Quote]**

By casting their opponents in such a negative light, stakeholders in growth disputes undermine any potentially valid arguments that opponents might bring to the table. By characterizing one's opponents as less than ethical or moral, this negative framing contributes a significant barrier to genuine, reasoned dialogue and fosters an implicit aversion to serious consideration of their views and perspectives. This contributes to a climate of intractability and prevents parties from truly meeting each other as equals at the bargaining table.

Last Settlers

Another characterization frame dominant in growth disputes is illustrated by the "last settler" syndrome. These last settlers are recently arrived newcomers who argue forcefully that the time has come for stringent growth controls. Although many are newcomers themselves, once they have secured property in the growth region, these individuals feel that no additional residential growth should be allowed within their respective communities. Native or longtime Colorado residents tend to negatively characterize the last settlers for their blindness to their own contribution to the growth and sprawl facing the region.

> People who've even moved here in the recent past have a tendency toward drawing up the drawbridge. In other words, [they say] "now that we're here, we need to stop this growth thing." **[Larimer 22]**

These longtime residents see the arguments of newcomers who advocate stopping sprawl and growth as largely hypocritical, and therefore not worthy of serious consideration. Because they have been living in the region for a much longer time than the newcomers, and because they have seen growth trends in a much wider historical perspective, the longtime residents of the region show a certain level of hostility toward newcomers, and characterize them accordingly.

Bureaucracy and Power

Advocates of freedom discussed in the identity framing section above often have unkind words to say about proponents of regulation and zoning. Because they see government regulation as a severe threat to their land-use rights, these individuals negatively characterize planners, governmental officials, and their supporters as greedy, antidemocratic, and hungry for power. These characterization frames are closely linked to individualist social control frames, which oppose government intervention through regulation.

In El Paso County this frame illustrates both a positive societal role and institutional characterization of this individual's core identity group—as independent, freedom-loving residents living east of the city—while simultaneously decrying the "enemy": those power-hungry and bureaucratic government officials. The following citizen quotes illustrate similar frames:

> . . . people who want to use other people's property without paying for it. **[El Paso 14]**
>
> [Government officials] who practice tyranny and despotism are known as tyrants and despots. **[El Paso 12]**
>
> [B]ureaucrats[, like you, are] hungry for power and for money. **[El Paso 11]**

Other residents frame the "bureaucratic government" not as simply a set of outsiders impinging upon their individual liberties and freedoms, but rather as a group impinging on the ability of business owners and developers to do what they please with their land and property:

> [Boulder's land-use policies make] it so unpleasant and so uncomfortable for [developers] that they don't [build] here. . . . [they require a] major site-review process, which is this totally nutty thing. Talk about cumbersome, expensive, unpredictable. **[Boulder 13]**

Not surprisingly, the negative institutional characterizations of planners and government officials who support growth control regulations tend to intensify hostilities and differences. And this, in turn, makes growth-related problems all the more intractable.

Environmental Meddling

A similarly inimical sentiment comes from opponents of strict environmental regulations. These individuals contend that environmentalists tend to go too far in their efforts to preserve the natural ecosystems surrounding growth regions. Environmentalists are often perceived negatively by their opponents, and are thus seen as having little or no concern for the welfare of the area's rapidly growing human population. Accordingly, environmentalists are characterized as caring only about the natural environment (and, perhaps, their own privileged access to it) and not about the costs and consequences of environmental activism.

> [I]deology should give way to working together. The Sierra Club has got a lot of angry people—that's not compatible with good politics. **[Larimer 6]**
>
> Exclusionary preservation isn't the solution. **[Larimer 11]**
>
> They publicly beat on their chests that the world is going to hell in a handbasket. **[Larimer 7]**

It is common for those interested in environmental protection to be characterized as fanatics, who believe that the rights of nonhuman species are more important than human welfare. This characterization permits environmental interests to be discounted since environmentalists are, by definition, true believers who are not interested in compromise or accommodation. This, in turn, fosters the idea that there is an all-out war between the human and natural environment.

Elitism

A few respondents were able to look beyond an initial good guy/bad guy frame, and explore, self-reflectively, the unintended negative consequences of their framing of the problem. By reflecting critically on the frames that they bring into the dispute, they are able to discern the irony and tension inherent in their own (or their own city's) positions on growth and sprawl:

> [P]retty strict growth regulations . . . preserved . . . Boulder geographically, but in doing that, [they drove up] property values to the point of being an elite community. **[Boulder 11]**
>
> Growth management inside cities has the potential to, in a sense, create another form of a "gated" community. **[Boulder 10]**

By remaining self-reflective in their analysis of the growth-policy dispute, these individuals take a more balanced approach to the conflict by realizing the paradoxes inherent in their own positions. Additionally, these self-imposed characterization frames illustrate recognition of potential negative characterizations that may be placed on them by others. The self-characterizers oppose the exclusionary outcomes presumably produced by "strict" growth controls because these outcomes threaten their self-image as Boulder residents (who want to be viewed by others as neither "elite" nor "exclusionary"). To be sure, however, by adopting a more self-critical characterization frame, these parties are more adequately equipped to find compromise or consensus because of their ability to weigh competing frames in the conflict, thus moving away from a potentially intractable wrangle of positions.

Conflict Management Frames

Conflict management frames shape the way people think about resolving or managing disputes. More important, however, these frames influence the methods and approaches people pursue in shaping the outcomes of public policy. Some individuals, for example, seek to advance their interests through the negotiation of cooperative agreements while others rely on market forces or seek a regulatory structure capable of introducing the preferred policy. Still others focus on threats of political or legal action or even violence. Possible approaches to conflict management that we consider include: avoidance, fact finding, appeals to authority, joint problem solving (including dialogue and consensus), adjudication (or third party intervention), political action, market approaches, or perhaps even violence or struggle.

Each of these approaches constitutes a unique conflict management frame, and influences not only the methods one seeks in resolving a particular conflict, but also how the participants perceive and interpret the conflict itself. In addition, viewing a particular conflict through a particular conflict frame can and often does contribute to "frame lock," a situation in which one holds steadfastly to a particular management frame, rather than considering the validity or feasibility of competing frames. In the Front Range communities we studied, conflict management frames tended to correspond to the interest-based identity frames defined earlier in the chapter. Those operating from a freedom-based identity frame tended to find value in market-based solutions, while those viewing the conflict through community or common identity frames tended to point to the political process or joint problem-solving approaches. These frames additionally have positive and negative components that lead people to frame positively those processes that they advocate while ridiculing those processes they oppose. While positing a set of preferable solutions to resolving growth conflicts, these frames also limit the potential for alternative approaches to ever make it to the bargaining table, thus limiting participants' ability to transcend intractable conflict situations.

Market Solution Frames

Market-based conflict frames point to private enterprise or what we commonly refer to as "the market" to cure our social ills. Stakeholders in the growth conflict we studied adopted this frame when they believed that government is excessively cumbersome and bound so firmly with bureaucratic red tape that it is ill equipped to deal effectively and efficiently with many social policy issues. Favoring free market to governmental intervention in policy disputes, disputants operating from this frame advocate leaving growth policy decisions to private interests and the invisible hand of the market. Especially prevalent among those who frame the growth issue in terms of private property, free enterprise, and liberty, this frame reflects beliefs that private developers and contractors should have a stronger voice in guiding competing visions of development:

> [Y]ou can't legislate nirvana. We need more developers . . . to embrace the new vision. **[El Paso 15]**

Some advocates of appeal to market frames also commented on efforts to force the market to offer unwanted developments such as the new urbanist projects—architectural designs that incorporate housing, commerce, and recreation into a mixed-use, planned community. They believed such developments are doomed to failure because market forces do not always lead to outcomes that government regulators believe are best for the long-term interests of the community as a whole. Developers tend to rely on market frames to drive their decision making regarding the types, structures, and arrangements of housing and commercial developments to be built in an area. Those residents using conflict management frames based on appeal to market solutions see consumer demand (or lack thereof) as the driving force for these new urbanist alternatives. These frames were exhibited by several people from Larimer County.

> [While a] new urbanist project can be viable financially, [we should not force developers to produce] a product that people around here don't want. **[Larimer 18]**
>
> Developers challenge their numbers . . . for not looking at what people are doing in other parts of the country. **[Larimer 19]**
>
> [M]arket forces will take care of it. . . . If the people don't want what the planners think they want, then this could all be an academic pipe dream. **[Larimer 4]**

By the same token, those with interest-based identities espousing freedom also adopted few appeal to political action frames or authority decides based on expertise frames, which they considered meddling impositions. These individuals see a limited role for government in resolving the logistical problems associated with growth and development regulations.

> Government should only do what people can't do for themselves. . . . [People] have decided it's the government's job to solve neighborly squabbles. But we've suddenly become a society that expects someone else to solve our problems. **[Larimer 1]**

Proponents of the appeal to market solutions frame fear the government will have undue influence in everyday decisions that were once hammered out between neighbors. Consequently, they adopt a growth management strategy that opposes appeals to political or expert authority.

Political Action Frames

Another parallel we observed between identity and conflict management frames was overlapping interest-based identity and political action frames. Those who see market approaches producing unregulated growth and inevitable "tragedies of the commons" tend to frame regulatory processes as preferable to free market alternatives.

> The bottom line is to convince elected officials that they have a duty to the people to contribute to the betterment of their community. **[El Paso 7]**
>
> [S]ome form of standard public notification and input process was preferable to unrestricted growth. **[El Paso 8]**
>
> But now we need something, I believe it to be an arbitrator or a referee. We need zoning out there. **[El Paso 9]**

Joint Problem-Solving Frames

Despite the differences in conflict management frames presented above, some residents in each of our three communities espoused joint problem-solving frames. Joint problem-solving frames favor approaching the problem through collaborative decision-making processes, many of which are characterized by dialogue and efforts to reach consensus. Operating from this frame, stakeholders feel that decisions are ultimately best left to the local community or citizenry to decide, but usually only after a careful and inclusive policy dialogue.

While the three communities in our study framed the growth issue quite differently, many expressed a desire to view the growth policy as a joint problem-solving exercise. In El Paso County, residents demonstrated a high level of involvement in public policy debates surrounding growth and development, but felt that the planners and politicians dominated the policy dialogue and thus skewed the problem-solving process toward their own ends. Many of these residents, especially those living in the rural, eastern portion of the county, would have preferred to pursue a collaborative approach that tried honestly and earnestly to balance competing goals. However, they abandoned this frame after they decided that the planners and politicians were committed to pursuing their own vision. As these residents perceived that their voices were neither being heard nor understood, their framing of the issue became dominated by frustration, skepticism, and mistrust of the joint problem-solving process:

> The inflammatory rhetoric . . . it's unproductive, it's hurtful, and it distorts the issue. . . . people do not feel heard or understood. **[El Paso 13]**

Although these residents indicated that they would have liked to see an inclusive, participatory policy dialogue, their perception that the process was unfair and unrepresentative shifted the framing to one that approached joint problem solving as an ideal that was, in this case, unrealistic.

As an alternative to what was regarded as a failed collaborative process, these individuals drew upon a political ideology that assumed each person involved in a dialogue should have an equal say in the policy outcome. This led citizens to advocate some type of vote that would quantitatively measure public sentiment. While this can be viewed as a return to the political action frame, it really represents a reputation of a political process that was viewed as failing to exercise its collaborative problem-solving responsibilities. Their remedy to this problem was direct democracy. These residents felt that this was even better than a collaborative and inclusive dialogue since it allowed all residents to feel that their voice is being heard and considered.

In both Boulder and Larimer Counties, however, residents took an active role in establishing a well-balanced policy dialogue that weighed and considered multiple perspectives, including those of environmentalists, developers, planners, residents, land-use advocates, and businesspeople. Throughout the multiple stages of the growth-policy dialogue, Boulder and Larimer Counties established public venues and hearings to monitor and evaluate public sentiment toward various policy options. Because of these institutionalized spaces and feedback channels, many residents adopted a frame that recognized the political process as one that had the best interests of the public in mind. Unlike the skeptical El Paso County residents, more people in Boulder and Larimer adopted a joint problem-solving frame that was characterized by mutual trust, optimism, and an understanding that truly collaborative decision making must weigh simultaneously multiple, competing perspectives. People subscribing to this frame advocated and worked hard to establish a more inclusive, open, and democratic policy process concerning growth.

Since a large portion of land-use policy and other local civic affairs take place at the local community level, coordinating cooperation and consensual dialogue across communities and countywide posed significant logistical problems. This was especially true since different communities with different impacts had competing visions of how best to handle growth. Coordinating and reconciling these differences became a hurdle that city and county officials as well as local residents recognized they must overcome. While joint problem solving is more commonly used to reconcile competing individual interests, some residents advocated applying these principles to competing municipalities to promote a climate of collaboration and cooperation:

> [We need] regional cooperation. . . . But there's still a lot of competition, distrust, big fish/little fish mentality. **[Larimer 17]**

By focusing on regional cooperation, these residents felt that spillover effects from one city to another could be ameliorated. This framing acknowledges that such an approach would overcome much of the mistrust, exclusivity, and power dominating noncollaborative dialogues.

Struggle and Violence

When conflicts have endured for an extended period of time and when frustrated parties perceive no end in sight, combatants adopt conflict management frames rooted in violence or struggle. Violent conflict management frames often emerge as a last resort, after other, more peaceful alternatives have been explored, and frequently indicate that a consensual or collaborative goal has been abandoned.

In this study, when traditional legislative, legal, governmental, or community-based processes failed to adequately satisfy each party's needs or interests, they saw little alternative but to escalate the scope and intensity of the conflict. Among those who felt that political and legal institutions were failing to protect their legitimate interests, there was a temptation to threaten and justify violence. Although none of the conflicts in the three towns we studied had reached this level of polarization, struggle, sabotage, and violence frames were most prevalent in El Paso County, our most highly escalated conflict, as the following quotes illustrate.

> We're going to take you to court every time you turn around and we will kick your ass. **[El Paso 3]**
>
> Every time you enchain these people you are driving them further and further towards civil war. . . . You've got citizens here who are pissed off at you, do you not listen? **[El Paso 4]**
>
> This is a sad day for the county we love. We are here with a bomb squad outside, surrounded by the police because you are afraid of the people. There's a choice between ballots and bullets. You've given us the bullets not the ballots. President Kennedy once said, "Those who make peaceful evolution impossible make violent revolution inevitable." **[New Quote]**

Conclusion

The frames presented here quite literally extend from one extreme of the political continuum to the other. Those at each extreme are, at a very fundamental level, quite incompatible. Not surprisingly, at least in the communities we studied, there was a tendency for people to self-segregate into communities with more homogeneous frames on growth issues. The system of multiple, local political jurisdictions, fortunately, allows different people, in different places, to live in different ways. This does much to limit the intensity of growth conflicts. The result is a region with diverse perspectives and policies on the growth issue.

Part V

Conclusion

Chapter 15

Lessons Learned about the Framing and Reframing of Intractable Environmental Conflicts

Michael Elliott, Barbara Gray, and Roy J. Lewicki

In the preceding chapters we have explored eight cases of intractable environmental conflict, paying particular attention to the ways that disputants in these conflicts have made sense of them. Now that we have scrutinized our cases in detail, we want to draw lessons from our work about framing and intractability in environmental conflicts. To do so we first take a step back to revisit the research questions we raised in the Introduction. Those questions were:

- How does framing affect conflict dynamics, particularly when the conflict is proving to be quite difficult to resolve?
- Why do intractable conflicts over environmental issues persist and how do differences in the way disputants frame conflicts affect their intractability?
- Why are some environmental issues able to be resolved in one locale while in others they remain contentious?
- Why do some conflicts find resolution while others carry on over decades?
- What is it about environmental conflicts that makes them particularly susceptible to intractability?

In this chapter we explore what we have learned from our cases to answer these questions. Additionally, we explore technologies for frame change since we have seen that, to the extent that frames are malleable, the potential exists to render intractable disputes more tractable. We suggest techniques for reframing that can be applied to other difficult-to-resolve conflicts. We close with some final thoughts for people who find themselves embroiled in difficult environmental conflicts.

Answers to Our Research Questions

Intractability Is a Dynamic Process

Out of the eight cases, Voyageurs appears to be the most intractable, remaining essentially frozen into a pattern that has changed little in twenty years, with frames that recur repeatedly through time. Still, even in Voyageurs, some changes have occurred as different disputes erupt and get resolved, new players enter, and the local, state, and national contexts evolve. Compared to Voyageurs, however, the conflicts in some of the other cases (e.g., Quincy, Drake, and Chattanooga) have changed considerably.

Despite some degree of evolution in all of these cases, the conflicts continue against a deeper and harder-to-resolve background of more basic concerns. Thus, when we look at the Edwards Aquifer case, we see a multitude of disputes that have been settled through adjudication, changes in public policy and market conditions, and creation of new institutions. The fundamental questions about the allocation and management of the aquifer, however, remain intensely controversial. In Lock Haven, even after the Drake Chemical site was remediated, the conflict over whether the incinerator was safe continues to echo in the community. And, while the stakeholders in the Quincy Library dispute dramatically transformed the dispute, proposing what those involved in the original agreement considered to be a full resolution of the issues, the agreement did not hold because other stakeholders, excluded from the original agreement, elevated the conflict to a broader decision-making forum. Hence, we offer our first conclusion:

Conclusion 1: Conflicts are dynamic processes. For intractable conflicts, in particular, even though actors change, contexts transform, and the arenas in which dispute episodes are staged shift, the conflict persists. Our data also suggest that framing has much to do with this intransigence and that shifts in frames can make a conflict more or less tractable.

Frames Act as Lenses

In each of these cases, we discovered a rich array of frames constructed by stakeholders. Stakeholders constructed these frames to make sense of the conflicts for themselves. The frames enabled stakeholders to identify and interpret significant elements of their experience within the conflict, and to sort, synthesize, and condense large amounts of information into manageable nuggets. Through the process of framing, they also discarded, devalued, or ignored information that was inconsistent with their chosen frames. These nuggets or chunks form disputants' "whole story" frames, which encapsulate the essence of the conflict for them. In addition, more elaborated frames were also constructed that reflect the disputants' own orientations to the issues (identity frames), their stance on what should be done about the conflict (conflict management frames), and their views about the others involved (characterization frames). As we have shown, environmental disputants also construct interpretations about who is winning and who is losing (loss/gain frames), about how power and control are exercised in society (power and social control frames, respectively), and about whether they perceive any danger in the situation (risk frames).

In addition to helping disputants make sense of the dispute for themselves, frames helped stakeholders represent and express their interpretations to others. Disputants also constructed and employed frames to convey to others how they interpreted actions that were taken and events that occurred. And they employed frames to persuade others to adopt their interpretation of the conflict, its causes and dynamics, and their preferred outcomes, and to mobilize them to take action on the issues (Snow et al. 1986, Taylor 2000). Disputants both constructed their frames about the conflict and re-created the conflict through their constructions. Thus framing is integral to creating and perpetuating the conflict. As long as disputants' interpretations about what is at stake differ (and these differences are not acknowledged or considered a legitimate basis for dialogue), the conflict will persist.

Frame Differences

In our cases we have seen that disputants' interpretations of what the conflicts were about differed substantially. For example, in the Edwards case, farmers and irrigators framed the issues as private property rights, while the U.S. Fish and Wildlife Service framed them as protection of endangered species, and even residents within the city of San Antonio failed to see eye to eye on what the issues were that were in contention. In Voyageurs, the presenting issues and the underlying issues differed. While skirmishes ostensibly erupt over decisions about use or preservation, the underlying conflict was as much about loss of identity and control as it was about whether a particular bay is open or closed to snowmobiling. Local opponents, in an effort to regain some control, continually framed the conflict in terms of unrequited losses, while the Park Service framed it in terms of future regulation. This mismatch in framing helps to explain the Park Service's unsuccessful efforts to hammer out deals with the locals on concrete plans for the future (such as whether to require camping permits). The parties were, essentially, trying to address two different conflicts.

Characterization frames also significantly influence conflict dynamics. Consider what happened in the Colorado growth cases when advocates of economic development were viewed as "thieves," "criminals," and those who seek "to profit regardless of the community's rights or goals," **[Colorado L2]** while advocates of open-space preservation were viewed as latecomers who want to "draw up the drawbridge," as bureaucrats who are "tyrants and despots" and "hungry for power and money," and "as a lot of angry people" who "publicly beat on their chests that the world is going to hell in a handbasket." **[Colorado L22, L7]** Such demonization of opponents fueled those conflicts by increasing polarization, reducing the capacity of parties to talk and listen to each other, and, in effect, preventing each from seeking a different outcome because, by blaming the others for the problem, they absolve themselves from any responsibility to do so. In Drake, similar reactions were engendered in Department of Environmental Protection representatives when one of their own was called a "liar."

Consider also how the disputants in the Ohio Antidegradation External Advisory Group (EAG) process constructed conflict management frames differently from each other. The negotiators were professionals, seeking to approach the dispute rationally. Yet each framed aspects of the dispute in significantly different ways. For example, consistent with their own identity frames as concerned citizens devoid of private interests and working collaboratively to promote the public good, the environmentalists viewed the Ohio Environmental Protection Agency as a mediator: "The best outcome for this EAG process would be to develop rules that the environmental and regulated communities and Ohio EPA would mutually agree upon. I'd like to have as much consensus as possible."**[Ohio 52]** Also consistent with their own identities as representatives and legal advocates for their clients' positions, the regulated community viewed the Environmental Protection Agency as an arbitrator: "The Agency is in the driver's seat; if we can't agree, the default is the Agency's position" **[Ohio 56]** and "Consensus is nice, but that's not why I'm here. I'm here to make my best possible arguments to the Agency that advance our position on how the rule should look. That's my job." **[Ohio 57]** The disputants were not in agreement about the intended purpose of their meetings. These frames led environmentalists to use the mediation meetings as a forum to make public interest–based arguments while representatives of the regulated community more consistently advocated specific client positions. Thus identity frames interacted with conflict management frames, and together produced changes in the behavior of the disputants and the conflict dynamics that fed intractability. This leads us to our second conclusion.

Conclusion 2: Frames act as lenses through which disputants interpret conflict dynamics, and these interpretations construct the conflict as more or less tractable.

Perhaps this seems self-evident in a book on framing, but the reader should recall that the cases were selected not because they were good examples of framing, but because they were intractable. Major differences in identity, characterization, and conflict management framing, therefore, appear to be a common feature of all eight intractable environmental conflicts that we studied. Additionally, in the natural resource conflicts, where site-specific decisions were linked with national policy issues, social control frames were usually more prominent, and differences in social control frames more often fueled a conflict. We discuss this further below as we turn our attention to the link between framing and intractability.

Framing and Intractability

Stability of Frames

For frames to perpetuate the intractability of disputes, they must remain stable over time or recur through time. This stability in how disputants understand the issues and the other parties reinforces the conflict, despite changing external conditions. And, although they represent only one perspective, disputants come to believe that theirs is the only appropriate interpretation. We see evidence of this in the cases, and hence draw our third conclusion.

Conclusion 3: Frames can remain remarkably stable, through many dispute episodes, thereby reinforcing conflict dynamics over time.

Evidence of how stability of frames generates intractability can best be seen in the Voyageurs case. The conflict is marked by particularly deep-seated identity and characterization frames. These frames have become mythologized, as one generation of disputants passes these frames to the next generation. The language used during the mid-1960s: "[The park is] once again taking away the right and freedom of individuals to truly make decisions regarding their lives and livelihoods in their own backyards" **[Voyageurs 3]** gets repeated in 1988: "[We need leaders to] make sure that people's freedoms are protected and not stripped away from them" **[Voyageurs 53]** and 2000: "What [environmentalists] don't understand is that every time they push that agenda further and further, they are taking away from the culture of the people who live here. . . . The people that live here are just constantly seeing our federal government chip away and chip away at the lifestyles and the culture." **[Voyageurs 26]** Freeze framing is also found in characterizations of outgroups with terms such as "crybabies," "spoiled brats," "selfish," "ecoterrorists," "motorheads," and "pawns for big business interests." The stability of these frames reinforces conflict dynamics, creating a long history of difficult relationships and unfulfilled expectations by all parties. Further, the embeddedness of the conflict in larger political dynamics in the state and nationally renders it like a pendulum with continually shifting winners and losers. In this case, the parties, the issues, the relationships, and even the social system conspire to keep the conflict from moving toward civil, constructive dialogue.

Frames may owe their stability to conditions that are inherent in the conflict itself and in the larger social system. In the Edwards Aquifer, conflict management frames grow from ambiguity in the social systems that make decisions concerning water withdrawal. Portions of the decision-making authority reside in state, regional, local, private, and federal institutions. This leads to fighting "a jillion fights" **[Edwards 70]** about water rights, a recurring pattern of needing "to fight for their rights," **[Edwards 25]** and efforts to keep other institutions from "overstepping their boundaries" **[Edwards 17, 18]** and the federal government from "taking over the aquifer." **[Edwards 69]** These concerns about protection of self and containment of others lead to preferences for political action and adjudicatory modes of conflict. Stakeholders prefer these conflict management processes because they hold open the possibility of obtaining "voice" and of protecting or recovering "rights." Continual suits and efforts to legislatively redefine the conflict, in turn, help keep the decision-making processes ambiguous as equally powerful groups move to block others from effective action. Thus frames and conditions can mutually reinforce each other over time. Moreover, in Edwards Aquifer, the social systems of decision making remain highly ambiguous, opening the possibility that stakeholders may revert to a narrower range of antagonistic conflict frames in the future.

Doan Brook also provides evidence of the mutually stabilizing effect of frames and external context. The conflict around Doan Brook is latent, in that stakeholders generally promote fact-finding strategies for managing differences but largely avoid addressing underlying concerns and values. This preference for conflict avoidance and fact-finding is reinforced by generally inclusive identities and positive characterizations of others:

> We are blessed with having an extremely sophisticated work group at the Joint Committee on Doan Brook watershed as a backbone for citizen outreach. **[Doan Brook 20]**

Still, the stakeholders hold significantly different beliefs about the nature of the problem, how differences should be resolved, and by whom. Stakeholders value the conflict management process because it provides them voice and information, but not because any real conflicts have been resolved. As one stakeholder indicated, "The process hasn't resolved any issues with the brook. It's been a process of examining and getting a better understanding of the brook." **[Doan Brook 19]** Another found satisfaction participating because "when the minutes came back and my concerns had been recorded in black and white, people heard me." **[Doan Brook 11]** And a third expressed limited expectations of the process: "You have to go a step beyond and say whose problem is this? Until there is an organization to deal with problems . . . , you can have a hundred ideas about what to do and how, and even where to get the money, and you won't do it because there is no one in charge." **[Doan Brook 13]** Thus, the interaction between positive identity and characterization frames that tend to mute conflict, conflict management frames that accept a lack of substantive progress, and the lack of mobilization within stakeholder groups, reinforce the latency of the conflict, despite gradually worsening conditions in the brook itself.

The Reinforcing Effects of Frame Interactions

What causes this stability? Just as a lens directs light rays so that they become concentrated, overlapping frames can reinforce their individual effects on intractability. In each of the examples cited above, the frames are reinforced either by other frames or by external conditions with which the frames interact. This interaction is important to our understanding of both framing and intractable conflicts. The cases portray other examples of interaction between frames as well. In some cases, those interactions do not produce frame stability, but rather allow frames to evolve over time. Thus we state our fourth conclusion.

Conclusion 4: Frame interactions can either mutually reinforce or dampen the stability of other frames and the intensity of the conflict.

Consider first the Quincy Library Group conflict. When the conflict began, environmentalists and timber workers each wrapped themselves in their interest-based identities, which spawned the conflict. These interest-based identity frames were reinforced during the "owls versus jobs" disputes of the 1980s. These conflict dynamics were repeated in many small communities throughout the Pacific Northwest, with national groups providing support and guidance for local disputants on each side. In Plumas County, however, a few key local leaders from both the local environmental groups and forest interest groups recognized that their interests were tied to their counterparts. According to the local environmentalists,

> The environmental community . . . know(s) what is wrong with present Forest Service activities and . . . how to fix it. . . . We also know that . . . for a complete solution to our common goals we need the wisdom of the people who have worked in the woods for the four generations that we have been logging Plumas County. **[Quincy 21]**

The forest interest groups expressed similar recognition of their interdependence (Gricar and Brown 1981):

> Without loggers, everyone else would have to rely on tourists. Without environmentalists, the loggers would have to put their faith in an unrestrained Forest Service to assure that there are trees for their grandchildren to cut. If it's "us against them," then it's all of us against the ninny bureaucrats who can never seem to do anything commonsensical. **[Quincy]**

With the U.S. Forest Service as a common enemy these two stakeholders sought to forge a dialogue to move past the stalemate that they perceived was damaging their community. In the process, the local environmentalists and loggers shifted from an interest-based identity to a place-based identity: "We sat down, and worked it out. In doing so, we began rediscovering our sense of community." **[Quincy 38]** This shift in identity altered several related frames. Negative characterizations were replaced with positive characterizations. Conflict mode frames shifted. As one participant described,

> The conversations, both formal and informal, that have occurred as a result of the efforts of the Quincy Library Group have been very positive. They have made us realize how dysfunctional a community we were before, always fighting each other, instead of trying to move forward on common goals. The social experiment of working together as neighbors is perhaps as important, or may be more important, than the forestry experiment we are now proposing. **[Quincy 38]**

This interrelationship between identity, characterization, and conflict management frames can also be seen in the Alton Park and Piney Woods neighborhoods in Chattanooga. The African American residents identify themselves as "victims," "fighters," and "protestors." They draw sharp distinctions around race, between neighborhood residents and the whites in the larger Chattanooga community. But in the context of environmental disputes, their identity shifts subtly. "One of the things about pollution and chemical companies, it is never a racial line. It draws a community together, both white and black . . . because everybody has a common ground in nature." **[Chattanooga 28]** This adoption of a larger collective identity created an opportunity for a shift in conflict management and characterization frames. As one environmental engineer explained,

> You have people who say, "Well I remember this release or this fire" and you go back and you find out they are talking twenty years ago, twenty-five, thirty, forty years ago. . . . But we have a lot of people in the neighborhood that are willing to take us at face value and help us get to a point of action. You can talk so much, but after awhile you got to act. **[Chattanooga 21]**

The failure to construct a common identity frame associated with place or with interests is epitomized by the controversy over incinerating the wastes located at the Drake Chemical site. There, the interactions among identity, characterization, and conflict management frames created an escalatory cycle, in which each group's negative characterization frames reduced their capacity to listen, narrowed their conflict management frames toward increasingly hostile alternatives, and reinforced each side's identity frames as victims of each other's tactics. As an environmental activist noted,

> You get to a point where you become very battle hardened and you realize that you are not going to get the truth from somebody unless you pull it out of them under oath. . . . The amount of our lives that we've put into this fight has been a tremendous investment of time. Emotion, time, money, health. I mean you name it, we've run ourselves ragged trying to stop this project and we've tried everything. We've tried conflict resolution, we've tried dialogue, we've tried everything right into court. And, here we are. **[Drake 17]**

This view is countered by a public official who is angered by a negative characterization of one of his colleagues:

> That was just wrong. . . . When they do stuff like that. If they called me names because I represent the government, I wouldn't like it but I'd tolerate it. When they called her a perjurer, that really made me mad. So, any consideration that I would have given him in the future is gone. He's done. **[Drake 16]**

We offer several conclusions about how frame differences contribute to intractability.

Conclusion 5: Frame differences foster intractability in the following ways: (a) Often the parties do not frame the underlying problem in the same way, which leads to repeated skirmishes that never address the underlying issues; (b) limited repertoires of conflict management frames lead disputants to adopt adversarial conflict management strategies that impede resolution and escalate conflict; (c) extensive and repeated use of characterization frames polarizes already antagonistic relationships; and (d) use of positional conflict management frames reinforces existing characterizations.

Additionally, in natural resource conflicts in particular, differences in social control frames are likely to be a critical source of intractability. As already noted, local decisions made in these conflicts are interwoven with national policy debates that create ambiguity about ultimate jurisdiction over the issues.

Conclusion 6: In natural resource conflicts, ambiguity in the social system coupled with disagreements among the parties about who should be making decisions about resource use and preservation (i.e., when the parties have different social control frames), increases the chances that the conflict will elude resolution.

In disputes over hazardous materials, differences in risk frames contribute to intractability. Disputants who frame risk differently generally have a difficult time seeing or honoring the way others are framing the issues (Vaughan and Siefert 1992). In our cases, fundamental differences in risk frames existed between Arrest the Incinerator Remediation (AIR) members and government agencies. Each constructed the risks using different bases (Elliott 1988), and these different conceptions were never judged by their counterparts to be legitimate. When parties operate out of unacknowledged differences in risk frames, they usually talk past one another and concentrate their efforts on blaming each other and delegitimating each other's frames. As

Table 15.1. Framing Effects on the Intractability or Tractability of Conflicts

Framing Effects Promoting Intractability	*Framing Effects Promoting Tractability*
Lack of common identity frames	Construction of common place-based identity frames
Unacknowledged threats to key identities	Acknowledgment of underlying identity issues
Unabated history of negative characterizations	Reduction in use of negative characterizations
Ambiguity about decision forum	Agreement about decision forum
Differences in conflict management frames	Common conflict management frame
Differences in social control frames	Agreement about social control frames
Repeated adoption of adjudication and struggle conflict management frames	Adoption of problem-solving conflict management frames with broad/authorized representation and clear understanding of and buy-in to the process by all parties
Failure to recognize different bases for understanding and assessing risk among disputants	Creation of a common, mutually acceptable understanding of and agreed-upon methods for assessing risk

Kasperson (1992, 155) has noted, "the defining of risk is essentially a political act."

Differences in risk frames arise from differing technical, social, and cultural experiences that influence individual and group definitions of hazards (Kasperson 1992; Wildavsky and Dake 1990). The Chattanooga case reveals differences in how exposure to hazards as well as risk perceptions varied by culture and class. For the largely African American community of Alton Park and Piney Woods, risk perceptions were based on personal histories and lived experience of community residents, whereas industrialists and government agencies relied on technical and epidemiological "data" to formulate their risk frames. In this case, however, unlike Drake, some shared bases for assessing risk began to evolve, albeit not until community mobilization efforts brought attention to the plight of the Alton Park/Piney Woods community. Thus another conclusion emerges from our toxics cases.

Conclusion 7: Until some common basis for describing and measuring risk can be agreed upon among disputants, conflicts over toxic pollutants will likely remain intractable.

In Table 15.1 we summarize the roles that frames play in fostering intractability or tractability in environmental disputes.

Reframing and the Potential for Promoting Resolution

The analyses of our eight cases suggest that disputants' frames not only can change but may well be changeable under the right circumstances. Frames may be transformed through mutually reinforcing, positive shifts in related frames. But this does not mean that changing frames is easy.

In fact, most of the cases provide considerable evidence that changing the frames of disputants in intractable disputes is a difficult process. In seven of the cases, efforts were made to consciously alter the conflict through dialogue processes. While none of these efforts was specifically directed at transforming the frames, they did seek to resolve the conflict through joint problem solving or public participation—processes that have the potential to generate frame change (Bush and Folger 1994, Moore 1996). Nonetheless, mediation efforts in Voyageurs had limited effects (it did create some agreements to which disputants referred in subsequent interactions), and relatively minor effects resulted in Edwards and the Ohio EAG. Moreover, public participation processes in both the Doan Brook and the Drake cases left frames essentially unchanged or reinforced. Yet, in both the Quincy Library Group and the Chattanooga cases, dialogue processes catalyzed substantial changes in both frames and the tractability of the conflict. We therefore draw our next conclusion.

Conclusion 8: In at least some conflicts, frames can be altered over time, through intentional actions and interventions. These changes in frames can render disputes more tractable.

The Quincy Library Group makes clear the potential power of dialogue processes and conscious efforts to reframe the dispute. In this case, the change began with an effort to reframe both characterization and identity frames, which in turn altered conflict management frames. The resulting dialogue process in turn reinforced the initial shifts in frames, creating a positive cycle of reframing and consensus building.

The Chattanooga case is perhaps even more compelling, because reframing is reflected not just in the neighborhood of concern, but also throughout the community. Chattanooga began a process of community consensus building in the early 1980s. The process was unrelated to the concerns of the Alton

Park and Piney Woods neighborhoods. Nonetheless, the successful application of these conflict management processes significantly altered conflict management frames throughout the community. While Alton Park and Piney Woods residents were largely uninvolved in these early processes, activists involved in citywide issues were intimately aware of these changes. By proactively promoting the use of joint problem solving, these activists created opportunities for initial dialogues between industrialists and residents. In turn, these processes altered negative identity and characterization frames. Over time, they also altered risk frames. Thus an engineer noted:

> A lot of us think, well, I am a rational person, I can figure out what my neighbors want. But that's not true. I found out from all the years on the advisory panel. . . . You have to ask people. **[Chattanooga 25]**

He went on to say:

> If you deal with residents like we do on the advisory panel, the first issue we have to address is like they do in the Middle East. You have to first acknowledge we all have the right to exist. You know it is easy to go in and say, "We just don't want you here, we want you out of here. We want zero emissions." That type of conflict is hard to resolve, because we rely on this job to feed our families. If we work past this issue, we can look at health effects of pollutants, how the company can better control pollutants, and whether cleaner substitutes can be made. **[Chattanooga 26]**

Similarly, residents note: "Racial integration, cooperation and working together has made the most difference to Chattanooga. If cooperation and communication were to happen, we wouldn't have all these other problems." **[Chattanooga 32]** And, in a more practical vein:

> EPA came up with the idea about the community advisory group. The community was so divided during that time and we just couldn't make decisions. One group is going one way and another going another. STOP [an environmental group] was knowledgeable about the environment, but we needed . . . to get full community input about what we should do. It was a good process, a timely process. At least in the '90s, we sat down at the table and discussed what was going to happen in the community. And from generating and discussion, things changed around. The govern-

ment turned around, and we began to see what could be done. **[Chattanooga 29]**

We can draw some tentative observations about reframing from these two cases. First, the interventions in both processes were rooted in the communities of interest and initiated by stakeholders who were in conflict with each other in those communities. While Chattanooga's process was promoted and assisted by stakeholders from outside the neighborhood, the Quincy process was largely initiated and managed by stakeholders from within the community. Second, the focal event for drawing disputants with competing interests together was their joint valuation of the place itself and a desire to maintain or improve something about that cherished place. In Quincy they sought to prevent economic decline of their town. In Chattanooga, the common motivation was to build a community-based ecology, economy, and equity. Third, in both cases, the processes started small, and grew with success. Initial efforts were not necessarily directed at resolving specific aspects of the conflict, but rather at exploring relationships and options. Successful progress in these arenas facilitated frame shifts, which in turn made joint problem solving more feasible. Still, the entrance into reframing for Quincy and Chattanooga was not the same for both communities. In Quincy the process started with a shift in identity frames, while in Chattanooga the process started with a shift in conflict management frames. In both cases, characterization frames changed dramatically. Drawing on these cases, our conclusions about how tractability can be increased in environmental conflicts are summarized in the right column of Table 15.1.

Additionally, our conflicts can be grouped according to two factors that distinguish the dispute resolution processes that were undertaken. Both reflect characteristics of the stakeholders who participated in the processes. The first deals with whether the participants formally represent constituencies from a distinct group or whether they are elected to participate as individual volunteers. We see these distinctions between the two water cases: In Doan the participants were volunteers with no formal representation, whereas in the Ohio EAG, a limited group of authorized representatives was seated. The second dimension that seems to distinguish the dispute resolution processes in our cases is the level of power and expertise that stakeholders have—that is, whether participants have balanced or unbalanced power at the table. For example, some have argued that representation in the Voyageurs mediation panel was unbalanced. Table 15.2 provides a matrix of these characteristics and lists the likely outcomes from each combination. Our cases are also arrayed on this table.

Table 15.2. Structuring Dispute Resolution Processes

Decision-Making Power and Expertise	*Representation*			
	Dispersed/Volunteer		*Limited/Authorized*	
BALANCED	Chattanooga; Quincy Library Group	Potential for shift to place-based identity Opportunity for new conflict mode frames	Edwards; Ohio External Advisory Group; Formal Forest Management Planning Process associated with Quincy	Potential elevation of conflict to higher authority Potential for strong institutional identification and characterization frames
UNBALANCED	Doan; Drake; Voyageurs Visitors' Use and Facility Planning Process; Colorado growth conflicts	Threat to trust Heightened sense of identity and characterization amongst groups Stronger social control frames	Voyageurs mediation process	Threat to legitimacy of deciion making process Significant polarization around institutional identity and characterizations

Strategies for Reframing Intractable Disputes

We now turn our attention to approaches that disputants and third parties can use to introduce constructive dialogue into intractable disputes. We have no illusions that diagnosis alone can shift intractable disputes into tractable ones. We also do not pretend that traditional dispute resolution techniques can easily transform conflicts that have so tenaciously resisted resolution. Nonetheless, our insights about how frames promote intractability suggest that efforts to promote understanding of frames held by disputants can lead to more constructive interactions among disputants, to frame enlargement, and even, at times, to reframing. We explore the potential for reframing in this section.

The Process of Reframing

We have mentioned that reframing occurs when disputants change their frames—that is, when they develop a new way of interpreting or understanding the issues in the dispute or a new way of appraising one or more of the other parties in the conflict. To reframe one's understanding of a conflict, some degree of "perspective-taking" is required. Perspective-taking involves standing back, observing, and reflecting on the fact that there is more than one way to view the issues. Reframing "depends on the ability of at least some of the actors to inquire into the intentions and meanings of other actors involved with them in the controversy" (Schön and Rein 1994, 171). As long as parties believe that their own view is the only legitimate way to understand the issues in dispute, they cannot reframe. But once they begin to realize that their frame depends on their own vantage point, this realization makes reframing possible. Reframing depends on the ability to entertain one or more perspectives other than the one you currently hold, to weigh the relative merits of each perspective, to allow for the possibility of alternative explanations, and to adopt alternative frames if one is convinced that other frames also make sense.

Since reframing requires taking on a new or different perspective, it is often not easy for parties to engage in reframing. This is particularly true when the conflict is intense or protracted, as such longevity tends to "lock" parties into their current frames (thereby contributing to the dispute's intractability). Under these circumstances, reframing often cannot occur without the help of a neutral third party or someone who does not have a direct stake in the conflict. For example, mediators explicitly describe their role as one of framing the issues for the parties and helping the parties to reframe the issues in a way that facilitates resolution (Lam, Rifkin, and Townley 1989; Moore 1986). Disputants typically present their frames (to each other and to the third party) in positional language, stating what their preferred outcomes are. By listening closely for the parties' underlying interests (their underlying needs) (Fisher, Ury, and Patton 1991), mediators attempt to "reinterpret" the conflict (reword, reformulate, and represent it to the parties) in a manner that incorporates both (or all) parties' interests.

As we have noted, shifts in contextual factors can promote reframing of a conflict. In these circumstances, some, many, or even all parties are often forced to reconsider their positions because the circumstances have worsened their no-agreement alternatives. For example, the economic slowdown of the early 1990s induced Quincy disputants to reappraise the consequences to their town of continuing to fight.

Absent such contextual change, reframing is most likely to occur when the parties engage in careful and constructive dialogue. Successful dialogues that promote reframing are conceptually similar to negotiations. These dialogues incorporate five general principles (Lewicki, Saunders, and Minton 1999): (1) Reduce tension and manage the de-escalation of hostility; (2) enhance communication, particularly to improve each party's understanding of the other's perspectives; (3) control the number and size of issues; (4) establish a common ground as a basis of agreement; and (5) enhance the desirability of the options and alternatives that one presents to the other parties. In the next section we incorporate these principles into a framework for reframing intractable environmental disputes. The framework focuses on tools for helping the parties reframe their views of the issues, themselves, and other stakeholders, and the mechanisms by which they seek to resolve the conflict. We start with reframing of conflict management frames because it often precedes the others. If the conflict has been particularly nasty or violent, it will be necessary to reduce tension and manage the de-escalation of hostility before other mechanisms for reframing can be attempted (Lewicki, Saunders, and Minton 1999).

Reduce Tension and Manage the De-escalation of Hostility

Efforts to de-escalate hostilities often require changes in patterns of conflict management and in patterns of communication. Escalation is reinforced when disputants progressively move away from direct communication toward increasingly confrontational modes of exchange. In like manner, de-escalation can be reinforced by movements in the opposite direction. Yet disputant frames often inhibit this shift. In particular, disputant conflict management frames can create considerable resistance to initial efforts to de-escalate hostility.

We emphasize the importance of conflict management frames because patterns of conflict management lay the framework upon which communication patterns are built. When disputants frame their conflict management options narrowly, they limit the options for communication. At the extreme, frames may limit interaction to struggle, sabotage, or violence. While adjudication allows for a wider range of options, these conflict management modes also inhibit effective communications. Thus effective reframing must often start with new forms of and forums for conflict management.

Our cases suggest that even in intractable conflicts, conflict management frames can be altered. We do not suggest trying to displace existing conflict management frames with newer frames. Rather, we suggest developing more flexible conflict management frames that allow for a wider range of communications. In most cases, the older frames remain active, at least in the short run, even as new forms of conflict management are incorporated into these frames. The disputants still distrust each other, still believe that struggle will be necessary, but hold open the potential for dialogue to ameliorate some of the problems generated by this struggle. They rarely give up the option for struggle until they have substantially reframed not only the conflict management aspects of the dispute, but also the identity, characterization, and substantive aspects as well.

How can we begin this process of reframing? Often, we must look for forums that promote more effective communication but do not preclude the continuation of current conflict management modes. We would suggest processes with limited objectives specifically designed to promote more effective communication about conflict management, identity, and characterization frames. Invite the parties to a meeting to foster understanding in which each will have an opportunity to share their "whole story frame" with other disputants and provide an opportunity for the others to ask questions to gain clarification and deeper understanding of why each stakeholder frames the dispute the way they do. Solicit a third party to facilitate a discussion among the stakeholders of how each sees the issues through different lenses (frames). Work with each group separately to increase their acknowledgment of the other party's right to a presence in the dispute and help the parties to adjust their understanding of and expectations for the other's behavior. Or, following interviews to elicit frames from disputants, present the framing notions to the stakeholders and ask them to discuss the frames that they see are getting in the way of their reaching agreement.

These mechanisms for reframing seek to reduce the level of tension and hostility between the parties by moving conflict management from the struggle, sabotage, and violence; avoidance; or appeal to political action frames (see Table 15.1) to joint problem-solving or fact-finding frames or other less confrontational, more problem-solving approaches. Such actions typically require the intervention of one or more third parties, who may function in a variety of roles—facilitators, diplomats, conciliators, mediators, and other intermediary roles—and who are actively involved in helping the parties reframe their views of the dispute resolution process, each other, and the issues. While our list of third party roles is not exhaustive (see Ury [2000] for an additional overview of third party roles), the following examples have proven useful in promoting reframing.

Study Circles

Study circles are democratic, highly participatory discussion groups, convened to address an issue of critical concern (see the Study Circles Resource Center, http://www.studycircles.org/). Facilitated discussions follow a framework laid out in discussion materials designed to explore the issue. These materials are often designed by a coalition of organizations that cut across the issues that divide the community. Participants are directed to first focus on how the issues affect themselves, examining larger questions only after basic perspectives are shared and understood. Study circles, which can be repeated throughout a community, can involve a large number of participants and often culminate in action forums, in which participants from small study circles come together to explore options for action.

Listening Project

In this approach disputants are given the task of interviewing other members of the community, including members who disagree with the perspective of the interviewer. Interviewers are trained in communication and conflict resolution skills before conducting the interviews. Interviewers seek first to understand the interviewee's concerns and perspectives, sufficient to summarize and explain those perspectives to other stakeholders (Dukes 1996).

Mediation

The literature on collaborative processes and mediation is rich, and will not be reiterated here (Bush and Folger 1994; Dukes, Piscolish, and Stephens 2000; Elliott 1999; Gray 1989; Moore 1986). By focusing on joint problem solving, mediation provides a context and incentives for delving into frames that act as barriers between disputants. At its best, it offers the potential for transforming conflicts by not only resolving the issues at hand, but also repairing the relationships between the disputants, such that they can more productively deal with their differences in the future.

Perspective Taking

Once disputants are open to new possibilities of conflict management, communications must be managed to improve each party's understanding of the other. Our research indicates that initiatives that help disputants examine their own perspectives and those of others are particularly helpful. Through this process disputants may enlarge or even reframe their views of themselves and of other parties. The objectives of reframing identity and characterization frames are to understand one's self more objectively and to see the other party in a more positive manner. A central tenet of these approaches is acknowledgment; that is, recognition that other disputants' views are valid and credible, especially in light of their vantage point and felt experience in the conflict. Moving disputants from hostility to acknowledgment requires construction of forums in which parties can express their deepest concerns without reprisal. This involves a capacity for deep listening and often generates empathic rather than dismissive responses from adversaries who can identify with the humanity of the other's experience. Our research suggests several approaches to reframing identity and characterization frames.

Acknowledging Critical Identities

As we have repeatedly shown in the cases in this book, parties in intractable disputes often have sharp and polarized definitions of their own identity and see the other parties in the dispute as posing a threat to that identity. Clyman and Gray (2002) speculate that identity issues often are not labeled as such by the parties, but instead are sublimated through zealous advocacy for particular issues, turf, or symbolic disputes and causes. Allowing the parties to acknowledge the importance of identity and to recognize the legitimacy of their own and others' identity claims helps to restore self-esteem and allow the parties to refocus their attention on the substantive issues. According to Montville, dialogue that explicitly acknowledges issues of identity can reactivate a necessary mourning process, through acknowledgment of past injustices, offers of contrition, and expressions of forgiveness by those who feel victimized (Montville 1995). The process encourages the development of empathy and seeks to restore a sense of worthiness among all disputants—a necessary precursor to substantively based problem solving. Often these dialogues are guided by a third party who enforces ground rules and ensures that listening takes place.

Examples can be drawn from the Oslo Accord, an effort to solve the Israeli–Palestinian conflict, in which the Palestinians and the Israelis explicitly reaffirmed the fundamental right of the other side to exist, restored the identity (or self-esteem) of each group, and hence allowed the parties to redirect their attention to problem solving about other specific issues in the conflict (Pruitt 2000, Smyth 1994). The devaluation of one's group and what it stands for evokes a natural human tendency to defend oneself—a stance that fuels escalation and perpetuates intractability. This escalating process can be seen in the Israeli-Palestinian dispute in 2002, as expressed in the Intefadeh and Israel's response to it.

Disputants seeking to more proactively address identity frames can employ the following specific mechanisms. Imaging focuses on reframing identities, whereas narrative forums and listening circles promote acknowledgment of the other party. In all of these approaches, parties are encouraged to use language more carefully (e.g., Tannen 1998) in stating their concerns, to work harder to listen to and understand the other, and to respond to the other's statements and declarations more judiciously. The techniques also try to help disputants identify how other parties might be framing the dispute (in ways that would be different from their own), to articulate underlying reasons why the others might have these interpretations, and to help disputants refrain from using flagrant, negative characterizations of the other parties.

Imaging

Imaging is one of several processes, usually facilitated by a consultant, that encourages parties in a dispute to specifically talk about their self-images (identities) and images of the other parties (characterizations) in the conflict (e.g., Alderfer 1977, Kelman 1996, Walton 1987). As a result of these discussions, disputing parties often clarify misperceptions, appreciate the validity of the other party's identity, agree to reduce negative stereotyping of the other, and sharpen the substantive issues that require focused negotiations.

Narrative Forums

Narrative forums seek to move beyond unidimensional frames that disputants create to explain the other (Dale 1999, Forrester 1999, Winslade and Monk 2000). Often, these focus on specific aspects of the other's characteristics and actions. By providing a forum in which more whole narratives can emerge and be recognized, such forums (whether imbedded in mediations or not) help destabilize the rigidity of the frames held by the other. They deconstruct dominant story lines by exploring their basis and the role of the various disputants in maintaining the frame. Often, they seek mutual acknowledgment of whole story frames told by disputants about themselves and their presence in the conflict.

Listening Circles

Used in many native cultures, such as Polynesian, Native American, and Hawaiian cultures, listening circles create a place of ritualized communication. The rituals slow down the pace of response, and value responses that thoughtfully acknowledge the words of the previous speakers. One version of this approach is the Psychodynamic Workshop (Fisher 1997; Volkan, Julius, and

Montville 1991) that has been employed in ethnic disputes, such as those in Cypress, Israel, and Estonia. These workshops are intensive, five-day events, in which participants are guided by psychiatrists through discussions of painful aspects of the conflicts, with the intention of emphasizing commonality of experiences of loss and anguish, promoting familiarity and trust amongst participants, and exploring means for breaking down barriers and developing cooperative activities. Such dialogues are designed to ensure the psychological safety of the participants, honor their identities, and eliminate or control the expression of negative characterizations.

Control the Number and Size of Issues

While our research focused primarily on conflict management, identity, and characterization frames, efforts to resolve intractable conflicts need to focus on substantive frames as well. In a classic work, Fisher (1964) described several actions that parties can use to reconfigure conflict dynamics: reduce the number of issues to be resolved, reduce the number of parties who are involved, break bigger issues into smaller, more manageable ones, shift "levels" on issues to make them either more specific or more general, and search for ways to resolve "this problem in this situation," rather than to create broad precedents or principles that will apply to numerous future disputes. Many of these strategies are widely used today by mediators to resolve environmental conflicts.

Such strategies often require mediators to intervene at two levels. First, mediators must alter the process rules, such that disputants are willing to suspend for a period their particular way of framing the substantive issues. For example, risk associated with a particular toxic waste site may be framed as a series of issues associated with contaminants and their pathways into the community, or more globally as an issue of environmental justice. The former frame provides more opportunities for resolution than does the latter, although arguably the latter may focus the dispute on more structural issues. Are these two frames mutually exclusive? Can the risks be reframed in ways that allow progress at both levels of discourse? While most mediators believe that smaller issues are easier to resolve than larger ones—both because the issues are more manageable and because smaller issues can always be repackaged into larger groupings as the resolution process evolves—our research into framing would suggest that this reframing must emerge from the disputants if it is to change the dynamics of an intractable conflict. Thus the mediator should seek to clarify the basis for the disputants' frames before seeking to reframe the issues to simplify the issues. Neither the mediator nor the disputants should assume that their way of framing the conflict is the only or the best way. Rather, our framing research would encourage disputants and mediators to assume that others will see it differently and have valid reasons for their perspectives.

Establish a Common Ground as a Basis of Agreement

Reframing also provides insights into how disputants can best establish a common ground for building an agreement. In particular, our framing research suggests that identifying common overarching goals or common enemies may provide the psychological space needed to reframe identity, characterization, and substantive frames. If parties can identify common goals or common enemies, this can help to bring them together.

Finding common ground often means establishing a superordinate goal—a goal that the parties cannot attain unless they coordinate to attain it (Sherif et al. 1988), banding together against a common enemy, or agreeing to follow a specific set of rules and procedures that will allow solutions to emerge. Common enemies unify the parties by requiring them to pool resources and develop a goal of minimizing the costly consequences of defeat. For example, the Deerfield River Hydroelectric Project allowed stakeholders to work together to develop a water flow management strategy on a dammed river that satisfied the needs of the power company, rafters and canoers, fishing enthusiasts, local environmental groups, and various groups within the local communities along the river. While the solution cost the power company more than building a simple dam across the river, the solution process allowed the parties to avoid costly litigation and appeals, avoid a potentially suboptimal judicial decision, and create solutions that invigorated the local economy (Ulman 1996).

Two processes, search for common ground and visioning/search processes, show considerable promise in efforts to reframe substantive goals.

Search for Common Ground

Without necessarily trying to address all the aspects of a dispute, it is possible to explore selected areas of mutual agreement; that is, search for common ground (see http://www.sfcg.org/). Such an exploration can take the form of a single forum, a longer-term dialogue, or shuttle diplomacy. Strong advocates of each side are facilitated to explore areas of agreement. Even in highly divisive conflicts (e.g., abortion, race relations, ethnic disputes), areas of agreement emerge that provide a basis for further exploration. Such areas of agreement may open up further communication and potential joint actions, thereby creating bridges and trust between groups that previously viewed each other as the enemy.

Visioning and Search Processes

The search process (Emery and Emery 1977, 1978; Emery and Purser 1996; Weisbord and Janoff 2000) is a participative planning process that encourages groups to identify desired futures that are shared between members of different stakeholder groups. This approach relies on enlarging the shadow of the future for participants. It is similar to the common argument of reframing the solution to a problem from a short-term perspective to a long-term perspective (or the converse, depending on the situation). Often, these processes seek to involve a full array of stakeholders, emphasize common ground among them, and develop small groups that are self-managing within the context of the full array of stakeholders. As such, it can be used for large group visioning efforts (Bunker and Alban 1997) such as those used in our Chattanooga case. Groups first identify their desired futures, revisit the history of their relationships, collectively anticipate trends likely to occur in the larger context that will affect their future interaction, and brainstorm joint actions they can take to move toward their desired futures. Search conferences have been used to address a number of conflictual multistakeholder issues such as the redesign of social service delivery systems and designing the jail of the future.

Enhance the Desirability of the Options and Alternatives

The fifth and final principle suggested by Lewicki, Saunders, and Minton (1999) focuses on enhancing the desirability of the options. Our research on substantive frames offers several strategies for how to reframe substantive issues in ways that will enhance the desirability of alternatives to the disputants. These strategies include repositioning the perceived payoffs for cooperating and competing, frame options and alternatives from the perspective of the other parties, and reframing perceptions of losses as gains.

Reposition the Perceived Payoffs for Cooperating and Competing

A number of experimental gaming studies (Clyman and Tripp 2000, Kelley and Thibaut 1978, Taylor 1987) have shown that decision makers can be influenced to make more cooperative versus competitive choices, depending on how the payoffs for self and other are framed for the parties. To the degree that one can reframe the individual payoffs so that they introduce a "coefficient of caring"—that is, include an increment to satisfy the other's concerns (Clyman and Gray 2002)—the more one can induce cooperative behavior from that party.

Frame Options and Alternatives from the Perspective of the Other Party

There are a number of ways that parties in conflict can "recast" the nature of alternative solutions so as to make them more palatable or acceptable to the other parties. Reformulating, repackaging, or rephrasing offers can often enhance the attractiveness of a proposed solution. Understanding their interests and offering them different options (Fisher, Ury, and Patton 1991) can remove a deadlock. Enhancing rewards and payoffs for picking desired alternatives can lead them to make a different choice, as can redefining which choice options are seen as most "fair" or viable.

Another approach that stimulates parties to reevaluate the existing alternatives is to adopt the perspective of bounded rationality (Clyman and Gray 2002). This approach requires a decision maker to take a "systems level perspective"—that is, to consider all parties' perspectives in their individual calculations of benefits and costs—and to consider what a "typical" rational decision maker would do in such a situation. Adopting this perspective often requires the decision maker to depersonalize the decision and simply do "what any rational decision maker would do in the situation." Adopting this perspective often allows the decision maker a simplified range of choice options, from which the cooperative alternative is often the most rational and clear-cut (Clyman and Gray 2002). Bazerman (2002) describes numerous other mechanisms that can be used to reduce bias in decision making.

Reframing Perceptions of Losses as Gains

Finally, in several of the cases, we noted that parties tended to frame a problem as a loss or a gain. In general, people tend to avoid taking risks when the decision they face is framed as a possible loss, but may be more willing to take a risk if the decision is framed as a possible gain. Hence, creative new solutions may emerge if what disputants initially perceived as a risk is framed differently (and in a positive light). If parties can see that they stand to gain something from a newly proposed option, they will be more likely to agree.

An Example of Substantive Reframing

Let's consider an example of a conflict between a state highway department and a rapidly growing township. To accommodate an expected increase in traffic, the highway department would like to build a road through a park in the township. The township, however, is not eager to give up its park. It appears that the parties are deadlocked; each holds firm to its position, to build or not build the road. However, when a third party starts asking questions of each party, it turns out that the problem is not necessarily so clear-cut. Conversation with the highway department reveals that they want to purchase the land for the new road now to save money, but they don't intend to build the road until sometime in the future when a greater increase in population warrants it. The township, on the other hand, wants to ensure that there is greenspace for its citizens, but it is not wedded to the particular location of the current park. Thus the conflict can be reframed by any of the parties, including the mediator, who realize that there are ways to "reposition" the arguments so solutions can be found that satisfy the interests of all parties. The mediator might reframe the dispute by asking the parties the following question: Can the state acquire the land now that it needs for the future highway, and still allow the city to have a park? If the answer is yes, the highway department can purchase the land now, but keep it as a park until the city (using the money from the purchase) can buy and construct a park somewhere else. Then the road can be constructed through the old park. While in this example, the reframing process produced an agreement that satisfied both parties, just because reframing occurs does not necessarily guarantee that the conflict will be resolved. Often, the parties themselves, and third parties, may have to reframe dispute issues many times to be able to move a dispute from intractable to tractable.

Reframing as an Aid to Conflict Resolution

As we have shown in this section, frame analysis and reframing strategies can enhance our range of conflict management options. The five major principles for promoting more effective conflict management can each be better understood from the perspective of the framing research explored in this book. Approaches to reframing described in the preceding text may be used (by the parties themselves or through a third party) separately or sequentially to help parties construct a forum for civil dialogue about intractable conflicts. Although these approaches are categorized separately here as a way to emphasize their dominant strategic intent, it is more likely that for intractable disputes many of the techniques will be used in tandem.

Conclusions

In this book we have applied a frame analysis to eight cases of environmental conflict. Our analysis reveals the important role that frames play in perpetuating the intractability of these conflicts as well as the potential that reframing can play in moving the conflicts toward resolution. Based on the case studies presented in this book, we conclude:

- Conflict is a dynamic process, and the processes that make a conflict more or less tractable to resolution are also dynamic.
- Frames act as lenses through which disputants interpret conflict dynamics, thereby making conflicts more or less tractable.
- Frames can remain remarkably stable, through many dispute episodes, thereby reinforcing conflict dynamics over time and rendering the conflicts intractable.
- Frames interact, and can either mutually reinforce or dampen the stability and intensity of other frames.
- In at least some conflicts, frames can be altered over time, through intentional actions and interventions as well as through changes in the larger context of the conflict. These changes may make the conflicts more tractable.

We introduced a typology of eight kinds of frames that environmental disputants employ to interpret the issues, their experience of the parties, and the conflict management context within which they interact with each other. Our analytic approach can be used both retrospectively and prospectively to diagnose virtually any environmental conflict—not only those that are particularly resistant to resolution. We believe this approach holds considerable promise for systematizing conflict assessment processes and determining whether a dispute can be mediated.

Finally, for those intractable conflicts that defy resolution, we believe this approach is particularly promising because it unlocks opportunities for deeper understanding of the dynamics that amplify these conflicts and keep disputants embroiled in them, often beyond their usefulness. By systematically uncovering the frames that operate for the disputants, it is possible to identify the real sticking points in the conflicts and then to design mechanisms that loosen these sticking points. We have been careful not to suggest that all intractable conflicts are resolvable. But we remain optimistic that by understanding how they are framed, we can begin to craft constructive processes in which disputants can explore the frames in operation, enlarge their own understandings of these conflicts, and, if they are inclined to do so, choose pathways that may make their conflicts more open to resolution.

Bibliography

Adler, R. W. 1995. Addressing barriers to watershed protection. *Environmental Law* 25:973–92.

Alderfer, C. P. 1977. Group and intergroup relations. In *Improving life at work: Behavioral science approaches to organizational change,* ed. R. Hackman and L. Suttle, 277–96. Santa Monica, Calif.: Goodyear.

Ashforth, B. E., and F. Mael. 1989. Social identity theory and the organization. *Academy of Management Review* 14:20–39.

Azar, L. 1990. *Twentieth century in crisis: Foundations of totalitarianism.* Dubuque, Iowa: Kendall Hunt.

Bantz, C. R. 1985. News organizations: Conflict as a crafted cultural norm. *Communication* 8:225–44.

Baron, J., and I. Ritov. 1994. Reference points and omission bias. *Organizational Behavior and Human Decision Processes* 59:475–98.

Bartlett, F. C. 1932. *Remembering: A study in experimental and social psychology.* Cambridge: Cambridge University Press.

Bateson, G. 1972. *Steps to an ecology of mind.* New York: Ballantine Books.

Baum, H. S. 2001. Why are school–community partnerships unlikely? Paper presented at the Urban Affairs Association Annual Meeting, March, 2001, Detroit, Michigan.

Bazerman, M. H. 1984. The relevance of Kahneman and Tversky's prospect theory on organizational behavior. *Journal of Management* 10:333–43.

Bazerman, M. H. 1998. *Judgment and managerial decision making.* 4th ed. New York: John Wiley.

Bazerman, M. H. 2002. *Judgment and managerial decision making.* 5th ed. New York: John Wiley.

Bazerman, M. H., T. Magliozzi, and M. A. Neale. 1985. Integrative bargaining in a competitive market. *Organizational Behavior and Human Decision Processes* 35:294–313.

Benford, R. D. 1993. You could be the hundredth monkey: Collective action frames and vocabularies of motive within the nuclear disarmament movement. *The Sociological Quarterly* 34:195–216.

Benford, R. D. 1997. An insider's critique of the social movement framing perspective. *Sociological Quarterly* 67:409–30.

Benson, R. D. 1996. The role of streamflow protection in Northwest River Basin Management. *Environmental Law* 26:777–85.

Berelson, B. 1952. *Content analysis in communication research.* New York: Hafner Press.

Bingham, G. 1986. *Resolving environmental disputes: A decade of experience.* Washington, D.C.: Conservation Foundation.

Bingham, G., ed. 1996. The growth of the environmental dispute resolution field. In *Resolving environmental disputes: A decade of experience,* ed. G. Bingham, 13–63. Washington, D.C.: Conservation Foundation.

Blomquist, W. 1992. *Dividing the waters: Governing groundwater in Southern California.* San Francisco: Institute for Contemporary Studies.

Bostrom, A., B. Fischhoff, and M. G. Morgan. 1992. Characterizing mental models of hazardous processes: A methodology and an application to radon. *Journal of Social Issues* 48(4):85–100.

Brooks, L. Quincy Library Group takes on Congress. *California County* July 8, 1994, pp. 7–8.

Bryant, B. 1995. *Environmental justice: Issues, policies, and solutions.* Washington, D.C.: Island Press.

Bryant, B., and P. Mohai. 1992. *Race and the incidence of environmental hazards: A time for discourse.* Boulder: Westview Press.

Buechler, S. M. 2000. *Social movements in advanced capitalism.* New York: Oxford University Press.

Bullard, R. D. 1990. *Dumping in Dixie: Race, class, and environmental quality.* Boulder: Westview Press.

Bullard, R. D., and B. Wright. 1989. Toxic waste and the African-American community. *Urban League Review* 13:67–75.

Bunker, B., and B. Alban. 1997. *Large group interventions.* San Francisco: Jossey-Bass.

Burgess G., and H. Burgess. 1995. Beyond the limits: Dispute resolution of intractable environmental conflicts. In *Mediating environmental conflicts: Theory and practice,* ed. J. W. Blackburn and W. Bruce, 101–19. Westport, Conn.: Quorum Books.

Burgess, H., and G. Burgess. 1996. Constructive confrontation: A transformative approach to intractable conflicts. *Mediation Quarterly* 13:305–22.

Burke, K. 1950. *A rhetoric of motives.* Berkeley: University of California Press.

Burton, J. 1987. *Resolving deep-rooted conflict: A handbook.* Lanham, Md.: University Press of America.

Bush, R. B., and J. Folger. 1994. *The promise of mediation.* San Francisco: Jossey-Bass.

Cannon, J. 2000. Choices and institutions in watershed management. *William and Mary Environmental Law and Policy Review* 25:260–78.

Carpenter, S., and W. J. D. Kennedy. 1988. *Managing public disputes.* San Francisco: Jossey-Bass.

Chilson, J. A. 1999. Keeping clean waters clean: Making the Clean Water Act's antidegradation policy work. *University of Michigan Law Review* 32:545–71.

Clyman, D. R., and B. Gray. 2001. Unraveling social dilemmas and frame discrepancies: The importance of reframing. Paper presented at the International Association for Conflict Management meeting, June 25, Cergy, France.

Clyman, D. R., and T. Tripp. 2000. Discrepant values and measures of negotiator performance. *Group Decision and Negotiation* May.

Coleman, P. T. 2000. Intractable conflict. In *The handbook of conflict resolution: Theory and practice,* ed. M. Deutsch and P. T. Coleman, 428–50. San Francisco: Jossey-Bass.

Crowfoot, J. E., and J. M. Wondolleck. 1990. *Environmental disputes: Community involvement in conflict resolution.* Washington, D.C.: Island Press.

Dahrendorf, R. 1959. *Class and class conflict in industrial society.* Stanford, Calif.: Stanford University Press.

Dake, K. 1991. Orienting dispositions in the perception of risk: An analysis of contemporary worldviews and cultural biases. *Journal of Cross-Cultural Psychology* 22(1):61–82.

Dake, K. 1992. Myths of nature: Culture and the social construction of risk. *Journal of Social Issues* 48(4):21–37.

Dale, N. 1999. Cross-cultural community-based planning. In *The consensus building handbook,* ed. L. Susskind, S. McKearnan, and J. Thomas-Larmer, 923–950. Thousand Oaks, Calif.: Sage.

de Raismes, J. N., III. 1999. From Lefthand to Coal Creek: Boulder's Open Space Program, 1999. http://www.ci.boulder.co.us/cao/x-opnsrl.html. Last visited August 7, 2002. Unpublished policy paper from Boulder city attorney's office. Available online:

de Raismes, J. N., III, H. L. Hoyt, P. L. Pollock, J. P. Gordon, and D. J. Gehr. Growth management in Boulder, Colorado: A case study. Unpublished policy paper from Boulder city attorney's office. Available online: http://www.ci.boulder.co.us/cao/x-bgmcs.html. Last visited August 7, 2002.

Deutsch, M. 1973. *The resolution of conflict.* New Haven: Yale University Press.

Diani, M. 1996. Linking mobilization frames and political opportunities: Insights from regional populism in Italy. *American Sociological Review* 61:1053–69.

Donnellon, A., and B. Gray. 1990. An interactive theory of reframing in negotiation, Pennsylvania State University, University Park, Pa., Center for Research in Conflict and Negotiation.

Donnelly, C. S. 1972. *The Hatfield–McCoy feud.* Parsons, W. Va.: McClain Printing.

Dore, J., and R. P. McDermott. 1982. Linguistic indeterminacy and social context in utterance interpretation. *Language* 58(2):374–98.

Duane, T. P. 1999. *Shaping the Sierra: Nature, culture, and conflict in the changing West.* Berkeley, Calif.: University of California Press.

Dukes, E. F. 1996. *Resolving public conflict: Transforming community and governance.* Manchester, UK: Manchester University Press.

Dukes, E. F., M. Piscolish, and J. B. Stephens. 2000. *Reaching for higher ground.* San Francisco: Jossey-Bass.

Dunlap, R. E., and K. D. Van Liere. 1978. The new environmental paradigm. *Journal of Environmental Education* 9(4):10–19.

Eakin, J. 1974. *The history of Doan Brook.* Cleveland: Nature Center.

Edwards Aquifer Authority. 2001. Historical chronology of the Edwards Aquifer Authority: 1996 to present. *Report to the Edwards Aquifer Legislative Oversight Committee, Texas State Legislature.* San Antonio, Tex.: Edwards Aquifer Authority.

Elliott, M. 1988. The effect of differing assessments of risk in hazardous waste facility siting negotiations. Unpublished manuscript, Georgia Tech University.

Elliott, M. 1999. The role of facilitators, mediators, and other consensus building practitioners. In *The consensus building handbook,* ed. L. Susskind, S. McKearnan, and J. Thomas-Larmer, 199–240. Thousand Oaks, Calif.: Sage.

Emery, F. E., and M. Emery. 1977. *A choice of futures.* Leiden, the Netherlands: Martinus Nijhoff.

Emery, M. 1982. *Searching: For new directions, in new ways . . . for new times.* Canberra, Australia: Australian National University.

Emery, F., and E. Trist. 1965. The causal texture of organizational environments. *Human Relations* 18:21–32.

Emery, M. R., and R. E. Purser. 1996. *The search conference: A powerful method for planned organizational change and community action.* San Francisco: Jossey-Bass.

Environmental Protection Agency (EPA). 1984. Record of decision (ROD) abstract. EPA/ROD/R03-84/002; 09/30/84.

Environmental Protection Agency (EPA). 1986. Record of decision (ROD) abstract. EPA/ROD/R03-86/033; 05/13/86.

Environmental Protection Agency (EPA). 1988. Record of decision (ROD) abstract. EPA/ROD/R03-88/058; 09/29/88.

Fan, D. P. 1988. *Predictions of public opinion from the mass media: Computer content analysis and mathematical modeling.* New York: Greenwood Press.

Feyerherm, A. E. 1995. Changing and converging mind-sets of participants during collaborative, environmental rule making: Two negotiated regulation case studies. *Research in Corporate Social Performance and Policy* Supplement 1:231–57.

Fischhoff, B., P. Slovic, S. Lichenstein, S. Read, and B. Combs. 1978. How safe is safe enough? A psychometric study of attitudes towards technological risks and benefits. *Policy Sciences* 9:127–52.

Fisher, R. 1964. Fractionating conflict. In *International conflict and behavioral science,* ed. R. Fisher. The Craigville Papers. New York: Basic Books.

Fisher, R. J. 1997. *Interactive conflict resolution.* Syracuse, N.Y.: Syracuse University Press.

Fisher, R. J., and L. Keashley. 1990. A contingency approach to third party intervention. In *The social psychology of intergroup and international conflict resolution,* ed. R. J. Fisher, 234–38. New York: Springer-Verlag.

Fisher, R., W. Ury, and B. Patton. 1991. *Getting to yes.* 2nd ed. New York: Penguin.

Floyd, D.W., ed. 1999. *Forest of discord.* Bethesda, Md.: Society of American Foresters.

Folger, J. P., M. S. Poole, and R. K. Stutman. 1997. *Working through conflict.* New York: Addison Wesley Longman.

Folk-Williams, J. A. 1988. The use of negotiated agreements to resolve water disputes involving Indian rights. *Natural Resources Journal* 28:63–103.

Forrester, J. 1999. Dealing with deep value differences. In *The consensus building handbook,* ed. L. Susskind, S. McKearnan, and J. Thomas-Larmer, 463–490. Thousand Oaks, Calif.: Sage.

Fraser, D. 1999. *Qualitative solutions and research: QSR NUD*IST NVivo reference guide.* Melbourne, Australia:Qualitative Solutions and Research Pty., Ltd.

Frohock, F. M. 1989. Reasoning and intractability. In *Intractable conflicts and their transformation,* ed. L. Kriesberg, T. A. Northrup, and S. T. Thorson, 13–24. Syracuse, N.Y.: Syracuse University Press.

Furniss, S. 1998. Factors contributing to the success of managed growth regimes: The effect of government leadership in northern Colorado. Unpublished manuscript presented at Western Social Science Association, April 18, Denver, Colorado. p. 6.

Gamson, W. A. 1992. The social psychology of collective action. In *Frontiers of social movement theory,* ed. C. M. Aldon Morris. New Haven: Yale University Press.

Gamson, W. A. 1997. Constructing social protest. In *Social movements and culture,* ed. M. Johnson and B. Klandemans, pp 85–106. Minneapolis: University of Minnesota Press.

Gamson, W. A., B. Fireman, and S. Rytina. 1982. *Encounters with unjust authority.* Homewood, Ill.: Dorsey.

Gamson, W. A., and D. S. Meyer. 1996. Framing political opportunity. In *Comparative perspectives on social movements.* ed. D. McAdam, J. D. McCarthy, and M. N. Zald, 275–90. New York: Cambridge University Press.

Getches, D. H. 1990. *Water law.* St. Paul, Minn.: West.

Glaser, B., and A. Strauss. 1967. *The discovery of grounded theory.* Chicago: Aldine.

Goffman, E. 1974. *Frame analysis: An essay on the organization of experience.* New York: Harper and Row.

Gooch, L. 1998. *Doan Brook: Understanding and protecting an urban stream and watershed.* Cleveland: Nature Center.

Gottlieb, R. 1993. *Forcing the spring: The transformation of the American environmental movement.* Washington, D.C.: Island Press.

Graham, L. 1999. The reborn American city: A place you might want to live. *Parade Magazine.* April 25, pp. 4–6.

Gray, B. 1989. *Collaborating: Finding common ground for multiparty problems.* San Francisco: Jossey-Bass.

Gray, B. 1997. Framing and reframing of intractable environmental disputes. In *Research on negotiation in organizations, Vol. 6,* ed. R. J. Lewicki, R. Bies, and B. Sheppard. Greenwich: JAI.

Gray, B. 1999. The development of global environmental regimes: Organizing in the absence of authority. In *Organizational dimensions of global change,* ed. D. L. Cooperider and J. E. Dutton, 185–209. Thousand Oaks, Calif.: Sage.

Gray, B., and D. Clyman. 2002. Difficulties in fostering cooperation in multiparty negotiations: Complexity, social dilemmas, and frame discrepancies in multiparty negotiations. In *International handbook of organizational teamwork and cooperative working,* ed. M. West, D. Tjosvold, and K. G. Smith. Chicester, U.K.: Wiley.

Gray, B., L. Putnam, and R. Hanke. 2002. The role of framing in intractable conflicts. Unpublished manuscript, Pennsylvania State University; Center for Research in Conflict and Negotiation.

Gricar, B., and A. Baratta. 1983. Bridging the information gap at Three Mile Island: Radiation monitoring by citizens. *Journal of Applied Behavioral Science* 19:35–49.

Gricar, B. and L. D. Brown. 1981. Conflict, power, and organization in a changing community. *Human Relations* 34: 877–93.

Gumperz, J. J. 1982. *Discourse strategies.* Cambridge, England: Cambridge University Press.

Harden, R. W. 1986. The Edwards connection. In *The Edwards Aquifer: An underground stream,* ed. J. Specht, 13–32. Seguin, Tex.: The Guadalupe-Blanco River Authority.

Hardin, G. 1968. The tragedy of the commons. *Science* 162:1243–48.

Hartzog, G. B., Jr. 1988. *Battling for the National Parks.* Mt. Kisco, N.Y.: Moyer Bell, Ltd.

Healy, M. P. 1997. Still dirty after twenty-five years: Water quality standard enforcement and the availability of citizen suits. *Ecology Law Quarterly* 24:393–460.

Heifetz, R.A. 1994. *Leadership without easy answers.* Cambridge, Mass.: Belknap Press.

Hilgartner, S. 1985. The political language of risk: Defining occupational threats. In *The language of risk: Conflicting perspectives on occupational health,* ed. D. Nelkin, 25–66. Beverly Hills: Sage.

Hird, J. 1994. *Superfund: The political economy of environmental risk.* Baltimore, Md.: Johns Hopkins University Press.

Hirt, P. W. 1994. *A conspiracy of optimism: Management of the national forest since World War Two.* Lincoln: University of Nebraska Press.

Hoare, C. H. 1994. Psychosocial identity development in United States society: Its role in fostering exclusion of other cultures. In *Race, ethnicity, and self: Identity in multicultural perspective,* ed. E. P. Salett and D. R. Koslow, 24–41. Washington, D.C.: National Multicultural Institute.

Hogg, M. A., D. J. Terry, and K. M. White 1995. A tale of two theories: A critical comparison of identity theory with social identity theory. *Social Psychology Quarterly* 58:255–69.

Hunter, S. 1989. The roots of environmental conflict in the Tahoe basin. In *Intractable conflicts and their transformation,* ed. L. Kriesberg, T. A. Northrup, and S. J. Thorson, 25–40. Syracuse, N.Y.: Syracuse University Press.

Ibarra, P. R., and J. I. Kitsuse. 1993. Vernacular constituents of moral discourse: An interactionist proposal for the study of social problems. In *Reconsidering social constructionism: Debates in social problems theory,* ed. J. A. Holstein and G. Miller. New York: Aldine de Gruyter.

Innes, J. E. 1996. Planning through consensus building: A new view of the comprehensive planning ideal. *APA Journal* Autumn:460–72.

Jennings, A., and K. Gardner. The evolution of flood risk and erosion damage in the Shaker Lakes/Doan Brook Urban Watershed. Available online: http://ecivwww.cwru.edu/civil/research/shaker.html. July 22, 2002.

Jensen, R. 1988. A new approach to regional water management: Two plans are developed to manage and protect the Edwards Aquifer. *Texas Water Resources* 14:1–6.

Kahneman, D., J. L. Knetsch, and R. H. Thaler. 1990. Experimental tests of the endowment effect and the Coase Theorem. *Journal of Political Economy* 98:1325–48.

Kahneman, D., and A. Tversky. 1979. Prospect theory: An analysis of decision under risk. *Econometrica* 47:263–91.

Kahneman, D., and A. Tversky. 1993. *Conflict resolution: A cognitive perspective.* Stanford, Calif.: Stanford Center on Conflict and Negotiation.

Kahneman, D., J. L. Knetsch, and R. H. Thaler. 1991. The endowment effect, loss aversion, and status quo bias. *Journal of Economic Perspectives* 5:193–206.

Kaiser, R. 1987. *Handbook of Texas water law.* Water monograph no. 87-1. College Station: Texas Water Resources Institute.

Kasperson, R. E. 1992. The social amplification of risk: Progress in developing an integrative framework. In *Social theories of risk,* ed. S. Krimsky and D. Golding, 53–78. Westport, Conn.: Praeger.

Kaufman, S., and J. Smith. 1999. Framing and reframing in land use change conflicts. *Journal of Architecture, Planning and Research* [special issue on managing conflict in planning and design]. 16(2):164–80.

Kaufman S., and K. Snape. 1997. Public attitudes toward urban infrastructure: The Northeast Ohio experience. *Public Works Management and Policy* 1(3):224–44.

Kawamoto, J. 1979. Oral interview by Voyageurs National Park historian, Mary Lou Pearson. International Falls, Minn.: Voyageurs National Park Archives.

Kelley, H. H., and J. Thibaut. 1978. *Interpersonal relations: A theory of interdependence.* New York: John Wiley & Sons.

Kelman, H. C. 1985. Overcoming the psychological barrier: An analysis of the Egyptian–Israeli peace process. *Negotiation Journal* 1:213–34.

Kelman, H. C. 1996. Negotiation as interactive problem solving. *International Negotiation* 1:99–126.

Kelman, H. C. 1999. The role of social identity in conflict resolution: Experiences from Israeli–Palestinian problem-solving workshops. Paper presented at the International Association of Conflict Management, June 22, San Sebastian, Spain.

Keltner, J. W. 1994. *The management of struggle: Elements of dispute resolution through negotiation, mediation, and arbitration.* Creeskill, N.J.: Hampton Press.

Kessler, E. H., C. M. Ford, and J. R. Bailey. 1996. Object valence as a moderator of the framing effect on risk preference. *Journal of Economic Behavior and Organizations* 30:241–56.

Knetsch, J. L. 1998. Reference states, fairness, and choice of measure to value environmental changes. In *Environment, ethics and behavior,* ed. M. H. Bazerman, D. M. Messick, A. E. Tenbrunsel, and K. A. Wade-Benzoni, 13–32. San Francisco: New Lexington Press.

Koerner, B., A. Wright, E. Cue, and C. Pritchard. 1998. Cities that work, *U.S. News and World Report,* June 8, via http://www.usnews.com.

Kriesberg, L. 1989. Conclusion: Research and policy implications. In *Intractable conflicts and their transformation,* ed. L. Kriesberg, T. A. Northrup, and S. J. Thorson, 210–20. Syracuse, N.Y.: Syracuse University Press.

Kriesberg, L. 1993. Intractable conflicts. *Peace Review* 5(4):417–21.

Kriesberg, L. 1998. *Constructive conflicts: From escalation to resolution.* Lanham, Md.: Rowman and Littlefield.

Kriesberg, L., T. A. Northrup, S. J. Thorson. 1989. *Intractable conflicts and their transformation.* Syracuse, N.Y.: Syracuse University Press.

Krippendorff, K. 1980. *Content analysis: An introduction to its methodology.* Beverly Hills, Calif.: Sage.

Kusel, J., S. C. Doak, S. Carpenter, and V. E. Sturtevant. 1996. The role of the public in adaptive ecosystem management. Sierra Nevada Ecosystem Project: Final report to Congress. *Assessments and Scientific Basis for Management Options,* vol. 2. Davis, Calif.: Centers for Water and Wildland Resources, University of California.

LaBianca, G., B. Gray, and D. Brass. 2000. A grounded model of organization schema change during empowerment. *Organization Science* 11(2): 235–257.

Lam, J. A., J. Rifkin, and A. Townley. 1989. Reframing conflict: Implications for fairness in parent–adolescent mediation. *Mediation Quarterly* 7(1):15–31.

Lederach, J. P. 1997. *Building peace: Sustainable reconciliation in divided societies.* Washington, D.C.: U.S. Peace Institute.

Lewicki, R. J., D. Saunders, and J. Minton. 1999. *Negotiation.* Burr Ridge, Ill.: McGraw-Hill Higher Education.

Little, J. B. 1995. The Quincy Library Group Posted: No... *American Forests* Jan. 2.

Littlejohn, S. W., and K. Domenici. 2001. *Engaging communication in conflict: Systemic practice.* Thousand Oaks, Calif.: Sage.

Luthanen, R., and J. Crocker. 1991. Self-esteem and intergroup comparisons: Toward a theory of collective self-esteem. In *Social comparison: Contemporary theory and research,* ed. J. Suls and T. A. Wills, 211–34. Hillsdale, N.J.: Lawrence Erlbaum.

Madison, C. 1997. The sustainable blue-collar town. *Utne Reader.* June/July, 9(2): 14–16.

Mather, L., and B.Yngvesson. 1980–81. Language, audience, and the transformation of disputes. *Law and Society Review* 15:775–821.

Mazmanian, D., and D. Morell. 1992. *Beyond superfailure: America's toxics policy for the 1990s.* Boulder, Co.: Westview Press.

McAdam, D., and R. Paulsen. 1993. Specifying the relationship between social ties and and activism. *American Journal of Sociology* 98:640–67.

McCall, G. J., and J. L. Simmons. 1978. *Identities and Interactions.* New York: Free Press.

McCusker, C., and P. J. Carnevale. 1995. Framing in resource dilemmas: Loss aversion and the moderating effects of sanctions. *Organizational Behavior and Human Decision Processes* 612:190–201.

McHarg, N. 2000. Park Service Chipping at [sic] Away at Our Rights. *Daily Journal,* September 5.

Merry, S. E., and S. Silbey. 1984. What do plaintiffs want? Reexamining the concept of dispute. *Justice System Journal* 9:151–77.

Milbrath, L. 1984. *Environmentalists: Vanguard for a new society.* Albany: State University of New York Press.

Minnesota Historical Society. 1964. Letter to Congressman John Blatnik from Jeno Pallucci: 1.

Minsky, M. 1975. A framework for representing knowledge. In *The psychology of computervisions,* ed. P. Winston. New York: McGraw-Hill.

Mitchell, R. C., and R. T. Carson. 1989. *Using surveys to value public goods: The contingent valuation method.* Washington, D.C.: Resources for the Future.

Montville, J. V. 1995. The nature and psychology of civil society. In *Social pathology in comparative perspective,* ed. J. Braun, 158–73. New York: Praeger.

Moore, C. W. 1986. *The mediation process: Practical strategies for resolving conflict.* San Francisco: Jossey-Bass.

Moore, C. W. 1996. *The mediation process: Practical strategies for resolving conflict.* 2nd ed. San Francisco: Jossey-Bass.

Morris, J. P. 2000. Who controls the water? Incorporating environmental and social values into water resources planning: Hastings West–Northwest. *Journal of Environmental Law and Policy* 6:117–33.

Motavalli, J. 1998. Chattanooga on a roll. *E, The Environmental Magazine* 92:14–16.

Mullins, G. W., and R. L. Vertrees. 1995. *Understanding Ohio's surface water quality standards.* Columbus: Ohio Environmental Protection Agency.

Neale, M. A., and M. H. Bazerman 1985. The effects of framing and negotiator overconfidence on bargaining behaviors and outcomes. *Academy of Management Journal* 28:34–49.

Neff, L. P. November 27, 1962. Memo to USFS Regional Forester George James. Duluth, Minn.: Superior National Forest Archives.

Newcomb, T. M. 1947. *Readings in social psychology.* New York: H. Holt.

Northrup, T. A. 1987. *Women's and men's conceptualizations of war, peace, and security: The relationship between sex, sex-role identification, and war/peace attitudes.* Syracuse, N.Y.: Syracuse University Press.

Northrup, T. A. 1989. The dynamic of identity in personal and social conflict. In *Intractable conflicts and their transformation,* ed. L. Kriesberg, T. A. Northrup, and S. J. Thorson, 55–82. Syracuse, N.Y.: Syracuse University Press.

Novak, P. 1998. Memorandum to External Advisory Group members and interested parties. Antidegradation External Advisory Group meeting, May 27, 1998.

Nute, G. L. 1969. *The Voyageurs highway.* St. Paul: Minnesota Historical Society.

Ohio Environmental Protection Agency. 2000. Current division of surface water external advisory groups (EAGs), Ohio Environmental Protection Agency. Available online: http://www.epa.state.oh.us/dsw/eag/antideg/groundru.pdf. Last visited August 27, 2002.

Ohio Environmental Protection Agency. June 14, 2000. Current division of surface water external advisory groups (EAGs). Available online: http://www.epa.state.oh.us/dsw/eag. June 23, 2002.

O'Leary, R., T. Yandle, T. Moore. 1999. The state of the states in environmental dispute resolution. *Ohio State Journal on Dispute Resolution* 14:515–613.

Ostrom, E. 1990. *Governing the commons: The evolution of institutions for collective action.* New York: Cambridge University Press.

Ostrom, E., R. Gardner, and J. Walker. 1994. *Rules, games, and common-pool resources.* Ann Arbor: University of Michigan Press.

Otway, H. J., D. Maurer, and K. Thomas. 1978. Nuclear power: The question of public acceptance. *Futures* 10:109–18.

Parkinson, P. D. 2000. Voyageurs National Park: General Management Plan, Environmental Impact Statement, Visitors Use and Facilities Plan. Review and Valuation. Two Harbors, Mn: The Parkinson Group.

Parmeter, D. 2000. Draft response to VNP Management Plan/EIS/Visitor Use and Facilities Plan. Memo to the Koochiching County Board. International Falls, Mn: Northern Resources Center: September 1.

Paulucci, J. 1964 or 1965. Vigorously opposed to Voyageurs National Park. Source unknown.

Pearce, W. B., and S. W. Littlejohn. 1997. *Moral conflicts: When social worlds collide.* Thousand Oaks, Calif.: Sage.

Perez, R. 1986. Potential for updip movement of saline water in the Edwards Aquifer. *Resource Investigations Report 86-4032.* San Antonio, Tex.: U.S. Geological Survey.

Peters, N. E., and M. Meybeck. 2000. Water quality degradation effects on freshwater availability: Impacts to human activities. *Water International* 25:185–93.

Pinkley, R. L., and G. B. Northcraft. 1994. Conflict frames of reference: Implications for dispute processes and outcomes. *Academy of Management Journal* 371:193–205.

Potter, J., and M. Wetherall. 1987. *Discourse and social psychology: Beyond attitudes and behavior.* London: Sage.

Pruitt, D. G. 2000. The tactics of third-party invervention. *Orbis* Spring. Available online: http://www.findarticles.com/cf_0/m0365/2_44/61943111/p1/article.jhtml.

Pruitt, D. G., and J. Z. Rubin. 1986. *Social conflict: Escalation, stalemate, and settlement.* New York: Random House.

Pruitt, D. G., and P. V. Olczak. 1995. Beyond hope: Approaches to resolving seemingly intractable conflict. In *Conflict, cooperation and justice,* ed. J. Z. Rubin and B. B. Bunker and Associates, 59–92. San Francisco: Jossey-Bass.

Pruitt, D. G., J. C. Parker, and J. M. Mikolic. 1997. Escalation as a reaction to persistent annoyance. *International Journal of Conflict Management* 5:284–98.

Putnam, L. L. 1994. Challenging the assumptions of traditional approaches to negotiation. *Negotiation Journal* 10:337–46.

Putnam, L. L., and M. Holmer. 1992. Framing, reframing, and issue development. In *Communication and negotiation,* ed. L. Putnam and M. E. Roloff, 128–55. Newbury Park: Sage.

Quincy Library Group. 1993. Community stability proposal. Quincy, Calif.: Quincy Library Group.

Riffe, D., and A. Freitag. 1997. A content analysis of content analyses: Twenty-five years of *Journalism Quarterly. Journalism and Mass Communication Quarterly* 73:515–24.

Roland, A. 1994. Identity, self, and individualism in a multicultural perspective. In *Race, ehnicity, and self: Identity in multicultural perspective,* ed. E. P. Salett and D. R. Koslow, 24–41. Washington, D.C.: National MultiCultural Institute.

Rolston, H., III. 1990. Science-based versus traditional ethics. In *Ethics of environment and development,* ed. J. R. Engel and J. G. Engel, 63–72. Tucson: University of Arizona Press.

Ross, A., and H. Chard. 1999. Solving wet-weather problems in the U.S.: An example in Ohio. *Splash* 4(1): 3.

Ross, L. 1977. The intuitive psychologist and his shortcomings: Distortions in the attribution process. *Advances in experimental social psychology,* vol. 10, ed. I. L. Berkowitz, 173–220. Orlando, Fla.: Academic.

Rothman, J. 1997. *Resolving identity-based conflict in nations, organizations, and communities.* San Francisco: Jossey-Bass.

Rubin, J. Z., D. G. Pruitt, and S. H. Kim. 1994. *Social conflict: Escalation, stalemate, and settlement.* New York: McGraw-Hill.

Schein, E. H. 1970. *Organizational psychology.* Englewood Cliffs, N.J.: Prentice Hall.

Schön, D. A., and M. Rein. 1994. *Frame reflection: Toward the resolution of intractable policy controversies.* New York: Basic Books.

Shedenfeld, M. 2000. Empowering stakeholders: Limits on collaboration as the basis for flexible regulation. *William and Mary Law Review* 41:619–30.

Sheppard, B. H. 1984. Third party conflict intervention: A procedural framework. In *Research on Organizational Behavior,* ed. B. M. Staw and L. L. Cummings, 6, 141–90. Greenwich, Conn.: JAI.

Sheppard, B. H., K. Blumenfield-Jones, and J. Roth. 1989. Informal thirdpartyship: Studies of everyday conflict intervention. In *Mediation research,* ed. K. Kressel, Dean G. Pruitt and Associates, 166–89. San Francisco: Jossey-Bass.

Sheppard, B. H., R. Lewicki, and J. Minton. 1992. *Organizational justice: The search for fairness in the workplace.* New York: Lexington Books.

Sherif, M. 1958. Superordinate goals in the reduction of intergroup conflicts. *American Journal of Sociology* 63:349–58.

Sherif, M., L. Harvey, B. White, W. Hood, and C. Sherif. 1988, 1961. *The Robber's Cave experiment: Intergroup conflict and cooperation.* Middletown, Conn.: Wesleyan University Press.

Sierra Club. 1997. Help Stop S.1028, the Quincy Logging Bill! Sierra Club Action Alert, Oct. 3.

Smyth, L. F. 1994. Intractable conflicts and the role of identity. *Negotiation Journal* 10:311–21.

Snow, D. A., and R. D. Benford. 1988. Ideology, frame resonance, and participant mobilization. *International Social Movement Research* 1:192–217.

Snow, D. A., and R. D. Benford. 1992. Master frames and cycles of protest. In *Frontiers in social movement theory,* ed. A. D. Morris and C. M. Mueller, 133–55. New Haven: Yale University Press.

Snow, D. A., B. Rockford Jr., R. D. Benford, and S. K. Worden. 1986. Frame alignment processes, micro-mobilization and movement participation. *American Sociological Review* 51:464–81.

Spyke, N. P. 1999. Public participation in environmental decision making at the new millennium: Structuring new spheres of public influence. *Boston College Environmental Affairs Law Review* 26:263–81.

Stamberg, S. 2001. National Public Radio, *Morning Edition.*

Staw, B. M. 1976. Knee-deep in the big muddy: A study of escalating commitment to a chosen course of action. *Organizational Behavior and Human Performance* 16:27–44.

Strauss, A., and J. Corbin. 1990. *Basics of qualitative research: Grounded theory procedures and techniques.* Newbery Park: Sage.

Stryker, S. 1968. Identity salience and role performance: The relevance of symbolic interaction theory for family research. *Journal of Marriage and the Family* 30:558–64.

Susskind, L., and J. Cruikshank. 1987. *Breaking the impasse.* New York: Basic Books.

Tajfel, H., and J. C. Turner. 1979. An integrative theory of intergroup conflict. In *The Social Psychology of Intergroup Relations,* ed. W. G. Austin and S. Worchel, 7–24. Monterey, Calif.: Brooks/Coleman.

Tajfel, H., and J. C. Turner. 1985. The social identity theory of intergroup behavior. In *Psychology of intergroup relations,* ed. S. Worchel and W. G. Austin, 7–24. Chicago: Nelson-Hall.

Tannen, D. 1979. What's in a frame? Surface evidence of underlying expectations. In *New directions in discourse processes,* ed. R. Freedle, 137–81. Norwood, N.J.: Ablex.

Tannen, D. 1998. How to turn a debate into a dialogue. *USA Weekend* Feb. 28–March 3:4–5.

Taylor, D. 2000. Advances in environmental justice: Research, theory and methodology. *American Behavioral Scientist* 43(4):504–80.

Taylor, D. M., and F. Moghaddam. 1994. *Theories of intergroup relations: International social psychological perspectives.* Westport, Conn.: Praeger.

Taylor, M. 1987. *The possibility of cooperation.* New York: Cambridge University Press.

Teger, A. I. 1980. *Too much invested to quit: The psychology of the escalation of conflict.* New York: Pergamon.

Texas Water Development Board. 1996. *Surveys of Irrigation in Texas—1958, 1964, 1969, 1974, 1979, 1984, 1989, 1994.* Austin, Tex.: Texas Water Development Board.

Thorson, S. J. 1989. Introduction: Conceptual issues. In *Intractable conflicts and their transformation,* ed. L. Kriesberg, T. A. Northrup, and S. T. Thorson, 1–10. Syracuse, NY: Syracuse University Press.

Tribe, L. H. 1992. *Abortion: The clash of absolutes.* New York: Norton.

Tversky, A., and D. Kahneman. 1981. The framing of decision and the psychology of choice. *Science* 211:453–458.

U.S. Department of Agriculture (USDA). 2001. *Record of decision: Sierra Nevada forest plan amendment environmental impact statement.* Vallejo, Calif.: U.S. Department of Agriculture, United States Forest Service, Pacific Southwest Region.

U.S. Forest Service (USFS). 1999. *Record of decision and summary: Herger–Feinstein Quincy Library Group Forest Recovery Act, final environmental impact statement.* Vallejo, Calif.: U.S. Department of Agriculture, Forest Service, Pacific Southwest Region.

U.S. Forest Service (USFS). 2001. *Record of decision: Sierra Nevada Forest Plan Amendment environmental impact statement.* Vallejo, Calif.: U.S. Department of Agriculture, Forest Service, Pacific Southwest Region.

U.S. Geological Survey (USGS). 1998. *Recharge to and discharge from the Edwards Aquifer in the San Antonio Area,* 1997. San Antonio, Tex.: U.S. Geological Survey.

Ury, W. 2000. *The third side.* New York: Penguin.

Ury, W., J. M. Brett, and S. Goldberg. 1993. *Getting disputes resolved: Designing systems to cut the cost of conflict.* San Francisco: Jossey-Bass.

Van Dijk, T. A. 1977. *Text and context.* London: Longmar Group.

Van Dijk, T. A. 1987. *Macrostructures.* Hillsdale, N.J.: Erlbaum.

Van Liere, K. D., and R. E. Dunlap. 1980. The social bases of environmental concern: Does it make a difference how it's measured? *Public Opinion Quarterly* 44:181–97.

Vaughan, E., and M. Seifert. 1992. Variability in the framing of risk issues. *Journal of Social Issues* 48(4):119–35.

Volkan, V. A., D. A. Julius, and J. V. Montville, eds. 1991. *The psychodynamics of international relationships.* Lexington, Mass.: Lexington Books.

Votteler, T. H. 1998. The little fish that roared: The Endangered Species Act, state groundwater law, and private property rights collide over the Texas Edwards Aquifer. *Environmental Law* 28:845–79.

Wagner, W. E. 2000. Restoring polluted waters with public values. *William and Mary Environmental Law and Policy Review* 25:279–301.

Walton, R. 1987. *Managing conflict: Interpersonal dialogue and third party roles.* Reading, Mass.: Addison-Wesley.

Weick, K. E. 1979. *The social psychology of organizing.* Reading, Mass.: Addison-Wesley.

Weick, K. E. 1995. *Sensemaking in organizations.* Thousand Oaks, Calif.: Sage.

Weisbord, M., and S. Janoff. 2000. *Future search: An action guide to finding common ground in organizations and communities.* New York: Berrett Kohler.

West, B. 1997. *Draft decision record for wildlife protection (WPA), Voyageur's National Park,* 1997–1998 season, December 2.

Westley, F., and H. Vrendenburg. 1991. Strategic bridging: The collaboration between environmentalists and business in the marketing of green products. *Journal of Applied Behavioral Science* 271:65–90.

Wiethoff, C., R. Hanke, J. Wunch, T. Bryan, J. Jones-Corley, and M. Momen. 1999. *Master codebook for the environmental framing consortium.* Center for Research in Conflict and Negotiation, Pennsylvania State University, September.

Wildavsky, A., and K. Dake. 1990. Theories of risk perception: Who fears what and why? *Daedalus* 119:41–60.

Winslade, J., and G. Monk. 2000. *Narrative mediation.* San Francisco: Jossey-Bass.

Witzig, F. 2000. *Eighty years in the making: A legislative history of Voyageurs National Park,* 1997–1998 season, December 2.

Wolff, N. 1997. *Mayor: An inside view of San Antonio politics, 1981–1985.* San Antonio: San Antonio Express News.

Wondolleck, J.M., and S. L. Yaffee. 2000. *Making collaboration work.* Washington, D.C.: Island Press.

Yaffee, S. L. 1994. *The wisdom of the spotted owl: Policy lessons for a new century.* Washington, D.C.: Island Press.

Zartman, I. W., and J. Aurik. 1991. Power strategies in de-escalation. In *Timing the de-escalation of international conflicts,* ed. L. Kriesberg and S. J. Thorson, 152–81. Syracuse, N.Y.: Syracuse University Press.

About the Contributors

Todd A. Bryan is a doctoral candidate in the School of Natural Resources and Environment at the University of Michigan where he is studying the relationship between public land management agencies and local communities. He is also an adjunct assistant professor in the Graduate School of Public Affairs at the University of Colorado–Denver. Todd has worked in the natural resources field for over twenty years and has spent the last ten years as a professional mediator, trainer, and organizational consultant. Todd's most recent publication, with Julia Wondolleck and Steven Yaffee, is titled "Tragedy Averted: The Promise of Collaboration," and is soon to appear in *The Proceedings of the Plum Creek Lecture Series* (Missoula: Montana School of Forestry). He is currently working on a book about the Quincy Library Group.

Guy Burgess received his Ph.D. in sociology with Kenneth Boulding in 1979 from the University of Colorado. Following several years as a consultant to a number of real world policy-making processes, he cofounded with other colleagues the University of Colorado Conflict Research Consortium. The Consortium, which he has codirected with his wife, Heidi, since 1988, is focused on the development of more constructive ways of approaching intractable conflicts. The Burgesses and the Consortium have also been at the forefront of efforts to harness the World Wide Web as a tool for better delivering conflict-related information to practitioners, educators, students, and disputants. He is codirector of two major Hewlett-funded initiatives: the Intractable Conflict Knowledge Base Project and CRInfo, the Conflict Resolution Information Source.

Carol Conzelman is a doctoral student of cultural anthropology at the University of Colorado–Boulder, and is studying democratization and development among rural agriculturalists in Bolivia. She is a board member of a non-governmental development organization and leads teams of volunteers to communities around the world for short-term service programs. She also periodically produces an international affairs program for Boulder's community radio station.

Craig B. Davis is professor of natural resources and professor of environmental science at the Ohio State University. His research areas included ecology and ecosystem management, and environmental security. Recent publications include "Soil, Sustainability and Security: The Importance of Ecosystem Integrity" (with F. E. Miller), in J. Wilson (ed.), *Soil Quality in Relation to Sustainable Development of Agriculture and Environmental Security in Central and Eastern Europe,* (Kluwer Academic Publishers 2000), and "Needed Behavioral Change: Steps toward Environmental Security," in N. Polunin and J. Burnett (eds.), *Surviving with the Biosphere* (Edinburgh University Press 1993).

Michael Elliott is an associate professor of planning and public policy at the Georgia Institute of Technology. He serves as director for research of the Consortium on Negotiation and Conflict Resolution and director of the Southeast Negotiation Network. He mediates and facilitates public policy consensus-building processes, designs dispute management systems, and conducts research in policy implementation and conflict management. Dr. Elliott received his Ph.D. in Urban and Regional Studies from Massachusetts Institute of Technology and his M.C.P. from the University of California, Berkeley.

Robert Gardner is a doctoral student in the Department of Sociology at the University of Colorado at Boulder. He received his B.A. in sociology at Bowling Green State University. Robert's academic interests include the areas of rhetoric, cultural studies, urban and community sociology, and cultural memory. He is currently working on his doctoral dissertation, which will explore the various ways that culture and cultural performance provide a source of history and tradition in a rapidly changing American West.

Barbara Gray is professor of organizational behavior and director of the Center for Research in Conflict and Negotiation at Pennsylvania State University. She has studied environmental conflict, mediation, and collaborative processes for over twenty-five years. Her many publications include *Collaborating: Finding Common Ground for Multiparty Problems* (Jossey-Bass 1989), "Framing and Reframing of Intractable Environmental Disputes" (1997), and "Organizing for Global Environmental Change" (1999). She has worked with numerous organizations, including the U.S. Fish and Wildlife Service, the National Park Service, the Federal Highway Administration, and the Pennsylvania Departments of Environmental Protection and Agriculture, on dispute resolution issues. She is the organizer and driving force behind the Interuniversity Consortium on the Framing of Intractable Environmental Disputes, the group that prepared this book.

Ralph Hanke is a Ph.D. candidate in Management and Organization and a research assistant at the Center for Research in Conflict and Negotiation at Pennsylvania State University. He earned an Honors B.A. and M.A. in philosophy (University of Waterloo) and a Master of Applied Philosophy (Bowling Green State University). He has studied environmental conflict, mediation, and facilitation processes. His main area of interest is framing and its role in intractable environmental conflicts. As a private-sector trainer, he developed and delivered numerous training programs and workshops on developing partnerships, negotiation and controversy, and team building.

Sanda Kaufman is professor of planning and public administration at Cleveland State University's Levin College of Urban Affairs. She holds degrees in architecture, planning, and public policy analysis. Her research areas include negotiations and third-party intervention in public, organizational, environmental, and school conflicts, as well as program evaluation. Her articles have been published in the *Journal of Conflict Resolution*, *Negotiation Journal*, the *International Journal for Conflict Management*, the *Journal of Planning Education and Research*, and the *Journal of Architecture Planning and Research*.

Roy J. Lewicki is the Dean's Distinguished Teaching Professor and professor of management and human resources at the Max M. Fisher College of Business, Ohio State University. Dr. Lewicki maintains research and teaching interests in the fields of negotiation and dispute resolution, trust in organizations, organizational justice, and ethical decision making. He is an author or editor of twenty-four books, including *Negotiation* (Irwin/McGraw-Hill 1999); *Negotiation: Readings, Exercises and Cases* (Irwin/McGraw-Hill 1998); and seven editions of *Research on Negotiation in Organizations* (JAI 1999). He was an organizer and chair of the Conflict Management Division of the Academy of Management, and is a past president of the International Association of Conflict Management.

Karen Mockler is a freelance writer living in Cody, Wyoming. Her recent work appears in *High Country News* and on Wyoming public radio. She was a corecipient of the 2001 Dolly Connelly Award for Excellence in Environmental

Journalism for her series on the Columbia River estuary. She holds a master's degree in environmental journalism from the University of Colorado.

Mehnaaz Momen is a doctoral student in public administration at the Levin College of Urban Affairs, Cleveland State University. Her dissertation, On Becoming Marginal: The State and the Citizen, explores the relationship between the state and the citizen in the context of the policy process. Her research interests are policy formulation, policy analysis, citizen participation, community development, and environmental and urban issues.

Tarla Peterson is an associate professor in the Department of Speech Communication at Texas A&M University. Dr. Peterson's current research involves the development of strategies to enhance public participation in decisions regarding watershed management, collaborative learning approaches to environmental disputes, and analysis of stakeholder perspectives in natural resource disputes. She is the author of *Sharing the Earth: The Rhetoric of Sustainable Development* (University of South Carolina Press 1997) and numerous articles on public policy and environmental issues. She has received funding to study environmental policy making from the Environmental Protection Agency, the National Science Foundation, and the Hewlett Foundation.

Linda L. Putnam is a professor in the Department of Speech Communication at Texas A&M University and director of the Program on Conflict and Dispute Resolution in the Institute for Science, Technology, and Public Policy at the George Bush School of Government and Public Service. Her current research interests include environmental conflict, negotiation and organizational conflict, and language analysis in organizations. She is the coeditor of five books, including *The New Handbook of Organizational Communication* (Sage 2001) and *Communication and Negotiation* (Sage 1992), and over ninety articles and book chapters in the areas of conflict management, negotiation, and organizational studies. She is the 1993 recipient of the Charles H. Woolbert Research Award for innovative research in communication and the 1999 recipient of the Distinguished Scholar Award from the National Communication Association, and is a fellow and past president of the International Communication Association and the International Association for Conflict Management.

Kim Sanchez attended the University of California at Davis, where she received undergraduate degrees in Environmental Policy Analysis and Planning and Spanish. She holds a master's degree in public policy from the University of Colorado–Boulder. She is currently working as special projects planner with Boulder County Land Use Department.

Carolyn Wiethoff is an assistant professor in the Management Department of the Kelley School of Business at Indiana University. In addition to her work on conflict framing, Carolyn also conducts research examining the effect of nonvisible diversity (e.g., sexual orientation and religion) on work teams, and the nature of trust and distrust in organizational relationships.

Julia M. Wondolleck is a professor at the School of Natural Resources and Environment at the University of Michigan where she teaches courses in environmental and natural resource conflict management; negotiation skills in resolving environmental disputes; and mediation of public disputes. Her current research focus is on the collaborative dimension of ecosystem management, and ways to ensure the accountability of collaborative processes when public resources are at stake. She was a member of the USDA Committee of Scientists that examined the national forest management process and recommended a new approach to planning that is grounded in principles of sustainability and pursued in a collaborative manner. She is the coauthor of *Making Collaboration Work: Lessons from Innovation in Natural Resource Management* (Island Press 2000); author of *Public Lands Conflict and Resolution: Managing National Forest Disputes* (Plenum 1988); and coauthor of *Environmental Disputes: Community Involvement in Conflict Resolution* (Island Press 1990).

Index